The Corporate Contract in Changing Times

The Corporate Contract in Changing Times

Is the Law Keeping Up?

EDITED BY STEVEN DAVIDOFF SOLOMON AND RANDALL STUART THOMAS

THE UNIVERSITY OF CHICAGO PRESS CHICAGO AND LONDON

The University of Chicago Press, Chicago 60637
The University of Chicago Press, Ltd., London

Published 2019
Printed in the United States of America

28 27 26 25 24 23 22 21 20 19   1 2 3 4 5

ISBN-13: 978-0-226-59940-3 (cloth)
ISBN-13: 978-0-226-59954-0 (e-book)
DOI: https://doi.org/10.7208/chicago/9780226599540.001.0001

Library of Congress Cataloging-in-Publication Data

Names: Davidoff Solomon, Steven, 1970– editor. | Thomas, Randall S., 1955– editor.
Title: The corporate contract in changing times : is the law keeping up? / edited by Steven Davidoff Solomon and Randall Stuart Thomas.
Description: Chicago ; London : The University of Chicago Press, 2019. | Includes bibliographical references and index.
Identifiers: LCCN 2018035074 | ISBN 9780226599403 (cloth : alk. paper) | ISBN 9780226599540 (ebook)
Subjects: LCSH: Contracts—United States. | Contracts—Delaware. | Corporations—Investor relations—United States. | Corporations—Finance—Law and legislation—United States.
Classification: LCC KF801.C677 2019 | DDC 346/.066—dc23
LC record available at https://lccn.loc.gov/2018035074

♾ This paper meets the requirements of ANSI/NISO Z39.48–1992 (Permanence of Paper).

Contents

Foreword

Leo E. Strine Jr.

As you read this provocative collection of incisive reflections on whether the corporate contract is keeping up with changing times, you might usefully reflect on this question: Is corporate law scholarship keeping up with a rapidly changing world?

This excellent gathering of thoughts from many of America's leading corporate law scholars brought this question to my mind as I considered how some of our best minds have approached new dynamics from what largely seem to be the same perspectives that have long shaped academic corporate law thinking. Writing a foreword that does justice to such a diverse collection of provocative essays is a task, as an evidence treatise would say, beyond my ken. What you take from the essays will inevitably depend on your perspective, the mood you are in when you dig into them, and your openness to new ideas.

Perhaps the only real service I can be to you, the reader, is to share a few reactions I had to the collection, with the idea that they may inspire you to consider how the various pieces, taken as a whole, might reveal some promising paths forward for new thinking and policy ideas.

As in most cases when various minds come together, the most interesting way to read this collection is to consider the dissonance of the various perspectives, and what that suggests about the state of thinking and of actual corporate governance dynamics. For example, several eminent scholars[1] suggest that Delaware has adopted a form of corporate law, of both the statutory and common law variety, that limits stockholder influence markedly.[2] They also seem to lament the relative scarcity of judicial injunctions, yearning nostalgically for another period such as 1985–1988, when they were all the rage.[3] By contrast, another learned commentator bemoans the extent to which Delaware corporate law has required directors, within the limits of their legal and ethical discretion, to make stockholder welfare the end of for-profit corporate governance, with other constituencies entitled to consideration only to the extent that doing so is consistent with advancing stockholder welfare.[4] Because of Delaware's prominence, he speculates that judicial rhetoric elevating other constituencies to the same level as the only constituency given rights in the Delaware General Corporate Law would have stimulated much different, other-regarding behavior by corporations. Still others suggest that recent Delaware efforts to adopt a form of for-profit corporation that explicitly requires that all corporate constituencies be treated as an end of governance and be treated with due regard are arguably unnecessary because all Delaware corporations can already do that.[5]

What I found curious in this clash, honestly, was the lack of a consistent focus on the power structure established by Delaware law (and utilized in concert with federally mandated disclosures and Rule 14a-8) that has affected the real world within which for-profit public entities that make products and deliver services must operate. Bemoaning the absence of injunctions under *Unocal* and *Revlon* in an era when structural defenses have been largely torn down and it has never been easier to take over a company without a fight seems to miss the most important reality. Suggesting that somehow Delaware judicial protection of the ballot box has been eroded in an era when proxy fights are more common than ever, dissident directors are regularly seated on boards, and companies back down constantly at the threat of a fight also seems to be misdirected. But then again, so, too, does suggesting that the world would be a different place if the Delaware judiciary had simply stated that directors of for-profit entities could regard constituencies such as workers and the community as equal ends of for-profit governance with the only citizens recognized by American corporate law—stockholders. After all, in jurisdictions in the United States where antitakeover and constituency statutes were adopted, there is no discernible trend toward protecting other constituencies. Outsourcing, offshoring, and regulatory shortcuts are just as, if not more, common, in corporations chartered in such states. Perhaps all that is different is that management has had more potential to use those statutes as leverage for itself. No trend of their use for workers exists.

Likewise, I yearned to see in the chapters a connection between the incentive systems within which key actors work and the policy points.

For example, the excellent chapter on the importance of director oversight in the context of financially important firms cries out for a recognition that market pressures on corporate governance may have led bank boards to be less equipped to manage externality risk and less willing to do so.[6] Firms that engaged in the activities that led to the financial crisis got a premium for that behavior before the bubble burst.[7] And of course, these very financial institutions had lobbied to relax the regulatory framework within which they conducted huge-scale financial activity, posing risks for our entire economy. Not only that, but the push for heightened independence standards and boards with large supermajorities of independent directors may have led to the seating of supposedly independent directors with no industry or professional experts to oversee risk effectively and who were more responsive to immediate market pressures than to the interests of long-term stockholders and the stability of the financial system more generally. Is it really that *Caremark*[8] with more teeth would do the trick? Or do we need to address the power dynamics that affect corporate boards, including the behavior of institutional investors and their priorities?

Put simply, I sense that clear-eyed and big-hearted thinkers such as Adolf Berle, as a corporate law specialist, or George Orwell, as a keen observer of human affairs, would be struck by the extent to which these learned thinkers let their priors and focus on past policy debates distract them from the more important overall trends in the real world over the past decades. The comparative strength of stock market forces over corporations has grown, just as all for-profit corporations have been forced to deal with intense international competition in product and services markets. In an environment where only one corporate constituency has power, when the legal moves have shifted power to the directors most sensitive to stock market pressures and the reputational threat of tangling with stockholder activists—professional independent directors with no strong ties to any company and with an ardent desire to stay in the independent director network—it is not surprising that corporations have increasingly adopted the business and governance policies that the most vocal in the market demand. The most vocal does not mean the most rational, and none of the chapters focus on this fact. Rather, the most vocal are the most active traders, the ones who deviate from stable buy-and-hold policies the most and, of course, those for whom corporate governance sport has become a hobby. As a result, corporate governance policies have moved in the direction of a "corporate California" approach, where plebiscites may be held routinely and where business strategies are highly responsive to market demands for higher payouts, more leverage, and a receptivity to acquisitions and spin-offs.

That none of the chapters commissioned on the cutting-edge topic of this collection addresses in a focused way the behavior and incentives of the class of fiduciaries who control the most capital of the most Americans—institutional investors such as mutual funds and pension funds—is a bit remarkable. So, too, is the comparative bloodlessness of the essays. Lost in these essays' expert and close focus on the mechanics of corporate law is a larger perspective on what our corporate governance system is supposed to do and why we charter for-profit entities with special rights such as limited liability and perpetual life spans.

The reality that almost every investor owes more to her ability to get a quality job than to her stock portfolio's performances is not a theme. The reality that externality risks—such as environmental degradation from climate change and pollution, dangerous working conditions, unsafe products, and the dislocating effect of events such as the financial meltdown—loom large for human investors is not a theme. The reality that most human investors do not have a say in the system and must effectively give money managers their wealth until retirement does not really get a mention. The reality that those to whom human investors must turn over their capital have fundamentally different interests than their human investors is barely touched upon.

In an era when corporate wealth and the wealth of other moneyed interests swamps the political system that is supposed to regulate the corporations society has created, pressures on the corporate law model are apparent, but they are not explored in these chapters. Traditionally, the argument has been that corporate law itself should not focus on the protection of other constituencies and the problem of externality risk, because that was a job for other bodies of positive law. But when corporations increasingly have no geographic identity and not even any basic national loyalty—consider the wave of inversions, which, put bluntly, involves forsaking American citizenship—there is little reason to think that boards will become more socially responsible absent strong external boundaries, which include not just norms but actual laws. And in a world where money management firms that do not breathe air, work in factories or stores, or have any of the other attributes of actual human investors are the direct stockholders, corporations are increasingly free to act on the political system itself, through large lobbying and political expenditures. These corporate efforts to determine who represents us and what they do in office can be expected to focus not on the larger public interest but on diminishing governmental regulation of specific industries and on seeking rents from taxpayers.

The cumulative effect of a corporate governance system that puts tremendous pressure on each company to deliver the highest profits at all times, that frees companies to act on the political process to increase returns without constraint from human investors, and that makes corporations increasingly subject to influence by immediate plebiscite is of questionable utility to the human beings for whom corporations were supposedly created. Most human beings invest for the genuinely long term. Bubbles do not help them; they wound them deeply, in the form of lost jobs, lower pay, and less wealth. Market forces that pressure corporations to externalize risks hurt them. Market pressures that encourage corporations to outsource, offshore, and otherwise reduce levels of employment and underinvest in human capital simultaneously make more scarce that which human investors need more than anything: access to quality jobs.

But that is not to say that these realities are entirely absent from this volume. Even when not explicitly addressed, many of these thoughtful essays acknowledge and begin to grapple with the clash of agents that can ill serve the humans for whom our system of corporate governance is supposed to work, even if they do so within the context of today's doctrine. For example, in their piece on changes in how the standards articulated in *Revlon* and *Unocal* are applied, Professors Davidoff Solomon and Thomas identify short-termism as a growing, potentially troubling phenomenon and observe that traditional common law constructs may not be sufficient to regulate short-term-focused behavior.[9] Similarly, Professor Bratton makes a workmanlike contribution to literature on how defensive measures could adapt to the reality that, today, one sort of agent—activist hedge funds—is more likely to threaten a corporation than the sort of agent—corporate raiders and takeover artists—for whom poison pills were originally engineered.[10] In addition to being likely to intrigue readers interested in fine-tuning or confounding corporate defenses, Professor Bratton's chapter implicitly highlights the limits of corporate law doctrine in addressing the gap between the long-term needs of human investors and the short-term forces unleashed by their agents. Although these pieces, and others in the volume, tend to highlight the limits of current doctrine, David Berger's consideration of what would be different if Delaware's corporate law recognized corporate duties to constituencies other than shareholders also should remind readers of the broad potential for defining the roles of the different actors in our corporate governance republic.[11] Berger usefully highlights the role that agents other than shareholders have historically played in our corporate governance republic,[12] which should serve as useful food for thought for readers inclined to contemplate the current state of our corporate governance republic. Likewise, Professor Pollman's forward-looking essay[13] warns of developments that herald a serious shift in power relationships within society, with judicial rulings and other developments tilting the balance of power in noneconomic spheres away from the society that gives life to business entities and toward these artificial creations, with worrisome implications for people trying to constrain corporate behavior that is socially harmful.

Like some of the best works of literature, the pieces by Professors Honigsberg and Jackson, and Professor Subramanian, invite the reader to help fill in the details of their ambitious, but admittedly sketch-form, examination of cutting-edge developments on the diverse topics of appraisal rights, financial technology, and the optimal balance of proscriptivity in corporate law. Although some might criticize their works as allowing readers with totally divergent views of the specific direction in which policies in these areas should point to claim these works for their own cause, these expansive, yet terse, expressions of the authors' viewpoints puts up a big tent at a time when many yearn for a more inclusive society.

In sum, I found these essays thought-provoking, and many of them bear consideration for useful progress on small-bore measures. In that vein, Professors Fisch and Winship dive into the realities of shareholder litigation and offer insightful analysis of the current balance of power between shareholders and boards in the litigation context.[14] So, too, does Professor Griffith advance a proactive proposal[15] to check rent seeking by stockholder plaintiffs. These important chapters give a sense of the increasing recognition that the hope that institutional investors would act to diminish litigation when it poses no benefits for investors and pursue claims only when there are bona fide reasons to do so has been dashed and that serious conflicts of interest between end-user investors and the most constant plaintiffs remain, and remain unaddressed.

Overall, this diverse and lively group of essays made me yearn to see these excellent thinkers dig deeper and reflect on this related question:

What precisely is the contract between the human beings for which society exists and the corporations that society creates? Is it one supposed to benefit human beings? Or is it to benefit the layers of agents who now feast on the wealth and power that the contract now bestows upon them, to the virtual exclusion of the human beings from which that wealth and power flows?

Notes

1. Robert B. Thompson, "Why New Corporate Law Arises: Implications for the Twenty-First Century," *infra* chapter 1; Steven Davidoff Solomon and Randall S. Thomas, "The Rise and Fall of Delaware's Takeover Standards," *infra* chapter 2.

2. *See* Thompson, *supra* note 1, at 7–9; Davidoff Solomon and Thomas, *supra* note 1, at 7–8.

3. *See* Davidoff Solomon and Thomas, *supra* note 1, at 4–8, 10–11.

4. David J. Berger, "In Search of Lost Time: What If Delaware Had Not Adopted Shareholder Primacy?," *infra* chapter 3.

5. Michael B. Dorff, "The Odd Couple: Delaware and Public Benefit Corporations," *infra* chapter 4.

6. Frank Partnoy, "Delaware and Financial Risk," *infra* chapter 6.

7. *See* William W. Bratton and Michael L. Wachter, *The Case against Shareholder Empowerment*, 158 U. Pa. L. Rev. 653, 718–21 (2010).

8. *In re* Caremark Intern. Inc. Derivative Litig., 698 A.2d 959 (Del. Ch. 1996).

9. Davidoff Solomon and Thomas, *supra* note 1, at 12, 15.

10. William W. Bratton, "Hedge Fund Activism, Poison Pills, and the Jurisprudence of Threat," *infra* chapter 7.

11. Berger, *supra* note 4.

12. *E.g.*, *id.* at 36, 46.

13. Elizabeth Pollman, "Corporate Governance beyond Economics," *infra* chapter 8.

14. Jill E. Fisch, "*Boilermakers* and the Contractual Approach to Litigation Bylaws," chapter 11; Verity Winship, "Litigation Rights and the Corporate Contract," *infra* chapter 12.

15. Sean J. Griffith, "Private Ordering Post-*Trulia*: Why No-Pay Provisions Can Fix the Deal Tax and Forum Selection Provisions Can't," *infra* chapter 13.

Introduction

Enormous changes are occurring in our capital markets as shareholder activists become increasingly prominent, institutional investors gain power, and capital markets intermediaries such as proxy advisory firms play increasingly important roles. Corporations, and their boards of directors, are also increasingly uncertain how to respond to these new dynamics and adhere to predefined fiduciary duties to stockholders. The uncertainty has led to schizophrenic responses, including the increasing use of dual-class stock and wholesale corporate governance changes of uncertain validity designed to fight off or placate certain shareholder groups.

We believe that these enormous changes merit a review of corporate law to examine needed adjustments for these revolutionary times. For example, much of the case law governing corporate conduct was created in another time—the 1980s—and designed to meet another disruptive force—hostile takeovers. Is it time to reexamine this case law and create new laws for possibly different threats? Alternatively, statutory laws such as the rules governing appraisal rights seem ripe for a complete review in the wake of appraisal arbitrage.

To examine these and related questions, the University of California, Berkeley, School of Law and Vanderbilt University Law School organized a conference on April 14 and 15, 2016, entitled "The Corporate Contract in Changing Times: Is the Law Keeping Up?" The conference was cosponsored by the law firm of Wachtell, Lipton, Rosen and Katz and spearheaded by us as well as Bill Savitt at Wachtell, Lipton.

The conference was a great success, with more than 250 attendees. It brought together leading judges, academics, practitioners, and other industry participants to discuss these and other related questions. Chief

Justice Strine and Chancellor Andre Bouchard of the Delaware Supreme Court and Delaware Chancery Court, respectively, participated.

This book is a collection of the papers presented at that conference, and a modest attempt to bring more understanding and cohesion to future corporate law.

Steven Davidoff Solomon
Randall S. Thomas

CHAPTER ONE

Why New Corporate Law Arises

Implications for the Twenty-First Century

Robert B. Thompson

Corporate law is facing calls for change that are more intense than those heard in decades. Shareholders are more aggressively pushing back against management. In turn, other corporate stakeholders are expressing increasing concern about shareholders' use of their power for selfish reasons and the perceived pernicious impact of shareholder wealth maximization as a guide for corporate law. Why does corporate law change, and how it might change now?

Corporate law changed regularly in the first half of our country's history. A series of innovations followed one after another during the nineteenth century, including limited liability, general incorporation statutes, a strong shift to director-centric corporate governance, authorization of corporations holding stock in other corporations, and the disappearance of ultra vires and other limits on corporate behavior. By the arrival of the twentieth century, all the key economic elements of the modern corporation were in view, and corporate law settled into a stable pattern we still see today. State law abandoned its prior regulatory approach and its continual change in favor of a director-centric structure with expansive room for private ordering that has remained remarkably stable. Federal law stepped in to restrain economic concentration (antitrust law), to protect employees and consumers against corporate power (done by industry regulation and employment and consumer laws, not corporate governance), to limit corporate political contributions, and to make recurring, if sporadic and noncomprehensive, efforts to enhance the role of shareholders against managers.

This chapter examines this history of change in corporate law in America, the dramatic and abrupt shift in the focus of state corporate law visible in the last decade of the nineteenth century, the interactive pattern of state and federal law that has grown up over the second half of the country's history, and prominent theories explaining what leads to corporate law change. Together these various strands suggest there will be no fundamental change in corporate law even in this time of visible stress to the now classic structure.

Prior Changes in Corporate Law

Over the first decades of the nineteenth century, for-profit corporations came to supplant religious, charitable, and quasi-public (bridge or turnpike) entities as principal users of the corporate form (Blumberg 1990). Corporate law changes reflected and facilitated this trend. By the end of the century, the modern corporation was in view with the economic characteristics that are familiar to twenty-first-century lawyers and business people. The 1890s presented a key inflection point for corporate law. States abandoned their regulatory approach to corporations in favor of permissive laws that were director-centric in their allocation of power and left ample room for market decision making, contracting, and private ordering. The government's regulatory impulse did not disappear, however, but came to be expressed in various regulatory regimes in federal law—for example, antitrust, worker protection, and the parts of federal securities laws that addressed corporate governance.

Changes over the Nineteenth Century

Corporations evolved dramatically over the nineteenth century in America, accompanied by recurring changes in corporate law. The legal changes occurred incrementally among the various states over multiple decades, often with each change occurring in partial steps in an individual state, making the national change seem even more incremental. The statutory changes in turn reflected fundamental economic and financial changes that were taking place on the ground that continued to evolve. By the end of the century, these various trends had jelled into a legal form we would recognize as the modern corporation and a regulatory structure that would be familiar to modern corporate lawyers.

The components of this dramatic transformation of the corporation and its regulatory structure included: (1) growth in the number of corporations and the increasing dominance of for-profit entities; (2) limited liability for shareholders becoming the usual rule; (3) the move from special legislative chartering of each corporation to general incorporation laws; (4) evolution in the corporate form to facilitate centralized management and the rise of middle management in business to take greater advantage of this corporate characteristic; (5) public trading of stocks; and (6) permitting corporations to own stock in other corporations.

GROWTH IN THE NUMBER OF INCORPORATIONS AND THE INCREASING DOMINANCE OF FOR-PROFIT ENTITIES. Joseph Ellis (2015) has described the move to the Constitution from the Declaration of Independence (and the weak Articles of Confederation that connected the newly independent states) as a second American revolution that turned on a change in the size of the world that Americans defined for themselves. In the colonial period, the geographic space citizens considered relevant for their political and business life was small, perhaps thirty miles; giving powers to a national government seemed too likely to reprise the oppression of the British crown against which the revolution had been fought. But the dysfunction of the confederation government, and perhaps some sense of the economic possibilities in a larger republic, led to a change in the form of government, which facilitated a broadened geographic frame of reference for politics that would soon be followed in American business. Over time there was opportunity, and a greater need, for enterprises that assembled the capital from more than one person (Livermore 1939), and over time improvements in transportation and machinery increased the size of the market in which entrepreneurs could compete effectively. The result was a dramatic increase in the number of corporations, particularly for-profit corporations, in the early nineteenth century.

Some of the most visible early nineteenth-century corporations were created for bridge or turnpike companies; these infrastructure projects were needed by the community but were financed with private funds under a governmental charter, leading to a close association in the minds of the public between specially chartered corporations and worries about privilege and monopoly. Banking corporations were common and the subject of much of the Supreme Court litigation of the period (Blair and Pollman 2015), raising questions of how to regulate entities affecting the money supply and similar issues that invoked core public issues. By the

1830s, manufacturing corporations exceeded those in banking, insurance, and public service and the number was growing (Blumberg 1990); more companies were incorporated in Illinois in the 1850s than in the entire first half of the century (Dodd 1936).

LIMITED LIABILITY. As the size of markets and the need for capital in a particular business grew, limited liability was seen as a way to encourage entrepreneurial risk taking. Several states adopted such rules in the first two decades of the nineteenth century. Massachusetts moved to limited liability for shareholders in 1830, and this rule became common in other states for corporations. Even so, it did not provide complete insulation from limited liability. Double liability, subjecting shareholders to personal liability for corporate obligations beyond their original investment up to an additional sum equal to that amount, remained the norm for the remainder of the century (and continued for California corporations and for national banks into the middle of the twentieth century) (Horwitz 1986).

GENERAL INCORPORATION STATUTES. Concerns about privileges provided to incorporated businesses at the expense of the larger population, mixed in with Jacksonian opposition to rechartering the Bank of the United States (banks generally being one of the most visible groups of incorporated entities), led to passage of general incorporation statutes in some states in the 1830s and 1840s and in almost all states by 1875 (Hamil 1999). This may be the largest single statutory change for corporate law over the nineteenth century, but consistent with the other changes, it happened incrementally—four states in the 1830s, three in the 1850s, and continuing to build (Hilt 2008). Even as the states moved to provide general incorporation, many of them did not prohibit state legislatures from continuing to provide special charters to individual companies on whatever terms the legislature desired. Delaware, for example, had a general incorporation statute as early as 1875 (and relaxed the conditions for the use of the general statute in 1883); even so, in 1897, just before Delaware's modern statute of 1899, the number of special charters (115) was more than eleven times greater than the ten entities that used the general incorporation law for that same year (Arsht 1976).

Eric Hilt traced the impact of Massachusetts's general corporation act of 1851, under which the state continued to retain special chartering from the legislature after enacting a general incorporation statute. Hilt found that "the firms created under the general act looked quite different" from firms chartered prior to 1851 (when special chartering was the only option) or firms that used the special charter route after 1851 (Hilt 2008, at 25). They were more diffuse in their industries and geography than the specially chartered firms, were significantly smaller with fewer shareholders, and had much higher degrees of managerial ownership (Hilt 2008).

CENTRALIZED MANAGEMENT. Centralized management has long been an advantage of the corporate form, but its use in business corporations changed dramatically in the nineteenth century, for both legal and economic reasons. Educational and other charitable and nonprofit corporations had previously received charters that put control in a board of trustees or directors. Livermore's treatment of land companies on the western frontier before and after the Revolutionary War shows some degree of centralized governance in these business firms even without charters in a setting where citizens were making "side" investments to their everyday commercial pursuits (Livermore 1939).

General use of centralized management was later in coming than the two characteristics of limited liability and general incorporation just described. New Deal Supreme Court Justice Wiley Rutledge, in his earlier role as a corporations law professor, observed that "the general incorporation laws of the nineteenth century were designed primarily to extend the privilege of limited liability to what may be termed 'incorporated partnerships' and relatively local joint stock companies rather than the creation of institutions national in the spread of their securities and activities" (Rutledge 1937 at 307). Noted business historian Alfred Chandler similarly described the increasing use of the incorporated stock company in the early nineteenth century, but through the 1840s he saw no change in the relatively decentralized governance characteristics that still proved satisfactory for most businesses (Chandler 1977).

Over the latter half of the nineteenth century, there was a gradual decline in the importance of the general meeting of shareholders as reflected in the broadening power exercised by directors. Dodd (1936) noted, for example, the very broad powers given directors in general incorporation acts such as that of Illinois in 1872. Horwitz (1986 at 182) identified this late nineteenth-century shifting of power away from shareholders to directors so that after 1900 directors were treated "as equivalent to the corporation itself."

The legal changes reflected the evolution in market and financial conditions after the Civil War, when innovations propelled by the Industrial Revolution and changes in transportation, manufacturing, and distribution increased the scope of markets in which firms could compete. Middle management that had not earlier existed became a common feature of corporations, and managers who did not own a majority of shares acquired effective control of many firms. Depending on how businesses became large in this new environment, some firms whose internal growth was sufficient to meet their capital needs became managerial under the control of the founders or family. By contrast, firms that needed outside capital to become large and take advantage of the new economies of scale were run by managers with only a minority of stock ownership (Chandler 1977). Once statutes provided for control by directors, as set out in the early Delaware general incorporation statutes described below, and provided for director appointment of other officers and agents, the statutory structure was sufficiently malleable to permit the growth of top executives and middle managers as economic conditions evolved.

PUBLIC TRADING OF STOCKS. Like the centralized control just described, public trading of stock reflected the changing possibilities provided by evolving markets and finance. Early general corporation statutes proclaimed stock to be personal property and provided for its sale by means set forth in the bylaws (Hilt 2015 at 9). After the Civil War, stock exchanges expanded to include a larger number of manufacturing firms that effectively provided free transferability across a broad range of America's largest firms without the need for any bylaw provision or private contracting (Navin and Sears 1955 at 107–8). By the end of the nineteenth century, free transferability had developed to the point where it became a usual characteristic of the modern conception of a corporation.

RECOGNITION OF HOLDING COMPANIES. The last characteristic of the modern corporation to appear in the nineteenth century was the statutory grant to corporations to own stock in other corporations. Changes in economic and financial conditions showed the benefit of controlling entities operating in multiple states. Yet doing business outside the state of incorporation presented some difficulty for corporations given a Supreme Court decision in 1839 that declined to find such a constitutional right for corporations.[1] Entrepreneurs such as John D. Rockefeller looked to trusts as a way to structure the burgeoning oil refinery business that he was assembling.[2] He organized the South Improvement Company in the 1870s and then made Standard Oil into a trust in the 1880s, providing the same centralized control available within the corporate form but without the limits in operating across state lines or owning stock in other corporations (Chandler 1977 at 323). When state courts in Louisiana, New York, and Ohio found trusts in cotton, sugar, and oil violated state corporations laws, New Jersey came to their rescue. In 1888 and 1889, amendments to the New Jersey corporations statute authorized corporations to own stock in other corporations (Horwitz 1986 at 195).

The Modern Corporation in View: The Inflection Point in the Late Nineteenth Century That Shaped Corporate Law

By the late 1880s, all the elements of the modern corporation were in view (if not yet spread to all corners of the country). It was a coming together of the expansion in the geographic and industrial scale that could be supported in the growing American economy and the administrative ascendancy of middle managers (Chandler 1977). Corporate law reflected and facilitated these changes; the liberalizations of New Jersey's general incorporation act of 1896 provided no limit on a corporation's duration, permitted incorporation for any lawful purpose and to carry on business in other jurisdictions, authorized mergers and consolidations, and enabled director amendments of bylaws (Strine and Walter 2015). New Jersey became the home not just of Standard Oil but of a substantial percentage of larger New York businesses. The race among the states was on, with New Jersey being the early favorite and Delaware stepping into New Jersey's shoes after that state's governor, Woodrow Wilson, pushed reform on his way to Washington to assume the presidency (Yablon 2007). This period also saw a decline in other traditional restrictions on corporations—the disappearance of ultra vires and quo warranto actions that had been used to limit corporations' acts—and a similar shriveling of state efforts to assert control over foreign corporations (Horwitz 1986).

Here we see a wholesale state law abandonment of the prior regulatory approach to corporations in favor of the permissive director-centric approach with more room for private ordering that still characterizes American corporate law. Joel Seligman (1976) termed it a "revolution wrought in the law of corporations" (264) that led to general incorporation statutes that "turned corporate law inside out" (273). Similarly, Justice (then Professor) Rutledge described the New Jersey law of 1887–1891 as "destined eventually to reverse the historic policy of the states [and] to place state policy fundamentally in opposition to that of the Federal government" (Rutledge 1937 at 311–12).

This point of inflection was recurringly described as following from the underlying changes in an economy where size seemed inevitable. Rutledge (1937 at 311–12) characterizes prior corporations statutes ("horse and buggy statutes" he called them) as "antiquated and inadequate to the needs of modern high-powered business organized, on a mass-production scale. . . . It may be that a society organized as broadly as ours is upon the basis of machines and under the capitalistic system, changing as rapidly as it has done during the last fifty years, can operate only with highly mobile industrial and financial organizations. If this is true, and the tendency certainly seems to have been in this direction . . . , the power phases of the recent corporate development have been necessary phases of that growth."

Morton Horwitz (1986), even less of a champion of big business than Rutledge, noted a "stunning reversal in American economic thought" in this period to "defend and justify as inevitable" the emergence of large-scale corporate concentration, pointing to the writings of economist Henry Adams and to the influence of the "natural entity" theory of the corporate entity whose main effect "was to legitimate large scale enterprise and to destroy any special basis for state regulation" (221). When Columbia University president Nicholas Murray Butler (1912) declared the limited liability corporation as "the greatest single discovery of modern times . . . [e]ven steam and electricity are far less important . . . and they would be of comparative impotence without it," he based his claim on this fundamental economic shift in society: "The era of unrestricted individual competition has gone forever . . . taken up into a new and larger principle of cooperation . . . It cannot be stopped. It ought not to be stopped. It is not in the public interest that it be stopped. . . . This new movement of cooperation has manifested itself in the last sixty or seventy years chiefly in the limited liability corporation" (82).

For some, this belief led to a conclusion that "legal forms cannot interfere with the natural evolution of the economy," expressed in support of general incorporation acts that did not restrict corporations (Bostwick 1899). The permissive approach to state corporate law that has prevailed since the late nineteenth century is consistent with this version. For others, including Butler and progressives of the day, this economic fact led to more support for intense federal regulation that found expression in antitrust and railroad regulation from the late nineteenth century (Butler 1912) or federal securities laws that increasingly provided mandatory federal rules of corporate governance. The reality is that the corporate law of the nineteenth century has continued in two streams: state corporations law that corporate lawyers of the late nineteenth century would still recognize as familiar and federal law of various flavors that has experienced a much greater degree of change. Justice Louis Brandeis's lament in his dissent in the Liggett case in 1933[3] that corporate law had been denuded of all its traditional constraints cannot be fully appreciated today with considering the mantle of regulation assumed by federal law in the time since.

Changes in Corporate Law in the Second Half of the Country's History

Since the point of inflection discussed in the previous section, the pattern of change in corporate law illustrates two divergent paths. State corporate law today is still the governance system whose core points would be recognized by the cutting-edge late nineteenth-century corporate lawyers who drafted the statutes of that period. Federal law reflects a completely different pattern of regular and diffuse changes. The two strands existing simultaneously are a necessary foundation to the theory of changes discussed below.

STATE CORPORATE LAW. Modern corporate law reflects three core principles that can be directly traced to nineteenth-century corporate law and to an important and sometimes overlooked fourth principle acknowledging how the business and economic foundation on which the law is placed fundamentally reshapes the reality of the initial three rules.

Rule 1: Directors rule (most of the time). This principle derives from a bedrock point of corporate law found in all American corporate statutes, including Delaware's § 141 and § 8.01(b) of the Model Business Corporation Act, that "all" corporate powers shall be exercised by the board. Empowering a centralized group to speak for the entity provides efficiency benefits in an economy where shareholding is widely dispersed. As a centralized decision maker, the board can negotiate on behalf of shareholders and other constituencies. The wording of today's section 141 comes directly from Section 20 of Delaware's 1899 General Corporation Act: "The business of every corporation organized under the provisions of this Act shall be managed by a board"[4] and tracks similar language in Delaware's 1883 statute (but not in Delaware's first general incorporation statute in 1875). The business judgment rule, a common law presumption of judicial deference to director decisions, reflects this same principle and also dates to the nineteenth century (Smith 1998). At the same time, directors with this broad power to direct other people's money might not pay as much attention to the enterprise that the shareholders would like them to or may use their power to benefit themselves or the managers who they fail to monitor sufficiently. This leads to rules 2 and 3.

Rule 2: Shareholders are empowered to do only three things—vote, sell, and sue, and only in limited doses. Shareholders are not given plenary powers to decide corporate policy (Thompson 2016). Rather, they are conceived as simple actors able to perform only three basic functions. First, they are permitted to elect directors once a year and vote on mergers and other fundamental changes (provided the directors have first agreed to such a transaction). Shareholder power to vote to amend the corporation's bylaws, in some situations without the board playing a gatekeeping role, has taken on broader importance in recent years. Second, shareholders can sell their shares, either in the market or in response to a tender offer made to them by a bidder seeking to acquire control. Third, they can, in some limited situations, sue for violation of statutes or fiduciary duties.

The current language of Delaware § 211(b) specifying stockholder election of directors at an annual meeting tracks the language of the 1899 act and parallels the same principle written into the 1883 act. [5] Today's language empowering stockholders to make and alter bylaws also dates from the 1899 statute, along with the enabling language that this authority may be conferred on directors. These precise specifications of shareholder power contrast to common provisions of special incorporation statutes that focused corporate governance on the general meeting of shareholders. Indeed, Delaware's first general incorporation act, enacted in 1875, was silent on director control. These limited powers retained for shareholders in the time since reflect the concern that directors, while providing the advantages of centralized control, may, if unconstrained, act in ways that benefit themselves or otherwise harm shareholders. Shareholders, so the argument goes, are best positioned as a residual claimant of the enterprise to perform this monitoring function (Thompson 2016).

Rule 3: Judicial review provides a check on agency power via fiduciary duties and resolves disputes at the boundary of director and shareholder power. American corporate law relies on courts to constrain director decisions (and possible abuse of their centralized power) by enforcing fiduciary duties of care and loyalty and sometimes resolving overlap between directors and shareholder realms. The early general incorporation acts were largely silent, as today's Delaware statute still is, as to directors' and officers' duties, so this space has been occupied by the courts and, more recently, the federal government. One of the key mid-twentieth-century drafters of the current Delaware statute concluded that in the post-1899 world, Delaware courts "promptly asserted the power of the Delaware judiciary to prevent corporate fraud and the inequitable use of corporate machinery by management" (Arsht 1976 at 1). That severely telescopes the build-out of Delaware common law of fiduciary duty that largely occurred much later in the twentieth century. "Entire fairness" cases can be found prior to World War II, but it took until the 1970s and 1980s to see the complex review structure of Unocal, Revlon, and Blasius and the even more elaborate use of special committees and other internal corporate governance to cleanse possible director incapacity that have followed (Davidoff Solomon and Thomas 2016).

Rule 4. Legal rules defer to the business and economic reality that managers usually are the first mover in corporate governance. Reading only the statutes or common law rules described above would leave one with a fundamental misunderstanding of American corporate governance. These legal rules have intentionally been placed atop a business and economic reality where there are efficiencies from a separation of function among shareholders, directors, and managers and where a managerial hierarchy will often be the most effective decision maker for the firm. This means that managers will usually be the first movers in corporate governance. That all-encompassing director power of rule 1 will only be used intermittently, when managers are disabled by conflict or in times of crisis or egregious shortfalls in care. Shareholder power in its more limited space described above will be used even more intermittently. This shared power governance structure leaves substantial room for private ordering as each of these groups pushes back against the other. Managers threaten not to cooperate (Badawi 2014). Shareholders push directors and management to change even without seeking to take over the company, as was more common in the hostile takeover world of the late 1960s and early 1980s. Delaware courts seem to understand that within this shared power system, keeping all players in the game is an important judicial function, so that each lives to fight another day, and effective governance requires the continued interaction of the parties (Thompson 2016).

This is not to say, however, that directors and managers do not have the central position under state law governance. It would be misdirection to characterize Delaware law as shareholder friendly because its law lacks some of the severe antitakeover statutes of other states. Delaware's early blessing of poison pills and its supreme court's refusal to rein in that use of director power in all but the most egregious cases is more telling than a host of rarely used antitakeover statutes. Relative to this chapter's focus on why law changes, this gives the governance structure in state corporate law a much more stable appearance while leaving considerable room for contracting and other private ordering within the broad boundaries set by the legal governance structure.

FEDERAL LAW AFFECTING CORPORATIONS. As state corporations law took a less regulatory approach at the end of the nineteenth century, federal law occupied the regulatory space that the states abandoned and also partially advanced into the manager-director-shareholder governance structure that became the focus of state corporations laws in the twentieth century. The first move focused on direct regulation of corporations because their conduct affects the public or subgroups such as consumers or workers (i.e., outsiders to the internal governance space just mentioned). The second move often sought to bolster shareholders in their interaction with boards and managers and to limit the broad space for those actors that state corporate law provided.

Regulating Corporate Conduct Affecting the Public and Outsiders: From the founding of the republic, corporate law had reflected mistrust of the corporate form based on, for example, size or fear of monopoly or special privilege, leading to recurring limits on purpose, size, or duration of these entities. As the state law changes discussed above embraced the potential for growth that the corporate form could provide in a changing economy, this regulatory impulse did not disappear;

rather, it moved to a different level of government. Even before New Jersey had completed its shift to a laissez-faire statute that freed Standard Oil and other large corporations of the traditional limits of state corporate law, Congress enacted the Sherman Antitrust Act in 1890, providing a federal venue to challenge monopolies and other forms of anticompetitive behavior. Direct industry regulation, such as over railroads, grew after enactment of the Interstate Commerce Act, passed shortly before the Sherman Act. In the early twentieth century, the Tillman Act limited the ability of corporations to make political contributions. The Federal Trade Act bolstered the antitrust powers of the federal government and provided consumer protection, largely against corporations. Another generation later, the New Deal brought a host of new governmental controls over the business activities of corporations vis-à-vis consumers, employees, and the public. Much of this regulation reflects the nature of the fears that had generated the direct regulation of corporations in the first half of the country's history, but which had disappeared from state corporate law with changes triggered in the late nineteenth century.

Regulating Internal Corporate Governance in the Space That State Law Had Retained: As state law narrowed its corporate law to focus on the relative governance rights of shareholders, managers, and officers, Congress did not provide a comprehensive set of federal rules as it had done in the areas just discussed, but neither was it willing to leave undisturbed the state law balance in corporate governance. The twentieth century saw three highly visible movements to federalize corporate law: during the Progressive movement at the beginning of the century, when three consecutive presidents favored federal incorporation statutes; during the beginning of the New Deal, when the government contemplated responses to the Great Depression; and in the latter part of the century in the debate over the "race to the bottom" versus the "race to the top." Federal incorporation did not result from any of those debates, but the result has been a series of federal intrusions into corporate governance and a bifurcation of corporate rule making between state and federal lawmakers that is highly relevant in the discussion of why corporate law changes (Thompson and Sale 2003):

- The disclosure requirements of the Securities Exchange Act of 1934, later expanded by the Williams Act in 1968, sought to empower shareholders (vis-à-vis directors and centralized managers) when they voted or sold their shares, a dramatic governance addition to state corporations statutes which still have very little in terms of what must be disclosed before shareholders act;

- Rule 14a-8 (promulgated in 1942) was one of many efforts of the Securities and Exchange Commission over the last eighty years to enhance the position of shareholders in the state governance structure described above by, for example, creating a forum for shareholders to pursue proposals about corporate governance;
- The federal government has been increasingly willing to fill in the duties of managers (about which state law is almost completely silent) by, for example, specifying legal duties of the chief executive officers and chief financial officers and providing clawback of compensation in certain circumstances;
- Twenty-first-century federal law has even specified the makeup of the board of directors, an issue at the very core of state governance, by requiring that boards have key committees made up of independent directors, something that state law is silent about, leaving such questions to private ordering.

Recurring changes that have taken place in the federal space present a completely different pattern than what has happened in state law. Predicting when law will change requires examining the prevailing approach followed at each level of government and, even more, the interaction between them.

Why Does Law Change?

Theories on Why Law Changes

Different theories have been suggested as to what would cause laws to change. Changes in the underlying economy, from inventions to demographic changes to trade relationships, would seem obvious reasons. The shifts in the American economy in the nineteenth century described at the beginning of this chapter suggest such a change. Changes in the legal system could have a similar effect, as was common in various countries after the fall of the Berlin Wall.

Stuart Banner suggests such a theory would be too broad. In the context of a discussion about the impact of technological advances on securities trading, Banner (1997, 855) argues such changes alone would not be sufficient: "If one wants to know what future events would be most likely to persuade governments [to enact new regulatory laws] the answer is not new developments in information technology. The answer is a crash." His conclusion, reflecting three hundred years of securities trading, is that as long as securities markets are rising or holding steady, new regulation is held in check "by the simple fact that too many people have been making too much money to favor regulation restricting trading. But when prices drop much of that opposition to regulation is removed. People who are proponents of securities trading in good times become critics in bad" (851).

That theory does well in explaining changes to American securities regulation—and the parts of corporate conduct that Congress has used the federal securities laws to reach. The crash of 1929 was followed by the Great Depression and the federal securities laws of the New Deal. The smaller market reaction at the time of the Enron scandal led to the Sarbanes-Oxley Act of 2002. The Great Recession of the late 2000s included a painful crash and precipitated the reforms of the Dodd-Frank Act of 2010. Together, those legal responses to financial crises cover the list of federal changes to "internal" corporate law identified in the previous section. But the theory seems to do less well in explaining the series of changes to state corporate law in the nineteenth century and the relative stability of state corporate law since then.

Much of the debate on the change in corporate law has focused on theories surrounding interest groups. William Cary, writing in 1974 but reflecting ideas going back to New Jersey's ascent in the 1890s, argued that states compete for incorporations by making their laws favorable to insiders who realistically make the choices as to where to incorporate, with the result being a race to the bottom among the states. Ralph Winter (1977) responded that if there is a race, it is to the top, not the bottom, propelled by the power of markets. Winter argued that if a corporation chose a place of incorporation that produced inferior results for its shareholders, those investors would move their money to invest in businesses from other jurisdictions with different rules.

Whatever the result of the debate about the direction of the race among the various states (and many articles have been written and much empirical data gathered as to the relative performance of corporations formed in Delaware and other states), the pattern of state and federal law set out above suggests the limitations of any such theory that considers only states competing against one another. Mark Roe (2003) has shown that even if Delaware has the instincts that Cary believed it did, the fear that the federal government will preempt all of state corporate law keeps Delaware from going very far in that direction. It seems, even more than Roe has suggested, that there is a lock-in; all state laws are locked in to a statute that prefers control in directors and managers and the ability of the parties to freely contract about the governance system. If economic conditions change so that is not the preferred result, then the new law will most surely come from the federal government, not the states, as discussed more fully below.

Projecting Change in Law Given the Contemporary Context

STRESS ON THE CLASSIC SYSTEM. Contemporary developments in the corporate space are putting more stress on the classic governance system. First, technology has dramatically lowered the costs of gathering and storing information and lowered the costs of communicating across markets, such as among shareholders in a publicly held corporation, making it easier for shareholders to challenge a centralized hierarchy. Second, changes in how the United States has chosen to fund worker retirement has created a different census of shareholders with incentives and conflicts that have diverged from traditional mom-and-pop shareholders that typified shareholders of publicly held corporations in earlier generations. Seventy percent or more of the equity in American public corporations is owned by institutions acting as intermediaries for beneficiaries such as individuals or nonprofit educational and charitable entities.

A majority of American stock is in the hands of a particular kind of institutional investor—mutual funds or similar investments as part of employer-sponsored retirement plans given preferred tax status by the federal government and providing a vehicle for employees to save for retirement or their children's education (Edelman, Thomas, and Thompson 2014). The business plan for these funds, directed toward getting employers to include the fund among the small number of funds offered in the plan made available to employees of that particular company, gives the funds little reason to vote the shares that they control (Gilson and Gordon 2013). Any money spent on corporate governance in portfolio companies only increases costs, while benefits are shared by other funds holding shares in the same portfolio company that have not incurred those costs. In such a setting, dollars spent for voting can lower the active fund's relative performance, a common metric that plan sponsors use in deciding which funds to include in a company's plan.

Yet federal agencies (first under laws protecting employees and their retirement and more recently under laws directed to protect investors) now require intermediaries to vote the shares that they control and have expanded the number of issues on which shareholders vote, as compared to the limited list specified in state corporate law. The urgent need of institutional investors to be informed about these votes, and their lack of incentive to spend much money in the process, created an opening for a new set of agents in the voting process—proxy advisory firms. Such firms focus on providing information and voting services to institutional investors by gathering information about each of the votes to be held at public firms and then distributing that information for a fee to the many institutional investors that own shares in that company. Their efficiencies extend to tracking and submitting tens of thousands of votes cast each year by institutions. Moreover, these advisory firms have developed expertise on issues of corporate governance. A small group of proxy advisory firms has grown up over the last twenty-five years, with Institutional Shareholder Services the most visible (Edelman, Thomas, and Thompson 2014).

For most of the history of American corporate law, it made little economic sense for shareholders to use the powers given to them under state corporate law even with the federal enhancements. The collective action problems were too great when one shareholder with a minuscule portion of the equity would have to spend an amount for litigating or voting that would quickly exceed what it could hope to get back from the pro rata change in the value of its stock from any successful outcome. The dominant strategy for shareholders unhappy with their managers was the Wall Street rule to simply sell the stock (Schwartz 1978). In the contemporary governance setting described above, one group of institutional investors—activist hedge funds—has figured out a way to make shareholder voting profitable. The organization, regulation, and business plans followed by hedge funds give them high-powered incentives to seek out relatively risky investments that can produce above-average returns. The subset of hedge funds focused on active governance seeks out situations where a change in the target company's financial strategy (e.g., a dividend or stock buyback) can produce short-term gains for shareholders. The activist shareholders' business plan (e.g., high leverage) means they do not want to commit funds sufficient to acquire control of the company. Crucially for their strategy, mutual funds and other institutional investors that own the bulk of the equity (and the proxy advisory firms who advise institutions) are sometimes willing to support such proposals. At least this combination has occurred enough to push directors and managers to share the usual levers of corporate power when activists come calling.

A concern about too much short-termism and possible shareholder overreaching has opened a new chapter of a long-running corporate governance debate. For example, Delaware's Chief Justice Leo Strine, a learned and prescient observer of all things corporate, has suggested a series of proposed governance changes designed to (1) align the intermediaries that control the funds invested in American equities with the long-term values of end users for whom those funds are invested; (2) reduce and sharpen the number of votes put before shareholders so as to not "overwhelm" the capacity of the institutional investor community "to actually think in a serious manner how to vote"; and (3) regulate the activist shareholders using current governance procedures by requiring more skin in the game for those making shareholder proposals and obtaining additional disclosure for those who are seeking shareholder votes on changes in corporate policy (Strine 2014).

HOW MIGHT CORPORATE LAW CHANGE IN THIS NEW SETTING?. What kind of changes in law might be expected given the changes and stresses just described? The governance issues raised in the activist shareholder context in the current period are at the core of traditional state corporate law, so we might expect the states to be the focal point for possible changes in law. The relative control rights of shareholders as compared to directors and managers has been the principal concern of state law since the reconfiguration of state and federal law in the corporate area that began in the 1890s. Further, the substance of what is being debated—concern about inappropriate shareholder interference with board governance—fits easily within the director-centric structure that has characterized Delaware law and most other states for more than a century.

Yet Delaware law has not gone very far in exploring possible responses when the governance problem is said to be shareholder overreaching. One reason is a mismatch with the toolbox currently available to state law. As already described, Delaware law lets shareholders do only three things—vote, sell, and sue, each in limited doses. In such a setting, its courts have never had to spend a lot of time developing tools to constrain shareholder overreaching. It has often been enough to rely simply on rule 1 above, which puts most corporate power in the hands of the board and lets them use that power to constrain particular exercises of shareholder power. See, for example, the ease with which the Delaware Supreme Court expanded director power in *Unitrin* to easily intrude on shareholder efforts to assert their right to sell in a takeover context. Similarly, other decisions have trimmed the more intense judicial scrutiny of the *Blasius* standard applicable to directorial interference with the shareholders' vote so that it is only "rarely applied" (Thompson 2016 at 420).

More specifically, the primary tool used by Delaware courts to resolve governance disputes would likely be difficult to adapt to the shareholder setting. Fiduciary duty is well developed in cases where a manager or a board of directors has used its control over other people's money in violation of duties of loyalty or care. These duties have occasionally been extended to controlling shareholders who occupy a similar position, and there have been some cases raising a parallel situation where a shareholder has a veto, but the activist setting would extend fiduciary obligations beyond traditional applications.

Thus, extending state corporate law would require building out a whole new set of rules beyond what is currently found in state law to address shareholding in public corporations in this new world of institutional shareholders. That is not to say it could not be done, or should not be done. The changes introduced in the 1890s were even more dramatic. More recent developments such as the special litigation committee and the poison pill originally arose from private ordering of entrepreneurial lawyers. Similar approaches could find a platform in addressing the activism question within state corporate law.

Some of the suggestions made in the current debate—for example, requiring institutional shareholders, such as mutual funds, to vote in compliance with their investment policy for their beneficiaries or permitting reimbursement of nonmanagement director nominees who cross a certain threshold of votes received—fit easily within the scope of traditional corporate law (Strine 2014). Others require changes in tax policy or regulation of retirement plan investment, which has not been the usual concern of state law. Other suggestions, such as reducing the frequency of shareholder votes, would require rolling back federal law that has consciously replaced state power.

Delaware's reluctance to take on this challenge reflects the historical pattern that has developed in which the state and federal governments share lawmaking space for corporate law. Delaware's preferred approach is a director-centric model that emphasizes contracting and other private ordering among key corporate constituencies. When the state wishes to intervene, its preferred tool is to adjust the rules applicable to directors. By contrast, the federal government has long seen the world of corporate governance through a lens shaded toward the role of shareholders. When a crash suggests the need to intervene in the state-based system, the federal government's preferred tool is mandatory rules focused on shareholder power. Of course, each actor is addressing aspects of the allocation of governance power in the corporation so that an adjustment to director power necessarily affects that allocated to shareholders and *vice versa* but that does not diminish the characteristic approach for each government. Congress has regularly provided rules for corporate governance but has not intruded on directors' core power to make corporate decisions. When a Delaware court needed to specify corporate disclosure obligations in advance of a shareholder vote where directors have a conflicting interest, it expressly eschewed promulgating state-based rules in favor of a blanket incorporation of federal law on the subject: "Federal regulations and exchange rules address disclosure of this kind in a detailed manner that balances the cost of disclosing all past relationships against the need to give stockholders information about some prior relationship that, while not rendering directors non-independent of each other, are important enough to warrant disclosure. Those bodies of authorities should not be lightly added to by our law."[6]

Several factors contribute to Delaware's disinclination to change its law. One is a strong preference for its longtime director-centric governance system with its ample room for private ordering and a shared power structure making use of the separate contributions of managers, directors, and shareholders, characteristic of Delaware law since the late nineteenth century. Another is the preferences of managers and institutional shareholders for such a structure—the two groups who could upset this equilibrium if they wanted by moving to other jurisdictions. Delaware has ample reason to get this right because it is home to about 60 percent of America's largest corporations, with 20 percent or more of its state budget coming from incorporations. Delaware also values the sophisticated corporate bar and its nationally recognized judiciary that focuses on corporate law, bringing fame and fortune to those groups well beyond what would be associated with a state forty-ninth in size and forty-fifth in population among the fifty states. In turn, these groups contribute to network effects and reduce the level of uncertainty, a reduction that consumers of a corporate governance system value (Klausner 1995).

To maintain this favorable position, Delaware needs to worry about possibly simultaneous challenges in two separate dimensions: First, one or more of the other states might seek to topple Delaware from its crown just as Delaware did to New Jersey in the previous century; second, Delaware, to the extent it is able, does not want to provoke federal action preempting the core of what remains of corporate law in the state domain. Any governance decision to alter the allocation of power between shareholders and managers, for example, could upset the equilibrium. In the competition with other states, the risks differ depending on which way Delaware might move—for example, toward a more director-empowering position or to a more shareholder-empowering position.

There has been little threat to Delaware's position from other states following a shareholder-empowering approach. North Dakota's intentionally shareholder-friendly statute of 2007 has come up practically empty in terms of attracting publicly held corporations. California's statute is the best example of an older statute with views different than those of Delaware, but our largest state punches well below its population's share in terms of number of corporations that have chosen to be governed by its law.

The challenge from states attempting to compete with Delaware by adopting more pro-management laws than Delaware has been somewhat stronger. Some states have passed more antitakeover statues than Delaware, although the trend has slowed since the early 1990s. More recently, a handful of states have enacted mandatory staggered boards for entities incorporated in their state, a provision seen as aiding management. The motivation driving such change and the effect of such statutes often seem to relate to a particular local company threatened by an unwanted takeover. Nevada has perhaps gone the furthest in separating itself from Delaware on this dimension, adding provisions that permit waiver of fiduciary duties of loyalty in addition to antitakeover statutes. Recent studies show its effect concentrated in small firms with low institutional shareholding but not in corporations more generally. Delaware, with its larger share of publicly held firms that would not value a tipping of the balance between various corporate constituencies, would, according to one study, lose 11 percent of its market share and between $35 million and $70 million per year in franchise taxes if it changed its laws to adopt stronger management protections, as in Nevada: "Nevada does not seem to create pressure on Delaware to cater to managerial interest" (Eldar and Magnolfi 2016 at 4). From the perspective of a race among the states, there seems little reason for Delaware to move from its sweet spot.

In looking at the interaction with the federal government, the result seems to be the same. The pattern for most of the past 120 years has been for the federal law to step in when the balance of state law goes awry (Roe 2003). This interaction has usually produced a change in one direction: toward greater empowerment of shareholders. If Delaware were to step in to limit the power of shareholders, such action increases the likelihood of a federal response, as has occurred twice already in this century, in Sarbanes-Oxley and Dodd-Frank. Even if Delaware wanted to legislate to increase the power of shareholders, it would be competing against an already large federal footprint. Why should the state modify corporate law rules to lean toward shareholders when the federal inclination in making laws relating to corporations over the past eighty years leans so much in the direction of adding provisions for shareholders? And why should Delaware modify corporate rules to lean toward directors or managers when it may simply provoke federal response to take more or all of corporate law under the wing of federal law?

Might a period of significant federal deregulation during the Trump administration change this pattern? After all, a prior such period in the early 1980s produced perhaps the most significant deviation from the lawmaking pattern described here, at least on the Delaware side. The Unocal, Revlon, and Blasius fiduciary duty standards developed in those years held the possibility of significant limits on director discretion (Davidoff Solomon and Thomas 2016). A couple of factors point to a narrow impact of such a scenario. The still interstitial footprint of existing federal corporate governance rules, even after eighty years of federal lawmaking, suggest that any particular federal action likely will not disrupt the overall pattern. The limited bang for the buck for any such interstitial rollbacks likely pushes such changes down the deregulatory agenda. On the state side, as discussed above, the director-centric approach of Delaware law and the judicial reliance on director fiduciary duty are not well suited to provide new rules focused on activist shareholders. Delaware corporate law remains focused on managers and, to a lesser extent, shareholders. Employees, consumers, and other corporate constituencies are still likely to prefer pursuing corporate lawmaking in the federal forum (Roe 2003). Benefit corporation legislation, opening up state corporate law to corporate purposes beyond shareholder wealth maximization, is another possible avenue of change in state law (Kassoy, Houlahan, and Coen Gilbert 2016). Ensconced in the nonmandatory, private ordering pattern of Delaware and other state corporations laws and therefore applicable only if managers and shareholders choose this alternative, this model also seems unlikely, at the moment, to substantially change the current balance at state law.

Conclusion

In the current federal-state world that has grown up in corporate law, there seems little likelihood of any significant move in state law. For 120 years Delaware has followed a director-centric structure to its corporate law that emphasizes ample room for private ordering and for key parties in the internal governance of the corporation to push back and forth among themselves about particular governance issues. For about the same amount of time, the federal government has periodically intervened with regulation aimed at large, publicly held corporations to protect consumers and workers and sometimes to empower shareholders, but not to erase the long-standing internal governance system of state corporations statutes. This bifurcated approach to corporate law contributes to the static nature of lawmaking in the state realm. Delaware's director-centric/private ordering approach for governance in large publicly held corporations faces little real challenge from other states that may seek to be more shareholder empowering than Delaware or more friendly to management. Delaware must pay constant attention to the possibility of federal incursion. Yet the pattern that each has chosen to follow—Delaware's focus on directors and the federal focus on shareholders—has facilitated a "stay in your lane" approach by each in terms of how they implement what are essentially inconsistent approaches to regulation. The result is likely to be a continued pattern of static state law and periodic change in federal law, likely in response to a crash.

Notes

1. Bank of Augusta v. Earle, 38 U.S. (5 Pet.) 517 (1839).

2. The trust concept had a long history in Anglo-American corporate law as a means to organize entities without a charter from the crown in earlier centuries. *See* Maitland (1902 at xxix) ("Behind the screen of trustees and concealed from the direct scrutiny of legal theories all manners of groups could flourish.").

3. Liggett Co. v. Lee, 288 U.S. 517, 550–54 (1933) (Brandeis dissenting).

4. Del. General Corporation Act (1899) § 20. The major difference is the phrase "or under the direction of" that was added late in the twentieth century. Delaware's 1899 act in large parts tracked the 1896 New Jersey statute.

5. 1899 § 20. 1899 § 17. The 1899 statute was the first in Delaware to contain consolidation (merger) provision by a supermajority vote of shareholders, which previously would have required unanimous action. 1899 § 54.

6. *In re* Netsmart Technologies, Inc. Shareholders Litigation, 924 A.2d 171, 206 (Del. Ch. 2007).

References

Arsht, S. Samuel, 1976, *The History of Delaware Corporation Law*, 1 DEL. J. CORP. 1.

Badawi, Adam, 2014, *Influence Costs and the Scope of Board Authority*, 39 J. CORP. LAW 675.

Banner, Stuart, 1997, *What Causes New Securities Regulation*, 75 WASH. U. L. Q. 849.

Blair, Margaret, and Elizabeth Pollman, 2015, *The Derivative Nature of Corporate Constitutional Rights*, 56 WM. & MARY L. REV. 1673.

Blumberg, Phillip A., 1990, *The Corporate Entity in an Era of Multinational Corporations*, 15 DEL. J. CORP. L. 283, 301.

Bostwick, C., 1899, *Legislative Competition for Corporate Capital.*

Butler, Nicholas Murray, 1912, *Why Should We Change Our Form of Government: Studies in Practical Politics.*

Cary, William, 1974, *Federalism and Corporate Law: Reflections upon Delaware*, 83 YALE L. J. 663.

Chandler, Alfred D. Jr., 1977, *The Visible Hand, The Managerial Revolution in American Business.*

Davidoff Solomon, Steven, and Randall S. Thomas, 2016, *The Rise and Fall of Delaware Takeover Standards.*

Dodd, E. Merrick, 1936, *Statutory Developments in Business Corporation Law 1886–1936*, 50 HARV. L. REV. 27, 40.

Edelman, Paul, Randall S. Thomas, and Robert B. Thompson, 2014, *Shareholder Voting in an Age of Intermediary Capitalism*, 87 S. CAL. L. REV. 1359.

Eldar, Ofer, and Lorenzo Magnolfi, 2016, Regulatory Competition and the Market for Corporate Law, Yale Law and Economics Working Paper 528.

Ellis, Joseph, 2015, *The Quartet: Orchestrating the Second American Revolution 1783–1789* (Alfred A. Knopf).

Gilson, Ronald J., and Jeffrey N. Gordon, 2013, *The Agency Costs of Agency Capitalism: Activist Investors and the Revaluation of Governance Rights*, 113 COLUM. L. REV. 863, 897.

Hamil, Susan Pace, 1999, *From Special Privilege to General Utility: A Continuation of Willard Hurst's Study of Corporations*, 49 AM. U. L. REV. 81.

Hilt, Eric, 2008, *Democratizing Incorporation: Law and the Industrial Enterprise in Massachusetts, 1830–1880.*

Hilt, Eric, 2015, Corporations Law and the Shift toward Open Access in the Antebellum United States, National Bureau of Economic Research Working Paper 21195.

Horwitz, Morton J., 1986, *Santa Clara Revisited: The Development of Corporate Theory*, 88 W.V. L. REV. 173.

Houlahan, Bart, Andrew Kassoy, and Jay Coen Gilbert, 2016, *Impact Governance and Management: Fulfilling the Promise of Capitalism to Achieve a Shared and Durable Prosperity* (Brookings Institution), https://www.brookings.edu/research/impact-governance-and-management-fulfilling-the-promise-of-capitalism-to-achieve-a-shared-and-durable-prosperity/.

Klausner, Michael, 1995, *Corporations, Corporate Law, and Networks of Contracts*, 81 VA. L. REV. 757.

Livermore, Shaw, 1939, *Early American Land Companies: Their Influence on Corporate Development* (Commonwealth Fund).

Maitland, William, 1902, Preface to Maitland's English translation of Otto Gierke, *Political Theories of the Middle Ages.*

Navin, Thomas R., and Marian V. Sears, 1955, *The Rise of a Market for Industrial Securities, 1887–1902*, 29 BUS. HIST. REV. 105, 106.

Roe, Mark, 2003, *Delaware's Competition*, 117 HARV. L. REV. 588.

Rutledge, Wiley D., 1937, *Significant Trends in Modern Incorporation Statutes*, 22 WASH. U. L. Q. 305.

Schwartz, Donald E., 1978, *In Search of Corporate Soul: The Structure of the Corporation; By Melvin Aron Eisenberg*, 87 YALE L. J. 685, 688.

Seligman, Joel, 1976, *A Brief History of Delaware's General Corporation Law of 1899*, 1 DEL. J. CORP. L. 249.

Smith, D. Gordon, 1998, *The Shareholder Primacy Norm*, 23 J. CORP. L. 277.

Strine, Leo Jr., 2014, *Can We Do Better by Ordinary Investors? A Pragmatic Reaction to the Dueling Ideological Mythologists of Corporate Law*, 114 COLUM. L. REV. 449.

Strine, Leo E. Jr., and Nicholas Walter, 2015, *Originalists or Original: The Difficulties of Reconciling Citizens United with Corporate Law History.*

Thompson, Robert B., 2016, *Anti-Primacy; Sharing Power in American Corporations*, 71 Bus. Law 381.

Thompson, Robert B., and Hillary A. Sale, 2003, *Securities Fraud as Corporate Governance: Reflections upon Federalism*, 56 Vand. L. Rev. 859

Winter, Ralph, 1977, *State Law, Shareholder Protection and the Theory of the Corporation*, 6. J. Legal Stud. 251.

Yablon, Charles, 2007, *Historic Race Competition for Corporate Charters and the Rise and Decline of New Jersey, 1880–1910*, 32 J. Corp. L. 355.

CHAPTER TWO

The Rise and Fall of Delaware's Takeover Standards

Steven Davidoff Solomon and Randall S. Thomas

Introduction

The takeover standards that we learn and teach in law school—*Blasius*, *Revlon*, *Unocal*, *Van Gorkom*, and *Weinberger*—appear to be in decline. Promulgated in the 1980s, these standards, named after the cases that created them, have been subject to judicial pruning or wholesale replacement in the last two decades. In some instances, they have been replaced with more structured standards providing for business judgment review. Alternatively, they have been transmogrified into tests that call for lower judicial scrutiny, such as reasonableness. At least one, the *Blasius* standard, appears to be on the chopping block. Another, the *Unocal* standard, has been described by some commentators as "dead" (Thompson and Smith 2001).

This is a remarkable turn of events.

In this chapter, we attempt to explain the rise and fall of jurisprudential takeover standards in Delaware. We theorize that these standards were created by Delaware courts in the mid-1980s to rectify a failure in the corporate governance system—principally, the failure of directors to act responsibly in the corporate governance ecosystem. At that moment in time, the Delaware courts issued new rules designed to regulate the conduct of takeovers. These new standards successfully channeled takeovers into certain preferred forms, but they also helped ameliorate the problematic practices of that period. These new standards collectively had another effect: encouraging the rise of private enforcement activities—initially by the raiders themselves, but once hostile transactions became a less significant force, through expanded shareholder litigation.

The costs of private litigation activities were justifiable when there was a governance gap that needed to be filled. Over time, as standards evolved, practitioners adapted to the new reality, and clear rules were set forth about how to conduct both friendly and hostile takeovers. The need for Delaware court intervention diminished, and it occurred only when players acted to substantially deviate from the now established norms of takeover contests.

In this new environment, private litigation became increasingly unnecessary, a fact that became quite apparent with the rise in litigation rates to 96 percent of all takeovers (Cain and Davidoff Solomon 2015). At the same time, several other changes occurred: the rise of institutional investors, coordinating bodies such as proxy solicitors, third-party voting advisers, hedge fund activism, and corporate governance movements as well as the expansion of federal securities law into areas such as executive compensation and board independence/monitoring. These new developments created alternative monitors to a culture of litigation that were perceived as substitutes for lawsuits and corrections to the market failures that had necessitated the 1980s court-ordered standards. The recent move to limit shareholder litigation further reflects the Delaware courts' renewed focus on reducing the burdens and costs of private enforcement in favor of other governance mechanisms. Our theory jibes with a paper by Vice Chancellor Laster (forthcoming), which argues that the turn toward reasonableness in Delaware was driven by the rise of institutional shareholders and a loss of faith in shareholder litigation due to its ubiquity.

Although these new developments spurred Delaware to back away from active judicial intervention, largely leaving private actors to engage in monitoring, this does not mean that everything is now perfectly frozen in time. This chapter concludes by drawing lessons from the rise and fall of Delaware takeover standards. The historical arc of takeover standards has largely been a positive development, though there may still be areas where court intervention may be more appropriate, such as in the realm of hostile takeover defenses and the staggered board. The lessons of this rise and fall also provide a theoretical construct for looking at Delaware's jurisprudence as well as parameters for when Delaware courts should consider future imposition of higher-level standards in takeovers and corporate governance. Indeed, the arc of Delaware corporate law generally has followed the arc in takeover law we trace. We develop this point by examining whether Delaware or private enforcement mechanisms should apply to regulate hedge fund shareholder activism, concluding that the current judicial hesitancy to wade into this debate appears appropriate.

The Rise of 1980s Standards

The 1980s began with little existing state regulation of takeovers.[1] Indeed, the 1970s had produced the first substantive state regulation, but only in a narrow subset of going-private transactions. The controversy over going-privates in the wake of the 1973 recession and the Securities and Exchange Commission (SEC) crusade against these takeovers led by SEC chairman Manuel F. Cohen spurred state action. In 1977, the Delaware Supreme Court adopted the business purpose test for evaluating going-privates, representing a step away from business judgment review in takeovers.[2] Delaware's move to regulate going-private transactions was also a sign of its willingness to protect shareholders against corporations, something of import in the wake of Cary's (1974) savage criticism of Delaware as engaged in a "race to the bottom."

But this was just the start. The early 1980s saw a sharp rise in the number and frequency of hostile takeovers, and of takeovers generally. The reasons for this are still debated, possibly spurred by relaxed antitrust enforcement under the Reagan administration, easy credit as a result of earlier Federal Reserve actions, and the invention of the high-yield debt market by Michael Milken (Jarrell 1992).

In this cauldron, the Delaware courts transformed the state's jurisprudence through a series of decisions that adopted heightened judicial review standards to takeover-related actions.[3] The first hostile takeover decision came in 1985 in *Unocal v. Mesa Petroleum*,[4] a decision that arose out of the raider T. Boone Pickens's two-tiered hostile offer for Unocal. The Delaware Supreme Court ultimately upheld the defensive self-tender conducted by Unocal. In doing so, the Court held that such defensive actions would be subject to a heightened standard of review. The *Revlon* case the following year was a decision in which the court weighed the actions of the Revlon board in fighting off another hostile raider, Ronald Perelman.[5] The Delaware Supreme Court this time sided with the hostile bidder, holding that, in a breakup or change of control of the company, a target was required to obtain the highest price reasonably available. Consequently, Revlon could not unduly favor another competing bid by a friendly private equity group.

The standards proliferated in a variety of settings. In *Weinberger*, decided two years before *Unocal*, the Delaware Supreme Court repudiated the business purpose standard and instead held that the entire fairness standard would apply for review of take-privates.[6] In the 1985 case *Smith v. Van Gorkom*,[7] the Delaware Supreme Court considered the takeover of the TransUnion Corporation and issued a decision specifying standards for duty of care violations in the takeover context.[8] The blizzard of standard setting was capped off in 1988, when Chancellor Allen, in *Blasius Indus. v. Atlas Corp.*,[9] imposed strict scrutiny on actions taken by the board with a primary purpose of impeding or impairing the shareholder vote. The *Blasius* case was notable for being about the efficacy of board defensive actions to fight off an early version of shareholder activist.

The consequence of the proliferation of standards was to insert the Delaware judiciary directly as arbiters of takeover contests. As Prentice and Langmore (1990, 478) wrote, summing up the decade of court action: "Whereas ten years ago, target boards could defeat hostile tender offers with virtually no scrutiny from the courts, today they must justify their actions under stringent standards of review and a presumption that creating an alternative transaction (at a higher premium) is the best form of defense. Litigation is expensive, but it is possible to conclude that using the courts to resolve such disputes is more cost-effective than alternatives which have been proposed, such as written contracts between shareholders and managers." Prentice and Langmore highlighted the rise of judicial enforcement mechanisms through shareholder litigation. Their analysis is notable in observing this shift but also for its narrow cabining of the available alternative enforcement mechanisms at the time. This would change, as would Delaware law.

The Shift Away

Late in the 1980s, Delaware began to back away from these standards. This was not an immediate process with clear rejection decisions. Rather, in response to changes in market forces we discuss below, the courts gradually backed away from the interventionist approach and new standards of the 1980s. The result over the period spanning from the 1990s until today are clear: a wholesale change in the application and use of these standards.

The first signs of Delaware's less interventionist approach came with the *Unocal* doctrine. In the 1980s *Unocal* appeared to have substantive content that would provide space for court intervention to provide an end to corporate control contests. In *City Capital Associates vs. Interco Inc.*[10] and *Grand Metropolitan PLC vs. The Pillsbury Company*,[11] Chancellor Allen had interpreted *Unocal* to permit the Chancery Court to play an active part in deciding takeover contests. But after the Delaware Supreme Court's decision in *Paramount Communications Co. v. Time, Inc.*,[12] *Interco* and *Pillsbury* were left for dead, directly repudiated by the higher court as contrary to Delaware law beginning with the *Time* decision in 1989.

In the wake of the *Time* decision, *Unocal* became a standard with limited substantive effect[13] as the courts continued to narrow *Unocal*'s effect in *Unitrin, Inc. v. American General Corp.*[14] and other cases. The gradual hollowing of *Unocal* was noted in a law review article by Thompson and Smith (2001). They surveyed the existing case law and came to the conclusion that *Unocal* was, in their words, "dead." *Unocal* was still invoked, but in the handful of times it was used to strike down board action, the court acted only to maintain preestablished rules of the road. Thus, in 1998 the *Unocal* standard was utilized by the Chancery Court to strike down a dead-hand poison pill before a separate ruling by the Delaware Supreme Court invalidating no-hand poison pills on statutory grounds.[15] By acting to prevent these more powerful forms of poison pill, the courts maintained an equilibrium that had been established between bidders and targets in hostile takeovers. The culmination of the court's backing away from intervention arguably came in the *Airgas* case.[16] There Chancellor Chandler refused to redeem a poison pill despite his apparent distaste for the *Time* holding and the offer being deemed fair. The decision validated the "just say no" defense and left targets wide latitude to resist takeover offers in accordance with the practices set up over the prior decades.[17]

The *Revlon* doctrine—the core doctrine governing friendly takeovers—was also reworked. Although the language of the standard remained the same, in *Lyondell Chemical Co. v. Ryan*,[18] the Delaware Supreme Court effectively viewed *Revlon* through the lens of good-faith analysis, holding that so long as the actions of the board were "reasonable" and in "good faith," they would not be challenged. The decision provided boards with wide latitude to choose how to sell themselves and the appropriate sale process. Once again, the court had removed itself from a more searching scrutiny, instead preferring in this instance to subsume *Revlon* within the general fiduciary duty of loyalty and its standard of good faith.[19] As Johnson and Ricca (2014, 209–10) wrote:

> Both the actual words and the clear "music" of the Lyondell opinion imposed a demanding liability standard for challenging director conduct in the Revlon setting. Thus, in the nearly quarter century from Revlon to Lyondell, the court—with a little help from the General Assembly—substantially redrew the director liability landscape on both the duty of care and duty of loyalty fronts, and then fitted the pre-existing Revlon doctrine into the larger arc of those fiduciary developments.
>
> In light of Lyondell, continuing assertions about the Revlon duty imposing a higher "reasonableness" standard of scrutiny than ordinary business judgment rule review, and requiring that directors carry an initial burden of proof, are, in the personal liability context, outworn and faulty doctrinal vestiges.

As for *Blasius*, it became a doctrine rarely applied. This was true despite the fact that the standard appeared tailor-made for the analysis of many shareholder activism situations. In one of the few cases in the last decade to apply a *Blasius* analysis, *Mercier v. Intertel*,[20] then vice chancellor Strine argued that the strict scrutiny standard should be abandoned and incorporated into the *Unocal* reasonableness standard. The then vice chancellor found for the first time that board action impeding or impairing the shareholder vote met *Blasius*'s compelling justification requirement, an implicit argument for adopting his revised standard.

In the turn of the millennium, there also occurred a sustained effort to turn back the *Weinberger* entire fairness standard, which addressed issues associated with minority/majority shareholder relationships. In a series of decisions that spanned fifteen years, the Delaware courts validated separate arrangements for business judgment review first for tender offers and later in the merger context. This line of cases culminated in a 2014 decision by the Delaware Supreme Court, *Kahn v. M&F Worldwide Corp.*[21] The transaction involved a controlling shareholder's squeeze-out of the minority shareholders in a public company—a case that under the *Weinberger* standard would have required fairness analysis. There the court determined that the approval of an empowered, independent special committee of directors coupled with a fully informed, noncoerced majority of the minority shareholder vote approving of the merger was sufficient to shift the standard of review to the business judgment rule. The result was that a principled standard—the *Weinberger* entire fairness test—was replaced with a more structured rule-like test for going-private transactions.

The rationale for this shift was explained earlier in the *Cox* decision of the Chancery Court.[22] Private litigation mechanisms through plaintiffs' law firms no longer functioned effectively. Meanwhile, the rise of independent directors and institutional investors had provided Delaware courts with alternative monitoring mechanisms. As then Vice Chancellor Strine wrote, the value of shareholder litigation in this context had been diminished, even though it appeared that deals pursuant to the old *Weinberger/Kahn* standard produced higher premiums than tender offers under the *Pure Resources* standard (Subramanian 2007). In other words, the view changed that judges were necessary to police this market as the courts recognized other private mechanisms.[23]

The collective result of these cases was a significant reduction in judicial oversight of takeovers. This idea was cemented in a recent law review piece written by now Chief Justice Strine (2015). He surveyed the landscape acknowledging that so long as there were independent and conflict-free directors and advisers, Delaware's role was to stand aside and let these private monitors function. He stated:

> You and your clients get to write the play. Not only is there nothing wrong with that, but done properly and with integrity, there is everything right with that. If the play is one where your clients appear to have made sensible, good faith judgments for legitimate, well-documented reasons, those judgments are likely to withstand judicial scrutiny. By focusing on the quality of the deliberative process, you maximize the directors' ability to bring their best collective judgment to bear on the difficult decisions they must make in the M & A context. And if avoiding legal embarrassment is a motivating factor for directors, use that factor for all it is worth to help them live up to what should be their overriding objective: doing the right thing for the company and its stockholders. (706)

In this world, Delaware's focus is on ensuring that directors serve their own role as independent monitors and ensuring that the "road" stays open. The importance of the independent director monitoring process explains Delaware's current exploration of financial adviser liability as well. Beginning with the *Del Monte* case,[24] and culminating in the *RBC Capital Markets v. Jervis*[25] decision, Delaware made it clear that independent directors have a duty to run the sale process independently. Directors who close their eyes and let financial advisers drive the deal without supervision create potential liability for themselves. However, if these private monitors do their job and follow the rules set forth in Delaware opinions, then a high scienter requirement will protect their financial advisers (and third-party acquirers) from liability.

The intersection of the financial adviser liability cases and the move away from close judicial scrutiny was reached in a recent Delaware Supreme Court decision, *Singh v. Attenborough*,[26] where the court dismissed an aiding and abetting claim against a board's financial adviser after a fully informed, uncoerced vote of disinterested shareholders. The court held that the business judgment rule should be applied in these circumstances. The end result of this movement is clear: The 1980s standards are gone, replaced by newer standards that rely on private monitoring.

Theoretical Foundations

Explaining the 1980s

The most commonly offered theoretical explanation for Delaware's actions in the 1980s is a political economy one. Delaware's constituency can be defined as the corporations that charter there and pay incorporation fees and taxes as well as the corporate bar (Macey and Miller 1987). The controversy over takeovers and corporate demands for protection pushed Delaware courts to adopt a jurisprudence meeting the needs of its corporate constituency. By acceding to corporate wishes, Delaware maintained its attraction for public incorporations and prevented an outward migration of charters to other states.

This explanation ignores the fact that, in many cases, Delaware did not go so far as to provide complete protection from hostile takeovers. The principal state legislative response was rather weak and consisted of the adoption of a business combination statute. Pennsylvania, in comparison, adopted six different types of antitakeover statutes. The Delaware courts also adopted the *Unocal* and *Revlon* doctrines, both of which limited a public corporation's ability to resist a hostile takeover, though *Unocal* itself turned out to be weak medicine.

This more particularized response has been explained by Roe (2003) and Davidoff (2007) as a possible consequence of fears of federal intervention. Delaware's response in the 1980s can be seen as one crafted to counter SEC pressure. At that time, the SEC was seeking to regulate takeovers and was opposed to hostile takeover defenses, instead openly advocating for a level playing field. Delaware's response can be seen as a preemptive one seeking to forestall SEC action while attempting to still cater to its corporate constituency.

We offer a complementary theory: Delaware's response, which we believe extended beyond takeover law, was also driven by a need to address existing corporate governance failures. Prior to the invention and validation of the poison pill, corporations were struggling to defend themselves against the hostile takeover. *Unocal* itself concerned Unocal's attempts to defend itself against what the court concluded was a coercive, two-tiered hostile tender offer. Against this struggle, there was real concern about the board conflicts created by these offers and the perception that a targeted board would not appropriately and in good faith consider a takeover offer. Instead, the concern was that the board would seek to entrench itself through takeover defenses.

Market mechanisms did not then exist to stem either of these problems. The role of institutional shareholders during this period was passive. Institutional and other shareholders did not actively engage with management or otherwise seek to affect the course of takeover offers or corporate governance generally. Other monitoring mechanisms were still developing. Proxy advisory services were in their infancy, as was the corporate governance movement. Boards at this time were mostly inside directors. The board as a majority of independent directors as a norm did not begin to take hold until the 2000s. Shareholder activism by hedge funds was also limited: There were some activist blockholders who targeted poorly performing companies, seeking asset divestitures or stock buybacks, but the market reaction to them was minimal. (Bethel, Liebeskind, and Opler 1998).

The Delaware courts' rapid promulgation of different standards during this period can be seen as an attempt to remedy this private market failure. The Delaware courts as regulator were providing a market good by establishing order and stability to the market when it otherwise could not provide this order itself. But the Delaware court's action was predicated on a lack of alternatives. When the market structure changed, so did Delaware's role.

The Effect of the 1980s

These standards had a significant number of short- and long-term effects. In the short term, the standards were regulatory in nature, setting rules of the road for takeovers generally and hostile takeovers in particular. These rules ultimately encouraged private ordering solutions around the poison pill. Later decisions would establish the proxy contest as the clear mechanism to circumvent the pill and allow for a hostile takeover to proceed. These decisions also set limits for what defensive actions could be taken and how boards should respond to hostile deals.

The insertion of standards of conduct made Delaware a regulator, but it was a regulator only when litigation was brought. These decisions thus created a culture of litigation, ultimately leading to litigation in almost every single takeover. In the longer term, this obviated the need for market enforcement. Instead, the courts (and plaintiffs' law firms) served as monitors.

In the 1980s, the Delaware court also established itself as the final arbiter of takeovers and for the institutionalization of litigation as an enforcement mechanism. The steady stream of litigation ensured that the Delaware court became both the rule maker and umpire in these takeover contests. As Rock (1997) has detailed, these decisions often took the form of morality opinions that detailed extensive rules of conduct. These lessons and rules initially established a neutral playing field that allowed hostile takeovers to proceed. Raiders now knew the limits of their bids and the structures that would pass muster. Companies knew that they could adopt certain takeover defenses but not others.

But the structure of the market changed over time. More powerful, and more pervasive, institutional shareholders appeared, providing an active monitoring force for corporate governance. This force was complemented by hedge fund activism. Hedge funds, empowered and backed by institutional shareholders, could police misconduct and oppose, support, or even instigate, takeovers. Similarly, the rise of proxy advisory services and corporate governance agents allowed for additional monitoring and collective action by shareholders. Finally, the expansion of federal securities law into areas such as executive compensation and board independence/monitoring allowed for a semiprivate form of monitoring.

The market of the 2000s thus looked very different from the market of the 1980s. In addition to empowered shareholders who were more empowered and active, boards were now comprised of a majority of independent directors who presumably were more willing to serve as a check against conflicted management responses. The federal government regulated broad areas of corporate governance. These market developments largely served to fix the market failures of the 1980s. In this brave new world, the need for a court regulator was diminished. Indeed, by 2010, the costs of such regulation were proving to be excessive due to widespread and, in some cases, frivolous litigation (Fisch, Griffith, and Davidoff Solomon 2015; Thomas and Thompson 2012; Thompson and Thomas 2004).

To be sure, this does not mean that the Delaware courts became irrelevant. The rules for takeovers were still set by the court in the 1980s and created the space for Delaware courts to later retreat. And the courts still serve to police outside conduct that does not fall within the allowed conduct. The difference today is that that the scope of permissible conduct is well defined and its range is broad so that most takeovers create little need for court intervention. The lack of widespread intervention these days is illustrated by the small number of cases that result in a significant monetary payment to shareholders or an injunction enjoining the deal from completion. In 95 percent of cases, the transaction completes as contemplated with little judicial intervention beyond the occurrence and quick settlement of litigation (Cain and Davidoff Solomon 2015).

We do not think that the current state of play is a paradise where all corporate law problems are resolved. To the contrary, there still exist market failures and areas where judicial intervention to correct market failures may be appropriate. And the Delaware courts may still act for political economy or strategic reasons to the detriment of market solutions (Davidoff 2012). In particular, we note the issues raised by the staggered board and poison pill in the face of a hostile bid may be a case for judicial intervention due to the heightened chance of market failure.[27] But we put forth this theory as a general explanation and guide for Delaware's conduct and actions.

We also do not put our theory forth as the sole explanation for the rise and fall of these standards. However, we believe that our theory offers a structure for when and where Delaware courts should step in to actively supervise corporate conduct—a topic we discuss in the next section. Our theory also jibes with a theory of the Delaware courts. Generally, Delaware law and its courts should be oriented toward free market solutions and private contracting. Although this is not always the case, and political economy considerations sometimes predominate, in many instances, left to themselves, the Delaware courts will let markets decide the issue except where there is a clear market failure. Where none is identified, then the courts will abstain from action. The evolution of the marketplace over the years permitted the Delaware courts to step back and allow the market to do its work.

The Future

It may be that the takeover standards of the 1980s are still evolving. Our theory—that these standards filled a corporate governance failure—provides a touchstone for future Delaware action. This would be in line with the view of the Delaware courts as market oriented, favoring private solutions. If a similar governance failure arose today, or in the future, a ratcheting back up of these standards, or the development of new ones, may be appropriate.

In today's market, the best candidates for such renewed interventions appear to be hedge fund activism and shareholder power generally. Critics have argued that activism and the increased power of shareholders have encouraged short-termist behavior. They have led to the adoption of corporate governance initiatives that some claim lack sound theoretical or empirical support, such as the separation of the chairperson and chief executive officer positions and the abandonment of the staggered board. In extreme cases, shareholder activism has led to significant harm to companies such as JCPenney, which experienced a substantial decline in revenue due to the implementation of a controversial plan promoted initially by a hedge fund, Pershing Square, which was later put in place after Pershing Square seized control of the company.

To date, there has been little judicial appetite for intervention in these matters. Chief Justice Strine, for example, has decried these developments but has offered policy proposals requiring more disclosure of activist intentions instead of new or revised judicial standards (Strine

2017). In line with Chief Justice Strine's writings, the Delaware courts have maintained the status quo, largely applying the toothless *Unocal* standard to deferentially review a number of prominent disputes about takeover contests. The most prominent example of this occurred in the Sotheby's case.[28] In that decision, the Delaware Chancery Court reviewed the adoption of a two-tiered poison pill that set a 10 percent trigger for all shareholders except passive institutional ones, which could acquire 20 percent of Sotheby's shares without triggering the poison pill. Sotheby's asserted that it had acted to influence and forestall the activist fund Third Point from building a bigger stake and to prevent it from cooperating with other hedge funds.

The initial question before the Chancery Court was the standard of review to apply, because this would in large part determine the outcome of the case. The court found that the adoption of the poison pill was not done for the "primary purpose" of interfering with the shareholder franchise, the touchstone of *Blasius* analysis, and so that standard did not apply to the poison pill adoption. Third Point had also requested that the Sotheby's board waive the 10 percent threshold to permit Third Point to accumulate a larger position to influence an upcoming proxy contest. This would seem to naturally implicate *Blasius*, but again Vice Chancellor Parsons refused to apply the standard. The vice chancellor called the question "uncomfortably close" but ultimately ruled that *Moran* had implied that the poison pill would have some deleterious effect on shareholder voting, and that while there was incidental voting power reduction here, the Sotheby's board's actions did not preclude a proxy contest.

Since *Blasius* did not apply to the Sotheby's board action, it was reduced to a *Unocal* case. Not surprisingly, given the weakness of the *Unocal* standard, the court ultimately upheld the poison pill and the refusal to waive the threshold as valid acts under *Unocal*. The court reasoned that the 10 percent threshold was appropriate because it was substantially higher than the board's cumulative offsetting ownership of 1 percent of Sotheby's. The 10 percent thus seemed reasonable given the larger stake a hedge fund could accumulate and its effect of forestalling a "wolf pack" of hedge funds from collectively accumulating a more significant, controlling stake.

The Sotheby's case is the latest in a string of cases—including the *Yucaipa* case involving an activist attack on Barnes and Noble—where the Delaware court utilized *Unocal* to analyze defensive measures against an activist. The fit could be questioned. *Unocal* was designed to address excessive measures taken by boards defending hostile takeovers, not activists, and each is a different situation. Given the markedly different contexts, the Delaware court could have easily created a different standard or perhaps utilized the *Blasius* standard, which seems more focused on the type of voting issues that occur in an activist situation. But the courts did neither, instead preferring an effectively abstentionist approach.

In the case of Sotheby's, we think the lack of a more substantive intervention made sense. The Sotheby's board may have acted aggressively, but there were still existing and plausible market mechanisms to check its behavior. Indeed, the day after the vice chancellor's decision, the Sotheby's board settled its proxy fight with Third Point, appointing a number of Third Point representatives to the Sotheby's board. It did so anticipating its imminent defeat in the proxy contest.

More generally, we also believe that the current market dynamics do not justify more searching standards on defensive actions against hedge fund activism. The market appears to be functioning with motivated large shareholders serving as a monitor, willing to take steps to remove and replace directors when their conduct oversteps bounds. For example, in the case of Darden Restaurants, the board acted to sell its Red Lobster restaurants despite protests of institutional shareholders and activist shareholders. The result was a replacement of the entire board at a proxy contest (see Stevenson 2014). Some may criticize institutional shareholders as unduly favoring activists, but in fairness they have been seen to be willing to act contrary to activists' demands in appropriate cases, such as Cracker Barrel and DuPont. This hesitancy is mirrored in the SEC's stated refusal to "take sides" in the shareholder activist battle despite the SEC's earlier willingness to intervene in the 1980s. And it is a force buttressed by the number of studies that have found that, in general, activism increases the value of firms.[29]

More broadly, there is the issue of short-termism and a board's ability to respond effectively to this pressure. We note at the outset that there is a widespread debate about the existence of short-termism. Theoretically speaking, short-termism should not exist if markets are functioning efficiently. Markets will simply price in this conduct and so shareholders and boards will avoid detrimental actions. Of course, there may be market malfunctions or imperfections that make the market unable to price these actions; that may be occurring here, but there is no definitive evidence either way.[30]

It is hard to see a role for the Delaware courts in addressing short-term behavior. Delaware already emphasizes the role of directors in corporate decision making as well as the clear right of shareholders to freely elect directors. The relationship of these two parties to each other and the role of the ballot box in affecting corporate behavior are still changing. We believe that the evolving situation mitigates forbearance on the part of the Delaware courts in order to provide space for boards and shareholders to establish their own private equilibrium. Moreover, an appropriate corporate law response to shareholder activism is unclear. Judicial action in this space would therefore seem both inapposite and uncertain in effect.

This does not mean that Delaware should be quiescent. Markets evolve rapidly, and there will no doubt be future market malfunctions in corporate governance. Delaware should be prepared to fill clear gaps with judicial enforcement mechanisms and a willingness to set rules of the road for new conduct in order to allow the development of private solutions. This may happen at a later date, but right now there appears to be limited need for Delaware to once again fulfill the role as regulator and rule maker in chief.

Notes

We thank Delaware Supreme Court Chief Justice Leo Strine, Delaware Chancery Court Vice Chancellor Travis Laster, Professors Sean Griffith, Frank Partnoy, and Robert Thompson as well as workshop participants at UC Berkeley, Fordham University, and Vanderbilt University for their helpful comments.

1. Congress had passed the Williams Act in 1968, which was largely disclosure-oriented but with a few substantive provisions that regulated the form of tender offers. 15 U.S.C. §§ 78m (d)–(e), 78n (d)–(f). One paper has found it had the effect of raising premiums in completed tender offers but lowering the overall completion rate (Jarrell and Bradley 1980).

2. Singer v. Magnavox Co., 380 A.2d 969 (Del. 1977).

3. There were two principal conflicts during this period that the Delaware courts confronted. The first was the clear conflict between a majority/controlling shareholder on one side and the minority shareholders in a going-private transaction. The second was less clear and involved possible conflicts among directors, managers, and shareholders in an arm's-length takeover. In the latter instance, the issue was a possible misalignment of interests due to management entrenchment, but such misalignment was not necessarily present and could be

counteracted by mechanisms such as the golden parachute, which would incentivize management to sell. The clear conflict of the going-private transaction gave rise to Delaware's initial foray into takeover jurisprudence, though by the middle of the 1980s, the approach and remedy (higher rather than lower standards) was arguably uniform. We thank Professor Robert Thompson for drawing our attention to this point.

4. 493 A.2d 946 (Del. 1985). Shortly thereafter, the same court upheld the validity of the poison pill defense in Moran v. Household International, Inc., 500 A.2d 1346 (Del. 1985).

5. Revlon, Inc. v. MacAndrews & Forbes Holdings, Inc., 506 A.2d 173 (Del. 1986).

6. Weinberger v. UOP, Inc., 457 A.2d 701 (Del. 1983).

7. 488 A.2d 858 (Del. 1985).

8. *Van Gorkom* was arguably the most controversial of these decisions, and was immediately met with a statutory response, when the Delaware legislature adopted DGCL 102(b)(7).

9. 564 A.2d 651 (Del. Ch. 1988).

10. 551 A.2d 787 (Del. Ch. 1988).

11. 558 A.2d 1049 (Del. Ch. 1988).

12. 571 A.2d 1140 (Del. 1989).

13. Thomas (1993): (Paramount "mark[s] the collapse of heightened judicial scrutiny for takeover defenses against hostile tender offers and a retreat to their deferential review under the business judgment rule.")

14. 651 A.2d 1361 (Del. 1995).

15. *See* Carmody v. Toll Bros., Inc., 723 A.2d 1180 (Del. Ch. 1998); Mentor Graphics v. Quickturn Design Systems, 721 A.2d 1281 (Del. 1998). The lower court opinion in *Mentor Graphics* had relied on *Unocal* to strike down the no-hand poison pill. Mentor Graphics v. Quickturn Design Systems, 728 A.2d 25 (Del. Ch. 1998).

16. Air Products and Chemicals, Inc. v. Airgas, Inc., 16 A.3d 48 C.A. No. 5249 (Del. Ch. Ct. Feb. 15. 2011).

17. The only deviation from this analogy was arguably the Omnicare decision in 2003—Omnicare, Inc. v. NCS Healthcare, Inc., 818 A.2d 914 (Del. 2003)—but it was met with fury by the corporate law bar (for reasons that have little to do with this discussion) and subsequently was also whittled away (see Davidoff 2008).

18. 970 A.2d 235 (2009). Revlon's reach had already been significantly narrowed by the Delaware Supreme Court in Paramount Communications, Inc. v. QVC Network, Inc., 637 A.2d 34 (Del. 1993) when it adopted the "change of control" test to determine the occurrence of a sale triggering the doctrine.

19. *See also In re* Synthes S'holder Litig., C.A. 6452 (Del. Ch. Aug. 17, 2012) (holding that a controlling stockholder could legitimately refuse to sell and find-

ing that even if *Revlon* applied, the board took "reasonable steps to maximize the sale price of the Company").

20. 929 A.2d 786 (2007).

21. 88 A.3d 635 (2014).

22. *In re* Cox Communications, Inc. S'holders Litig., 879 A.2d 604 (Del. Ch. 2005).

23. Appraisal litigation may remain the one area where Delaware judges are actively involved in evaluating the terms of mergers (Jiang, Li, Mei, and Thomas 2016). However, recent case law suggests that these judges are moving in the direction of setting rules of the road for valuation cases and being deferential to the price set by deal makers. Council of the Corporation Law Section (2015) (Delaware courts have "suggested that a market test of a transaction will serve as a proxy for fair value in appraisal suits, so that arm's-length deals with adequate market checks do not create appraisal risks for buyers.").

24. *In re* Del Monte Foods Co. S'holders Litig., 25 A.3d 813 (Del. Ch. 2011).

25. No. 140 (Del. Sup. Ct. Nov. 30, 2015).

26. No. 645 (Del. Sup. Ct. May 16, 2016).

27. Even here, though, we see evidence of powerful market forces at work as institutional investors have pushed hard to declassify boards at US public companies in recent years, and this has led to significant reductions in the prevalence of these devices (Shareholder Rights Project 2015). These efforts, however, have been somewhat offset by the increased incidence of classified boards in the charters of companies going public for the first time (Hall 2016).

28. Third Point LLC v. Ruprecht, C.A. No. 9469-VCP (May 2, 2014).

29. Griffith and Reisel (2016) document instances when the Delaware courts have imposed higher standards in the case of dead-hand proxy puts—an example where market mechanisms appear to have broken down and thus intervention is warranted.

30. In this regard we do note that there is certainly evidence of short-termism in the responses of companies to increased shareholder activism and the rise of share buybacks as a partial response.

References

Bethel, Jennifer, Julia Liebeskind, and Tim Opler, 1998, "Block Share Purchases and Corporate Performance," *Journal of Financial Economics* 53: 605–34.

Cain, Matthew D., and Steven Davidoff Solomon, 2015, "A Great Game: The Dynamics of State Competition and Litigation, *Iowa Law Review* 100: 465–99.

Cary, William L., 1974, "Federalism and Corporate Law: Reflections upon Delaware," *Yale Law Journal* 83: 663–705.

Council of the Corporation Law Section, Delaware Bar Association, 2015, "Section 262 Appraisal Amendments."

Davidoff, Steven M., 2007, "The SEC and the Failure of Federal Takeover Regulation," *Florida State University Law Review* 34: 211–69.

Davidoff, Steven M., 2008, "The Long, Slow Death of Omnicare," *New York Times DealBook*, August 28, http://dealbook.nytimes.com/2008/08/28/the-long-slow-death-of-omnicare.

Davidoff, Steven M., 2012, "Airgas and the Value of Strategic Decision-Making," *Columbia Business Law Review* 2012:502–51.

Fisch, Jill, Sean Griffith, and Steven Davidoff Solomon, 2015, "Confronting the Peppercorn Settlement in Merger Litigation: An Empirical Analysis and a Proposal for Reform," *Texas Law Review* 93: 557–619.

Griffith, Sean, and Natalia Reisel, 2016, "Shareholders, Creditors, and Dead Hand Proxy Puts," unpublished working paper.

Hall, Joseph, 2016, "The Impact of ISS' New Policy on IPO Company Director Elections," https://corpgov.law.harvard.edu/2016/08/10/the-impact-of-iss-new-policy-on-ipo-company-director-elections/.

Jarrell, Gregg A., 1992, "The 1980s Takeover Boom and Government Regulation," *Regulation* 15: 44–53.

Jarrell, Gregg A., and Michael Bradley, 1980, "The Economic Effects of Federal and State Regulation of Cash Tender Offers," *Journal of Law and Economics* 23: 371–407.

Jiang, Wei, Tao Li, Danqing Mei, and Randall Thomas, 2016, "Appraisal: Shareholder Remedy or Litigation Arbitrage?" *Journal of Law and Economics* 59: 697–729.

Johnson, Lyman and Robert Ricca, 2014, "The Dwindling of Revlon," *Washington and Lee Law Review* 71: 167–227.

Laster, J. Travis, forthcoming, "Changing Attitudes: The Stark Results of Thirty Years of Evolution in Delaware M&A Litigation," in HANDBOOK OF SHAREHOLDER LITIGATION, edited by Sean Griffith, David Weber, and Verity Winship.

Macey, Jonathan, and Geoffrey Miller, 1987, "Toward an Interest Group Theory of Delaware Corporate Law," *Texas Law Review* 65: 469–523.

Prentice, Robert A., and John H. Langmore, 1990, "Hostile Tender Offers and the 'Nancy Reagan Defense': May Target Boards 'Just Say No'? Should They Be Allowed To?" *Delaware Journal of Corporate Law* 15: 377–481.

Rock, Edward B., 1997, "Saints and Sinners: How Does Delaware Corporate Law Work?" *UCLA Law Review* 44: 1009–106.

Roe, Mark J., 2003, "Delaware's Competition," *Harvard Law Review* 117: 588–646.

Shareholder Rights Project, 2015, "121 Companies Agreed to Move towards

Annual Elections," http://www.srp.law.harvard.edu/companies-entering-into-agreements.shtml.

Stevenson, Alexandra, 2014, "Activist Hedge Fund Starboard Succeeds in Replacing Darden Board," *New York Times*, October 11, B6.

Strine, Leo E., 2015, "Documenting the Deal: How Quality Control and Candor Can Improve Boardroom Decision-Making and Reduce the Litigation Target Zone," *The Business Lawyer* 70(3): 679–706.

Strine, Leo E., 2017, "Who Bleeds When the Wolves Bite? A Flesh-and-Blood Perspective on Hedge Fund Activism and Our Strange Corporate Governance System," *Yale Law Journal* 126, 1600–971.

Subramanian, Guhan, 2007, "Post-Siliconix Freeze-Outs: Theory and Evidence," *Journal of Legal Studies* 36: 1–26.

Thomas, Randall S., 1993, "Judicial Review of Defensive Tactics in Proxy Contests: When Is Using a Rights Plan Right?" *Vanderbilt Law Review* 46: 503–60.

Thomas, Randall S., and Robert B. Thompson, 2012, "A Theory of Representative Shareholder Suits and Its Application to Multi-Jurisdictional Litigation," *Northwestern University Law Review* 106: 1753–820.

Thompson, Robert B., and Gordon D. Smith, 2001, "Toward a New Theory of the Shareholder Role: 'Sacred Space' in Corporate Takeovers," *Texas Law Review* 80: 261–326.

Thompson, Robert B., and Randall S. Thomas, 2004, "The New Look of Shareholder Litigation: Acquisition Oriented Class Actions," *Vanderbilt Law Review* 57: 133–207.

CHAPTER THREE

In Search of Lost Time

What If Delaware Had Not Adopted Shareholder Primacy?

David J. Berger

Introduction

Ideas go in cycles. So it is with corporate law. Since at least the mid-1980s, we have lived in a world of shareholder primacy.[1] In this world, the primary duty of directors is to maximize the value of the corporation for the benefit of the stockholders. Directors who reject this notion, who take actions that are for the primary benefit of other so-called stakeholders in the corporation—be they employees, customers, the communities served by the corporation, or others—have their ideas rejected in the boardroom, may be the subject of scorn and derision in the business press and with their peers, can be voted out of their positions by shareholders, and can even be found to have breached their fiduciary duty to the company and its shareholders. The reason for this breach is simple: The primary—or fundamental, fiduciary—obligation of the director is to the corporation's stockholders, and while directors can take actions that benefit nonstockholder constituencies, the ultimate purpose of all such actions must be to benefit the company's stockholders.

Yet it was not always so. As first described by the US Supreme Court, the corporation was "an artificial being, invisible, intangible and existing only in contemplation of law. Being the mere creature of law, it possesses only those properties which the charter of its creation confers upon it, either expressly or as incidental to its very existence. These are such as supposed best calculated to effect the object for which it was created."[2] Corporate charters typically do not state that the corporation must be run for the benefit of stockholders, and nothing in Chief Justice Marshall's opinion in *Dartmouth* indicated that the corporation was to be run for the exclusive benefit of the shareholders. Rather, as discussed below, the stockholder primacy notion is a modern concept that only gained widespread acceptance in the mid-1980s and is based on common law (i.e., judicial decisions rather than statutes) and academic theories that were substantially aided by regulatory developments, not statutory changes or changes to the company's charter.

Fast-forward from Chief Justice Marshall's opinion in *Dartmouth* to the twentieth century. During this period, the US economy changed dramatically, from the development of the railroads and economic growth in in the late nineteenth century (associated with business leaders such as Rockefeller, Mellon, and Carnegie, described variously as captains of industry or robber barons depending on one's point of view), followed by the development and rise of antitrust law and other regulations designed to limit the economic (and political) power of large corporations; the decade of the 1920s, with the stock market bubble, followed by the market crash and the Great Depression; the response of President Franklin D. Roosevelt to this crisis, including the creation of the Securities and Exchange Commission and the passage of the critical legislation that still forms the basis of US federal securities laws today; World War II and its aftermath in the 1950s, which led to an era of even greater government regulation in the market, the rise of unions, and the concept that corporations had a duty to all their stakeholders, including their employees and the communities in which they operated, as well as being good corporate citizens by (among other things) paying taxes and sponsoring artistic and cultural events; to the advent of stockholder capitalism in the 1980s, perhaps best personified by Gordon Gekko's famous speech about "greed, for lack of a better word, is good," but whose lineage is perhaps best traced in popular culture to Milton Friedman's famous 1970 article in the *New York Times Magazine*, which stated that "there is one and only one social responsibility of business—to use its resources and engage in activities designed to increase its profits."[3]

The influence of Friedman's article as well as Michael Jenson and William Meckling's 1976 "A Theory of the Firm" article,[4] the deregulation environment championed by President Reagan, and the takeover wars of the mid-1980s led directly to the decline of the countervailing forces that had acted as a constraint on corporate power in the approximate half century between the Great Depression and the mid-1980s, when the leading Delaware cases that form the rules of the game that continue to govern director conduct were decided. These cases, including *Revlon*[5] and *Unocal*,[6] as well as more recent cases such as *eBay*[7] and *Trados*,[8] emphasize that in today's world, the board's ultimate duty is to the company's shareholders. As the court noted in the *eBay* case, having chosen "a for-profit corporate form . . . directors are bound by the fiduciary duties and standards that accompany that form. Those standards include acting to promote the value of the corporation for the benefit of its stockholders. The 'Inc.' after the company name has to mean at least that. Thus, I cannot accept as valid . . . a corporate policy that specifically, clearly, and admittedly seeks not to maximize the economic value of a for-profit Delaware corporation for the benefit of its stockholders."[9]

Yet, as described above, the concept that the core duty of directors is to "maximize the economic value of . . . the corporation for the benefit of the shareholders" is neither required by statute nor deeply (or permanently) ingrained in judicial or economic precedent. Indeed, while the origins of shareholder primacy are now often traced to the Michigan Supreme Court's decision in *Dodge v. Ford Motor Co.*,[10] no less an authority than former Delaware Chancellor Bill Allen noted that, in the 1960s, there was "scant attention" paid to this case, and it "seemed that every interesting question in corporation law had been answered and that nothing remained" to be discovered in the study of corporate law.[11] Thus, the notion of stockholder primacy is a rather recent development, arising out of the regulatory and academic arguments that became broadly influential beginning in the early 1980s, eventually becoming part of the Delaware common law in the mid-1980s, and can be seen as part of a broader response to the takeover wars and the academic and legal debate that was occurring during this time.[12]

In this essay, I ask the question: What if?[13] That is, how might directors and investors manage corporations if we did not live in a world of stockholder primacy? I think this is a critical question to ask for at least two reasons. First, as I will discuss below, while the concept of stockholder primacy currently dominates Delaware law, the courts in Delaware have held this view for a relatively short time. Indeed, no less an authority than Delaware Chief Justice Leo Strine wrote that the "Delaware Supreme Court first grappled with the question" of shareholder primacy in the late 1980s, in its decisions in *Unocal* and *Revlon*.[14] In the history of corporate law, the stockholder primacy notion is just a youth, still capable of further development.[15]

However, despite the youth and geographic limitations on the concept of stockholder primacy, the doctrine's influence cannot be overstated. As one who has been advising corporate boards for more than twenty-five years, my own experience in the boardroom, in the courtroom, and in the business community demonstrates that corporate directors, business leaders, institutional investors, legal practitioners, politicians, and pundits, including the business press, all take for granted that the sole duty of corporate directors today is to maximize stockholder value.[16] Any change from this consensus view would have enormous implications for director decision making on all basic board issues.

Second, while stockholder primacy may currently be the cornerstone of Delaware law, the law can change. The reason for this is not particularly complicated: Delaware corporate law is based on principles of common law and equity, while the Delaware General Corporate Law (DGCL) is, as is well known, an enabling body of law, allowing directors to take most actions they choose unless specifically prohibited by the DGCL or—and here we are back to fiduciary principles—equity.[17]

In simpler terms, this means that the foundation underlying stockholder primacy in Delaware are the views of the distinguished jurists who presently sit on the Delaware Court of Chancery and the Delaware Supreme Court, and have come to hold those positions since the mid-1980s (i.e., during and after *Unocal* and *Revlon* and their progeny). While these judges correctly view themselves as constrained by certain precedents, the historical basis of the courts of equity must also be remembered: Such courts were created as an alternative to the law courts, to allow judges to apply principles of equity based on many sources to achieve a just outcome rather than simply apply the law as was then written. Further, many of these judges have not hesitated to make clear where they departed from precedent and have urged the Delaware Supreme Court (or the Delaware legislature, as appropriate) to change existing Delaware law and/or practice.[18]

This does not mean, of course, that the shareholder primacy rule that currently dominates in Delaware will disappear tomorrow. However, it does make it worth considering a world where stockholder primacy may not be the sole duty of directors in Delaware, including a world where these other constituencies may even have standing to sue to enforce any obligations that may be owed to them or, even in some faraway world, be granted voting rights to elect directors, as Delaware's common law often develops and changes in response to new facts and circumstances.[19]

The purpose of this essay is fourfold. First, and most simply, the essay demonstrates that stockholder primacy is a relatively recent development. While there was debate over the purpose of the corporation in the half century from the mid-1930s to the mid-1980s, by the mid-1950s, no less a shareholder advocate than Adolf Berle recognized that corporate "powers [are] held in trust for the entire community" and that therefore the debate between him and Merrick Dodd "has been settled (at least for the time being) squarely in favor of Professor Dodd's contention."[20] As one who frequently advises directors and speaks with young corporate lawyers thinking about this topic, the mere awareness of a world before stockholder primacy is an important understanding for business leaders and many of their advisers.

Second, the essay attempts to recognize the broader historical and social constraints on corporate behavior in an effort to show that the question of whether we live in a world of stockholder primacy or director primacy is ultimately too narrow a question. Instead, historically the greatest constraints on corporate behavior have traditionally been not shareholders (or even the courts) but rather various countervailing forces in the form of employees (particularly when bargaining collectively as unions); local, state, and national communities (both through individual citizens groups and when acting through their respective government regulators); suppliers and creditors; the public; the press; and other institutional authorities that have the ability to meaningfully affect corporate behavior. At present these countervailing forces can only exist outside the corporation, because, as Delaware Chief Justice Strine has recognized, to "expect that corporate directors elected by stockholders will foreswear the chance to reap materially higher post-tax profits for the benefit of their stockholders is naïve and even immature . . . the solution must come from other bodies of positive law that constrain corporate behavior such as the tax code itself, and cannot rationally rest on calls for corporate directors to 'be patriotic.'"[21]

Thus, a third purpose of this essay is to note that there was a time (not so long ago) when corporate directors had to respond not just to a different tax code, but even more fundamentally to a different regulatory and structural regime. This regime sought to include a variety of constituents who could influence the corporation to consider different interests, whether they be unions forcing corporations to distribute more of the corporation's profits to workers rather than shareholders or environmentalists arguing that trees and other inanimate objects should have the same standing to sue that corporations do.[22] With respect to corporate law, if standing to sue were extended to those affected by corporate decisions (not to mention voting rights under certain circumstances), including employees, communities, and others, one suspects that the "bodies of positive law that constrain corporate behavior" could be substantially expanded.

The fourth purpose of the essay is the most modest: to simply recognize that the law, including the most basic tenets of corporate law, are subject to change. Former Chancellor Bill Allen recognized this reality long ago, when he described corporate law as "schizophrenic" precisely because our view of the corporation changes along with our relative views of "efficiency concerns, ideology and interest group politics."[23] Thus, what seems permanent and solid today may someday change again, to something old or new.

The remainder of this essay is divided into four sections. The next section reviews the purposes of the corporation, including the rise of countervailing powers during most of the twentieth century, only to be replaced by the rise of stockholder primacy beginning in the mid-1980s. This section includes a discussion of some of the political, economic, and other factors that led to these developments and attempts to place the stockholder primacy argument within the broader context of the various regulatory and other developments that allowed stockholders to gain primacy.

A later section examines Delaware law, not to interpret what the state of the law is—again, I believe the duties of directors of a Delaware corporation are currently well established, as is the corporate purpose in Delaware—but rather to review how Delaware law might be different if it had gone down a different path. To accomplish this objective, I consider separately the various constituencies identified by Justice Moore in *Unocal* and ask what if the law had developed to allow these constituencies to participate in corporate decision making.[24]

The essay concludes by noting the potential for changes in corporate law, even in Delaware. I point out again some of the various elements that can lead to a change in the law and how the law reacts to calls for change. Sometimes, of course, these changes occur outside the law, and, again, for much of the twentieth century, corporate behavior was constrained by powerful countervailing forces. The essay thus concludes by noting that many recent decisions have changed the way we view corporations, as well as changed the ability to regulate corporate behavior, and that these recent decisions may ultimately lead to significant changes in corporate law beyond those that seem possible to imagine today.[25]

Quick Look in the Rearview Mirror: What Was the Corporation For?

A World before Shareholder Primacy

One need not go back centuries to find the generally accepted notion that directors owed duties to all corporate stakeholders. In fact, as I have previously discussed, the dominant view of corporate law for most of the twentieth century eschewed the notion of shareholder primacy, and still the modern corporation managed to exist quite nicely.[26] For example, as recently as 1946, the chairman of Standard Oil described the goal of the modern corporation as maintaining "an equitable and working balance among the claims of the various directly interested groups—stockholders, employees, customers and the public at large."[27] Just a few years later, George Merck, then president of Merck & Co., stated that the purpose of Merck was to develop medicine "for the patient. We try never to forget that medicine is for the people. It is not for the profits. The profits follow, and if we have remembered that, they have never failed to appear. The better we have remembered it, the larger they have been."[28]

The views of these business leaders were echoed in the law and in the marketplace. For example, in the 1930s, Professor Adolf Berle engaged in a series of debates with E. Merrick Dodd in the *Harvard Law Review* about the purpose of the corporation.[29] As Chief Justice Strine has noted, Berle argued that managers should "operate within a binding accountability structure that demonstrated adequate regard for those affected by corporate conduct and that would therefore help managers act more in keeping with the better angels of their nature."[30] The question, of course, was where this "binding accountability structure" urged by Berle would come from. Berle and Dodd agreed that it was not going to come from shareholders, and by the mid-1950s, Berle made clear his belief that the accountability would also not come from courts holding directors accountable to shareholders. Rather, in a series of lectures in

1954 at Northwestern Law School, Berle argued that the world had developed to a point where shareholders had little power, and the increasing power and wealth of the corporation made it less reliant on publicly invested capital.

Given the limited power and role of stockholders in the market, by the mid-1950s, Berle concluded that management accountability had to come from regulators, employees, consumers, and others in the public sphere, because these were the only entities that had sufficient power to oversee and monitor corporate conduct. Thus, Berle conceded that the debate between him and Dodd "has been settled (at least for the time being) squarely in favor of Professor Dodd's contention."[31]

Berle's views played out in the marketplace, where the countervailing powers to corporate (and board) action were not shareholders, but employees, regulators, and others. For example, in the so-called Treaty of Detroit, entered into in 1950 by the United Auto Workers (UAW) and General Motors (GM), the primary power pushing GM for information about its business, profitability, and costs was the union negotiating for better wages, not shareholders. The agreement GM reached with the UAW, following years of difficult negotiations (as well as strikes) between the UAW and the various automakers, provided for a five-year contract between GM and the UAW, whereby the UAW gave up certain bargaining rights in exchange for extensive health, unemployment, pension, and other benefits.[32] Since 1950, the Treaty of Detroit has been the subject of considerable economic and political debate, and the merits of a labor agreement are obviously far beyond the scope of this essay.

However, there are at least two reasons why this agreement is significant in the context of an essay on corporate governance. First, when the UAW began negotiations, it sought documents from GM, similar to the type of documents shareholders now seek under Delaware Section 220, to determine the value and profitability of the company. GM initially resisted production of many of these documents, arguing that the documents sought went beyond what was necessary for the negotiations and that there was no requirement for their production (these arguments will sound familiar to corporate litigators who have been involved in Section 220 disputes). Ultimately, the federal government required production of most of these documents to the UAW to help the UAW determine GM's financial condition as part of these negotiations. No one suggested that the UAW should make a demand *as a shareholder* for these documents pursuant to Michigan (or Delaware) law.

Second, at the time GM entered into the treaty, GM's shareholders do not appear to have had any role or taken any position on the impact of this agreement on GM's shareholders, while the government and the broader social good of this type of an agreement were topics of heated debate. Again, one can debate whether ultimately this labor agreement was a positive or negative benefit, and whether there should have been more concern for shareholder interests. The point of this essay, however, is that during the 1950s, and carrying through until the takeover boom in the 1980s and early 1990s (and the decisions by the Delaware courts arising out of these corporate control battles), was that the notion of stockholder primacy was far from decided.[33]

Even as late as the early 1980s, stockholder primacy, while being widely discussed in academic circles, still was far from the prevailing view in business or law. For example, as late as 1981, the chairman of the Business Roundtable wrote the following in the *New York Times*, in support of the roundtable's "Statement of Corporate Responsibility":

> [T]he character of shareholders has changed. At one time most of them were long-term, personally involved individual investors. Now large numbers of them are grouped in institutions as unidentified short-term buyers most interested in maximum near-term gain. Such interest must be balanced with a long-term perspective. *The simple theory that management can get along by considering only the shareholder has been left behind in old economic dissertations.*
>
> Chief executive officers who have been out there facing reality know that corporations are surrounded by a complicated pattern of economic, social, ethical, and political ideas and expectations. They know that they have to be concerned not only about shareholders but about such constituent groups as customers, employees, communities, suppliers and society at large. And they believe a corporation best serves its shareholders by carefully balancing the legitimate interests of all constituents.[34]

In short, for the period beginning at least with the New Deal in the 1930s until the early 1980s, corporations and corporate law generally recognized that a corporate board was responsible to the broader corporate stakeholders, including its customers, employees, communities, and suppliers.[35]

Equally significant, enforcing the obligations on corporations was not a single task or even within the exclusive province of corporate law;

rather, it belonged to many of these same constituencies, including, employees (particularly when acting collectively through unions), communities (when acting through their various local, state, and federal representatives as government regulators), individual citizens (when acting as activists and bringing attention to the roles of particular corporations), and even the media and the public, in a system that was described as one of "countervailing powers."[36] Contractual and other rights, both internal and external to the corporation, formed the basis for corporate regulation; this was coupled with a general public sense that the corporation owed duties to constituencies in addition to stockholders.

It is important to note that the purpose of this essay is not normative, and I am not suggesting here that the governance system that existed during the period before the stockholder primacy regime we now live under was better (or worse) than what is often (erroneously) described as the stakeholder primacy system that existed from the 1930s until the mid-1980s.[37] Rather, the point of this essay is to confront the largely lost reality that there have been long periods in the United States when corporate leaders recognized that they had obligations to nonshareholder constituencies, that the rights of these nonshareholder constituencies were broadly recognized and enforced through a variety of different forums, that corporations (and the broader economy) managed to do just fine during these periods, and that it is entirely possible that the tides will turn again such that one day our system will no longer be one of shareholder primacy.

The Growth of Shareholder Primacy: Deregulation and the Takeover Wars

As noted above, the 1970s were a period of debate about the purpose of the corporation. Importantly, this discussion did not occur in a vacuum; to the contrary, the debate occurred in the context of multiple, fundamental changes to the US economy in the late 1970s and early 1980s, including "stagflation," the election of President Reagan—whose view of economics and government regulation differed fundamentally from the Keynesian consensus that had governed since at least the end of World War II, which led his administration to adopt policies that would substantially reduce the ability of the countervailing powers that had limited corporate power in the postwar period to perform this function—the stock market decline in the 1970s, the rise of the so-called corporate raiders in the 1980s, and the growing power of institutional investors in the market.

In addition, the legal/academic debate over the role of the corporate board of directors came into focus during this period as the takeover wars grew, with Marty Lipton's seminal piece "Takeover Bids in the Target's Boardroom" advocating for courts to give greater deference to decisions by the company's board of directors.[38] The response to Lipton came from Professor (now Judge) Frank Easterbrook and Dan Fischel, two of the leading proponents of the "law and economics" movement, who advocated that shareholder wealth should be the ultimate goal of the corporation.[39] Their article, in the *Harvard Law Review*, titled "The Proper Role of a Target's Management in Responding to a Tender Offer," advocated for a more "shareholder friendly" response to tender offers, and that the "proper" role of directors in responding to a tender offer was to be passive so that shareholders could make their own decisions.[40]

During the same period, Michael Jensen and Eugene Fama wrote a series of highly influential articles that reframed the Berle and Means debate over corporate control. Jensen and Fama argued that shareholders contract for the residual right to the corporation's net cash flows, and in return allow management and the board to make the basic decisions about the company, subject to the right of shareholders to vote on matters reserved for their ratification.[41] Under this theory, day-to-day business decisions were the province of managers, while the role of the board (and, to the extent appropriate, other monitors) was to ensure that managers did not improperly expropriate for themselves cash flows that "belonged" to the residual claimants—that is, the stockholders.

Changes in regulatory and enforcement rules and practices also helped foster this movement as the role of the countervailing powers that had constrained the corporation had begun to erode by the 1980s. For example, the 1980s saw a significant decline in the role of unions in the United States as President Reagan eased regulations allowing companies to avoid collective bargaining, while many companies, particularly manufacturing companies, moved from the Midwest to states that had so-called right-to-work laws, limiting the ability of unions to form.

The Securities and Exchange Commission also provided greater flexibility to companies by, for example, allowing companies to repurchase their own shares in the market. Thus, in 1982, the commission adopted

Rule 10b-18 of the Securities Exchange Act.[42] This rule gave a "safe harbor" against manipulation claims to companies making open market purchases of their own stock so long as, among other things, the company informed the public of the general repurchase plan and did not buy more than 25 percent of the previous four weeks' average daily trading volume. Rule 10b-18 led to a substantial expansion of shareholder buybacks by companies at a time when companies were under increased pressure from governance advocates and others to more closely link executive compensation to the company's stock price, thereby increasing the significance of stock (and stock options) as part of executive compensation packages. These actions, and the regulatory developments supporting this trend, expanded the use of stock buybacks as a way of returning capital to shareholders rather than through dividends.[43] Another effect of this rule was to incentivize senior management and the board to increase share prices, even at the expense of reinvestment in the company for such things as research or increased compensation for employees who did not own substantial amounts of stock, since a greater percentage of executive compensation was linked to increases in the company's share price.[44]

In addition to the decline in the power of unions and a more relaxed regulatory environment, the 1980s saw a dramatic decline in the role of antitrust enforcement. New theories of antitrust regulation, based on then-novel financial theories, were widely adopted by the Reagan administration. These theories, as well as the Reagan administration's broader philosophical opposition to much government regulation, led to a decline in the role of government as a countervailing force pushing corporations to consider broader constituencies, including consumers and others.

As a result of these changes, the period of the mid-1970s through the mid-1980s saw an erosion of influence by many of the parties that had traditionally been involved in the corporate governance debate, including labor, various regulators, and other countervailing powers.

At the same time the corporation was gaining influence over the traditional countervailing powers that had sought to limit corporate power, the courts and leading scholars were advocating for greater stockholder influence in corporate governance. Thus, the growing influence of stockholders in corporate governance was occurring at the same time that power of other corporate stakeholders was on the decline.

Unocal, *Revlon*, and the Growth of Stockholder Primacy in Delaware

As this debate was going on, the Delaware courts were relatively quiet about the issue of corporate purpose.[45] The Delaware courts did not confront the issue of corporate purpose until 1985, in the case of *Unocal v. Mesa Petroleum Co.*[46] In *Unocal*, the Delaware Supreme Court considered whether a board facing a takeover bid may consider nonstockholder constituencies when deciding how to respond to the offer. In answering this question, the court held that, in "the board's exercise of corporate power to forestall a takeover bid our analysis begins with the basic principle that corporate directors have a fiduciary duty to act in the best interests of the corporation's stockholders."[47] However, the court then noted that a board could consider corporate constituencies in addition to stockholders:

> If a defensive measure is to come within the ambit of the business judgment rule it must be reasonable in relation to the threat posed. This entails an analysis by the directors of the nature of the takeover bid and its effect on the corporate enterprise. Examples of such concerns may include: inadequacy of the price offered, nature and timing of the offer, questions of illegality, the impact on "constituencies" other than shareholders (*i.e.*, creditors, customers, employees and perhaps even the community generally), the risk of nonconsummation and the quality of securities being offered in the exchange. While not a controlling factor, it also seems to us that a board may reasonably consider the basic stockholder interests at stake, including those of short term speculators, whose actions may have fueled the coercive aspect of the offer at the expense of the long term investor.[48]

The court cited an article by Marty Lipton to support the proposition that directors could consider constituencies in addition to stockholders.[49] The court also specifically rejected the Easterbrook and Fischel theory that the board should take no action to block shareholders from accepting a tender offer, finding that "[i]t has been suggested that a board's response to a takeover threat should be a passive one. However, that clearly is not the law of Delaware, and as the proponents of this rule of passivity readily concede, it has not been adopted either by courts or state legislatures."[50]

Not surprisingly, many supporters of stockholder primacy and the law and economics movement sternly criticized the *Unocal* decision. For example, Michael Jensen described the decision as a "stunning loss for Unocal shareholders and society" because the "evidence indicates that takeovers are beneficial."[51]

Shortly thereafter, in *Revlon*, the Delaware Supreme Court had the opportunity to, in its own words, "address for the first time the extent to which a corporation may consider the impact of a takeover threat on constituencies other than shareholders."[52] The court's answer to this question was clear: "While concern for various constituencies is proper when addressing a takeover threat, that principle is limited by the requirement that there be some rationally related benefits accruing to the stockholders."[53] As recently described by Delaware's current chief justice, Leo E. Strine, the "understanding in Delaware is that *Revlon* could not have been more clear that directors of a for-profit corporation must at all times pursue the best interests of the corporation's stockholders, and that it highlighted the instrumental nature of other constituencies and interests. Non-stockholder constituencies and interests can be considered, but only instrumentally, in other words, when giving consideration to them can be justified as benefitting the stockholders."[54]

Revlon planted the Delaware flag firmly in the ground of stockholder primacy. In the years since *Revlon*, the foundation of stockholder primacy has been solidified in Delaware.[55] For example, in *eBay Domestic Holdings, Inc. v. Newmark*,[56] the founders and controlling shareholders of craigslist, Inc. argued that the company should be allowed to favor its users and communities over shareholders by, among other things, choosing to not monetize its site.[57] Because the directors and majority shareholders of craigslist admitted that they were favoring the interests of a nonstockholder constituency over stockholder interests, the court found that these directors had breached their fiduciary duties:

> As an abstract matter, there is nothing inappropriate about an organization seeking to aid local, national, and global communities by providing a website for online classifieds that is largely devoid of monetized elements. Indeed, I personally appreciate and admire [the founders'] desire to be of service to communities. The corporate form in which craigslist operates, however, is not an appropriate vehicle for purely philanthropic ends, at least not when there are other stockholders interested in realizing a return on their investment. [The founders] opted to form craigslist, Inc. as a *for-profit Delaware*

> *corporation*, and voluntarily accepted millions of dollars from eBay as part of a transaction whereby eBay became a stockholder. Having chosen a for-profit corporate form, the craigslist directors are bound by the fiduciary duties and standards that accompany that form. Those standards include acting to promote the value of the corporation for the benefit of its stockholders. The "Inc." after the company name has to mean at least that. Thus, I cannot accept as valid . . . a corporate policy that specifically, clearly, and admittedly seeks *not* to maximize the economic status of a for-profit Delaware corporation for the benefit of its stockholders.[58]

The Delaware Court of Chancery's decision in *eBay* came nearly twenty-five years after the Delaware Supreme Court's ruling in *Revlon*, yet the philosophical consistency of the two decisions is beyond dispute. As these decisions (as well as the many more recent articles by Chief Justice Strine) all make clear, Delaware is now squarely in the camp of shareholder (or director) primacy. Based on these same decisions, it is equally clear that Delaware law prior to the *Unocal* and *Revlon* decisions on corporate purpose was less clear, since, as the Delaware Supreme Court noted in *Revlon*, that case presented the court with the opportunity to "address *for the first time* the extent to which a corporation may consider the impact of a takeover threat on constituencies other than stockholders."[59]

What If Shareholder Primacy Was Not the Rule in Delaware?

Delaware today is firmly entrenched in the shareholder/director primacy camp. However, as described above, this has been the rule in Delaware only since the mid-1980s, and it was not always obvious that Delaware's jurisprudence would adopt this view. The remainder of this essay explores the question of what might have happened if Delaware had gone down a different path and how corporate governance—and the broader economy—might be different. In particular, I look at some ways the various economic stakeholders in the corporation may have been affected had Delaware not concluded that the primary purpose of the corporation was to maximize wealth for stockholders.

To begin on this path, let's assume that, instead of adopting the stockholder primacy rules set forth in *Revlon* and its progeny, Delaware's courts chose to expand upon the court's words in *Unocal* and ruled generally that directors had *the obligation* to consider "the effect" of *any corporate action* "on the corporate enterprise," which included "the impact on 'constituencies' other than stockholders (*i.e.*, creditors, customers, employees, and perhaps even the community generally)." This encompasses "the basic stockholder interests at stake, including those of short term speculators, whose actions may have fueled the coercive aspect of the offer at the expense of the long term investor."[60] Further, assume that we have a court that allows (or even mandates) directors to consider the other corporate stakeholders identified in *Unocal* to the same extent it considers stockholder interests when making decisions and (most importantly) allows these stakeholders to enforce these rights, whether at the ballot box on certain fundamental corporate decisions and/or grants standing as applicable to those stakeholders in a court of equity to enforce those rights.[61] What if Delaware's law developed in this fashion since the mid-1980s through the present?[62]

What If the Corporation Owed Duties to Creditors?

Beginning with the first item on the list set forth in *Unocal*: What if the corporation owed duties to the company's creditors? This question seems particularly appropriate because, as recently explained by Vice Chancellor Laster, Delaware law with respect to the fiduciary duties owed to creditors has changed fairly dramatically over the last decade. According to Laster, before 2007:

- The fiduciary duties owed by directors extended to creditors when the corporation entered the vicinity of insolvency;
- Creditors could enforce the fiduciary duties that directors owed them through a direct action for breach of fiduciary duty;
- Under the trust fund doctrine, the directors' fiduciary duties to creditors included an obligation to manage the corporation conservatively as a trust fund for the creditors' benefit;
- Because directors owed fiduciary duties both to creditors and stockholders, directors faced an inherent conflict of interest and would bear the burden of demonstrating that their decision were entirely fair; and
- Directors could be held liable for continuing to operate an insolvent entity and incurring greater losses for creditors under a theory known as "deepening insolvency."

However, by at least the end of 2010, according to Laster, "none of these assertions remain true." In their place is a different regime in which the following principles are true:

- There is no legally recognized "zone of insolvency" with implications for fiduciary claims. The only transition point that affects fiduciary duty analysis is insolvency itself;
- Regardless of whether a corporation is solvent or insolvent, creditors cannot bring direct claims for breach of fiduciary duty. After a corporation becomes insolvent, creditors gain standing to assert claims derivatively for breach of fiduciary duty;
- The directors of an insolvent firm do not owe any particular duties to creditors. They continue to owe fiduciary duties to the corporation for the benefit of all of its residual claimants, a category which now includes creditors. They do not have a duty to shut down the insolvent firm and marshal its assets for distribution to creditors, although they make a business judgment that this is indeed the best route to maximize the firm's value; and
- Delaware does not recognize the theory of "deepening insolvency." Directors cannot be held liable for continuing to operate an insolvent entity in the good faith belief that they may achieve profitability, even if their decisions ultimately lead to greater losses for creditors.[63]

So how could corporate law, and the economy more generally, look differently if Delaware law further changed the duties owed to creditors by extending fiduciary duties to creditors? Although the literature on this issue is limited, there is at least some evidence that "firms are more likely to circumvent debt covenants when directors owe fiduciary duties only to shareholders than when they owe them to creditors as well . . . [and] that imposing fiduciary duties toward creditors reduces financial-reporting conflicts between equity and debt-holders, and consequently reduces the likelihood of manipulations that favor equity holders' over creditors' interests."[64]

More broadly, studies to date indicate that financial reporting and board governance generally are positively associated when fiduciary duties are owed to creditors. As was recently reported, "board quality improves financial-reporting quality for the stakeholder to whom directors owe fiduciary duties."[65]

This should not be surprising; directors, as Chief Justice Strine has noted, respond to those who have power to compel their performance and the right to remove them if that performance does not favor their interests.[66] One such response is to tailor financial reporting (within legal bounds) to represent the interests of shareholders more favorably, even if such reporting results in less reliable information being available to creditors.

This should also not be surprising, because, to the extent directors feel obligated to maximize stockholder interests and stockholder value, they (along with management) may be incentivized to present the company's financial statements in the manner that demonstrates the greatest financial value to the company's stockholders, even if this results in a portrayal of these financial statements in less creditor-friendly terms. Yet given how the Delaware courts have changed the scope and nature of duties to creditors over the last decade, one must wonder whether the potential benefits of greater financial transparency and disclosure should be a factor that could influence the courts as they continue to explore the duties owed to creditors.

Another potential implication of increased duties to creditors is empowering employees who are owed pensions by the corporation to protect their interests in those pensions. In 1983, the Reagan administration determined that corporations could terminate pension plans not just in narrow cases of "business necessity," but also generally so long as the company bought an annuity for the existing benefits from an insurance company.[67] The rule change allowed a board to terminate plans for the benefit of stockholders and at the expense of employees, who were creditors of the company by virtue of their interests in the company's pension plan.

As is by now well known, many boards took advantage of this change to terminate plans and distribute the "excess" from the pension plans to shareholders without compensating the employee/creditor for the risks of the new plan or providing any of the "profits" from the plan to enhance the plans themselves.[68] Although the battle over which stockholder (or group of stockholders) should receive the excess from the pension plans was often litigated in Delaware, the courts did not address whether the board had a fiduciary duty to the original beneficiaries of these pension plans, to ensure that they received any excess before it was paid out to stockholders.[69] This had an enormous impact on the economy, because it effectively redistributed wealth from a group of long-term creditors/employees—pension plan beneficiaries—to the company's stockholders. This had important consequences for workers and corporate governance that remain to this day, and obviously would have been different had Delaware imposed duties on boards to consider the interests of employee/creditors as part of any termination of a pension plan.[70]

What If the Corporation Owed Duties to Customers?

Delaware has generally not allowed claims by customers to be brought against directors, nor allowed customers to claim that they are owed duties by directors. At the same time, the notion that a company should be run for the benefit of its customers has a long tradition (arguably longer than the notion that the company should be run for the benefit of its shareholders). For example, Peter Drucker some time ago wrote: "Asked what a business is, the typical businessman is likely to answer an organization to make a profit. The typical economist is likely to give the same answer. The answer is not only false, it is irrelevant. To know what a business is, we have to start with its purpose. Its purpose must lie outside the business itself. In fact, it must lie in society since business enterprise is an organ of society. There is only one valid definition of business purpose: to create a customer."[71]

A similar view was expressed a few years later by Ken Mason, then president of Quaker Oats, who wrote in *Businessweek* that Milton Friedman's "profits are everything" philosophy represents "a dreary and demeaning view of the role of business and business leaders in our society. . . . Making a profit is no more the purpose of a corporation than getting enough to eat is the purpose of life. Getting enough to eat is a requirement of life; life's purpose, one would hope, is somewhat broader and more challenging. Likewise with business and profit."[72]

This view continues today with many of this country's leading companies. For example, Steve Jobs stated that Apple "existed to delight customers first" and that the philosophy of putting its customers first benefited all the company's stakeholders.[73]

What would the economy look like if law allowed boards to prioritize customers over shareholders? According to Roger Martin, former dean of the University of Toronto's School of Management, the effect of prioritizing shareholders over customers creates incentives for executives to meet the "expectations market" of the public stock exchanges rather than the "real world market," where "customers are the focus and the central task of companies is to find ever better ways to serve them."[74]

According to Martin, the focus on the expectations market has had significant negative consequences for companies, the economy, and even for stockholders. Martin argues that rules requiring a company, its board and executives to emphasize shareholder value above all else leads to short-term profits at the expense of long-term investment, a focus on stock price rather than building better products, and even a business environment where there is incentive to take business and ethical risks to meet market expectations because share price expectations must be met at all costs.

In contrast, prioritizing customers over stockholders incentivizes executives to create the greatest products and services. This incentive system creates an opportunity to build for the long-term rather than short-term, and because this "real market" is focused on customers, employees, and products, it tends to create broader benefits for the employees and companies that create these products, which provides greater benefits for the broader economy and society.[75]

Martin compares the stockholder-focused rules that govern corporations with the focus in the National Football League, which he says attempts to maximize "customer satisfaction." This comparison leads Martin to analogize chief executive officers and boards managing for the stock market to quarterbacks and coaches who seek to meet the point spread rather than win games. Martin advocates for a system where stockholder interests are secondary to the interests of customers (and other stakeholders), on the theory that if customers are the focus of corporations and boards, then the long-term value of corporations and shareholders is more likely to be created.[76]

Martin is far from alone in his view of the harm caused by focusing on shareholders rather than customers.[77] Again, however, the point here is not normative, to argue that one approach to management theory—or legal duties—is preferable. Rather, it is simply to point out an alternative—maximizing customer satisfaction rather than stockholder value—that has a number of business, management, and economic advocates and may have several positive consequences for the economy and even stockholders.[78]

What If the Corporation Owed Duties to Employees?

The next constituency identified in *Unocal* was employees.[79] As an initial matter, there can be no dispute that employees are critical to the success of a company. Employees improve the company by, for example, the exercise of skill and effort beyond the minimum necessary to merely obtain their compensation. There is also no question that employees truly take risks and "invest" in the company through their work; workers obtain education, experience, and skill for their employers, and they make substantial sacrifices for their employers.

Yet even if one were to dispute the added value, efforts, risks, and investment made by employees in their company, the law often imposes fiduciary obligations on employees—including duties of care and loyalty—that are more generally associated with directors without imposing similar duties upon the employer. To the contrary, many employees are required as a condition of employment to sign employment agreements that expressly waive any obligations the company may have to the employee, while also limiting certain of the employee's rights (i.e., requiring disputes to be resolved in arbitration rather than in court, perhaps limiting the employee's rights to sue in other ways, and expressly setting forth the employee's duties to the company).

Interestingly, while courts have held that employees can and generally do owe fiduciary duties to their employers, employers generally do not owe such duties to their employees.[80] Delaware is consistent with this view (which is also in the Restatement (Second) of Agency), and places a fiduciary duty on employees to act in good faith, loyalty, and fairly with their employer—an obligation that is similar to the duties directors owe to shareholders.[81] However, such a duty is typically *not* imposed upon a company toward its employees.

What if the situation was changed, such that directors and companies had similar legal and equitable duties and obligations to each other, directors had the right to place employee interests above shareholder profits, and employees had the rights to elect a certain number of directors and/or standing to bring a lawsuit against directors for breach of fiduciary duty if the directors took actions that harmed employees?[82] What would the corporation look like, and is it possible that a board that is obligated to consider the welfare of its employees before considering shareholder profits may, in fact, be more successful than a corporation that focuses on maximizing shareholder value? Again, given the hypothetical nature of this discussion, it is not practical to expect a definitive answer, but there is at least some evidence that when employees do better, the corporation as a whole (as well as society) does better.[83]

Many economists have long argued that corporations that pay higher wages have more productive employees.[84] Multiple studies have shown, for example, that paying higher wages motivates employees to work harder and leads to less job turnover;[85] higher wages attract more talented, qualified, and capable employees;[86] and better pay leads to increased customer satisfaction and service.[87] Many business leaders, including such prominent figures as Howard Schultz at Starbucks and Steve Easterbrook at McDonalds, support the view that when companies focus on improving wages and benefits for employees, the corporation is the ultimate beneficiary, not just because it achieves higher profits but because these employees provide better customer service, are more loyal to the corporation, and generally are more productive.[88]

These steps have obviously been taken within the existing structure, where companies are obligated to give primacy to stockholder interests, and the benefits paid to employees under these circumstances have been supported by the notion that stockholders benefit from the investments in employees. However, a potential next step if directors owed duties to employees could include, for example, duties to (1) share productivity gains with employees and not just stockholders, (2) focus on creating wealth for their employees as well as stockholders, and (3) require some relationship between pay at the top of the organizational structure and pay to all the company's employees. In a world where a director's duties include creating value for the company's employees, and employees have the right to enforce that duty, there are many ways that more profits may be allocated to employees, which ironically may also benefit shareholders (but, at least under this definition, would not be done for that purpose).

What If Directors Owed Duties to Their Communities?

The growth of corporations since the takeover wars of the 1980s has also led communities to focus on how these corporations disclose and manage their social and environmental activities as well as their financial condition.[89] While multinational corporations have been around for decades, the dramatic growth of the world's largest corporations over the last few decades is unprecedented. For example, by 2012, the largest 1,000 public corporations (the Global 1000) were responsible for half of the total market value of all of the world's more than 60,000 public companies; had $34 trillion in revenues; directly employed more than 73 million people (and millions more in their multiple supply chains); and had a total market capitalization of more than $28 trillion.[90]

The Global 1000 are larger than many nations. For example, Dow estimates that it consumes as much energy on a daily basis as Australia, while the sales of Royal Dutch Shell and Walmart are each higher than the gross domestic product of all but about thirty countries.[91] The concentration of power in a few large corporations exists across industries. For example, when Google's search engine went down for five minutes in 2013, it caused global Internet traffic to drop by 40 percent; Monsanto controls more than 90 percent of the global genetically modified seed market; and just six companies—Comcast, Disney, News Corp., Time Warner, Viacom, and CBS—control an estimated 70 percent of cable broadcasting in the United States.[92]

The concentration of power in large, global companies has created a demand for these companies to focus more on their communities and other stakeholders, which is challenging for these communities given the size and scope of these companies.[93] It should come as no surprise that a large, multinational company may be less inclined to focus on a local community than a smaller company that hires most of its employees locally and sells its products locally. As one commentator noted, for "an oil and gas company that extracts oil in Equatorial Guinea and sells downstream in the US the interests of customers, employees, suppliers and local communities are likely to diverge significantly."[94]

In response to this growing power, citizens and regulators are already challenging corporations to serve communities over stockholders. For example, surveys show that globally more than 80 percent of citizens want chief executive officers to shift their focus from short-term profits to broader business and social issues such as income inequality and society's interests.[95] Corporations and boards have also felt pressure to focus on stakeholder issues in their public disclosures. For example, in 1992, just twenty-six companies issued sustainability reports (i.e., reports that contained social, environmental, or other governance information but did not include financial information); by 2012, that number had grown to more than 6,000.[96]

All of this has occurred, of course, in a world where boards have not had a fiduciary obligation to consider the interests of communities as equal to (or above) the interests of stockholders. However, the growth of corporations (including the widely recognized growing political influence of corporations) has led to greater demand for more disclosure of nonfinancial issues by corporations. If boards and corporations had fiduciary obligations to communities, then we would presumably see even greater development of the corporation functioning as an integral part of the broader economic and social part of society—a role that apparently a vast majority of people expect, particularly in light of the growing power of corporations.

What If Boards Could Consider the Basic Stockholder Interests at Stake, Including Those of Short-Term Speculators?

The last set of constituencies identified in *Unocal* are the "basic stockholder interests at stake, including those of short-term speculators" who may have created the situation that creates the need for defensive actions by the board.[97] If directors could consider the basic stockholder interests at stake and choose to prioritize one group of stockholders over another, how would directors choose between various classes of stockholders?

Again, it is worth starting with a few basic points. First, although it is often stated that most Americans invest in the stock market, this is, in fact, not the case. Rather, recent evidence demonstrates that about half of all Americans have nothing invested in the stock market, and of those who do invest in the market, the vast majority have very little invested.[98] Roughly speaking, about one-third of the stock market is owned by the richest 1 percent (or less) of the country; another one-third of the market is owned by the richest 5 percent; and the remaining one-third is spread out among the remaining 95 percent of the population that owns stocks.[99] Because share ownership is so concentrated among the wealthy (and very wealthy) in the United States, maximizing share value at the expense of the company's other stakeholders means that if shareholder wealth maximization is the ultimate goal of the corporation, then the wealthy will benefit disproportionately as a result since they own the vast amount of stock traded in the country.

Second, stock trading, as opposed to stock ownership, has come to dominate the market. As Chief Justice Strine has noted, even the mutual funds that serve as the primary investment vehicle for most Americans who do invest in the market trade on a "gerbil-like" basis, with turnover rates of more than 100 percent on an annual basis in their portfolio, and even pension funds engage in a similar turnover of their equity investments.[100] Further, the domination of trading by institutions means that the trading of stocks on all exchanges in the United States regularly exceeds 100 percent, rendering most institutions "more short-term speculators than committed, long-term investors."[101] The result is that the holding periods for stocks has declined substantially in recent years, at the same time that individuals have become less involved in the market.[102]

Consistent with the notion that stock markets today favor *traders* rather than *investors* is the simple reality that today's investors are not actually buying stock in a company; rather, they are simply buying shares from another trader, with the hope that those shares will increase in value without any financial interest or investment directly in the company. For example, Apple raised $97 million in its initial public offering in 1980;[103] since then, although Apple has had four stock splits, it has not sold any stock to the public. Thus, buyers of Apple stock today are hoping that they can eventually sell that stock for an even higher price, but Apple as a corporation does not receive anything from either the purchase or the sale of its stock.

This trend has substantially accelerated in recent years. From 2000 to 2010, net issuance of corporate equity in the United States was a *negative $287 billion* according to information provided by the Federal Reserve. In addition, initial public offerings have dramatically declined over the last several years. Together, this indicates that, although the stock market involves a great deal of trading, the corporations whose stock is traded directly receive only a fraction of the proceeds from these trades.[104]

Yet, at the end of the day, does the time horizon of a company's stockholder base really matter? Company executives certainly believe it does, as studies have found that more than 90 percent of executives believe that a company with long-term investors is more likely to grow market share and invest more in new products, while a company whose investor base is focused on short-term results is more likely to engage in share repurchases, cost reductions, and other actions designed to impact stock price rather than longer-term growth initiatives and strategic planning.[105]

These results seem to lead back to the court's decision in *Unocal*, as many advocates today would argue that one reason companies are less inclined to engage in long-term investment is precisely because of the pressure created by short-term investors. If a firm that does not "heavily buy and sell its own shares" benefits when managers focus on the long term, then it is worth questioning whether structures should be established that allow those who have a greater long-term interest in the corporation to influence corporate behavior so that the debate about how the corporation should act is not dominated by those solely focused on immediate actions that may result in a temporary increase in stock price.

Conclusion

Economic disruption over the last decade has raised fundamental questions about many of our leading institutions, including government, the financial sector, and corporations. The disruption and anxiety have been fueled, at least in part, by growing wealth disparities in the country, and there is substantial evidence that the wealth disparities can be linked to the stockholder primacy philosophy of corporate governance, which requires that shareholder wealth be maximized over all other corporate constituencies.[106] This essay does not challenge the dominance of stockholder primacy in today's world. To the contrary, given the analysis by, among others, Delaware Chief Justice Leo E. Strine about the current state of Delaware law, as well as my own experience in advising directors and others on the duties of directors (including directors of companies incorporated in states other than Delaware), there can be little question about the dominance of shareholder primacy in the corporate community today.

Rather, the purpose of this essay is threefold. First, I emphasize that shareholder primacy is a relatively recent development. The origins of shareholder primacy are now often traced to the Michigan Supreme Court's decision in *Dodge v. Ford Motor Co.*,[107] but as former chancellor Bill Allen noted, in the 1960s this case drew scant attention, and it "seemed that every interesting question in corporation law had been answered and that nothing remained" to be discovered in the study of corporate law.[108] It was not until the 1980s—with the takeover boom, the growth of institutional investors, the changing regulatory environment, the rising law and economics movement, and developments in corporate finance as well as other macroeconomic events—that shareholder primacy came into full force. Prior to that time, and in particular from the New Deal until the mid-1980s, directors managed companies for all corporate stakeholders, and the primary enforcement mechanism for stakeholder capitalism was the countervailing power of other large institutions, including employees (largely through labor unions), customers and suppliers (often through consumer federations and other organizations), and communities (whether acting individually or through their representatives in local, state, and national government regulators).[109] It was these countervailing powers that directors had to answer to, and responding to these powers precluded any notion of shareholder primacy. Further, by whatever measurement one chooses, the evidence shows that, during this period, US corporations were, on the whole, very successful.

Second, although in hindsight it seems inevitable that Delaware would adopt a shareholder primacy model, at the time there was considerable debate about how this issue would be resolved in the Delaware courts. In particular, both *Unocal* and *Revlon* were vigorously litigated, and it was far from certain that the Delaware Supreme Court in *Revlon* would rule in favor of Perelman and against the board, particularly following Justice Moore's decision in *Unocal*.[110] Further, it is important to note that by the time of these decisions, many of the countervailing powers that had served to limit corporate power since the 1930s—including, most notably, private unions and government regulatory agencies—had weakened significantly by the mid-1980s. Thus, while *Revlon* may be seen as enhancing shareholder rights at the expense of other stakeholders, *Unocal*, *Revlon*, and their progeny would also come to be viewed as placing considerable process constraints on boards, particularly in the takeover context. In this way, one can view the Delaware courts as becoming a (moderate) new countervailing power to corporate director conduct, particularly in the takeover context.

The final purpose of this essay is to note that, even though we live in a world dominated by stockholder primacy, this could change (again) in the future. Ideas and legal theories move in cycles, and while lawyers, directors, and business people are judged by current standards, that does not mean that these standards are frozen in time. To the contrary, the reality—indeed, the likelihood—is that today's standards will be discarded in the years to come, and it is more a question of when, not if. As then chancellor Allen wrote more than two decades ago (and less than a decade after both *Unocal* and *Revlon* had been decided):

> I suppose that there will be no final move in defining the nature or the purpose of the business corporation. It is perhaps asking too much to expect us, as a people—or our law—to have a single view of the purpose of an institution so large, pervasive, and important as our public corporations. . . . Thus I conclude that we have been schizophrenic on the nature of the corporation, but as a society we will probably always be so to some extent. The questions "what is a corporation?" and "for whose benefit do directors hold power?" are legal questions only in the sense that legal institutions will be required at certain points to formulate or assume answers to them. But they are not simply technical questions of law capable of resolution through analytical rule

manipulation. Even less are they technical questions of finance or economics. Rather in defining what we suppose a public corporation to be, we implicitly express our view of the nature and purpose of our social life. Since we do disagree on that, our law of corporate entities is bound itself to be contentious and controversial. It will be worked out, not deduced. In this process, efficiency concerns, ideology, and interest group politics will commingle with history (including our semi-autonomous corporation law) to produce an answer that will hold for here and now, only to be torn by some future stress and to be reformulated once more. And so on, and so on, evermore.[111]

Notes

The author would like to thank William Chandler, the Honorable Leo Strine, Jesse Fried, Rob Daines, Steven Davidoff Solomon, Larry Sonsini, Ignacio Salceda, Herb Fockler, and Aaron Benjamin for their insights and comments. Obviously all views are solely those of the author and not those of his firm or anyone else. "In Search of Lost Time" is the English translation of the title of Marcel Proust's great novel *À La Recherche du Temps Perdu*. As Proust noted in one of the volumes of his oeuvre, "a powerful idea communicates some of its power to the man who contradicts it." *See* 2 Marcel Proust, In Search of Lost Time: Within a Budding Grove 186 (C. K. Scott Moncrieff and Terrence Kilmartin trans., Modern Library 1992) (1981).

1. While the debate about whether directors or stockholders control the corporation remains an active one in US corporate law—*see, e.g.*, Stephen M. Bainbridge, The New Corporate Governance Theory and Practice (2008); Charles R. T. O'Kelley, *The Entrepreneur and the Theory of the Modern Corporation*, 31 J. Corp. L. 753 (2006)—as will be discussed in more detail below, for purposes of this essay, the differences between stockholder control and director control are less significant because the issue posed in this essay is whether non-stockholder constituencies should have the opportunity to enforce rights in addition to stockholders and directors. For this reason, I use the term *stockholder primacy* to refer to both stockholder and director primacy.

2. Trs. of Dartmouth Coll. v. Woodward, 17 U.S. 518, 636 (1819).

3. Interestingly, the end of Friedman's sentence, which is critical to his thesis, is often forgotten. The full sentence states: "There is one and only one social responsibility of business—to use its resources and engage in activities designed to increase its profits so long as it stays within the rules of the game, which is to say, engages in open and free competition without deception or fraud." Milton Friedman, *The Social Responsibility of Business Is to Increase Its Profits*, N.Y. Times Mag., Sept. 13, 1970. As has been persuasively argued by, among others, Robert

Reich, the key is to determine the "rules of the game" by which corporations (and markets) exist. *See generally* Robert B. Reich, Saving Capitalism for the Many, Not the Few 5 (2015) ("A market—any market—requires that government make and enforce the rules of the game. In most modern democracies, such rules emanate from legislatures, administrative agencies, and courts. Government doesn't 'intrude' on the 'free market.' It creates the market."). These rules are frequently changed, often in little-noticed ways that have the effect of favoring one industry over another or impacting legal regulations.

4. *See* Michael Jensen and William Meckling, *A Theory of the Firm: Managerial Behavior, Agency Costs, and Ownership Structure*, 3 J. Fin. Econ. 305 (1976).

5. Revlon, Inc. v. MacAndrews & Forbes Holdings, Inc., 506 A.2d 173 (Del. 1986).

6. Unocal Corp. v. Mesa Petroleum Co., 493 A.2d 946 (Del. 1985).

7. eBay Domestic Holdings, Inc., v. Newmark, 16 A.3d 1 (Del. Ch. 2010).

8. *In re* Trados S'holder Litig., C.A. No. 1512-VCL (Del. Ch. Aug. 16, 2013).

9. *eBay*, 16 A.3d at 34.

10. 170 N.W. 668 (Mich. 1919).

11. William T. Allen, *Our Schizophrenic Conception of the Business Corporation*, 14 Cardozo L. Rev. 261, 263 (1992).

12. Stockholder primacy is also rather limited in its geographical scope; in particular, its principle locus is the state of Delaware, which, for reasons beyond the scope of this chapter, is the "most important jurisdiction" for corporate law in the United States. Further, a majority of states have laws expressly allowing directors to consider stakeholders in addition to stockholders. However, the statutes in these states have limited effectiveness, in part because the statutes generally do not allow these other constituencies to elect directors or even bring a lawsuit to protect their interests, while stockholders do have such rights. *See generally* Lyman Johnson, *Relating Fiduciary Duties to Corporate Personhood and Corporate Purpose* at 11, in Research Handbook on Fiduciary Law (D. Gordon Smith and Andrew Gold eds., 2016), https://ssrn.com/abstract=2814231. The federal government, as well as the listing rules on the stock exchanges, generally defer to the states on the duties of directors. *See, e.g.*, CTS Corp. v. Dynamics Corp. of Am., 481 U.S. 69 (1987) (corporations generally governed by state of incorporation). As a result, Delaware corporate law remains the most influential body of law in the country today, as it is the state of incorporation for well over half of US public companies (as well as a substantial number of private companies). Given Delaware's influence, this chapter focuses on the development of stockholder primacy in that state.

13. Many historians have noted that asking What if? can also help eliminate what has been called "hindsight bias." *See* Stephen E. Ambrose et al., The Collected What If? Eminent Historians Imagine What Might Have Been

xiv (Robert Cowley ed., 2001). I find that helpful in this context because the prevailing wisdom of shareholder primacy is so strong. The potential for hindsight bias has also been recognized as a risk in director decision-making process. *See* CDX Holdings, Inc., v. Fox, C.A. No. 8031-VCL (Del. Ch. July 28, 2015), *aff'd*, No. 526 (Del. June 6, 2016); *see also* Travis J. Laster, *Cognitive Bias in Director Decision-Making*, 20 Corp. Gov. Advisors 1 (Nov.–Dec. 2012).

14. Leo E. Strine Jr., *The Dangers of Denial: The Need for a Clear-Eyed Understanding of the Power and Accountability Structure Established by the Delaware General Corporation Law*, 50 Wake Forest L. Rev. 761 (2015).

15. That said, I wish to make clear that I am not challenging the view, so eloquently set forth by Chief Justice Strine in *The Dangers of Denial* as well as by such learned jurists as former chancellors Chandler and Allen, that Delaware law currently requires directors to "make stockholder welfare their sole end, and that other interests may be taken into consideration only as a means of promoting stockholder welfare." *See id.* at 771–72; *see also eBay*, 16 A.3d at 34; TW Servs., Inc. v. SWT Acquisition Corp., 14 Del. J. Corp. L. 1169, 1183–84 (Del. Ch. 1989). Rather, as discussed in more detail below, the purpose of this essay is to review some of the broader, nonlegal developments that coincided with the development of this case law as well as to consider what might have happened if the law had not developed in this fashion.

16. A study by the Brookings Institution found that the top twenty law schools and top twenty business schools in the United States routinely teach that maximizing shareholder value is "settled law" and that students are taught that their job as "corporate leaders" is to "enhance shareholder value and not to follow broader concepts of the corporation." *See* Darrell M. West, *The Purpose of the Corporation in Business and Law School Curricula*, Governance Studies at Brookings, July 19, 2011, at 17–19, https://www.brookings.edu/wp-content/uploads/2016/06/0719_corporation_west.pdf.

17. *See, e.g.*, Myron T. Steele and J. W. Verret, *Delaware's Guidance: Ensuring Equity for the Modern Witenagemot*, 2 Va. L. & Bus. Rev. 189, 191–92 (2007) (noting that the "Delaware Court of Chancery, as an equity court, has wide latitude to craft remedies and mold precedent to fit particular fact patterns in the tradition of the English High Court of Chancery. This fact has allowed the Court of Chancery to maximize efficiency in resolving disputes while undercutting the future applicability of precedent, which has led to a tension between efficiency and predictability.").

18. For example, and as discussed in more detail below, in just the last decade, the Delaware courts have fundamentally changed the duties owed to creditors. Similarly, but perhaps more notably for those focused on M&A litigation, over the last few years, the Court of Chancery has, for example, developed new laws allowing forum-selection bylaws and changed prior law relating to the settlement of merger litigation, and in particular disclosure settlements in the con-

text of merger litigation. *See, e.g.*, Boilermakers Local 154 Ret. Fund v. Chevron Corp., 73 A.3d 934 (Del. Ch. 2013) (upholding the validity of exclusive forum provision); *In re* Trulia, Inc. Stockholder Litig., 129 A.3d 884 (Del. Ch. 2016) (rejecting disclosure-only settlement and providing a new standard for approval of such a settlement).

19. Former chancellor Allen expressed this notion long ago in his seminal article on the "schizophrenic" development of corporate law. See Allen, *Our Schizophrenic Conception* at 262 ("Corporation law and, indeed, the law generally, is not simply what it may seem at first, a comprehensive system of legal rules. While it is that, it is also a great deal more. People who think of law as a system of legal rules alone fail to understand that law is a social product, inevitably complex, at points inescapably ambiguous, and always dynamic—always becoming something new. Of course, it is essential . . . to understand the legal rules that at any moment constitute the most elemental part of that body of law. But . . . [i]n order to grasp the dynamic feature of legal rules, it is necessary to see them in their historical and social context. For while, in one sense, legal rules exist 'out there,' constituting shared interpretations of our common legal culture, they are, as well, continually re-created within that culture through interpretation.").

20. Adolf A. Berle Jr., THE 20TH-CENTURY CAPITALIST REVOLUTION 169 (1954). For a lengthier discussion of this issue, *see* David J. Berger, *One Practitioner's Random Thoughts on Shareholders' Rights in the Modern World*, in THE ACCOUNTABLE CORPORATION: ESSAYS IN CORPORATE GOVERNANCE 121 (Marc J. Epstein and Kirk O. Hanson eds., 2006).

21. Strine, *The Dangers of Denial* at 797.

22. *See, e.g.*, Sierra Club v. Morton, 405 U.S. 727, 742 (1972) (J. Douglas dissenting). As Justice Douglas recognized, many inanimate objects have standing to sue when their "rights" are impacted, including ships, corporations, various associations, and other groupings.

23. Allen, *Our Schizophrenic Conception* at 281.

24. In taking this position, I do not assume that Justice Moore in *Unocal* anticipated providing rights to nonstockholder constituencies, that *Revlon* was in any way a change from the court's decision in *Unocal*, or that the Delaware courts should have supported a nonstockholder constituency regime. Instead, I simply try to envision what a legal structure that protected the different constituencies identified by Justice Moore might look like, including assuming that these different constituencies had the right to enforce the obligations owed to them by the board.

25. For a longer discussion of some recent cases that have changed the way we currently view corporations and corporate law as well as a discussion of the potential impact of these decisions, *see* Leo E. Strine Jr., *Corporate Power Ratchet: The Courts' Role in Eroding "We the People's" Ability to Constrain Our Corporate Creations*, 51 HARV. CIV. RTS.-CIV. LIBERTIES L. REV. 423 (2016) (discuss-

ing recent federal decisions that have changed the power of corporations and limited the ability to regulate corporate behavior).

26. *See generally* Berger, *One Practitioner's Random Thoughts.*

27. *See id.* at 123.

28. George W. Merck, Med. Coll. of Va. at Richmond, MEDICINE IS FOR THE PEOPLE, NOT THE PROFITS (Dec. 1, 1950), https://www.merck.com/about/our-people/gw-merck-doc.pdf.

29. Adolf A. Berle Jr., *Corporate Powers as Powers in Trust*, 44 HARV. L. REV. 1049 (1931); E. Merrick Dodd Jr., *For Whom Are Corporate Managers Trustees?* 45 HARV. L. REV. 1145 (1932); Adolf A. Berle Jr., *For Whom Corporate Managers Are Trustees: A Note*, 45 HARV. L. REV. 1365 (1932). As is by now well known, Berle and Dodd started from the same assumption: that the corporation would be run by its managers, largely free from stockholder interference. (Berle analogized corporate managers to "princes and ministers." *See* Berle, *For Whom Corporate Managers Are Trustees: A Note* at 1366).

30. Strine, *The Dangers of Denial* at 1 n.1. Berle and Dodd also differed substantially on the purpose of the corporation, with Berle arguing that the corporation should focus on maximizing shareholder wealth and Dodd arguing that corporations have a "social service as well as a profit-making function." Dodd, *For Whom Are Corporate Managers Trustees?* at 1148.

31. Berle, THE 20TH-CENTURY CAPITALIST REVOLUTION at 169.

32. *See generally* Frank Levy and Peter Temin, *Inequality and Institutions in 20th Century America* (National Bureau of Economic Research Working Paper No. 13106, 2007), http://www.nber.org/papers/w13106.pdf (discussing the background and impact of the Treaty of Detroit).

33. For example, Professor Berle, the leading proponent of running the corporation for the benefit of its stockholders, had articulated his vision in 1931 as follows: "[A]ll powers granted to a corporation or to the management of a corporation, or to any group within the corporation, whether derived from statute or charter or both, are necessarily and at all times exercisable only for the ratable benefit of all the shareholders as their interest appears." Berle, *Corporate Powers as Powers in Trust* at 1049. However, as noted earlier, by the mid-1950s, Professor Berle had changed his view, writing that "[t]wenty years ago the writer had a controversy with the late Professor E. Merrick Dodd, of Harvard Law School, the writer holding that corporate powers were powers in trust for shareholders while Professor Dowd argued that these powers were held in trust for the entire community. The argument has been settled (at least for the time being) squarely in favor of Professor Dodd's contention." Berle, THE 20TH-CENTURY CAPITALIST REVOLUTION at 169.

34. Andrew C. Sigler, *Business Forum; Reader Comment; Roundtable Reply*, N.Y. TIMES, Dec. 27, 1981, http://www.nytimes.com/1981/12/27/business/business-forum-reader-comment-roundtable-reply.html (emphasis added); *see*

generally The Business Roundtable, Statement on Corporate Responsibility (Oct. 1981) (stating that "corporations have a responsibility, first of all, to make available to the public quality goods and services at fair prices, thereby earning a profit that attracts investment to continue and enhance the enterprise, provide jobs, and build the economy. . . . Business and society have a symbiotic relationship: The long-term viability of the corporation depends upon its responsibility to the society of which it is a part. And the well-being of society depends upon profitable and responsible business enterprises.").

35. Another concept that did not exist at this time was that of corporate governance. For example, neither Berle nor Dodd ever even used the term. Rather, the phrase "corporate governance" first came into widespread use in the mid-1970s, first as part of a Ralph Nader–led project to "democratize" and control large corporations, followed by Securities and Exchange Commission hearings in the late 1970s. *See generally* Robert Teitelman, Bloodsport: When Ruthless Dealmakers, Shrewd Ideologues, and Brawling Lawyers Toppled the Corporate Establishment 82 (2016).

36. For the origins of this system, *see* John Kenneth Galbraith, American Capitalism: The Concept of Countervailing Power (rev. ed. 1993). For a more detailed discussion of this system and its evolution to a shareholder primacy system, *see generally* Ralph Gomory and Richard Sylla, *The American Corporation*, 142 Daedalus, no. 2, 2013, at 102.

37. I find the term *stakeholder primacy* not particularly helpful; like *stockholder primacy* and *director primacy*, these concepts have become politically loaded and not particularly meaningful. Rather, in my experience, the real question is who gets to write the rules, elect directors, and enforce rights. Simply giving directors the option to consider nonstockholder constituencies (as many states have done) has proven to be largely meaningless in the absence of giving these other constituencies the right to hold directors accountable if directors did not consider their interests. *See generally* Nathan E. Standley, *Lessons Learned from the Capitulation of the Constituency Statute*, 4 Elon L. Rev. 209 (2012).

38. *See* Martin Lipton, *Takeover Bids in the Target's Boardroom*, 35 Bus. Law. 101 (1979).

39. Fischel and Easterbrook were leading members of the fast-growing "law and economics" movement, then led by academics associated with the University of Chicago. The law and economics movement also had significant support within the Reagan administration. *See generally* Jane Meyer, Dark Money: The Hidden History of the Billionaires behind the Rise of the Radical Right (2016) (discussing the relationship between the law and economics movement and the Reagan administration); Steven M. Teles, The Rise of the Conservative Legal Movement: The Battle for Control of the Law (2008).

40. *See* Frank H. Easterbrook and Daniel R. Fischel, *The Proper Role of a*

Target's Management in Responding to a Tender Offer, 94 HARV. L. REV. 1161 (1981).

41. *See* Eugene F. Fama and Michael C. Jensen, *Separation of Ownership and Control*, 26 J. L. & ECON. 301 (1983); Eugene F. Fama and Michael C. Jensen, *Agency Problems and Residual Claims*, 26 J. L. & ECON. 327 (1983); *see also* Michael C. Jensen and Kevin J. Murphy, *Performance Pay and Top Management Incentives*, 98 J. POL. ECON. 225 (1990) (arguing that top management should be paid primarily in stock to better align their incentives with the company's shareholders).

42. For a good discussion of the history leading to the adoption of Rule 10b-18 as well as some of the rule's current effects, *see* William Lazonick, *Profits without Prosperity*, HARV. BUS. REV., Sept. 2014, https://hbr.org/2014/09/profits-without-prosperity.

43. There were, of course, many changes during the 1980s and 1990s that further supported shareholder primacy. For example, the growth of the institutional investor and the newly adopted requirements under the US labor code that institutional investors vote their proxies solely for the economic benefit of the beneficiary, without regard to other interests, led to labor and other unions voting in support of transactions that resulted in many of their members losing their jobs and/or benefits. The Reagan administration also supported the benefits of shareholder primacy and an active M&A market. *See, e.g.*, COUNCIL OF ECONOMIC ADVISERS, ECONOMIC REPORT OF THE PRESIDENT (Feb. 1985) (arguing that shareholders are the "true owners" of the corporation and that serving their interests is "socially beneficial); *see generally* Teitelman, BLOODSPORT at 180–86 (discussing the impact of the Council of Economic Advisers report).

44. For a lengthier discussion of the benefits and costs of expanded stock buybacks, *see* Lazonick, *Profits without Prosperity*. More recently, scholars have argued that companies that do not engage in substantial share repurchases are more likely to benefit from long-term investors, but the benefits to (and from) long-term investors are less clear if (as is now typical) a company engages in substantial repurchases of its own stock. *See, e.g.*, Jesse Fried, *The Uneasy Case for Favoring Long-Term Shareholders*, 124 YALE L. J. 1554 (2015).

45. Delaware had been the subject of some academic attacks during this period. *See, e.g.*, William Cary, *Federalism and Corporate Law*, 83 YALE L. J. 663 (1974) (arguing that Delaware had a vested interest in maintaining its dominance in corporate law and that the federal government should consider adopting minimum corporate standards). The criticism of Delaware was heightened following the Delaware Supreme Court's decision in Smith v. Van Gorkom, 488 A.2d 858 (Del. 1985), a decision that some called "one of the worst decisions in the history of corporate law." *See* Daniel R. Fischel, *The Business Judgment Rule and the Trans Union Case*, 40 BUS. LAW. 1437, 1455 (1985).

46. 493 A.2d 946 (Del. 1985).

47. *Id.* at 955.

48. *Id.* at 955–56 (citation omitted).

49. *Id.* (citing Martin Lipton and Andrew R. Brownstein, *Takeover Responses and Directors' Responsibilities: An Update* at 7, in ABA National Institute on the Dynamics of Corporate Control (Dec. 8, 1983)).

50. *Id.* at 955 n.10 (citation omitted).

51. Michael C. Jensen, *When Unocal Won Over Pickens, Shareholders and Society Lost*, Financier, Nov. 1985, at 50–52; *see generally* Teitelman, Bloodsport.

52. Revlon, Inc. v. MacAndrews & Forbes Holdings, Inc., 506 A.2d 173, 176 (Del. 1986).

53. *Id.*

54. Strine, *The Dangers of Denial* at 773. As described by Chief Justice Strine, Revlon also led to substantial criticism, but this time from the proponents that the corporation should serve constituencies in addition to stockholders. *Id.*

55. Much of the remainder of this section is based on several recent articles written by Chief Justice Strine, who is both among the finest corporate law scholars of this era and, as the chief justice of the Delaware Supreme Court, presumably the most knowledgeable person on the current state of Delaware law. *See, e.g.*, Strine, *The Dangers of Denial*; Leo E. Strine Jr., *Making It Easier for Directors to "Do the Right Thing*, 4 Harv. Bus. L. Rev. 235 (2014); Leo E. Strine Jr., *One Fundamental Corporate Governance Question We Face: Can Corporations Be Managed for the Long Term Unless Their Powerful Electorates Also Act and Think Long Term?* 66 Bus. Law. 1 (2010) [hereafter cited as Strine, *Corporate Governance Question*]. Obviously all errors about the current state of Delaware law (or anything else in this essay) are solely the responsibility of the author.

56. 16 A.3d 1 (Del. Ch. 2010).

57. *Id.* at 8.

58. *Id.* at 34 (emphasis in original).

59. *Revlon*, 506 A.2d at 176 (emphasis added).

60. *Unocal*, 493 A.2d at 955–56.

61. While many states have adopted so-called stakeholder constituency statutes, these statutes are largely ineffective because they don't give these other stakeholders the opportunity to enforce their rights, either by the ballot or in court. As a result, these statutes have been criticized for simply giving directors greater discretion to act contrary to the interests of shareholders without any meaningful check on the scope of this expanded authority.

62. Again, at the risk of being redundant, I am not disputing what Delaware law is, as currently articulated by (among others) Chief Justice Strine. I have been privileged to litigate many cases before Chief Justice Strine (including when he was both chancellor and vice chancellor) as well as many of the other distinguished jurists on the Delaware courts, and completely defer to their views

on what Delaware law currently is. I am only asking What if? and, by this, hypothesizing what Delaware law could be and how the world might be different if the law had developed differently.

63. Quandrant Structured Prods. Co. v. Vertin, 115 A.3d 535, 543–45 (Del. Ch. 2015).

64. Shai Levi et al., *Does Fiduciary Duty to Creditors Reduce Debt-Covenant-Avoidance Behavior?* (Mar. 26, 2016), https://ssrn.com/abstract=2800724.

65. *Id.*

66. *See, e.g.*, Strine, *Corporate Governance Question* at 7–9; *see also* Leo E. Strine Jr., *Toward a True Corporate Republic: A Traditionalist Response to Bebchuk's Solution for Improving Corporate America*, 119 HARV. L. REV. 1759 (2006). This is again why the current regime of stakeholder constituency statutes outside of Delaware have proven to be largely ineffective; the constituencies these statutes were designed to benefit have no ability to remove or challenge the directors if their rights are not considered.

67. *See* Martin Gelter, *The Pension System and the Rise of Shareholder Primacy*, 43 SETON HALL L. REV. 909, 933–36 (2013); Richard A. Ippolito, *Tenuous Property Rights: The Unraveling of Defined Benefit Contracts in the US*, in PENSION POLICY IN AN INTEGRATING EUROPE 175–76 (Onotato Casellino and Elsa Fornero eds., 2003) (describing the specific regulatory changes and some of the policy implications).

68. There were about 580 terminations between 1980 and 1985, and more than 1,500 in 1986 alone, at the height of the takeover boom. Between 1980 and 1989, 1,635 plans were terminated, yielding an aggregate of $18 billion (corresponding to 45 percent of these plans' assets) to shareholders. *See generally* Gelter, *The Pension System* at 935–36.

69. *See, e.g.*, *In re* Anderson, Clayton S'holders Litig., 519 A.2d 680 (Del. Ch. 1986) (noting that the board had decided to terminate "certain overfunded pension plans" for the benefit of shareholders, and assuming *sub silentio* that such termination did not create any obligation to share the excess in those pension plans with the beneficiaries of the plans).

70. As the *Wall Street Journal* recently reported, many companies eliminated their pension plans in favor of 401(k) plans to cut expenses, while others simply eliminated all types of pension plans. The result is that nearly half of all households have no retirement savings at all, and retirement savings at virtually all levels of income are below recommended amounts. *See* Timothy Martin, *The Champions of the 401(k) Lament the Revolution They Started*, WALL ST. J., Jan. 2, 2017, http://www.wsj.com/articles/the-champions-of-the-401-k-lament-the-revolution-they-started-1483382348.

71. Peter F. Drucker, THE PRACTICE OF MANAGEMENT (2006).

72. Steve Denning, *The Origin of "The World's Dumbest Idea": Milton Friedman*, FORBES, June 26, 2013.

73. *See* Ben W. Heineman Jr., *Steve Jobs and the Purpose of the Corporation*, Harv. Bus. Rev., Oct. 12, 2011.

74. Roger L. Martin, Fixing the Game: Bubbles, Crashes, and What Capitalism Can Learn from the NFL (2011).

75. *Id.*

76. *Id.*; *see also* Roger Martin, *Fixing the Game: The Problem with Expectations*, Huffington Post, May 4, 2011, http://www.huffingtonpost.com/roger-martin/the-problem-with-expectat_b_857458.html.

77. *See, e.g.*, Michael E. Porter and Mark R. Kramer, *Creating Shared Value*, Harv. Bus. Rev., Jan.–Feb. 2011; Steven Pearlstein, *Social Capital, Corporate Purpose and the Revival of American Capitalism*, Ctr. of Effective Pub. Mgmt. at Brookings, Jan. 2014, https://www.brookings.edu/wp-content/uploads/2016/06/BrookingsPearlsteinv5_Revised-Feb-2014.pdf.

78. *See* Martin, Fixing the Game (noting that total stockholder returns during the period of stakeholder capitalism from about 1933 to 1976 was 7.5 percent compounded annually, while in the years of shareholder capitalism from 1976 to 2010, the S&P total return was 6.5 percent compounded annually).

79. *Unocal*, 493 A.2d at 955.

80. *Compare, e.g.*, Espinoza v. Aaron's Rents, Inc., No. 01–14–00843-CV, 2016 Tex. App. LEXIS 423 (Tex. Ct. App. Jan. 14, 2016) and Beverick v. Koch Power, Inc., 186 S.W.3d 145,153 (Tex. Ct. App. 2005) (holding that under Texas law an employer does not owe a fiduciary duty to an employee or manager), with Johnson v. Brewer & Pritchard, P.C., 73 S.W.3d 193, 200 (Tex. 2002) (quoting Restatement (Second) of Agency § 13 cmt. a (1958)) (concluding that "when a fiduciary relationship of agency exists between employee and employer, the employee has a duty to act primarily for the benefit of the employer in matters connected with his agency").

81. *See, e.g.*, Triton Constr. Co. v. E. Shore Elec. Servs., Inc., No. 3290-VSP, 2009 Del. Ch. LEXIS 88 (Del. Ch. May 18, 2009) (holding that an employee in Delaware law owes fiduciary duties to his employee, as under "fundamental principles of agency law, an agent owes his principal a duty of good faith, loyalty and fair dealing).

82. As I have already noted, Delaware courts have held that corporations have standing to sue employees for breach of fiduciary duty, and many countries, such as Germany, have companies that include employees. Query whether the lack of these types of structural safeguards allowed boards to conclude that they had no obligation to share any excess from the employee pension funds with their employees, and courts to generally not place such an obligation on the board.

83. Some may point to the failures of some companies, such as various airlines like United, that failed in the late 1990s and early 2000s despite having significant ownership by employee stock ownership plans (ESOP"). However, con-

siderable analysis suggests that these airlines failed for reasons other than the ESOPs, and that notwithstanding the ESOPs, employee interests were not sufficiently considered. *See, e.g.*, Cory Rosen, *Observations on Employee Ownership: United Airlines, ESOPs and Employee Ownership*, National Center for Employee Ownership, 2002, https://www.nceo.org/observations-employee-ownership/c/united-airlines-esops-employee-ownership. In contrast, Southwest Airlines, one of the most successful airline companies over the last half century, publicly proclaims that it puts its "employees first, customers second and shareholders third" and that this policy is the reason for its success. *See* Emmie Martin, *Southwest Puts Employees First*, Business Insider, July 29, 2015, http://www.businessinsider.com/southwest-airlines-puts-employees-first-2015-7.

84. *See, e.g.*, Justin Wolfers and Jan Zilinsky, *Higher Wages for Low-Income Workers Lead to Higher Productivity*, Peterson Inst. for Intl. Econ., Jan. 13, 2015.

85. Michael Reich, Peter Hall, and Ken Jacobs, Living Wages and Economic Performance: The San Francisco Airport Model (Mar. 2003), http://laborcenter.berkeley.edu/pdf/2003/sfo_mar03.pdf; *see also* John Pepper, *Workers and Businesses Benefit from a Higher Minimum Wage*, US Dept. of Lab. Blog (Aug. 7, 2014), https://blog.dol.gov/2014/08/07/workers-and-businesses-benefit-from-a-higher-minimum-wage/.

86. *See, e.g.*, Ernesto Dal Bó et al., *Strengthening State Capabilities: The Role of Financial Incentives in the Call to Public Service*, 128 Q. J. Econ. 1169 (2013); *see also* Stephen V. Burks et al., *The Value of Hiring through Employee Referrals*, 130 Q. J. Econ. 805 (2015) (discussing how higher wages can lead to more employee referrals and how such employees are more productive than nonreferred workers).

87. *See, e.g.*, Wolfers and Zilinsky, *Higher Wages*.

88. *See, e.g.*, Phil Wahba, *McDonald's CEO Says Better Worker Benefits Boosting US Sales*, Fortune, Apr. 22, 2016; Myles Udland, *Starbucks Giving Every US Employee a Raise Is Part of the Biggest Economic Story in America*, Business Insider, July 11, 2016.

89. *See generally* George Serafeim et al., *The Role of the Corporation in Society: Implications for Investors*, Calvert-Serafeim Series, Sept. 2015 [hereafter cited as Serafeim et al., *Calvert Paper*]; George Serafeim, *The Role of the Corporation in Society: An Alternative View and Opportunities for Future Research*, Harvard Bus. Sch. (May 2014) [hereafter cited as Serafeim, *Role of the Corporation*].

90. *See* Serafeim, *Role of the Corporation* at 6. Fewer than 4,000 companies are actively traded on the New York Stock Exchange and Nasdaq, with another approximately 15,000 stocks traded over the counter in the United States. The remaining companies are traded on various exchanges and in markets across the globe. However, this figure does not include the growth of companies con-

trolled by private equity firms, which has also increased dramatically in recent years. For example, Blackstone alone has a portfolio of more than 81 companies, with $70 billion in combined annual revenue, and directly employs more than 560,000 people around the world. *See Private Equity*, BLACKSTONE, http://www.blackstone.com/the-firm/asset-management/private-equity. Many private equity firms have entered the market for services that were traditionally provided by governments, which has given rise to entirely new issues. *See, e.g.*, Danielle Ivory et al., *What Can Go Wrong When Private Equity Takes Over a Public Service*, N.Y. TIMES, June 25, 2016.

91. *Id.*

92. *Id.*; *see also* Serafeim et al., *Calvert Paper* at 6–7.

93. It is worth noting that as the Global 1000 have increased in size, institutional investors have also increased in size. For example, as of 2011, the ten largest institutional investors in the world collectively held 27.1 percent of the outstanding shares, on average, across Global 1000 companies. *See* Serafeim, *Role of the Corporation* at 9.

94. *Id.* at 7.

95. *2016 Edelman Trust Barometer Global Report*, EDELMAN, Jan. 17, 2016, at 34, http://www.slideshare.net/EdelmanInsights/2016-edelman-trust-barometer-global-results.

96. *See* Serafeim, *Role of the Corporation* at 11.

97. *Unocal*, 493 A.2d at 955–56.

98. *See, e.g.*, Heather Long, *Over Half of Americans Have $0 in Stocks*, CNN, Apr. 10, 2015, http://money.cnn.com/2015/04/10/investing/investing-52-percent-americans-have-no-money-in-stocks/; Justin McCarthy, *Little Change in Percentage of Americans Who Own Stocks*, GALLUP, Apr. 22, 2015, http://www.gallup.com/poll/182816/little-change-percentage-americans-invested-market.aspx (finding that 55 percent of Americans are invested in the stock market, which includes individual stocks, mutual funds, and 401(k) and other retirement plans).

99. *Id.*; *see also* Ralph Gomory, *Inversions Are Revealing the Ugly Face of Shareholder Value*, HUFFINGTON POST (Sept. 9, 2014), http://www.huffingtonpost.com/ralph-gomory/inversions-are-revealing-_b_5785376.html.

100. *See* Strine, *Corporate Governance Question* at 10–11.

101. *Id.* at 11. Historically the growth in trading over holding is even more extreme. For example, the average holding period for an equity traded on the New York Stock Exchange in the 1950s was about seven years; today, it's about six months. Similarly, households owned more than 90 percent of the US-based public companies, while today institutions (both domestic and foreign) own the vast majority of equity traded in the United States, and it is these institutions that are engaged in the most active trading. *See generally* Justin Fox and Jay Lorsch, *What Good Are Shareholders?* HARV. BUS. REV., July–Aug. 2012.

102. I have previously written about this phenomenon and offered some modest suggestions for trying to encourage stockholders to have a longer-term focus. *See, e.g.*, David J. Berger, Steven Davidoff Solomon, and Aaron Benjamin, *Tenure Voting and the US Public Company* (Mar. 1, 2016), https://ssrn.com/abstract=2740538.

103. WSGR represented Apple in its IPO.

104. See generally Fox and Lorsch, *What Good Are Shareholders?* 102.

105. *See, e.g.*, Anne Beyer et al., *Does the Composition of a Company's Shareholder Base Really Matter?* Stanford Closer Look Series, July 2014.

106. By far the most thorough explanation of the correlation between wealth and income inequality is Thomas Piketty, Capital in the 21st Century (Arthur Goldhammer trans., President and Fellows of Harv. Coll. 2014) (2013); *see also* Joseph E. Stiglitz, The Price of Inequality: How Today's Divided Society Endangers Our Future (2012).

107. 170 N.W. 668 (Mich. 1919).

108. Allen, *Our Schizophrenic Conception*. In recent years, many scholars have also challenged the validity and/or soundness of *Dodge v. Ford*. *See, e.g.*, Lynn A. Stout, *Why We Should Stop Teaching Dodge v. Ford*, 3 Va. L. & Bus. Rev. 163 (2008).

109. *See generally* Galbraith, American Capitalism.

110. *See generally* Teitelman, Bloodsport.

111. *See* Allen, *Our Schizophrenic Conception* at 280–81.

CHAPTER FOUR

The Odd Couple

Delaware and Public Benefit Corporations

Michael B. Dorff

Introduction

Of all the social and economic challenges to the current state of Delaware corporate law, perhaps the most potentially revolutionary is the shift in attitudes about the very purpose of the corporation. Delaware corporate law holds as a core precept that the corporation's goal is to maximize shareholder value.[1] Corporations' freedom to serve the goals of other corporate constituencies (such as employees, customers, or the communities in which the companies operate) or to serve broader goals (such as protecting the environment or aiding the poor) is constrained by the requirement that any such efforts be primarily aimed at improving the bottom line for the benefit of the companies' shareholders.[2] With its recent authorization of public benefit corporations, Delaware has made it possible for entrepreneurs to change this shareholder primacy rule by choosing a business entity form that is required to pursue the social good as well as profits.[3]

Not all observers agree that traditional Delaware corporations must exclusively pursue profits. Progressive corporate legal scholars such as Margaret Blair and Lynn Stout have long asserted that corporate boards must balance the interests of different corporate constituencies, which sometimes means sacrificing profits to assist workers, lenders, or communities.[4] And the Delaware courts themselves have not always been clear on this point. For example, in the famous case of *Unocal Corp. v.*

Mesa Petroleum Co., the Delaware Supreme Court stated that one of the issues a corporate board could consider when determining whether a hostile acquisition offer constituted a threat to the corporation was the offer's impact on constituencies other than shareholders, such as "creditors, customers, employees, and perhaps even the community generally."[5] The court soon backtracked from this position, however, in *Revlon, Inc. v. MacAndrews & Forbes*.[6] There, the court stated that, "while concern for various corporate constituencies is proper when addressing a takeover threat, that principle is limited by the requirement that there be some rationally related benefit accruing to the stockholders."[7] Today, it seems reasonably clear that Delaware corporate law requires boards of directors to attempt to maximize shareholder profits, at least as a default rule.[8]

Entrepreneurs who want to pursue social goals to the *exclusion* of profits may form nonprofit corporations. But Delaware's corporate law historically provided no ready-made option for entrepreneurs who wanted to create an entity that balanced traditional profit seeking with the pursuit of other social goals.[9] The Delaware legislature changed this with the adoption of a public benefit corporation statute in 2013, making it the fourteenth state to do so.[10]

The benefit corporation form has often received poor reviews from corporate law experts.[11] Commentators have argued that the new freedom to pursue other goals will exacerbate agency costs by interfering with the ability of the market for corporate control to police boards and executives.[12] And the very idea that balancing the needs of other constituencies such as workers is a worthy goal is highly controversial.[13] Plus, for-profit corporations already possess substantial freedom to undertake tasks that do not have an immediate profit as their goal, such as charitable donations.[14] All of which prompts the question: Why risk Delaware's sterling reputation with the corporate bar and the directorate class by endorsing this untested and controversial new form of business organization?

In thinking about this question, we should bear in mind how corporate law is formed and why Delaware's role in this area is so critical. Corporate governance law primarily deals with conflicts that may arise among shareholders, officers, and directors, often with directors and officers on one side of the dispute and shareholders on the other. The law that governs these disputes, or the "internal affairs" of the corporation, is the law of the state of incorporation. Boards of directors can therefore choose which state's law will govern the company's internal affairs by choosing the state of incorporation. In addition, boards can change their state of incorporation relatively easily by reincorporating elsewhere.

There are two dominant theories of how legislatures and courts shape corporate governance law. The first, often called the "race to the bottom" theory, argues that states choose corporate governance rules to help them compete for corporate franchise tax fees. When a corporation registers in a state, it must pay a special annual tax to the state, called a franchise tax. A state that manages to capture a large share of corporate registrations will also receive substantial tax revenue. This revenue could be especially significant to a small state, such as Delaware, permitting it to offer better services or lower taxes to its citizens. Because corporate directors choose the corporation's state of incorporation, the race to the bottom theory argues that states compete for corporate registrations by providing corporate governance laws that favor directors in their contests with shareholders. That is, the states race to the bottom in the sense that they adopt legal rules that are the worst possible rules for shareholders, though the best for directors.[15]

Some theorists contend, however, that the competition for corporate charters will have precisely the opposite effect. These advocates of the "race to the top" theory argue that directors will incorporate in states with the best possible law for their shareholders. To do otherwise would suppress earnings, increase the costs of capital, lower share prices, and risk hostile takeovers that would replace boards. State governments will therefore compete for corporate charters (and franchise taxes) by providing legal rules that advantage shareholders over directors.[16]

While it is debatable which of these theories better describes state corporate governance law, one fact is clear: In the states' competition for corporate registrations and their associated franchise taxes, Delaware is the clear winner. Delaware has found a formula that has attracted a clear majority of the major corporations in the United States.[17] Delaware law is the gold standard. Delaware's tremendous success in the corporate governance arena makes its relatively early adoption of benefit corporations particularly puzzling. If the new movement flops, Delaware's early endorsement may damage its brand, perhaps providing space for some ambitious competition, such as Nevada, to gain ground. With so much at stake, why lend the state's credibility to an untested and controversial new form of business organization?

To explore this issue, I begin with a brief introduction to the history of benefit corporations (known as public benefit corporations or PBCs in Delaware). I then discuss Delaware's motives as revealed by published documents and through interviews with two of the principal players involved in the benefit corporation legislation. These sources reveal that Delaware was primarily trying to induce social entrepreneurs to register their companies in the state. To better understand whether the statute will be a success, I also discuss the results of interviews I conducted of twenty-five founders or senior executives of benefit corporations about why they chose the benefit corporation form.

Social entrepreneurs cite a variety of reasons for choosing the PBC (or benefit corporation) form, but the most important is a desire to signal their commitment to a more socially responsible form of capitalism. If Delaware's PBC statute is to succeed, then, it must ensure that PBC status communicates a meaningful signal of prosocial corporate behavior.

History of Benefit Corporations

Benefit corporations are largely the invention of B Lab, a nonprofit organization that certifies for-profit companies as "meet[ing] rigorous standards of social and environmental performance, accountability, and transparency."[18] In 2008, B Lab began lobbying state legislatures to persuade them to pass benefit corporation statutes.[19] B Lab had its first success in Maryland, whose statute became effective in 2010.[20] Four states followed with benefit corporation statutes that became effective in 2011 (New Jersey, Vermont, Virginia, and Hawaii)[21] and five more in 2012 (California, New York, South Carolina, Louisiana, and Massachusetts).[22] Washington's social purpose corporation statute, a close analogue, also became effective in 2012.[23] By the time Delaware's governor signed Delaware's public benefit corporation statute on July 17, 2013,[24] statutes were also effective in Illinois, Pennsylvania, and Washington, DC, with Arkansas's becoming effective the very next day.[25]

By the time Delaware acted, the benefit corporation movement had substantial momentum, with over a dozen states having effective statutes, including major commercial states such as California, New York, and Illinois. Still, these states together do not have the impact on corporate law that Delaware does. Nearly two-thirds of Fortune 500 corporations are incorporated in Delaware, and in 2014, 89 percent of all corporations that engaged in initial public offerings chose Delaware for their state of incorporation.[26] Delaware carries so much credibility in the corporate law arena that had it chosen to reject the new form, the benefit corporation movement might well have withered and died. Transactional lawyers might have pointed to Delaware's decision as grounds to avoid the new form, and investors and entrepreneurs might reasonably have regarded it with much greater suspicion.

Delaware's impact can be seen in the effect its blessing had on states' decisions. While it took four years for fifteen states to authorize some version of the benefit corporation before Delaware acted, it took only about half that time to double the number once Delaware passed its version.[27]

As of this writing, thirty-five states have passed some form of the benefit corporation statute.[28] These states cross traditional party divides, encompassing both blue states (such as California and New York) and red states (such as Louisiana and Arkansas). Similarly, the states that have not yet adopted the new form include blue states such as Maine, and red states such as Texas and Alabama. According to B Lab, five more states are working on enabling legislation,[29] and that does not include Iowa, which introduced legislation this year.[30]

Although benefit corporations are proving enormously popular with state legislatures, it is less clear that they are finding a receptive audience among entrepreneurs. It is not possible to be certain of the precise number of benefit corporations, since many states are not categorizing them separately. But a few scholars have attempted to count them over the past few years, and B Lab also tracks them. Based on the data we have, the numbers are fairly anemic. There were approximately 1.1 million legal entities registered in Delaware at the end of 2014,[31] yet fewer than 300 of these were active public benefit corporations.[32] Other states have similarly small numbers. As of April 2015, Nevada had the most, with 675, followed by Oregon with 403 and Colorado with 230.[33] New York had only 139, and California 118.[34]

Although the absolute number of benefit corporations is still rather small, the growth rate is impressive. In July of 2013, when Delaware had just passed its public benefit corporation statute, there were about 251 benefit corporations in the entire country.[35] By April 2015, the total number had grown to 2,144.[36] By January, 2016, B Lab's head of legal policy, Rick Alexander, claimed that there were over 3,000,[37] representing nearly a twelve-fold increase in just thirty months. If that rate continues, and if growth in adoptions is geometric, as it was for limited liability companies, in five years there could be over 400,000 benefit corporations.

At this point, any statement about the future popularity of benefit corporations is highly speculative. Benefit corporation statutes are too new to judge their likely success. Still, while a projection of 400,000 benefit corporations in just five years is almost certainly too optimistic, there is good reason to think a meaningful demand will develop as entrepreneurs and their lawyers and investors become more familiar with the new form. There is increasing demand among entrepreneurs, employees, and consumers for companies with a broader purpose than earning money—especially among millennials—and PBCs may play a critical role in meeting this demand.[38] Limited liability companies' early growth was uneven as well, yet the LLC ultimately became an enormously successful form of business organization.[39]

Delaware's Motives

Now that we have a sense of the historical context for Delaware's adoption of PBCs, we are ready to examine Delaware's motivations. Delaware already had a successful formula before adopting PBC legislation: It was the leading state for corporate law and the state of choice for incorporations, especially for public companies.[40] The benefit corporation is a new, largely untested idea that has been received with substantial skepticism by corporate law scholars.[41] Why, then, did the Delaware legislature feel the need to risk its credibility by adopting a benefit corporation statute?

Although it is difficult to ascribe with certainty a particular purpose to a legislative process that involves so many individuals, each of whom may have had their own ideas about why PBCs would benefit Delaware, we can gain a reasonably good sense of what the state had in mind from official statements and interviews of some of the players.

Delaware governor Jack Markell issued a statement upon signing the bill authorizing PBCs. He said: "We've all heard about corporations wanting to 'do well' while also 'doing good.' With this new law, Delaware corporations will now have the ability to build those dual purposes into their governing documents. We have heard repeatedly that public benefit corporations can fill a market need. But just as important, they will also fill a societal need."[42] Governor Markell cited two purposes for passing the PBC legislation: to allow corporations to institutionalize a social purpose, thereby helping the public, and to fill market demand for a form of business organization that permits this.

The legislators who sponsored the PBC legislation echoed similar themes. The leading sponsor of the bill in the Delaware Senate, Senator David Sokola, stated, "I'm proud that Delaware now has a corporate vehicle to offer business leaders and investors that want to create value that extends well beyond owners and managers to society and the public as a whole."[43] Senator Sokola, like Governor Markell, indicated that he had two related goals in championing the PBC legislation: to offer entrepreneurs a business form they desire and to assist them in helping the broader society.

Similarly, Representative Byron Short, who cosponsored the PBC bill, stated, "I'm happy to have co-sponsored this law which because of our State's unique role in Corporate America will make benefit corporations a viable option for entrepreneurs and investors in Delaware and throughout the nation."[44] Representative Short also seemed concerned with providing a form of business organization that entrepreneurs wanted, lending Delaware's credibility and its legal institutions to the benefit corporation form of business organization.

The official press release issued by the governor's office upon the PBC bill's signing listed some more specific goals within the same two themes. It stated, "This new corporate structure helps businesses combat short-termism, attract talent and customers, and accelerate the growth of a big investment opportunity to meet the needs of people who want to both make money and make a difference."[45] Again we see the theme of meeting the needs of social entrepreneurs, but there is also a hint of advocacy, making the claim that PBCs will assist entrepreneurs in achieving their pecuniary goals as well as their charitable ambitions. According to the press release, PBCs will attract and retain talented employees better than traditional for-profit corporations do and will also draw customers who might not patronize an ordinary for-profit. The press release does not cite any evidence for these claims.

Delaware corporate statutes, unlike most legislation, often originate not with the legislature but with a committee of the Delaware State Bar Association: the Corporation Law Council of the Corporation Law Section (the Council). The PBC legislation followed this pattern.[46] I therefore interviewed Frederick "Rick" Alexander, who chaired the Council when it was considering and drafting the benefit corporation statute.[47]

At the time, Mr. Alexander was a partner at Morris, Nichols, Arsht & Tunnell LLP, a leading corporate law firm in Delaware.[48] He has since become head of legal policy at B Lab.[49] Mr. Alexander has also written about the history of the Council's decision to adopt benefit corporation legislation in the introduction to his book, *The Public Benefit Corporation Guidebook: Understanding and Optimizing Delaware's Benefit Corporation*.[50] Mr. Alexander spoke only for himself, not the Council, but was often able to provide his impression of the Council's views.

Mr. Alexander ultimately shared Governor Markell's two goals in adopting benefit corporation legislation, though he was quite skeptical when B Lab first approached the Council. The Council's initial view was that corporate law already functioned quite well and that the best way to restrain corporate conduct that had a negative impact on society or the environment was through direct regulation, not by tinkering with corporate governance law.[51] The Council was eventually persuaded, however, after B Lab introduced the members to entrepreneurs, businesses, and investors who desired to organize their companies as benefit corporations.[52] The Council concluded that Delaware ought to offer businesses the flexibility to adopt social goals.[53]

Some members of the Council—including Mr. Alexander—also came to believe that benefit corporations could influence all corporations to operate more sustainably and responsibly.[54] Mr. Alexander was greatly swayed by the respective work of two scholars—Lynn Stout and Colin Meyer—and by institutional investors' tendency to diversify their investments by owning stock in many or even all publicly traded companies.[55] He concluded: "I remain convinced that the for-profit corporation remains the best vehicle for raising and allocating capital (other than for certain public goods that remain the responsibility of government and NGOs). However, given the challenges that our planet and society face, I also believe we must look for a way to allow that vehicle to operate with a recognition of the interdependence of our complex globe, and the responsibility that follows. The benefit corporation provides such a path."[56]

To gain additional perspective on the Council's views, I also interviewed Council member Professor Lawrence Hamermesh. Although—like Mr. Alexander—Professor Hamermesh spoke only for himself, and not the Council, he is a prominent scholar of corporate law and is highly respected in corporate legal circles. His views were therefore likely very influential. Professor Hamermesh is the Ruby R. Vale Professor at Widener University's Delaware Law School, where he teaches corporate law, and has been a member of the Council since 1995.[57] He served as chair of the Council from 2002 to 2004.[58]

Professor Hamermesh said he believed the primary purpose of passing the PBC statute was to provide another option to businesses that wanted it. He did not think there was a significant cost to providing an additional form, especially since investors who wanted a business form that permitted them to foster goals other than maximizing wealth for the owners could also do so through a limited liability company. He stated: "The public benefit corporation statute is very much in the mold of the enabling approach that characterizes all of the Delaware business entity statutes. This is just saying that here's another form that—if the participants want to embrace it—they can. It's got certain constraints, it is a corporation, a corporation with a somewhat different model in terms of purpose, but it's there on the shelf ready for people to take it down and use it if they want to."[59]

Professor Hamermesh believed there was demand for the new form but was not especially troubled by criticism that investors might be reluctant to invest in an entity that diverted some of its resources to nonshareholder constituencies. He replied to this criticism by saying, "If you believe investors ought to have the prerogative of choosing the form that suits them, we've built it and either they'll come or they won't."[60]

Professor Hamermesh acknowledged that Governor Markell may have also had the goal of furthering social goals by harnessing the power of private enterprise. But he told me that, for him, the primary motivation was to provide a form that some investors wanted. He said, "I think what really did it for me was that I was hearing from investors who said they really want this vehicle and when you hear that, it's a little hard to say, well no, we'd rather not give it to you when we're prepared to say you can take an LLC and do it anyhow."[61]

Delaware's two purposes in passing PBC legislation are intertwined. The goal of aiding society can only be met if entrepreneurs choose to adopt PBCs (and if PBCs empower entrepreneurs to aid society). Similarly, the goal of filling a market need can only be met if socially minded entrepreneurs find the PBC legislation amenable to their purpose.

For the PBC legislation to meet Delaware's goals, then, it is critical that it fulfill the needs of social entrepreneurs. As a theoretical matter, one can imagine a wide and diverse set of motivations for social entrepreneurs to want a specialized form of business organization. Founders might select a PBC in hopes that it will help the business appeal to an important group such as customers, employees, for-profit investors, foundations, or donors, or to signal a dual purpose for some other reason (*brand*). They might also choose a PBC because of its ability to distribute profits to owners (*earn*), something a nonprofit cannot do; because of its regulatory simplicity as compared to a nonprofit (*simplify*); because it might serve to push managers to adopt prosocial policies that will also help improve profitability (*manage*); or because the hybrid form may provide greater protection against hostile acquisitions (*keep*).

These are all pecuniary motives for choosing a PBC, but founders may also choose a PBC for purely idealistic motivations, because they believe that businesses should strive to do more than earn profits for their owners. Founders may believe that businesses have a moral obligation to aid their employees, communities, customers, or other corporate constituencies, even when doing so will reduce the company's profits. They may wish to adopt a business form that expresses these ideals and perhaps inspires others to follow their example (*express*). Similarly, the founders may want to shield themselves from liability for adopting prosocial policies that reduce earnings, thereby encouraging such policies (*protect*) or to ensure that the company continues to embody their values even after they lose control to their heirs or to eventual buyers (*endure*).

These eight goals are not mutually exclusive. A company's founders might well want to achieve several of these goals or even all of them. Nevertheless, it seems likely—and interviews with social entrepreneurs support this theory—that most social entrepreneurs will have one or two of these goals primarily in mind when opting for a PBC, though some or all of the others may provide a subsidiary motivation. Delaware seems to have focused on *brand*, a desire to attract and retain employees, customers, and investors, and to a lesser degree on *express*, a sincere desire to pursue a social mission.

To learn which of these goals loom largest in the minds of social entrepreneurs, I interviewed founders or senior executives of twenty-five benefit corporations and asked them why they chose the benefit corporation as the legal entity for their business. This was not intended as a statistically valid study. The subjects were not chosen at random but rather based on my ability or my research assistant's ability to find them—often starting with B Lab's list—and on their willingness to be interviewed.[62] The interview subjects do not represent a statistically valid sample, and their companies are registered in many different states, not just Delaware. Most of the companies were small, with fewer than five employees, though some had over one hundred employees and revenues in the millions. All were closely held. This was a qualitative empirical study, not a quantitative one.[63] Its purpose was to gather a sense of company founders' rationale for choosing this new form. The results of these interviews are summarized in Table 4.1.

Delaware's stated goal of aiding society is broadly shared by the social entrepreneurs I interviewed. The goal entrepreneurs cited most was *express*: an ideology or social mission, a sense that businesses should be about more than money. The majority of the entrepreneurs communicated a belief that companies should care about the welfare of their employees, the environment, and the broader impact they have on society and should sometimes sacrifice profit to pursue these other goals. Representatives of nineteen of the twenty-five companies I contacted mentioned this as one of the reasons they chose the benefit corporation form.

The vast majority of the entrepreneurs cited the *express* goal in its purely communicative, nonpecuniary sense. For many, the choice of form was important mostly for its ability to express their values, often with the hope of persuading others to adopt them. Entrepreneurs wanted to demonstrate their commitment to running their companies in accordance with their ethical values and in the way they believed all companies should be run, separate and apart from any tangible benefit the form might convey.

Relatedly, nearly half the entrepreneurs cited *protect*, the protection from liability benefit corporations provide to officers and directors who choose to prioritize a social mission over profit. The thrust of the en-

TABLE 4.1 **Reasons for Selecting Public Benefit Corporation Status**

Why Did You Choose a Public Benefit Corporation?	Number of Responses
Ideology/mission (nonpecuniary)	19
Attract customers	14
Hire/retain/motivate employees	13
Liability protection/freedom to protect mission	11
Attract investors	7
Administrative costs of nonprofit status	4
Governance weaknesses in nonprofits	2
Financial sustainability problems with nonprofits	2
Better deals from other businesses	1

trepreneurs' concern here seemed to be permissive; that is, they wanted this protection so that they could operate their companies in accordance with their social values, free from worry that their investors would sue them for sacrificing profit for the social good. Many cited the example of Ben & Jerry's, the famously progressive[64] ice cream maker that sold itself to Unilever, the multinational consumer goods conglomerate.[65]

The commonly told story is that Ben & Jerry's founders, Ben Cohen and Jerry Greenfield, wanted to retain ownership but felt that their duties to their public shareholders required them to sell.[66] Although some have argued that Cohen and Greenfield did not have an obligation to sell the company[67]—and Unilever has arguably not only allowed Ben & Jerry's to continue to pursue its social values but has adopted some of these values itself[68]—the concern that a socially conscious company would be forced to sell itself to a buyer and abandon its social mission in the process plagues the social entrepreneurship movement. Benefit corporations offer entrepreneurs the legal authority to reject buyout offers that would harm their social mission or nonshareholder constituencies such as employees by requiring them to balance these interests with those of shareholders.[69]

These concerns may be ill founded, or at least premature, since all the companies I interviewed are closely held, and few have outside investors. But many of the founders hope to have outside investors at some point, and these investors' financial interests may conflict with the founders' desire to pursue social goals.

In addition to the *express* motivation, the social entrepreneurs often also mentioned pecuniary rationales for choosing a benefit corporation, or at least appreciated that the form conferred pecuniary benefits even if they were not the rationale that drove the decision. In particular, they often cited versions of the *brand* motivation. Over 50 percent of the entrepreneurs said that they had an easier time recruiting and/or retaining employees because of their social mission, and a similar percentage said they were better able to attract customers.

It is important to note, however, that it seems to have been the social mission itself that was instrumental in conferring these pecuniary benefits rather than the company's status as a benefit corporation. The entrepreneurs expressed some frustration that neither audience—employees or customers—knew very much about benefit corporations and often had not even heard of the form. Once the entrepreneurs explained that being a benefit corporation meant making an enforceable, transparent commitment to the social mission, however, employees and customers reacted very favorably. The entrepreneurs frequently expressed hope that as benefit corporations became more widely known, these pecuniary benefits would come without the need to educate the target audiences.

Entrepreneurs were far less likely to claim that their company's status as a benefit corporation (or PBC) was helping them to attract outside investors. Only about a quarter of the entrepreneurs felt that their entity status was helpful in this regard, and few of these had actually secured significant capital from investors whose decision was heavily influenced by their choice of entity. Some had had conversations with investors where the entity status had seemed a bonus factor, while others just anticipated that it would be. On the other hand, some entrepreneurs expressed concern that investors—especially very large investors—would have hesitations about the form. These concerns did not take the shape critics have generally anticipated—that the company's mission would soak up resources and reduce investors' financial return—but rather centered on the form's unfamiliarity to investors and their counsel. The concerns, in other words, generally mirrored those investors have had with limited liability companies and had little to do with the prosocial aspects of benefit corporations or PBCs.[70]

Delaware's focus seems to have been on why entrepreneurs might choose a PBC over a traditional for-profit corporation, but for social entrepreneurs, often the strongest competitor to the PBC is a nonprofit corporation. Nonprofits can be complex to set up and maintain, especially for those desiring 501(c)(3) status.[71]

Benefit corporations are comparatively simple, though they do not offer the same tax advantages. Sixteen percent of the social entrepreneurs I interviewed cited this explanation for avoiding nonprofit status. A smaller percentage alternatively cited governance weaknesses perceived in nonprofits or concerns about the sustainability of an enterprise that depends on donations to survive. Only one entrepreneur cited both the complications of a nonprofit corporation and sustainability concerns; there was otherwise no overlap among these responses.

Conclusion

Delaware's motives in authorizing public benefit corporations were twofold: to encourage social entrepreneurs to register their businesses in

Delaware and to harness the power of capitalism to solve social problems. These goals are interrelated. To meet the first goal, the statute must provide a form that helps entrepreneurs pursue their various ambitions. Those included protection from liability when sacrificing profits for social ends; helping to attract or retain investors, customers, and employees; and expressing entrepreneurs' ideals and inspiring others to follow them. Meeting Delaware's second goal requires legal mechanisms that encourage or even require public benefit corporations to aid society.

As I explain in other work, the public benefit corporation statute seems unlikely to achieve Delaware's goals on its own.[72] The statute lacks the necessary enforcement mechanisms to persuade the relevant audiences that PBCs will be more socially constructive than run-of-the-mill for-profit corporations.[73] Without some intervention, the benefit corporation experiment—noble as it is—therefore seems unlikely to succeed. But private ordering arrangements, such as certification and auditing services provided by organizations such as B Lab, have the potential to fill the gaps left by the statute.[74] The fate of this experiment in social entrepreneurship rests, then, in the hands of organizational entrepreneurs. If millennials want corporations to embrace a different purpose in these changing times, then they will have to take an active role in persuading them to go beyond the bare requirements of Delaware's public benefit corporation statute.

Notes

I would like to thank Afra Asharipour, William Bratton, Jill Fisch, Ronald Gilson, Sean Griffith, Frank Partnoy, Elizabeth Pollman, Gordon Smith, Hillary Sale, Steven Davidoff Solomon, Randall Thomas, Robert Thompson, and Verity Winship for helpful comments and suggestions. I would also like to thank Eman Al-Hassan for her outstanding research assistance in finding benefit corporation founders and persuading them to be interviewed for this project. Most of this chapter has appeared previously as part of Michael B. Dorff, *Why Public Benefit Corporations?* 42 Del. J. Corp. L. 13 (2017).

1. The most recent statement of this legal principle in Delaware came in eBay Domestic Holdings, Inc. v. Newmark, 16 A.3d 1, 34 (Del. Ch. 2010):

> The corporate form in which craigslist operates, however, is not an appropriate vehicle for purely philanthropic ends, at least not when there are other stockholders interested in realizing a return on their investment. Jim and Craig opted to form craigs-

> list, Inc. as a *for-profit Delaware corporation* and voluntarily accepted millions of dollars from eBay as part of a transaction whereby eBay became a stockholder. Having chosen a for-profit corporate form, the craigslist directors are bound by the fiduciary duties and standards that accompany that form. Those standards include acting to promote the value of the corporation for the benefit of its stockholders. The "Inc." after the company name has to mean at least that. Thus, I cannot accept as valid for the purposes of implementing the Rights Plan a corporate policy that specifically, clearly, and admittedly seeks *not* to maximize the economic value of a for-profit Delaware corporation for the benefit of its stockholders—no matter whether those stockholders are individuals of modest means or a corporate titan of online commerce.

Id. at 34 (internal note omitted). *See also* Dodge v. Ford Motor Co., 170 N.W. 668, 684 (Mich. 1919) (stating, though arguably in dicta, "[I]t is not within the lawful powers of a board of directors to shape and conduct the affairs of a corporation for the merely incidental benefit of shareholders and for the primary purpose of benefiting others, and no one will contend that, if the avowed purpose of the defendant directors was to sacrifice the interests of shareholders, it would not be the duty of the courts to interfere."); Leo E. Strine Jr., *Our Continuing Struggle with the Idea That For-Profit Corporations Seek Profit*, 47 WAKE FOREST L. REV. 135, 151 (2012) (lambasting those who object to the view that, "as a matter of corporate law, the object of the corporation is to produce profits for the stockholders and that the social beliefs of the managers, no more than their own financial interests, cannot be their end in managing the corporation.").

2. Revlon, Inc. v. MacAndrews & Forbes, 506 A.2d 173, 176 (Del. 1986).

3. *See* 8 Del. Gen. Corp. Code §§ 361–68.

4. *See* Margaret M. Blair and Lynn A. Stout, *A Team Production Theory of Corporate Law*, 85 VIRGINIA L. REV. 248 (1999); Lynn A. Stout, THE SHAREHOLDER VALUE MYTH: HOW PUTTING SHAREHOLDERS FIRST HARMS INVESTORS, CORPORATIONS, AND THE PUBLIC (2012).

5. Unocal Corp. v. Mesa Petroleum Co., 493 A.2d 946, 955 (1995).

6. Revlon, Inc. v. MacAndrews & Forbes, 506 A.2d 173 (Del. 1986).

7. *Id.* at 176.

8. *See* Strine, *Our Continuing Struggle* at 151. It is possible that a provision in a corporations' certificate of incorporation that changed this rule would be enforced. *See* 8 Del. Gen. Corp. Code § 102(b)(1) (authorizing corporate charter provisions "for the management of the business and for the conduct of the affairs of the corporation, and any provision creating, defining, limiting and regulating the powers of the corporation, the directors, and the stockholders, or any

class of the stockholders, or the governing body, members, or any class or group of members of a nonstock corporation; if such provisions are not contrary to the laws of this State."). While a provision changing the corporation's goal would seem to fall squarely within both "management of the business" and "conduct of the affairs," it still might run afoul of the exception for charter provisions that are "contrary to the laws of this State." No statute requires corporations to maximize shareholder value, but the principle is sufficiently strong in the common law that a court might find that charter provisions that contradict it are invalid. The opposite result, of course, is also quite possible, making the outcome of this issue difficult to predict.

9. A Delaware limited liability company could likely be crafted to require balancing profits with other goals, given Delaware's emphasis on the malleability of the LLC form, but the LLC is not designed as an off-the-shelf option for this purpose. *See* Elf Atochem North America, Inc. v. Jaffari, 727 A.2d 286, 290–92 (Del. 1999) (stating that the Delaware Limited Liability Company Act is designed to give "maximum effect to the principle of freedom of contract" and that "only where the [operating] agreement is inconsistent with mandatory statutory provisions will the members' agreement be invalidated."). *See also* Frederick H. Alexander, The Public Benefit Corporation Guidebook: Understanding and Optimizing Delaware's Benefit Corporation Governance Model 45–46 (2016): ("Benefit corporations are increasingly popular structures for entrepreneurs looking to achieve both profit and social benefit, but similar goals can be accomplished in Delaware with a limited liability company.").

10. *See* 8 Del. Gen. Corp. Code §§ 361–68. The states that adopted a benefit corporation statute prior to Delaware's were, in order: Maryland, New Jersey, Vermont, Virginia, Hawaii, California, New York, South Carolina, Louisiana, Massachusetts, Illinois, Pennsylvania, and Arkansas. Washington, DC, had also passed a benefit corporation statute prior to Delaware, on February 8, 2013. The state of Washington authorized social purpose corporations, a similar form, in March 2012, also ahead of Delaware. It is likely, however, that a Delaware LLC could be crafted to achieve similar ends. *See supra*, note 9.

11. *See, e.g.*, Sherwin Abrams, *Decisions, Decisions: Helping Clients Choose the Right Business Entity*, 101 Ill. B. J. 530 (2013) ("The L3C and benefit corporation are mere marketing devices and should never have been authorized."); J. William Callison, *Putting New Sheets on a Procrustean Bed: How Benefit Corporations Address Fiduciary Duties, the Dangers Created, and Suggestions for Change*, 2 Amer. U. Bus. L. Rev. 85, 92 (2012) (arguing that the Model Statute "will ultimately discourage corporations from becoming benefit corporations and will discourage outside investment in benefit corporations and consumer validation of the benefit corporation status."); Brian Galle, *Social Enterprise: Who Needs It?* 54 Boston College L. Rev. 2025, 2041 (2013) ("It turns out, though, that the widespread legislative popularity of social enterprise has

little to do with its merits. Social enterprise is the product of a race to the bottom."); David Groshoff, *Contrepreneurship? Examining Social Enterprise Legislation's Feel-Good Governance Giveaways*, 16 U. Pa. J. of Bus. Law 233, 277 (2013) ("The material purpose and tax aims of these organizations can be achieved by existing business law structures, particularly because entities created by state law cannot alter the federal taxation schemes relative to invested equity capital and distributions to owners."); Robert A. Katz and Antony Page, *Sustainable Business*, 62 Emory L. J. 851, 865 (2013) (arguing that none of the enforcement mechanisms available to participants in benefit corporations are likely to prove successful); Mark Loewenstein, *Benefit Corporations: A Challenge in Corporate Governance*, 68 Bus. Lawyer 1007, 1011 (2013) (directors of benefit corporations will make suboptimal balancing decisions); Keren Raz, *Toward an Improved Legal Form for Social Enterprise*, 36 N.Y.U. Rev. L. & Soc. Change 283 (2012) (criticizing benefit corporations for having an overly broad definition of social mission and because the beneficiaries of a company's social mission cannot sue to enforce it); Dana Brakman Reiser, *Benefit Corporations—A Sustainable Form of Organization?* 26 Wake Forest L. Rev. 591, 593 (2011) (the benefit corporation statute does not provide sufficient mechanisms for enforceability of both the profit-seeking and prosocial purposes); Strine, *Our Continuing Struggle* at 150 ("[Benefit corporations exist in] a fictional land where you can take other people's money, use it as you wish, and ignore the best interests of those with the only right to vote. In this fictional land, I suppose a fictional accountability mechanism will exist whereby the fiduciaries, if they are a controlling interest, will be held accountable for responsibly balancing all these interests.").

12. Galle expresses this point particularly well: "Consider next the costs of contracting. There is nothing about running a for-profit business that makes the difficulty of contracting for the production of charitable goods easier, and indeed the opposite is very likely true. Suppose the entrepreneur and her investors jointly agree that they want to divert some of the firm's revenues to the charitable activity. But how much charity will the firm do, at what quality, and at what cost? Now the investors have two worries: that the manager will do too little charity, and also that she will do too much." Galle, *Social Enterprise* at 2031 (internal notes omitted). *See also* Groshoff, *Contrepreneurship* at 277 ("Despite the ostensible social good inherent in the names ascribed to SEL-related enterprises, these organizations structurally exacerbate equity investors' ability to control corporate agents effectively, thereby leading to less disclosure of agent activity and reduced ownership control capabilities."); Strine, *Our Continuing Struggle* at 150.

13. As Easterbrook and Fischel wrote: "To sum up: self-interested entrepreneurs and managers, just like other investors, are driven to find the devices most

likely to maximize net profits. If they do not, they pay in lower prices for corporate paper. Any one firm may deviate from the optimal measures. Over tens of years and thousands of firms, though, tendencies emerge. The firms and managers that make the choices investors prefer will prosper relative to others. Because the choices do not generally impose costs on strangers to the contracts, what is optimal for the firms and investors is optimal for society." Frank H. Easterbrook and Daniel R. Fischel, *The Corporate Contract,* 89 COLUMBIA L. REV. 1416, 1421 (1989). *See also* Stephen M. Bainbridge, *Director Primacy: The Means and Ends of Corporate Governance*, 97 NW U. L. REV. 547, 576 (2003) ("[S]hareholder wealth maximization is not only the law, but also is a basic feature of corporate ideology.); Stephen M. Bainbridge, *In Defense of the Shareholder Wealth Maximization Norm*, 50 WASH. & LEE L. REV. 1423, 1427–28 (1993) ("Directors thus cannot be loyal to both shareholders and nonshareholder constituencies. Rather, their role as stewards requires them to prefer the interests of their shareholder masters."); Michael C. Jensen and William H. Meckling, *Theory of the Firm: Managerial Behavior, Agency Costs and Ownership Structure*, 3 J. FIN. ECON. 305, 311 (1976) (firms have no social responsibility because they are legal fictions, not individuals); Milton Friedman, *The Social Responsibility of Business Is to Increase Its Profits,* N.Y. TIMES, Sept. 13, 1970, § 6 (Magazine) at 32, 33 (directors who pursue their social responsibilities at the expense of corporate profits are spending shareholders' money).

14. *See* Michael B. Dorff, *Can a Corporation Have a Soul?* THE ATLANTIC, Oct. 20, 2016, http://www.theatlantic.com/business/archive/2016/10/can-a-corporation-have-a-soul-dorff/504173/.

15. *See* William Cary, *Federalism and Corporate Law: Reflections upon Delaware*, 83 YALE L. J. 663 (1974).

16. *See* Ralph K. Winter Jr., *State Law, Shareholder Protection and the Theory of the Corporation*, 6 J. LEGAL STUD. 251 (1977).

17. *See* Delaware Division of Corporations, *2014 Annual Report*, https://corp.delaware.gov/Corporations_2014%20Annual%20Report.pdf (nearly two-thirds of Fortune 500 companies are incorporated in Delaware).

18. *See* B Lab, *What Are B Corps?* http://www.bcorporation.net/what-are-b-corps.

19. *See* B Lab, *Our History*, http://www.bcorporation.net/what-are-b-corps/the-non-profit-behind-b-corps/our-history.

20. Maryland Corp & Assn Code §§ 5–6C-01 *et seq. See* John Tozzi, *Maryland Passes "Benefit Corp." Law for Social Entrepreneurs*, BUSINESSWEEK (April 13, 2010), http://knoxblogs.com/rantsraves/wp-content/uploads/sites/8/2010/04/benefit_corp_bi.html.

21. *See* Haw. Rev. Stat. §§ 420D-1–420D-13; N.J. Rev. Stat. §§ 14A: 18-1–18-11; Vt. Stat. Ann. tit. 11A, §§ 21.01–21.14; and Va. Code Ann. §§ 13.1-782–13.1-792.

22. *See* Cal. Corp. Code §§ 14600–31; La. Stat. Ann. §§ 12:1801–12:1832; Mass. Gen. Laws ch. 156E, §§ 1–16; N.Y. BSC Law §§ 1701–09; and S.C. Code Ann. §§ 33-38-110–33-38-600.

23. *See* Wash. Rev. Code §§ 23B.25.005–23B.25.150.

24. *See Governor Markell Signs Public Benefit Corporation Legislation*, July 17, 2013, http://news.delaware.gov/2013/07/17/governor-markell-signs-public-benefit-corporation-legislation/.

25. *See* Ark. Code §§ 4-36-101–4-36-401; 805 Ill. Comp. Stat. §§ 40/1–40/5.01; 33 Pa. Cons. Stat. §§ 3301–31; and D.C. Code §§ 29-1301.01–29-1304.01

26. *See* Delaware Division of Corporations, *2014 Annual Report*, https://corp.delaware.gov/Corporations_2014%20Annual%20Report.pdf.

27. As of this writing, the following states have passed some version of the benefit corporation statute that became effective after Delaware's: Arizona, Connecticut, Colorado, Florida, Idaho, Indiana, Minnesota, Montana, Nebraska, Nevada, New Hampshire, Oregon, Rhode Island, Tennessee, Utah, West Virginia, and Wisconsin. *See* Ariz. Rev. Stat. §§ 10-2401–10-2442; Conn. Gen. Stat. §§ 33-1350–33-1364; Colo. Rev. Stat. §§ 7-101-501–7-101-509; Fla. Stat. §§ 607.601–607.613; Idaho Code Ann. §§ 30-2001–30-2013; Ind. Code §§ 23-1.3-1-1–23-1.3-10-6; Minn. Stat. §§ 304A.001–304A.301; Mont. Code Ann. §§ 35-1-1401–35-1-1412; Neb. Rev. Stat. §§ 21-401–21-414; Nev. Rev. Stat. §§ 78B.010–78B.190; N.H. Rev. Stat. Ann. §§ 293-C:1–293-C:12; Or. Rev. Stat. §§ 60.750–60.770; R.I. Gen. Laws §§ 7-5.3-1–7-5.3-13; Tenn. Code Ann. §§ 48-28-101–48-28-109; Utah Code §§ 16-10b-101–16-10b-402; and W. Va. Code § 23b.25.005–23b.25.150; 2017 Wisconsin Act 77.

28. *See supra*, notes 18–23, 25, and 27.

29. *See* B Lab, *State by State Status of Legislation*, http://benefitcorp.net/policymakers/state-by-state-status. Note that B Lab does not count Washington's statute, although Washington's social purpose corporation is very similar to a benefit corporation and, as of this writing, had not yet included Wisconsin, which enacted its benefit corporation statute on November 27, 2017. *See* 2017 Wisconsin Act 77.

30. *See* Elizabeth K. Babson, *Year in Social Enterprise: 2015 Legislative and Policy Review, The National Law Review*, Feb. 4, 2016, http://www.natlawreview.com/article/year-social-enterprise-2015-legislative-and-policy-review.

31. *See* Delaware Division of Corporations, *2014 Annual Report*, https://corp.delaware.gov/Corporations_2014%20Annual%20Report.pdf.

32. *See* Ellen Berrey, *How Many Benefit Corporations Are There?* May 5, 2015, http://ssrn.com/abstract=2602781. This number is as of April 2015, while the total number of entities comes from the end of 2014.

33. *See id.*

34. *See id.*

35. *See* Haskell Murray, *How Many Benefit Corporations Have Been*

Formed? SocentLaw, July 23, 2013, http://socentlaw.com/2013/07/how-many-benefit-corporations-have-been-formed/. This number included Maryland benefit LLCs but excluded incorporations in New Jersey or South Carolina for lack of data. *Id.*

36. *See* Berrey, *How Many Benefit Corporations Are There?*

37. *See* Nicole Fallon Taylor, *Becoming a Benefit Corporation: Is It Right for Your Business?* BUSINESS NEWS DAILY, Jan. 22, 2016, http://www.businessnewsdaily.com/8734-benefit-corporation.html.

38. *See* Punit Renjen, *Millennials and Purpose: The Message Is Clear for Business Leaders*, POLITICO, Sept. 24, 2015, http://www.theatlantic.com/business/archive/2016/10/can-a-corporation-have-a-soul-dorff/504173/.

39. *See* William J. Carney, *Limited Liability Companies: Origins and Antecedents*, 66 U. COLO. L. REV. 855, 858 (1995); Bruce H. Kobayashi and Larry E. Ribstein, *Evolution and Spontaneous Uniformity: Evidence from the Evolution of the Limited Liability Company*, ECONOMIC INQUIRY 34, pp. 464–83 at 472–73 (1996); Larry Ribstein, *Statutory Forms for Closely Held Firms: Theories and Evidence From LLCs*, 73 WASH. U. L. Q. 369, 430 (1995).

40. *See* Delaware Division of Corporations, *2014 Annual Report*, https://corp.delaware.gov/Corporations_2014%20Annual%20Report.pdf.

41. *See* Steven Davidoff Solomon, *Idealism That May Leave Shareholders Wishing for Pragmatism*, N.Y. TIMES, Oct. 13, 2015, http://www.nytimes.com/2015/10/14/business/dealbook/laureate-education-for-profit-school-public-benefit.html.

42. *See Governor Markell Signs Public Benefit Corporation Legislation*, July 17, 2013, http://news.delaware.gov/2013/07/17/governor-markell-signs-public-benefit-corporation-legislation/.

43. *Id.*

44. *Id.*

45. *Id.*

46. *See* Alexander, THE PUBLIC BENEFIT CORPORATION GUIDEBOOK at 8–9.

47. *See id.*

48. *See id.*

49. *See id.* at 9.

50. *Id.*

51. *Id.* at 9.

52. *See Interview of Frederick H. Alexander*, March 15, 2016, on file with author.

53. *Id.*

54. *See* Alexander, THE PUBLIC BENEFIT CORPORATION GUIDEBOOK at 9–10; *Interview of Frederick H. Alexander.*

55. *See* Alexander, THE PUBLIC BENEFIT CORPORATION GUIDEBOOK at 9–10, discussing Colin Mayer, FIRM COMMITMENT: WHY THE CORPORATION IS FAIL-

ING US AND HOW TO RESTORE TRUST IN IT (2013) and Lynn Stout, THE SHAREHOLDER VALUE MYTH: HOW PUTTING SHAREHOLDERS FIRST HARMS INVESTORS, CORPORATIONS, AND THE PUBLIC (2012).

56. *See* Alexander, THE PUBLIC BENEFIT CORPORATION GUIDEBOOK at 10.

57. *See* http://delawarelaw.widener.edu/current-students/faculty-directory/faculty/112/.

58. *Id.*

59. *See Interview of Professor Lawrence Hamermesh*, March 11, 2016, on file with the author.

60. *Id.*

61. *Id.*

62. *See* Delbert C. Miller and Neil J. Salkind, HANDBOOK OF RESEARCH DESIGN AND SOCIAL MEASUREMENT 192 (2002) (subjects are generally not randomly selected in qualitative research).

63. *See id.* at 143 ("Qualitative research methods are often used when the scientist is interested in obtaining detailed and rich knowledge of a specific phenomenon"). Qualitative research has been defined as follows: "Qualitative research is a situated activity that locates the observer in the world. It consists of a set of interpretive, material practices that makes the world visible. These practices . . . turn the world into a series of representations including fieldnotes, interviews, conversations, photographs, recordings, and memos to the self. At this level, qualitative research involves an interpretive, naturalistic approach to the world. This means that qualitative researchers study things in their natural settings, attempting to make sense of, or to interpret, phenomena in terms of the meanings people bring to them." Dawn Snape and Liz Spencer, *The Foundations of Qualitative Research* in Jane Ritchie and Jane Lewis eds., QUALITATIVE RESEARCH PRACTICE: A GUIDE FOR SOCIAL SCIENCE STUDENTS 2–3 (2003), quoting Denzin and Lincoln, HANDBOOK OF QUALITATIVE RESEARCH 3 (2d ed. 2000).

64. It is worth noting that Ben & Jerry's product, while delicious, is far from healthy. In that sense, the company is perhaps less progressive than its reputation, despite its admirable policies in other areas such as employment and the environment.

65. *See* Constance L. Hays, *Ben & Jerry's to Unilever, With Attitude*, N.Y. TIMES, Apr. 13, 2000.

66. *See* Jenna Lawrence, *Making the B List, Stanford Social Innovation Review* (Summer 2009), http://ssir.org/articles/entry/making_the_b_list (arguing that Cohen and Greenfield did not want to sell the company but had no choice because it was public).

67. *See* Antony Page and Robert A. Katz, *Freezing Out Ben & Jerry: Corporate Law and the Sale of a Social Enterprise Icon*, 35 VERMONT L. R. 211 (2010).

68. *See* David Gelles, *How the Social Mission of Ben & Jerry's Survived Be-*

ing Gobbled Up, N.Y. TIMES, Aug. 21, 2015, http://www.nytimes.com/2015/08/23/business/how-ben-jerrys-social-mission-survived-being-gobbled-up.html.

69. *See* 8 Del. Gen. Corp. L. § 365 (directing boards of PBCs to balance the interests of shareholders against the company's social mission and the interests of other corporate constituencies, and permitting companies to include a provision in their articles of incorporation protecting directors from liability for any disinterested failure to balance these interests appropriately).

70. Entrepreneurs often incorporate rather than form an LLC, in large part because of investors' greater familiarity with the corporate form, despite the potential tax advantages of the LLC. As Victor Fleischer has written: "[T]he uncertainty of the LLC form increases legal costs and is an unwelcome addition to a negotiating atmosphere already laden with uncertainty and distrust. In particular, entrepreneurs who are accustomed to running corporations might resist trying out a new and unfamiliar entity. For start-ups that hope to incorporate within a few years anyway, adding an extra layer of legal costs, complexity, and uncertainty is unappealing, creating another reason why entrepreneurs and venture capital professionals prefer the C corp structure." Victor Fleischer, *The Rational Exuberance of Structuring Venture Capital Start-Ups*, 57 TAX. L. REV. 137, 175 (2004).

71. Corporations that qualify under 26 U.S.C. § 501(c)(3) are exempt from taxation, and donations to such entities are tax deductible to the donor. See 26 U.S.C. § 501(c)(3).

72. *See* Michael B. Dorff, *Why Public Benefit Corporations?* 42 DEL. J. CORP. L. 77 (2017).

73. *See id.*

74. *See* Michael B. Dorff, *Assessing the Assessment: B Lab's Effort to Measure Corporate Benevolence*, 40 SEATTLE L. REV. 515 (2016) (analyzing B Lab's assessment tool).

CHAPTER FIVE

Delaware's Diminishment?

Hillary A. Sale

In the world of corporate law, Delaware reigns—or so the theory goes. This chapter examines the reality of that statement, focusing on directors and their fiduciary duties in the context of the nexus-of-contracts theory, Delaware's default-based system of governance, and the expansion of the federal government's role in the corporate space. I argue that the nexus-of-contracts approach fails to explain the reality of today's corporate governance structure, and that the same is true with respect to Delaware's role as a nexus in the nexus-of-contracts world. Instead, the private, contract-based space, to the extent it ever existed, has been occupied, both directly and indirectly, by the federal government, and the public, for quite some time. Two theories developed in other works are key to this analysis: the theory of publicness[1] and the information-forcing-substance theory, or the manner in which federal securities disclosure provisions develop and expand director fiduciary duties.[2]

A considerable amount of scholarship is devoted to the theory of the firm as a nexus of contracts.[3] This metaphor, as some have termed it,[4] defines the firm as an entity for which rights and obligations are determined by contract. Credit, employee, and other agreements are explicit contracts and extend beyond the governance realm.[5] Other contracts are implied and devolve from the default rules, or the rules that the legislature has designed to be those to which the parties, or the stakeholders, would have agreed in the absence of a contract.[6] In theory, because they are default rules, they are subject to change via explicit contracts.[7] As is typical of economic theory, there is a key assumption at work here: Information is sufficient such that the resulting contracts will be efficient and maximize outcomes, or wealth, for the parties and thus be socially optimal.[8]

This nexus-of-contracts metaphor, as Jim Cox points out, has considerable "substantive bite."[9] Implicit in the approach is that firms are private and that the law governing them is also part of the so-called world of private law. Default rules are essentially publicly provided, private law, stand-ins subject to change.[10] Thus, firms can opt out of norms and into their own structures, including, at least theoretically, their own governance systems. In this sense, firms and their governance structures are perceived to be consensual.[11]

Less frequently discussed, however, is the permissive nature of firms and how they devolve from the public. To be sure, the fact that corporations exist as "private" entities with public permission is not new. Indeed, many of the early corporations were created through legislative grants, on a case-by-case, contract-by-contract, basis.[12] The United States followed the British model here, with legislatures taking the place of the king and parliament.[13] Not surprisingly, in the early years, many of the most visible entities granted the privilege of incorporation were public-focused, with some resembling what are often "authorities" today. For example, an entity formed to build a bridge, with private funds, was granted the right to incorporate.[14] Today, we have airport authorities, port authorities, and more. In addition, as the number and type of entities grew, additional concerns about public impact arose. For example, as banking corporations increased in number, their potential impact on the money supply became a subject of discussion and concern.[15] Thus, whether these early entities were authority-like or more typical of today's corporations, they became functional private entities only as defeasible from, and with the permission of, the legislature, and, through it, the public.

This defeasible status is important, because regardless of the perceived private nature of the firm, its strategy and choices can impact the economy and citizens. As a result, we now supplement—and have for a very long time supplemented—the allowed private ordering with regulation ex ante and enforcement ex post.[16] Indeed, regulation and enforcement serve as bounds on the private space or the space in which contracting is allowed to occur. For example, a broad spectrum of regulation and enforcement is aimed at classic externalities, such as environmental regulation.[17] Although these types of regulation form boundaries on the concept of the firm as a nexus of contracts, they are not the subject of this chapter. Instead, the focus here is on the regulatory space that is connected to the state-based default statutes and particularly to director fiduciary duties. Here, corporate law provides limits on director action and is subject to judicial control and change and, thus, operates outside of the so-called contractual space.[18] Further, as we shall see, both the federal government and the public play an increasingly significant, if not dominant, role in regulating fiduciary choices and conduct.

Despite the rhetoric surrounding the private law and the nexus-of-contracts theory, firms have been publicly regulated for a long time, and the nature and source of the regulation has changed considerably in recent years. Although we often describe the enforcement mechanisms as both public and private, these categories may be inaccurate—particularly for publicly held firms. "Private" enforcement, for example, comes in the form of class actions, which are a method of monitoring behavior and providing accountability.[19] Yet the ability to bring a class action derives from both the Federal Rules of Civil Procedure and the judiciary.[20] Moreover, the markets are public, and the harm from fraud, when it occurs, is also public.[21] In this sense then, the class action is arguably a public mechanism designed to counteract shirking and agency costs by providing balance. Indeed, class actions are an example of one way in which the law evolves to provide protections for what might otherwise be deemed "private" decisions.[22]

In Delaware, "private" litigation comes largely in two forms: class and derivative actions.[23] The key difference between the two is the nature of the claim, with derivative claims being those where the shareholder brings the claim on behalf of, and to right a wrong to, the entity.[24] Because the Delaware statutory system is largely default in nature, with few mandatory features, even the fiduciary duties are based on common law.[25] This alone erodes the contractual metaphor, despite the fact that the focus of the case law is heavily on process and not on defining the content of the duties.[26] Put differently, it is possible that the bounds of the law, the fiduciary duty, or the contractual understanding might change, ex post, for a fiduciary.[27] When that happens, the fiduciary must adjust to the new expectations.[28] Indeed, although it is rare for such cases to result in damages in Delaware, the cases certainly outline areas in which directors must do better.[29] Delaware does play a significant role in this space. Nevertheless, it turns out, that publicness has been trimming Delaware's default-rule space for quite some time.

What is publicness? In the context of corporations, the theory of publicness makes clear that the private nature of the entity, as well as the contract theory we associate with it, is defeasible from the public. Indeed, the status of a corporation as private is not a right, but a privilege.[30] Corporations do not arise "solely by consent," but instead require state permission, through filings and other formalities.[31] As a result, this status is subject to erosion, over time and particularly in response to crises.[32] This should not be a surprise, because the status is a choice by legislatures and, through them, the public.[33] Publicness, then, operates as a constraint on the contractual theory of the corporation.

Why? Because corporations are powerful. They control jobs and wealth. Their actions impact the markets, of course, but many other aspects of people's lives as well, such as the environment. In fact, their outputs impact people both positively (think pharmaceuticals) and negatively (think toxics). In the interests of capital formation, corporations enjoy limited liability.[34] This status, however, is a gift from the state, and therefore the public.[35] Yet the health and wealth of the entity extends beyond its bounds and its shareholders, and the impact of corporate missteps, screwups, and frauds can be deep and lasting. Consider Enron and Worldcom and the effect of their collapse on the economy and on people's faith in the fairness and integrity of the securities markets.[36] Or consider the investment banks and the 2008–9 financial crisis, which resulted in foreclosures, job losses, and more.[37] Indeed, the impact of the 2008–9 financial crisis is ongoing, with the economy suffering from slow growth rates and other challenges.[38]

Crises force legislatures to take action, and, in the context of corporations, the result has been federal regulatory surges.[39] The cycle is common, and it is a form of publicness.[40] Here, publicness is what society demands from powerful institutions—accountability and transparency.[41] When society pushes back, the reality—that the private realm of corporate contracts exists in the shadow of the public—becomes transparent.[42] Thus, publicness accounts for the contraction of the space that used to be the domain of "private" contracts between shareholders and directors. And when Delaware's space is consumed by the federal regulatory structure, it is publicness at work. In short, the private, default-rule space gives way to the public, increasingly federal, regulatory space.[43]

In fact, no matter how you categorize it, the federal government's role in director regulation has increased. Often, the regulatory change occurs through the Securities and Exchange Commission (SEC) with both direct and indirect regulatory outcomes. Importantly, each new requirement, in addition to resulting from publicness, chips away at Delaware's space and the so-called private realm. Indeed, as the federal government has increased the range of its involvement in corporate decision making, the actual independence of Delaware and the private space of its corporate citizens has decreased. There are countless examples, including direct regulations that provide definitions of and mandatory requirements for numbers and types of directors and, thus are very direct in nature. There are also new federal information-forcing-substance regulations that, in an indirect manner, create fiduciary duties for directors. Moreover, in some cases the regulations, in conjunction with federal case law, have developed fiduciary duties that are similar to duties under Delaware law—including some duties that are largely unenforceable in Delaware because of the development of its common law. In short, although the federal regulatory changes are both direct and indirect in nature, the justification for both types of changes is the publicness of the securities markets and, when resulting from a crisis, the harm that has occurred to those markets and the economy.

Consider several recent, direct forms of federal regulation that have occupied what used to be Delaware's space and were preserved for director decision making, including regulations that define the type of directors and committees that boards must have. These regulations focus on director independence, a concept in Delaware's common law.[44] As it has developed, Delaware's approach to fiduciary duties and director independence is largely transaction based. Thus, over the years, the Delaware judiciary has set forth a set of standards for scrutinizing financial conflicts as well as the "beholdenness" of directors. The latter standard focuses on directors' state of mind and whether they, individually, as a group, or a special committee or subset, are able to conduct a process and make a decision in a manner that is sufficiently independent of those that might be conflicted.[45]

These standards usually work well enough—at least on a transaction-by-transaction basis. They allow for decision making to occur as needed and for some level of confidence in, for example, strategic combination decisions and going-private transactions. Notably, the standards are process oriented and transaction based. The question is whether the directors are sufficiently disinterested and independent to exercise reasonable business judgment with respect to a particular decision or transaction. These standards, however, do not address whether the questioned judgment was reasonable, or good, or perhaps even excellent. Instead, the goal is to prevent backward-looking judicial hindsight by focusing on the potentially conflicted state of mind of those running the process and making the decision.[46]

Although Delaware's role in prescribing independence ends there, the federal government's does not. Consider the requirements contained in the Sarbanes-Oxley Act, passed by Congress in the wake of Enron, Worldcom, and other corporate frauds. One requirement in that legislation was that the SEC promulgate regulations to ensure that a majority of the members of the board of directors were independent.[47] Note the living nature of this requirement; it is not tied to a specific transaction. Accomplished through stock exchange listing standards subject to SEC approval, the independence measures are largely financial and check-the-box in nature but nevertheless in effect.[48] Generally speaking, if a company is listed on an exchange, a majority of its board members must, at all times, meet these requirements and be independent.[49] The result is a cap on the number of insiders, or corporate officers and employees, as well as the number of outsiders who consult for and work with the corporation, who can serve on the board.[50]

Before Sarbanes-Oxley, the background and relationships of the directors on the board or on any committee was not legislated or regulated. It was viewed as a private decision, in theory as part of the contract between shareholders and the board, and was subject to review only through adjudication when an appearance of impropriety occurred. Moreover, even then, for any given transaction, there might have been an available cleansing mechanism. Now, however, due to publicness and the resulting federal law, a majority of the directors on the board of a publicly held company must be independent at all times.

Federal regulation of the boardroom and director decision making did not stop here. Instead, the Sarbanes-Oxley Act also provided that the board must have an audit committee composed solely of independent directors.[51] Additionally, after the financial crisis of 2008–9 and the resulting Dodd-Frank Act, every public company board must now also have compensation and nomination and governance committees, both of which must also be composed solely of independent directors.[52] Whether independence correlates with good business outcomes is a subject of some debate.[53] The premise, however, is that limitations on managerial overreaching are important to the willingness of shareholders and others to provide credit to firms and to the fairness and efficiency of the securities markets.[54] Indeed, Sarbanes-Oxley also made the practice of issuers making personal loans to directors and officers illegal, except for issuers in the business of making loans.[55] This provision, a form of direct regulation, also intervened in the state law space, which still allows for such loans.[56] And it, too, was a response to perceptions of managerial overreaching. These examples reveal that the existence of regulations and pressure to create changes in and limits on board decision making is present and not going away. It is also formally regulated. You can see this as the federal government occupying Delaware's space or as the erosion of the nexus of contracts, but either way, the space for directors to exercise decision making on these issues is now gone. The decisions are no longer, if they ever truly were, the subject of private law. Instead, the government now controls them.

How did this happen? Publicness. Corporations interact with and impact the public in various ways, and the public, in turn, pushes back. For example, corporate insiders develop corporate strategies and, in conjunction with the requirements of the federal securities laws and regulations, determine how to share that information with those outside the corporation.[57] When this occurs, the groups involved in the process expand beyond the shareholder-officer-director governance triad.[58] Thus, the legally defined governance triad is narrower than those who in fact impact governance and decision making. For example, outside actors—including analysts, regulators, media, and regular citizens—absorb, reframe, and critique those disclosures.[59] This interplay is part of publicness, and it impacts the delegation of power and responsibilities between shareholders, officers, and directors.[60] The dialectic also affects corporate outcomes—forcing changes in decisions, directors, and governance structures.[61]

Another outcome of this dialectic is that the federal government has become an increasingly important player in this space, developing corporate regulations in response to pressure.[62] Pressure, of course, comes from various interest groups, and it grows in response to market crashes and perceptions of fraud, greed, and corruption.[63] In this sense, publicness expands both as a result of decisions that corporate actors make as well as those that they fail to make.[64]

In addition to the federal regime's direct regulation of qualifications, committees, and committee composition is a second, complex, and indirect, system: the information-forcing-substance regime.[65] Here's how it works. The regulations are rooted in the Securities Act of 1933, which regulates offerings of securities.[66] The design of the securities regulatory system is one based on disclosure.[67] Thus, the government does not evaluate the merits of an offering; instead, it reviews disclosures for completeness and clarity.[68] The purpose of the disclosures is to allow buyers to form opinions about an offering.[69] In the initial public offering context, the idea is that the insiders of the issuer have significant information advantages over potential purchasers.[70] As I have argued elsewhere, initial public offerings are the most dramatic example of insider trading, and the disclosure provisions are the cure for this informational asymmetry.[71] These provisions are also supported by a very strong private cause of action contained in Section 11 of the 1933 Securities Act.[72]

In addition, there are also provisions that apply to aftermarket securities purchases, or trades in the market. The regulatory lever here is the 1934 Securities Exchange Act and accompanying regulations.[73] Here, too, there are private enforcement provisions—most prominently, Section 10 (and Rule 10b-5).[74] Thus, for both the 1933 and the 1934 acts and regulations, the basic premise is that disclosure, supplemented with back-end enforcement, will increase transparency and help develop fair and efficient markets in which purchasers are willing to trade.[75] Indeed, fairness and efficiency go hand in hand, because no one wants to play in a rigged market.

This federal securities regulatory apparatus is very robust and requires disclosure of information on many topics—from legal compliance to descriptions of financial conditions and operations.[76] For the purposes of this chapter and publicness, however, the key aspect of the regulations is how they develop and expand corporate fiduciary duties, or, put differently, how they cabin the space for contracting around default rules. In essence, regardless of the type of disclosure demanded, the fact that it is required and made means (at least normatively) that there is information underlying it. Indeed, directors (and certain officers) must sign the offering document (registration statement) and the issuer's annual report (10K). All those who sign the registration statement are potentially liable under Section 11 for any misstatement or omission of a material fact.

This cause of action is a strict liability provision, with a due diligence defense.[77] To avail themselves of the due diligence defense, the directors must in fact have a reasonable belief that the information contained in the documents is accurate. This is where the information-forcing-substance regime develops traction. To have the reasonable belief, of course, means that the signatories have to, at a minimum, ask questions, and in many cases do more, to ensure that the information provided to them is sufficiently accurate to be disclosed.[78] Indeed, law firm memos and other materials prescribing best practices emphasize that directors need to meet with both management and counsel to confirm, before signing, that the documents are accurate.[79] Thus, federal law dictates and expands directors' fiduciary duties.

This space, between the required disclosure, and the process for developing the system that allows for compliance with the disclosure requirement, is the home of the information-forcing-substance theory. Here, the regulatory approach is both direct (the disclosure regulation) and indirect (the reasonable belief requirement). It is also potentially very expansive. Each new required disclosure creates its own demands for information. Collecting, managing, reporting, and certifying the information all emphasize both adherence to fiduciary duties and the expansion of those duties.[80] In addition, when disclosures are litigated, further potential for expansion occurs as judicial interpretations develop the level of information and knowledge that directors should have when they sign the documents.[81] Thus, as we shall see below, the regulations become information forcing substance in nature both as a result of the regulatory demand and search for information to comply with it as well as through the judicial opinions interpreting those obligations.[82] In this manner, the regulatory apparatus drives both the process and substance of how directors are supposed to execute business judgments and can even supersede the state law–based fiduciary duties and corporate contract.

Consider a specific example, the disclosure of risk factors required by Regulation S-K, Item 503. Regulation S-K, through the integrated disclosure provisions, requires that offering documents and annual reports include descriptions of and changes in financial conditions, results of operations, and known risks and trends. The purpose of this provision, and the many others like it, is to ensure that potential investors receive information about risks. At the core of the information-forcing-substance theory is the work that goes on behind the disclosure. The first choice is whether a risk requires disclosure. If it does, the next step is to determine how much and what type is necessary to comply with the securities regulations, including the proviso that disclosures must be sufficiently complete so as not to be misleading.

To be sure that the disclosure is accurate, the board must actually plan for risk, understand risk, discuss risk, and oversee management's compliance procedures to control it. When directors sign the registration statement, they are in effect certifying that they have done sufficient work to hold a reasonable belief that the disclosures are accurate. Of course, the board members are not expected to do the underlying risk management work. They do not, and should not, implement programs. That is for management. Nevertheless, board members must engage in an active conversation with and oversight of management, or they cannot attest to the disclosures.[83] Further, when the disclosures are financial, the board should be satisfied that the company's statements accurately present its financial condition and results of operations, that other disclosures about the company's performance convey meaningful information about past results as well as future plans, and that the company's internal controls and procedures have been designed to detect and deter fraudulent activity.[84] It is in this manner that the regulatory disclosure demand drives behavior: pressing for active monitoring and discussions on the part of the fiduciaries. The goal is richer processes and more accurate and transparent disclosures.[85] In short, the demand for information forces substantive, fiduciary behavior.

Importantly, these regulations do not function in a vacuum. They are supported by both public and private enforcement regimes. For example, as discussed above, Section 11 of the 1933 Securities Act supports the disclosure system through its express, strict liability provision. It is a big stick, designed to urge compliance in providing appropriately fulsome and truthful disclosures. To be sure, the due diligence defense tempers the cause of action; nevertheless, it is also a driver of fiduciary duty. In fact, as designed, Section 11 presses directors (and other potential defendants) to scrutinize statements in offering documents and insist on information to ensure accurate and complete disclosures—and a lack of liability. Thus, Section 11 is information forcing substance in action.

Case law amplifies the power of this statute and reveals how the courts have insisted that corporate directors use their skills and knowledge to improve offering documents and, thereby, their oversight of corporate officers.[86] Indeed, that same case law contains criticisms of the failure of directors to engage in robust discussions with management about the contents of offering documents.[87] This type of dialectic between directors and officers is the fabric of which fiduciary duties are made. In economic theory terms, when the directors engage in this fashion, they are mediating the agency cost space between shareholders and managers.[88] Legal scholars have long attributed this role to directors through the state law–based fiduciary system, but as the analysis in this chapter reveals, the federal government staked a claim on the space early on, and its occupation of the fiduciary zone continues to expand.[89] At the core is the information-forcing-substance regime: regulations paired with causes of action (as well as SEC enforcement) pressing directors to ask questions and question answers and forcing the development of knowledge behind the required disclosures.

Next, consider the fact that the categories of information that must be disclosed continue to grow in number and complexity. The result is that in today's world, when directors sign off on a filing, the breadth of the required information is significant. For every disclosure, the directors' role is to ensure that the information is in accord with their understanding of the corporate information. Some of the categories, as Don Langevoort and I have written elsewhere, correlate directly with what were once solely discussed as state law–based fiduciary duties, such as risk management.[90] Now, however, federal regulation dictates that the disclosure must be made and through the due diligence requirement, and case law in other contexts, inserts the directors into the process.

The role of the federal government in developing and regulating director duties expands beyond the required ex ante disclosures. As mentioned above, ex post enforcement is a key disclosure incentive. As a result, at different points in time, the SEC has engaged in active monitoring of directors, even holding some liable for their fiduciary failures. Recently, although the circumstances were quite specific, the SEC issued complaints against directors in two public companies. In 2013, it settled with eight former directors of Regions Morgan Keegan open- and closed-end funds.[91] Although the liability at issue here arises out of a particular statute, this settlement is really one about the directors' failure to fulfill basic duties under the securities laws, here setting the methodology for determining the fair value of certain portfolio securities and then, in turn, determining that fair value. In addition to actual enforcement actions, former SEC chair Mary Jo White spoke publicly about the important role that engaged, question-asking directors can play in ensuring strong, ethical corporate environments.[92] Thus, she pressed the issue with directors, reminding them of their fiduciary roles.

The federal role also extends to the Department of Justice, which, with the introduction of the Yates Memo, became officially involved in the fiduciary zone as well.[93] The basic premise of the Yates Memo is that corporations seeking criminal or civil cooperation credit must provide information about the actual people involved in any wrongdoing.[94] The Department of Justice has been engaged in enforcement actions of this sort for a long time, but the Yates Memo goes further. The goal is to decrease the number of negotiated outcomes that result in corporate agreements, without prosecution of those who engaged in the wrongdoing.[95] In doing so, the Yates Memo elaborates a policy that is focused on finding individuals who willfully, and therefore criminally, failed to fulfill their fiduciary duties. It inserts the federal government directly into the director-officer relationship. The board's fiduciary duty, of course, is to the company, not to officers or individuals.[96] As a result, the Yates Memo's requirement that the company reveal the individuals involved in wrongdoing requires the board to assure itself that it knows what happened and is aware of all the individuals involved, some of whom might well be officers.[97] Directors now need to ask for the information and provide it to the federal government.[98] Although this information demand is retrospective, it still requires directors to be fully engaged in these discussions, and perhaps even to become the drivers of the investigatory process.[99] Thus, the memo arguably incentivizes independent decision making by the directors, who have to run the investigations. Moreover, like the securities regulatory regime discussed above, the Yates Memo also plays an indirect role in the fiduciary space. It pushes directors to be engaged fiduciaries that, for example, ensure appropriately robust compliance systems on the front end.

There are many other examples of the ways in which the federal government has developed fiduciary duties and occupied the corporate governance space, including proxy regulations as well as settlement agreements that insert the government directly into the boardroom conversation. Or regulation of disclosure around executive compensation coupled with shareholder votes, even though nonbinding, on officer pay. In the end, however, all of these examples point out that the so-called private realm of corporate decision making is considerably more constrained than either academic or other discourse might reveal. In fact, the extensive emphasis on the nexus-of-contracts theory in the corporate literature is impoverished and, as a result, may well contribute to the growth of the federal regime and the role of publicness, simply by failing to include them in its analysis. In short, as the analysis in this chapter makes clear, the public-private distinction is a construct, and the nexus-of-contracts theory must give way to further analysis of publicness and the role of the government in the corporate contract.

Notes

Thanks for comments go to Randall Thomas and Steven Davidoff Solomon, Jill Fisch, Frank Partnoy, Don Langevoort, Bob Thompson, and participants in the conference for this volume. Thanks for research assistance go to Kelsey Bolin, Alana Siegel, and Liz Sinclair.

1. Hillary A. Sale and Robert B. Thompson, "Market Intermediation, Publicness, and Securities Class Actions," *Washington University Law Review* (2015): 493; Hillary A. Sale and Donald C. Langevoort, "'We Believe': Omnicare, Legal Risk Disclosure and Corporate Governance," *Duke Law Journal* 66 (2016); Donald C. Langevoort and Robert B. Thompson, "'Publicness' in Contemporary Securities Regulation after the JOBS Act," *Georgetown Law Scholarly Commons* (2013): 340; Hillary A. Sale, "J.P. Morgan: An Anatomy of Corporate Publicness," *Brooklyn Law Review* (2014); Hillary A. Sale, "The New 'Public' Corporation," *Law and Contemporary Problems* (2011); Hillary A. Sale, "Public Governance," *George Washington Law Review* (2013).

2. Sale and Langevoort, "We Believe"; Sale, "J.P. Morgan; Sale and Thompson, "Market Intermediation."

3. *See, e.g.*, Frank H. Easterbrook and Daniel R. Fischel, "Voting in Corporate Law," *Journal of Law and Economics* (1983); Frank H. Easterbrook and Daniel R. Fischel, "Close Corporations and Agency Costs," *Stanford Law Review* (1985); Frank H. Easterbrook, "Corporate Control Transactions," *Yale Law Journal* (1981); Michael C. Jensen and William H. Meckling, "Theory of the Firm: Managerial Behavior, Agency Costs and Ownership Structure," *Journal of Financial Economics* (1976); William W. Bratton Jr., "Nexus of Contracts Corporation: A Critical Appraisal," *Cornell Law Review* 74 (1989).

4. Marcel Kahan and Michael Klausner, "Path Dependence in Corporate Contracting: Increasing Returns, Herd Behavior, and Cognitive Biases," *Washington University Law Review* (1996): 347; James D. Cox, "Corporate Law and the Limits of Private Ordering," *Washington University Law Review* (2015): 5. Jensen and Meckling refer to it as a theory. Jensen and Meckling, "Theory of the Firm." While others refer to it as a conclusion. Bratton, "Nexus of Contracts Corporation," 410. Regardless of the name, the nexus-of-contracts approach to analyzing the corporate form gained considerable traction and is still present.

5. Kahan and Klausner, "Path Dependence," 347.

6. Lucian A. Bebchuk, "Limiting Contractual Freedom in Corporate Law: The Desirable Constraints on Charter Amendments," *Harvard Law Review* (1989): 1847.

7. Frank H. Easterbrook and Daniel R. Fischel, "The Corporate Contract," *Columbia Law Review* (1989), 1428. *See also* ATP Tour, Inc. v. Deutscher Tennis

Bund, 91 A.3d 554, 558 (Del. 2014); Boilermakers 154 Retirement Fund v. FedEx Corp., 73 A.3d 934, 956 (D.C. 2013).

8. Kahan and Klausner, "Path Dependence," 347; Easterbrook and Fischel, "The Corporate Contract," 1431.

9. James D. Cox, "Corporate Law and the Limits of Private Ordering," *Washington University Law Review* (2015): 6.

10. *Id.* at 8. For a Delaware case exploring these issues, see Boilermakers Local 154 Retirement Fund v. Chevron Corp, 73 A.3d 934 (Del. Ch. 2013).

11. Easterbrook and Fischel, "The Corporate Contract," 1427. Scholarly work has increasingly recognized the limits of the nexus-of-contracts theory. One of the most prominent articles is the seminal work by Henry Hansmann and Reinier Kraakman, "The Essential Role of Organizational Law." In this article Professors Hansmann and Kraakman posit that at least with respect to asset partitioning, or the protection of the entity's assets from the creditors of its owners or managers, property rights play an important role. The asset-partitioning function, which is property law–based, allows for efficiencies in bonding and monitoring that, they argue, is key to the growth of large-scale enterprises. Henry Hansmann and Reinier Kraakman, "The Essential Role of Organizational Law," *Yale Law Review* (2000): 110. More recently, Morgan Ricks has expanded on the property focus, arguing that organizational law, including in organizations beyond the corporate form, has more than one property law aspect. His theory, which he supports with deep historical analysis, focuses on the important role of property relinquishment between co-owners. In this manner, Ricks's work expands the debate about the theory of the firm to include an examination of entity insiders. Both articles press on the nexus-of-contracts theory, revealing that how we define entities and their powers exceeds the more limited dimension of the nexus-of-contracts theory and, in both cases, in the interests of efficiency and growth. Both works are also focused on actors who are participating in or with the corporation. Publicness, however, reaches beyond to those on the outside, pressing on our understanding of who is in fact governing the rights of the entity participants.

12. Robert B. Thompson, "Why New Corporate Law Arises: Delaware's Golden Age and Likely Changes in the 21st Century," (2016): 2.

13. *Id.* at 4.

14. *Id.* at 3.

15. *Id.* at 3.

16. This is true even for closely held corporations. Cox, "Corporate Law," 12–15.

17. Classic externalities and how we regulate them; Easterbrook and Fischel, "The Corporate Contract," 1415; *see, e.g.*, Resource Conservation and Recovery Act, 42 U.S.C. §§ 6901–6992k (1976).

18. *See generally* Smith v. Van Gorkom, 488 A.2d 858 (Del. 1985) (providing an example of a judicial change in duty ex post which resulted in pushback). *See* Daniel R. Fischel, "The Business Judgment Rule and the Trans Union Case," *The Business Lawyer* (1985): 1440–41; Mercer Bullard, "Caremark's Irrelevance," *Berkeley Business Law Journal* (2013): 21; Larry E. Ribstein, "Takeover Defenses and the Corporate Contract," *Georgetown Law Journal* (1989): 96. Indeed, self-interested and conflicted behavior is proscribed and results in a shift in the burden of proof to the fiduciary, further undercutting the nexus of contracts metaphor. Cox, "Corporate Law." See also Debora DeMott, "Beyond Metaphor: An Analysis of Fiduciary Obligation," *Duke Law Journal* (1988): 900.

19. McLaughlin on Class Actions § 1:1 (12th ed.).

20. Fed. R. Civ. P. 23.

21. Private Securities Litigation Reform Act, 15 U.S.C. 78 (1995); Dodd-Frank Wall Street Reform and Consumer Protection Act 12 U.S.C. 5301 (2010); Halliburton Co. v. Erica P. John Fund, Inc., 134 S. Ct. 2398 (2014).

22. It is no surprise that the modern class action evolved from another area where the decision making was "private" and the harm needed monitoring—employment. § 1776 Class Actions for Injunctive or Declaratory Relief Under Rule 23(b)(2)—Civil-Rights Actions, 7AA Fed. Prac. & Proc. Civ. § 1776 (3d ed.). (Before Rule 23 was amended to expand the use of class actions, class actions were used to litigate alleged discrimination in employment.)

23. For an empirical evaluation of the relative role of class actions and derivative litigation in Delaware, see Robert B. Thompson and Randall S. Thomas, "The New Look of Shareholder Litigation," *Vanderbilt Law Review* (2004): 51.

24. Zapata Corp. v. Maldonado, 430 A.2d 779, 780 (Del. 1981).

25. *See, e.g.*, Smith v. Van Gorkom, 488 A. 2d 858 (Del. 1985); Broz v. Cellular Info. Sys., Inc., 673 A.2d 148 (Del 1996); Sinclair Oil v. Levien, 280 A.2d 717 (Del 1971).

26. Cox, "Corporate Law," 12.

27. The classic case here is Smith v. Van Gorkom, 488 A.2d 858 (Del. 1985).

28. Cox, "Corporate Law," 18.

29. *See, e.g.*, Edward B. Rock, "Saints and Sinners: How Does Delaware Corporate Law Work?" *UCLA Law Review* (1997): 1011; Brehm v. Eisner, 746 A.2d 244 (Del. 2000); Smith v. Van Gorkom, 488 A.2d 858 (Del. 1985).

30. Hillary A. Sale, "The New 'Public' Corporation," *Law and Contemporary Problems* (2011): 137–48.

31. Cox, "Corporate Law," 32.

32. Sale, "J.P. Morgan," 1654; Langevoort and Thompson, "Publicness in Contemporary Securities Regulation."

33. *Id.* As others have argued, the line between the public and private is a construct. *See, e.g.*, Martha Minow, "*Making All The Difference: Inclusion, Exclusion, and American Law*" (1990) ("Tracing the presence of state power in the

family sphere, historically described as removed from the state, suggests something powerful about boundaries: both sides of a boundary are regulated, even if the line was supposed to distinguish the regulated from the unregulated."); Laura A. Rosenbury, "Federal Visions of Private Family Support," *Vanderbilt Law Review* (2014) (examines the alleged line, or balance between state and federal authority over the family).

34. Joy v. North, 328 F.2d 880 (2d Cir. 1982).

35. Cox, "The Limits of Private Ordering," 32.

36. Jean Eaglesham, "The Shadow of Enron Still Lingers," *Wall Street Journal*, October 17, 2011, http://www.wsj.com/articles/SB10001424052970204774604576633413245885214; Jill E. Fisch and Hillary A. Sale, "The Securities Analyst as Agent: Rethinking the Regulation of Analysts," *Iowa Law Review* 88 (2003): 1079; William W. Bratton and Adam J. Levitin, "A Transactional Genealogy of Scandal: From Michael Milken to Enron to Goldman Sachs," *Southern California Law Review* 86 (2013): 832–34. *See also* Urska Velikonja, "The Cost of Securities Fraud," *William and Mary Law Review* 54 (2013) (arguing that the harm of fraud extends beyond shareholders, creating economic distortions that impact risk assessments and human and financial capital decisions).

37. Eduardo Porter, "Recession's True Cost Is Still Being Tallied," *New York Times*, January 21, 2014, http://www.nytimes.com/2014/01/22/business/economy/the-cost-of-the-financial-crisis-is-still-being-tallied.html?_r=0.

38. Porter, "Recession's True Cost."

39. Sale, "Public Governance," 1013–14. Some have criticized this move. *See, e.g.*, Jill Fisch, "Leave It to Delaware: Why Congress Should Stay Out of Corporate Governance," 37 *Delaware Journal of Corporate Law* 731 (2013). In addition, regulatory oversight surges after a market crash are common, in part due to public support for political entrepreneurs who oppose powerful interest groups. Such passion is short-lived, however, and wanes as the market returns to normalcy. *See also* John C. Coffee Jr., "The Political Economy of Dodd-Frank: Why Financial Reform Tends to Be Frustrated and Systemic Risk Perpetuated," *Cornell Law Review* 97 (2012): 1020–29.

40. Langevoort and Thompson, "Publicness in Contemporary Securities Regulation," 373–78.

41. Langevoort and Thompson, "Publicness in Contemporary Securities Regulation," 340; Sale, "Public Governance," 1032–35.

42. Langevoort and Thompson, "Publicness in Contemporary Securities Regulation," 378–83; Sale, "Public Governance," 1032–35.

43. The key work in this space is Mark Roe's article, "Delaware's Competition," *Harvard Law Review* 117 (2003). In this piece, Professor Roe challenged the long-standing, race-to-the-bottom argument, analyzing the role of the federal government in providing competition to Delaware in regulating entities. For additional works by Professor Roe in this space, see "Delaware's Politics," *Har-*

vard Law Review 118 (2005) and "Delaware's Shrinking Half-Life," *Stanford Law Review* 62 (2010).

44. *In re* Ltd., Inc., No. CIV.A. 17148-NC, 2002 WL 537692 (Del. Ch. Mar. 27, 2002).

45. *In re* Ltd., Inc., No. CIV.A. 17148-NC, 2002 WL 537692 (Del. Ch. Mar. 27, 2002); Beam ex rel. Martha Stewart Living Omnimedia, Inc. v. Stewart, 845 A.2d 1040 (Del. 2004).

46. Although the nexus-of-contracts proponents see these fiduciary duties as private, they are not. They "yield important externalities," including compensation to those injured and support for investment through protection for overreaching. Cox, "The Limits of Private Ordering," 33; DuPont v. Delaware Trust Co., 320 A.2d 694 (Del. 1974).

47. Sarbanes-Oxley Act sec. 301, § 10A, 116 Stat. at 775–77; 17 C.F.R. 240.10A-3.

48. John C. Coffee Jr. and Hillary A. Sale, "Redesigning the SEC: Does the Treasury Have a Better Idea?" *Virginia Law Review* 95 (2009): 769.

49. 17 C.F.R. 240.10A-3.

50. 17 C.F.R. 240.10A-3; Johnathan Macey and Hillary A. Sale, "Observations on the Role of Commodification, Independence, and Governance in the Accounting Industry," *Villanova Law Review* 48 (2003): 1183–87.

51. Sarbanes-Oxley Act sec. 301, § 10A, 116 Stat. at 775–77.

52. Dodd-Frank Act sec. 952, § 10C, 124 Stat. at 1900; 17 C.F.R. 229, 240 XX.

53. For articles questioning the value of independence requirements, *see* Sanjai Bhagat and Roberta Romano, "Event Studies and the Law: Part II: Empirical Studies of Corporate Law," *American Law and Economics Review* 4 (2002): 403; Sanjai Bhagat and Bernard Black, "The Non-Correlation Between Board Independence and Long-Term Firm Performance," *Journal of Corporation Law* 27 (2002): 231; Sanjai Bhagat and Bernard Black, "The Uncertain Relationship between Board Compensation and Firm Performance," *Business Law* 54 (1999): 922; Lisa M. Fairfax, "The Uneasy Case for the Inside Director," *Iowa Law Review* 96 (2010): 131. And for articles arguing that independence correlates with positive financial and governance outcomes, *see* Dain C. Donelson, John McInnis, and Richard D. Mergenthaler, "The Effect of Governance Reforms on Financial Reporting Fraud," *Journal of Law, Finance, and Accounting* 1 (2016) 235 (finding that increases in board independence produced significant decreases in rates of fraud); Vidhi Chhaochharia and Yaniv Grinstein, "CEO Compensation and Board Structure," *Journal of Finance* 64 (2009): 232 (finding that a significant decrease in CEO compensation occurred at firms required to implement stock exchange board oversight requirements, including majority board independence, after the 2001 and 2002 corporate scandals); James F. Cotter, Anil Shivdasani, and Marc Zenner, "Do Independent Directors Enhance Target Shareholder Wealth during Tender Offers?" *Journal of Financial Economics* 43

(1997): 214 (finding that independent boards enhance target shareholder gains from takeovers); Michael S. Weisbach, "Outside Directors and CEO Turnover," *Journal of Financial Economics* 20 (1988): 457 (finding that independent boards are more likely to replace a CEO in response to poor performance).

54. James D. Cox, "The Social Meaning of Shareholder Suits," *Brooklyn Law Review* 64 (1999): 7–40.

55. Sarbanes-Oxley Act sec. 401, § 10A, 116 Stat. at 775–77.

56. 8 Del. C. § 143.

57. Sale, "J.P. Morgan," 1630–31.

58. *Id.* at 1643–55.

59. Although the process often results from regulation, it occurs in both publicly-held and privately-held entities through press releases and the like. Sale, "J.P. Morgan," 1630–35.

60. Sale, "J.P. Morgan," 1630–31.

61. *Id.* at 1643–55.

62. Donald C. Langevoort, "The SEC as Lawmaker: Choices about Investor Protection in the Face of Uncertainty," *Washington University Law Review* 84 (2006): 1598–603. Sale, "J.P. Morgan," 1654–55.

63. Robert B. Thompson and Hillary S. Sale, "Securities Fraud as Corporate Governance: Reflections upon Federalism," *Vanderbilt Law Review* 56 (2003): 870–78. Sale, "J.P. Morgan," 1634–35.

64. Sale, "J.P. Morgan," 1634–35. This theory of publicness connects with institutional questions about compliance, regulation, legitimacy, and social license. *See, e.g.*, Jodi Short and Michael Toffel, "Making Self-Regulation More Than Merely Symbolic: The Critical Role of the Legal Environment," 55 *Administrative Science Quarterly* 361 (2010). Compliance is key to whether organizations and directors will encounter push back from the public. For an article examining the role of culture in compliance, *see* Donald C. Langevoort, "Cultures of Compliance," *American Criminal Law Review* 54 (2017): 733.

65. Bob Thompson and I began to develop the theory of this information-forcing-substance regime elsewhere and have continued to work on it. Thompson and Sale, "Securities Fraud," 875. Hillary A. Sale, "Independent Directors as Securities Monitors," *Business Lawyer* 61 (2006): 1375.

66. Securities Act of 1933, 15 U.S.C. § 77a *et seq*; Hillary A. Sale, "Disappearing without a Trace: Sections 11 and 12(a)(2) of the 1933 Securities Act," *Washington Law Review* 75 (2000): 430–34; Langevoort and Thompson, "Publicness in Contemporary Securities Regulation," 375–79.

67. Sale, "Disappearing without a Trace," 430–34; Langevoort and Thompson, "Publicness in Contemporary Securities Regulation," 375–79.

68. Securities Act of 1933, 15 U.S.C. § 77a *et seq*. Sale, "Disappearing without a Trace," 472. Langevoort and Thompson, "Publicness in Contemporary Securities Regulation," 352.

69. Securities Act of 1933, 15 U.S.C. § 77k. Sale, "Disappearing without a Trace," 470. Langevoort and Thompson, "Publicness in Contemporary Securities Regulation, 69.

70. Securities Act of 1933, 15 U.S.C. § 77k. *See also* Sale, "Disappearing without a Trace," 470; Langevoort and Thompson, "Publicness in Contemporary Securities Regulation," 352.

71. *See* Sale, "Disappearing without a Trace," 470; Thompson and Sale, "Securities Fraud as Corporate Governance."

72. Securities Act of 1933, 15 U.S.C. § 77k.

73. Securities Exchange Act of 1934, 15 U.S.C. § 78(a) *et seq.* Section 13 of the 1934 Securities Exchange Act actually works in conjunction with the 1933 Act requirements through what is referred to as integrated disclosure. Securities Exchange Act of 1934, 15 U.S.C. § 78(m).

74. *See* Securities Exchange Act of 1934, 15 U.S.C. § 78(j) and Employment of Manipulative and Deceptive Devices, 17 C.F.R. § 240.10b-5 (2015). *See also* Sale and Thompson, "Market Intermediation," 872.

75. *See* Sale and Thompson, "Market Intermediation," 872.

76. *See* Sale and Langevoort, "We Believe." *See also* Sale and Thompson, "Market Intermediation."

77. The 10b-5 cause of action is the provision for 10Ks. Employment of Manipulative and Deceptive Devices, 17 C.F.R. § 240.10b-5 (2015). *See also* Sale, "Disappearing without a Trace," 472.

78. *See, e.g., In re* WorldCom, Inc. Sec. Litig., 346 F. Supp. 2d 628 (S.D.N.Y. 2004) and Escott v. BarChris Construction Corp., 283 F. Supp. 643, 688 (S.D.N.Y. 1968).

79. *See, e.g.*, "SEC Issues Final Rules on CEO/CFO Certification under Section 302 of the Sarbanes-Oxley Act." Skadden, Arps, Slate, Meagher & Flom LLP. September 2002. https://www.skadden.com/sites/default/files/publications/841library.pdf. Jeff G. Hammel and Robert J. Malionek, "Statements Made and Not Made: An Auditor's Duty to Correct, and the Scope of Liability for Statements Made by Others," Latham & Watkins Securities Litigation and Professional Liability Practice (First Quarter 2007), https://www.lw.com/thoughtLeadership/securities-litigation-and-professional-liability-practice-issue-15. Paul Vizcarrondo Jr., "Liabilities under the Federal Securities Laws: Sections 11, 12, 15, and 17 of the Securities Act of 1933 and Sections 10, 18, and 20 of the Securities Exchange Act of 1934," Wachtell, Lipton, Rosen & Katz (August 2013), http://www.wlrk.com/docs/OutlineofSecuritiesLawLiabilities2013.pdf.

80. *See* Robert B. Thompson, "Federal Corporate Law: Torts and Fiduciary Duty," *Journal of Corporation Law* 31 (2006). *See also* Sale and Langevoort, "We Believe"; Sale and Thompson, "Market Intermediation." The Corporate Laws Committee, "Corporate Director's Guidebook—Sixth Edition." Business Lawyers 61 (Aug. 2011): 985, 987.

81. *See* Sale and Langevoort, "We Believe."

82. The scienter requirement under 10b-5 is intended to limit what might otherwise be a very flexible cause of action. Nevertheless, it could have the unintended consequence of decreasing the incentive of directors to develop knowledge. Jennifer H. Arlen and William N. Carney, "Vicarious Liability for Fraud on the Securities Markets: Theory and Evidence," *University of Illinois Law Review* 691 (1992): 714–15.

83. Indeed, in an additional indirect layer, the directors' behavior will drive management behavior, thereby enforcing yet another set of fiduciary duties. Sale and Langevoort, "We Believe." *See also* Sale, "Independent Directors," 1382.

84. *See* 2016 Principles of Corporate Governance, Business Roundtable 8 (Aug. 2016), https://businessroundtable.org/sites/default/files/Principles-of-Corporate-Governance-2016.pdf.

85. This is true whether the process drives a change in a proposed disclosure or no change. Sale and Langevoort, "We Believe."

86. *See, e.g.*, Escott v. BarChris Construction Corp., 283 F. Supp. 643, 688 (S.D.N.Y. 1968) and *In re* WorldCom, Inc. Sec. Litig., 346 F. Supp. 2d 628 (S.D.N.Y. 2004).

87. *Id.* at 683–93 (analyzing the relevant conduct of each director).

88. *See* Sale and Langevoort, "We Believe."

89. *See* Thompson, "Federal Corporate Law." *See also* Thompson and Sale, "Securities Fraud as Corporate Governance." *See also* Jill E. Fisch, "Federal Securities Fraud Litigation as a Lawmaking Partnership," http://ssrn.com/abstract=2869523 (exploring the relationship between Congress and the federal courts in further developing securities law).

90. *See* Sale and Langevoort, "We Believe."

91. https://www.sec.gov/News/PressRelease/Detail/PressRelease/136517157487. *See also* https://www.sec.gov/News/PressRelease/Detail/PressRelease/1365171514096.

92. *See* Sale and Langevoort, "We Believe."

93. Sally Quillian Yates, "Individual Accountability for Corporate Wrongdoing," Department of Justice (Sept. 9, 2015), https://www.justice.gov/dag/file/769036/download.

94. *Id.* at 1

95. *Id.* at 3.

96. Corporate Laws Committee, "Corporate Director's Guidebook," 985, 987.

97. Holly J. Gregory, "Board-Driven Internal Investigations," The Governance Counselor: Capital Markets and Corporate Governance (May 2016), http://www.sidley.com/~/media/publications/may-2016-practical-law-journal.pdf.

98. *See* Sale and Langevoort, "We Believe."

99. *See* Gregory, "Board-Driven Internal Investigations."

CHAPTER SIX

Delaware and Financial Risk

Frank Partnoy

Introduction

In this chapter, I argue that financial risk poses unique challenges that justify a differential application of the *Caremark*[1] oversight standard. In terms of this book's framework, I focus on changes in the corporate contract with respect to financial risk and the implications of those changes for director oversight duties. My target is primarily financial institutions, but my argument applies with equal force to nonfinancial institutions with significant exposure to financial risk. *Financial risk* refers to the risk associated with a firm's financial transactions and financial exposure, as contrasted to *business risk*, which refers to the risk inherent in a firm (see Gabriel and Baker 1980).

Unlike other scholars who have discussed director duties in the aftermath of the financial crisis, I do not argue for any change in the *Caremark* standard itself. Instead, my argument is that Delaware law already provides ample support and justification for holding directors to a higher standard with respect to the oversight of financial risk. Indeed, such a conclusion is consistent with—not in opposition to—the 2009 decision in *Citigroup*,[2] in which Chancellor Chandler dismissed claims of director oversight failure with Citigroup's subprime mortgage-related losses. In my view, the problem with the application of *Caremark* in cases involving financial risk stems not from *Citigroup* but from the federal court decision in *JPMorgan*,[3] the recent case applying Delaware law in the "London Whale" episode. To be clear, the target of my criticism is *JPMorgan*, not *Citigroup*.

I am not the first to address director oversight in the aftermath of the financial crisis. Bainbridge (2009) stressed the important distinctions in cases involving risk management failures. Pan (2009/2010) was skeptical about whether business risk should be treated differently from legal risk. Miller (2010, 123) rejected proposals to expand director oversight of risk management, arguing that risk management is "about smoothing returns, and the question of how smooth returns should be is a business decision." Miller (2010) argued that expanding the board's risk management oversight duties would amount to a repeal of the business judgment rule. Gevurtz (2010) argued that one should not look to state corporate law to limit excessive risk taking by financial institutions. Orenstein (2011) proposed a gross negligence standard for financial firm directors. Jones and Welsh (2012) advocated public enforcement of director oversight duties. Hill and McDonnell (2013) argued for an expanded duty to oversee business risk. Armour and Gordon (2014) argued for limited business judgment rule protection for systemically important financial firms. Tsuk Mitchell (2015) critiqued the historical development of the duty to monitor under Delaware law. To the extent Delaware judges or legislators are interested in changing the legal standards for director oversight duties, there is the above menu of options. To date, nothing has been ordered.

My argument here differs from those advanced by my predecessors: In my view, there is jurisprudential space within *Caremark* and its progeny for judges to embrace the notion that board oversight duties regarding financial risk should be more expansive than those with regarding business risk generally. Generalized business risk, where the courts rightly have expressed skepticism about claims, differs from financial risk, where there are reasons for courts to question more closely whether the board consciously failed to exercise reasonable oversight.

Indeed, Delaware judges already have demonstrated particular expertise with financial issues and financial risk. Although judges might have concerns about judicial second-guessing in the business context generally, as in the assessment of the Caremark board's oversight of pharmaceutical product marketing, the assessment of financial risk is categorically different. Delaware judges frequently assess financial risk. In a range of cases outside the *Caremark* context, Delaware judges have engaged in independent assessments of financial risk, have included detailed descriptions of financial risk and valuation issues, and have pointed out flaws in the analyses of financial experts. For example, in two recent cases, *In re: Appraisal of Dell* and *In re ISN Software Corp. Appraisal Litigation*, the Delaware courts demonstrated a capacity to engage in a sophisticated critique of expert valuations and to make independent financial assessments using discounted cash flow analyses.[4] Likewise, the descriptions of complex financial issues in Delaware cases have been cogent and complete,[5] and the Delaware courts have addressed financial institution conflicts of interest in a balanced way, without exposing such institutions to unwarranted liability in every case.[6] All of these cases suggest that, even if business risk generally is not in a Delaware judge's wheelhouse, financial risk is.[7]

The steps in my argument are as follows. First, I show how modern firms with significant exposure to financial risk are different in fundamental ways that matter crucially to the application of *Caremark*. (Most obviously, based on the financial crisis, modern firms generate significant externalities, though financial innovation has generated a range of difficult and complex internalized costs as well.) Second, I argue that, notwithstanding these differences, *Citigroup* was correctly decided, though the result might have been the opposite if the complaint been framed differently, with relevant and important facts. Third, I demonstrate that *JPMorgan* was wrongly decided.

In my view, much of the scholarly criticism of *Citigroup* arises not from Chancellor Chandler's approach or reasoning but from the feeble allegations in the *Citigroup* complaint. That complaint failed to plead facts to support a *Caremark* claim, even recognizing the unique challenges that arise with respect to financial risk. Given the weak allegations in *Citigroup*, that decision explicitly left an opening for a well-framed complaint in a later case to survive a motion to dismiss. As Chancellor Chandler stated, it might be possible for plaintiffs to prevail "under some set of facts."[8]

The case that presented just such a set of facts was the litigation surrounding the $6 billion "London Whale" loss at JPMorgan's Chief Investment Office (the "London Whale" was the nickname of the employee whose trades were at issue). The London Whale episode involved colossal oversight failures by the JPMorgan board with respect to risks arising from massive positions in complex credit derivatives. These oversight failures were described in detail as part of several government investigations, and JPMorgan's board admitted to facts regarding these failures in several settlements with regulators. Most important for this chapter's purposes, the details surrounding these oversight failures were included in the complaint in the *JPMorgan* derivative litigation. Whereas the *Citigroup* complaint relied primarily on press releases and rhetorical skepticism of the directors' judgments about risk, the *JPMorgan* complaint included numerous specific facts demonstrating the board's knowledge of sustained and systematic oversight failures over an extended period. Simply put, the difference between the *Citigroup* and *JPMorgan* complaints was night and day.

Nevertheless, the Honorable George B. Daniels of the Southern District of New York dismissed the *JPMorgan* complaint with prejudice, in a thirteen-page order, relying on *Citigroup*. In my view, *JPMorgan* was incorrect and should not be followed. As I will show, Judge Daniels, a federal judge attempting to apply Delaware law, misunderstood the meaning and import of *Citigroup* and, as a result, misapplied that case. The Delaware courts undoubtedly will adjudicate future director oversight disputes involving financial risk, and they will have an opportunity to distinguish *JPMorgan*. My goal is to persuade them to do so.

The complexities of financial risk pose unique challenges that the Delaware courts should take into account when assessing director oversight failures. Such an approach would not require abandoning *Caremark*. It would not subject directors to unwarranted exposure for oversight failures or have negative implications for business, and it would not change Delaware's approach to cases that do not involve financial risk. To be clear, I am not suggesting that complaints alleging oversight failures with respect to financial risk always should survive motions to dismiss, or even that they should survive frequently. Instead, I am simply rejecting the notion implicit in *JPMorgan* that such complaints can never survive.

The Delaware courts also have demonstrated a capacity to respond to changes in the corporate contract—notably in *Caremark* itself, where Chancellor Allen recognized that the modern corporate practice of oversight had changed and that the courts should change accordingly. Director oversight of financial risk is merely the most recent area in need of this kind of incremental judicial change.

Financial Risk and the Modern Corporate Contract

My first point should be uncontroversial: Financial risk is different. The modern corporation is a complex web of contracts and relationships among not only shareholders and managers but also potentially derivative counterparties, subsidiaries, variable interest entities, employees, joint venture participants, and a plethora of capital structure claimants (Partnoy 2009). Moreover, in the aftermath of the financial crisis, corporations with significant exposure to financial risk today face categorically different regulatory and incentive challenges than do other firms (Partnoy and Eisinger 2013).

As a result of these differences, the job of director oversight has been fundamentally transformed at firms with respect to financial risk. Directors of firms with significant exposure to financial risk necessarily must be far more aware of potential oversight challenges than their counterparts at other firms (Federal Reserve 2013). Financial institution boards in particular receive far more financial information than other firms, at more granular levels. The job of a financial institution director requires an awareness of the unique problems of agency costs and information asymmetry posed by their complex business.

At the outset, I want to note that I am discussing oversight duties broadly, not only for banks but for other firms that present the challenges I describe here regarding the modern corporate contract and financial risk. I am not proposing to limit the treatment exclusively to banks or based on other regulatory distinctions such as those in the 2010 Dodd-Frank Act. For example, the board of small bank might face fewer financial risk challenges than the board of a large insurance company. Moreover, a nonbank corporation could face substantial exposure to financial risk. Consider Enron during the early 2000s, or AIG during 2007–8, or General Electric before it recently divested GE Capital's most complex business lines. In addition, my argument is directed at a range of characteristics associated with financial institutions, not exclusively systemic risk. Armour and Gordon (2014) address the specific question of whether fiduciary treatment should vary based on the presence of systemic risk.

Of course, the question about whether differential treatment might be warranted depends on the issue and context. If the oversight question involves a relatively straightforward problem faced by firms in general—such as employment discrimination or bribery—no differential treatment might be warranted. For example, although *Stone v. Ritter* involved a financial institution, AmSouth, the compliance failures at issue in that case more closely resembled those in *Caremark* than in *JPMorgan*. They did not involve complex financial risk. Similar conclusions might hold for the recent problems with unauthorized new customer accounts at Wells Fargo, even though that company is a large, complex bank.

In contrast, if the oversight question is related to the complexities of financial risk—for example, involving "super-senior" exposure to synthetic collateralized debt obligations or large notional positions in credit default swaps based on credit indices—then the differential treatment would more likely be justified. The key question in the analysis becomes: How much different is the oversight function in context?

It can be helpful in answering this question to consider the specific ways in which institutions with significant exposure to financial risk can differ fundamentally from other firms. There is a large body of literature on these differences. For an overview, see Partnoy (2015). I will now summarize several aspects of that literature.

First is moral hazard. Firms with exposure to significant financial risk face greater moral hazard, which creates differential incentives among corporate actors. In particular, large firms that are potentially "too big to fail" face the temptation to take on risk in the presence of an anticipated bailout. Moral hazard can be pervasive at every level of such firms, including among lower-level employees with incentives to take on substantial asymmetric risks: If their bets win, they will be well compensated; if their bets lose, they will not suffer those losses. Directors of such firms necessarily are aware of this moral hazard in ways that directors of other firms typically are not. Indeed, moral hazard is a fundamental attribute of firms with exposure to complex financial risk, and much of a board's job involves oversight of the financial risk that accompanies moral hazard.

Second is leverage. Firms with substantial exposure to financial risk frequently have far greater leverage, and the role of debt claimants can be more varied and substantial than is the case for other firms. Indeed, such firms typically have more intricate capital structures—so much so that the question of who is the residual claimant can become unfathomably complex. Prior to the financial crisis, the residual claimants of financial institution's cash flows were arguably employees (or future taxpayers), not shareholders, who were in a position that more closely resembled a fixed claimant. Another difficulty is the role of various debt claimants: Highly leveraged financial institutions can frequently be in the vicinity of insolvency, particularly intraquarter. In any event, board oversight becomes far more important to the extent a firm is leveraged.

Third is agency costs. The history of financial risk is one of significant agency costs, including not only rogue traders but employees throughout the institution who face differential incentives (Partnoy 2009). Directors of firms with substantial exposure to financial risk necessarily are aware of the history of pervasive agency costs and the high risks associated with individuals with high-powered incentives. Another significant aspect of agency costs is short-termism: Financial institution employees have a relatively short time horizon, even with compensation vesting and potential clawbacks. Employees who take on substantial risks are rarely punished, and frequently are not even employed when losses occur. Financial institutions employ substantial numbers of employees who violate laws or regulations; one recent study found that 7 percent of employees in the financial and insurance sector have misconduct records (Egan, Matvos, and Seru 2016).

Fourth is information asymmetry. Financial risk generates high information costs. Even firms that are perceived as relatively conservative, such as Wells Fargo, have trillions of dollars of positions in over-the-counter derivatives, variable interest entities, and other complex structured finance transactions (Partnoy and Eisinger 2013). The reality is that directors of firms with substantial exposure to financial risk necessarily must have much more information than directors of simpler firms; this is one reason why director compensation at such firms is so high. To the extent financial risk management systems are working, they should deliver much more information to the boards of firms that have substantial exposure to financial risk than to the boards of firms that do not. On the other hand, to the extent those systems are not working, directors of firms with substantial exposure to financial risk potentially will be deprived of important information that might not even exist at other firms.

Fifth is regulatory scrutiny. The corporate contracts for most financial institutions, including bank charters, typically include explicit counterparty relationships with governmental entities, such as the Federal Reserve, the Office of the Comptroller of the Currency (OCC), or the Federal Deposit Insurance Corporation. For example, commercial banks are given access to the Federal Reserve discount window. Deposits at many financial institutions are insured. Financial institutions have assigned inspectors, many of whom work on-site at the institution. In the aftermath of the financial crisis, regulators became counterparties who purchased various financial assets using the Maiden Lane vehicles; they also played a significant role in bank mergers (Davidoff Solomon and

Zaring 2008). Indeed, large banks arguably play a macroeconomic role, including a role in the generation, and potentially contraction, of money supply (Ricks 2016). Finally, bank directors in particular already are held to significantly higher standards than nonfinancial institution directors: According to the OCC, effective risk management requires multiple lines of defense and involves much more than simply setting up a monitoring system.[9] Likewise, the Federal Reserve sets forth duties and responsibilities that recognize the unique role played by directors of regulated financial institutions. The Federal Reserve Commercial Bank Examination Manual states: "Directors who fail to discharge their duties completely or who are negligent in protecting the interests of depositors or shareholders may be subject to removal from office, criminal prosecution, civil money penalties imposed by bank regulators, and civil liability."[10] In addition, nonbank firms, such as insurance companies, can face similar regulatory scrutiny.

Perhaps the easiest way to illustrate the differences between the issues that arise with financial risk, as opposed to generalized business risk, is to consider *Caremark* itself. Recall that Caremark was a health care company. Its businesses included the marketing of prescription drugs. The complaint in *Caremark* arose out of a 1994 federal indictment alleging that Caremark and two of its employees had violated a law prohibiting health care providers from paying doctors to induce the referral of Medicare or Medicaid patients. The indictment alleged that the employees had paid a doctor over $1.1 million to distribute Protropin, a human growth hormone drug marketed by Caremark. (The complaints ultimately referenced later similar indictments as well.)

In 1994, Caremark's board had three committees: audit, nominating, and compensation. Its audit committee had limited responsibilities and was not explicitly charged with risk management. Indeed, even the audit committee duties concerning internal controls were limited: merely "to consider the adequacy of the accounting and internal control systems."[11] Moreover, although Caremark had sizable retail operations—it was among the top ten drug store chains in the United States by various measures, with 1,137 pharmacies—its business was relatively straightforward. Caremark's Form 10-K filing for 1994 was eighty-five pages, but that relatively slim volume was padded with several dozen pages of documents such as bylaws and retirement agreements. Caremark's financial statements were straightforward: The company had little debt, no derivatives, and minimal descriptions in its financial and accounting footnotes. Caremark's entire Management's Discussion and Analysis of Financial Condition and Results of Operations was less than four pages.[12]

In terms of the factors described above, moral hazard and leverage were largely absent at Caremark. Caremark's regulatory burdens were far less than those facing firms with significant exposure to financial risk, and Caremark was subject to far less regulatory scrutiny. Caremark faced challenges from agency costs and information asymmetry, but those challenges were comparable to those facing firms of similar size in other industries. Accordingly, with respect to board oversight, unless the board was aware of specific agency cost or information asymmetry challenges concerning prescription drugs, the policy of deference in *Caremark* made economic and legal sense. Boards cannot be expected to eliminate agency costs and information asymmetry, so there is a strong rationale for deference to board oversight, provided that directors have implemented a reasonable monitoring system.

In addition, imposing a heightened oversight duty on directors in a Caremark-like situation might both deter qualified people from serving as directors and disincentivize good performance by directors who choose to serve. As Chancellor Allen concluded, "a demanding test of liability in the oversight context is probably beneficial to corporate shareholders as a class, as it is in the board decision context, since it makes board service by qualified persons more likely, while continuing to act as a stimulus to good faith performance of duty by such directors."[13]

In contrast, holding directors of a firm with significant exposure to financial risk to a heightened oversight standard in contexts where the above factors are present would not likely deter or disincentivize directors. Instead, heightened scrutiny would merely make corporate law consistent with the other regulatory regimes and challenges facing the board. In addition, to the extent corporate law has some comparative advantage over other regulatory regimes, because of the advantages of private enforcement and ordering, it would be preferable to include corporate law among the menu of options in cases involving financial risk. In any event, heightened oversight duties for directors of firms with significant exposure to financial risk might not substantively impact their behavior, given the scrutiny already arising from other legal requirements, including regulatory and reputational risk arising from government prosecution and federal securities fraud class actions. As Cox and Thomas (2016) argue, federal securities fraud class actions in particular are evolving in various ways as substitute governance mechanisms to address managerial agency costs.[14]

As Chancellor Allen made clear in *Caremark*, "only a sustained or systematic failure of the board to exercise oversight—such as an utter failure to attempt to assure a reasonable information and reporting system exists—will establish the lack of good faith that is a necessary condition to liability."[15] Chancellor Allen's statement of the relevant factor—a "sustained or systematic failure of the board to exercise oversight"—was based in part on the context of that dispute. In other words, the application of his language varies depending on the context and type of risk. Specifically, what is "reasonable" depends on context, and my argument is that what constitutes the existence of "a reasonable information and reporting system" should be different for financial risk than for generalized business risk. A firm with significant exposure to financial risk that merely set up a monitoring system but did not address other granular aspects of risk management arguably could be exercising less oversight than a firm without such financial risk exposure that did not set up a monitoring system at all.

Citigroup

Citigroup involved allegations of board oversight failures with $55 billion of financial risk exposure related to subprime mortgage loans. The risk involved second-order exposure to mortgage loans, not through Citigroup's ownership of the loans themselves but through derivative securities based on those loans. In particular, Citigroup experienced substantial losses on super-senior positions in synthetic collateralized debt obligations and liquidity puts related to some collateralized debt obligations.

The central problem with the complaint in *Citigroup* was that it did not allege any facts to support a conclusion that the board failed in its oversight responsibilities with respect to these risks. As Chancellor Chandler noted, "plaintiffs' allegations do not even specify how the board's oversight mechanisms were inadequate or how the director defendants knew of these inadequacies and consciously ignored them"; instead, the *Citigroup* complaint contained "little more than portions of public documents that reflected the worsening conditions in the subprime mortgage market and in the economy generally."[16]

In *Citigroup*, Chancellor Chandler applied the same *Caremark* standard discussed above, as approved by the Delaware Supreme Court in *Stone v. Ritter* (which held that the framework for assessing director oversight liability is embedded in the fiduciary duty of loyalty and is based on the concept of good faith).[17] My analysis here would not require changing one word of Chancellor Chandler's formulation of board oversight duties, or even his emphasis: "to establish oversight liability, plaintiff must show that the directors *knew* they were not discharging their fiduciary obligations or that the directors demonstrated a *conscious* disregard for their responsibilities such as by failing to act in the face of a known duty to act. The test is rooted in concepts of bad faith; indeed, a showing of bad faith is a *necessary condition* to director oversight liability."[18]

Conclusions about the key terms in Chancellor Chandler's formulation obviously depend on context. For example, consider inferences about director mental states based on the facts alleged in a complaint. In cases where knowledge is inferred based on circumstantial evidence, the differences between allegations related to financial risk, as opposed to generalized business risk, can be significant. One might not expect that the directors at Gibson Greetings, or even at Procter & Gamble, would have *known* they were not discharging their obligations if they had reviewed the terms of a massive and complex interest rate swap with Bankers Trust during the 1990s (Partnoy 2009, 49–61). But if a board had reviewed those terms, then or now, or was aware of the firm's significant exposure to financial risk more generally, it would be more reasonable to assume the board *knew* or *should have known* particular facts. Moreover, given the sophisticated and comprehensive nature of many financial risk management systems, one might infer board knowledge of particularly large risks, depending on the facts.

Suppose the complaint in *Citigroup* had focused not on newspaper articles and other public warnings but on nonpublic information the board learned from Citigroup's management. For example, the Financial Crisis Inquiry Commission (FCIC) investigation of Citigroup found that at least some directors were aware of Citigroup's $55 billion of super-senior exposure by late summer 2007. Staff notes from the FCIC indicate that "based on FCIC interviews and documents obtained during our investigation, it is clear that CEO Chuck Prince and Robert Rubin . . . knew this information"; the notes suggest that Prince and Rubin knew these details "no later than September 9, 2007."[19] If the allegations had been that a majority of directors had known such facts, perhaps much earlier,

Citigroup might have been decided differently. (Citigroup officials represented during a October 15, 2007, analyst call that its subprime exposure was just $13 billion.)

Alternatively, suppose the complaint had alleged that Citigroup's board policy was that it would be informed about any positions with an aggregate notional amount or value-at-risk measure in excess of a particular value. Given the differences between firms that have significant exposure to financial risk and firms that do not, it might be reasonable to infer that directors who were informed about a $55 billion notional exposure to super-senior and liquidity put positions based on subprime mortgage-backed collateralized debt obligations but did nothing in response had consciously disregarded risks.

My purpose in raising these hypotheticals is not to relitigate *Citigroup* but rather to argue that the decision left room for board oversight allegations related to financial risk to survive a motion to dismiss, depending on the context. To reiterate, Chancellor Chandler stated that it might be possible for plaintiffs to prevail on claims related to business risks "under some set of facts."[20] Indeed, it is worth remembering that *Caremark* included just such an invitation to future claims as well, noting that the board's oversight responsibilities included an obligation to ensure that "information and reporting systems exist in the organization that are reasonably designed to provide to senior management and to the board itself timely, accurate information sufficient to allow management and the board, each within its scope, to reach informed judgments concerning both the corporation's compliance with law and its business performance."[21]

Would a reporting system be "reasonably designed" to permit the board to reach informed judgments if it did not elevate to the board information about financial risk positions with $55 billion of exposure to complex derivatives? Obviously, failing to implement *any* information or reporting system or controls would be an oversight problem for a board under Delaware law. But no board of a firm with significant exposure to financial risk would ever be in such a situation; every such institution has some information or reporting system and some controls. The question in *Caremark* is about the *design* of the system, not merely its existence. The "reasonably designed" question remains open.

What constitutes a red flag in financial risk cases also can vary, depending on context. Suppose the allegations in *Citigroup* had included facts showing that the board was aware of the increasing notional size of its super-senior exposure in 2006. That, on its own, might constitute a red flag. In other words, what directors *know* and what would count as a *conscious disregard for their responsibilities* or *bad faith* with financial risk should differ from what these terms mean with business risk generally.

Given the complexity of Citigroup's business, one might have expected at least some mention of super-senior and liquidity put exposure at the board level before late 2007. Indeed, the absence of facts suggesting any discussion of such exposure at the board level was striking. However, the complaint included no allegations that the board was aware of the increasing notional size or risks associated with these areas. There were no allegations of facts supporting a conclusion that the board's approach to risk management of these areas was flawed. There were no allegations that directors were even aware that these areas were generating abnormally large returns or profits. There were no allegations that directors received information from internal reports indicating that these areas had changed from low-risk hedging to high-risk proprietary trading. There certainly were no allegations that the board had received warnings from regulators about these particular areas. (Spoiler alert: All of the above facts in this paragraph were alleged in *JPMorgan*.)

It might not have been possible for the plaintiffs in *Citigroup* to gather sufficient information to support the above conclusions, at least not immediately. In that event, it might have been a better strategy for plaintiffs to wait for facts to arise from government investigations instead of rushing to court. It is notable that Citigroup settled related securities fraud class action litigation, which proceeded at a more deliberate pace and included a wider scope of factual allegations, for $590 million.[22] Alternatively, perhaps there were no facts to support a claim of board oversight failure in *Citigroup*, because Citigroup's risk management systems were reasonable but nevertheless failed to elevate any such information to the level of the board or senior management. In any event, *Citigroup* left room for allegations of board oversight failure with respect to financial risk, depending on the facts.

JPMorgan

And then there was the London Whale.

Prior to *JPMorgan*, it remained unclear how *Citigroup* would apply to allegations of director oversight failure based on substantially stronger allegations.[23] *Goldman Sachs*, another business risk case, involved allegations that the board put in place compensation practices that incentivized risky behavior and that the board therefore should have overseen the risky practices it incentivized.[24] Vice Chancellor Glasscock determined that, to the extent there was a duty to monitor business risk, it was not violated in *Goldman*. Compensation practices alone did not establish oversight failure, but perhaps other allegations would.

Unlike the claims in *Citigroup* or *Goldman*, the complaint in *JPMorgan* was based on a wide-ranging factual investigation by the US Senate Permanent Subcommittee on Investigations. The Permanent Subcommittee Report included numerous details about JPMorgan's risk management failures, including oversight failures at the board level.[25]

Two legal scholars have written excellent articles discussing the London Whale events. Sale (2014) argues that the episode and JPMorgan's response are powerful examples for exploring the theory of "publicness." Fisch (2015) cites the London Whale episode as an illustration of the potential limitations of shareholder empowerment and the risk that it will foster excessive risk taking. In addition, Zeissler, Ikeda, and Metrick (2015) provide a series of useful business school case studies about the London Whale.

However, the academic literature has not yet addressed the shareholder derivative case in *JPMorgan*. That case was brought under Delaware law, but in federal court in the Southern District of New York, before the Honorable George B. Daniels. As noted above, in a thirteen-page order, Judge Daniels dismissed the London Whale derivative claims with prejudice. In a subsequent four-page order, he also rejected a motion for reconsideration based on new evidence that arose from several regulatory settlements by JPMorgan. (In a companion case to *JPMorgan*, Vice Chancellor Glasscock did not reach the merits, because he found that collateral estoppel applied with respect to the previous New York adjudication.[26])

The claims in *JPMorgan* were focused on the chief investment office (CIO), which managed as much as $350 billion in assets until the $6 billion London Whale losses in 2012. The losses involved complex credit derivatives based on credit indices. The central claim in the complaint was that the JPMorgan board knew or should have known about the risks posed by the CIO but engaged in sustained and systematic failures to oversee those risks. Unlike the complaint in *Citigroup*, the complaint in *JPMorgan* pleaded facts demonstrating that the board had been warned on several occasions about specific problems and risks related to derivatives trading at the CIO. The facts that follow are from the *JPMorgan* complaint.[27]

The *JPMorgan* complaint alleged that in 2006—six years before the London Whale losses—the JPMorgan board became aware that the CIO had shifted away from its previously conservative, low-risk hedging strategy to trading in synthetic credit derivatives. This fact was significant, because the directors knew from their professional experience and from JPMorgan's involvement in previous scandals that trading in such instruments could pose substantial and devastating risks to the firm.

Then, according to the complaint, in 2007, the board learned that an internal JPMorgan audit had labeled these credit derivatives positions "proprietary"—as opposed to "hedging"—and also found multiple "calculation errors." By 2008, the board learned that the increasingly risky trades were held in an account known as the "synthetic credit portfolio," or SCP. According to the complaint, the board was aware of the SCP's high and volatile profits: $1 billion in 2009 alone. Moreover, the complaint alleged that, as of December 2010, the board was aware of substantial increases in the risk metrics for the CIO, including value at risk (VaR), as well as the fact that the CIO had generated a total of $2.8 billion in "economic value" and annual returns of 100%. According to the complaint, "no board member questioned how a supposed hedging strategy could generate such outsized annual returns. Nor did any Board member implement or even suggest an appropriate risk management approach that would be commensurate with a highly risky strategy that was generating 100% annual returns."[28]

The complaint's allegations about financial risk limits were specific. Starting as early as March 18, 2011, the entire board had received a series of letters from a major JPMorgan shareholder, CtW Investment Group, explaining concerns about JPMorgan's approach to monitoring risk limits. The complaint described the role of "the VaR limit, the Credit Spread Widening 01 ('CS01') limit, the Credit Spread Widening 10% ('CSW10%') limit, stress loss limits, stop loss advisories, and, more generally, the Comprehensive Risk Measure, or CRM" and the fact that directors were not only aware of the importance of closely monitoring these measures but had been involved in periodic review of and changes in risk limits.[29] These were not ordinary directors monitoring ordinary business risk: They had unique knowledge and expertise, given their experience with JPMorgan's role as the largest participant in the credit derivatives market and JPMorgan's role in various derivatives problems, including Long-Term Capital Management, Enron, and the recent financial crisis. No similar allegations were present in *Citigroup* or *Goldman Sachs*.

The *JPMorgan* complaint also alleged that in 2010 the board was informed that JPMorgan's primary regulator, the OCC, had issued a "Report on Examination" stating that the CIO lacked basic risk management functions such as a "documented methodology" or "clear record of decisions" underlying its increasingly risky trades.[30] This allegation was not about public information, as was alleged in *Citigroup*, but was a nonpublic report from a regulator, with specific findings about financial risk management failures.

The complaint's allegations further documented the board's knowledge and approval, through 2011, of the skyrocketing notional value of the SCP's derivatives positions. During 2011 alone, the notional value of the SCP's derivatives positions increased from $4 billion to $51 billion. Moreover, notwithstanding these substantial new financial risks, as of December 2011, the SCP's profits were essentially flat for the year, a notable red flag given the increasing notional value Figure 6.1, depicting the quarterly growth in the SCP, in billions of dollars, is from the Senate Permanent Subcommittee on Investigations; it is worth a thousand words.

The complaint further alleged facts supporting an inference of knowledge by the JPMorgan directors. Inferences of knowledge are an area where understanding how financial risk differs from generalized business risk is particularly important. Given the massive increases in the SCP's positions and profits, it would be reasonable to assume that a well-functioning board would have asked questions and received information about that increase.

Facts that the JPMorgan board allegedly "should have known" include the following. In September 2011, the CIO began shorting tranches of the CDX.NA.HY, a complex credit index, effectively betting that several high-risk companies would declare bankruptcy before the position expired on December 20, 2011. To offset this short position, the CIO also bought a long position in the CDX.NA.IG9, which tracked lower-risk companies.

Likewise, the complaint alleged should-have-known facts about a surprisingly large short-term credit default swap gamble by the CIO in 2011: that American Airlines would declare bankruptcy. Fortunately for

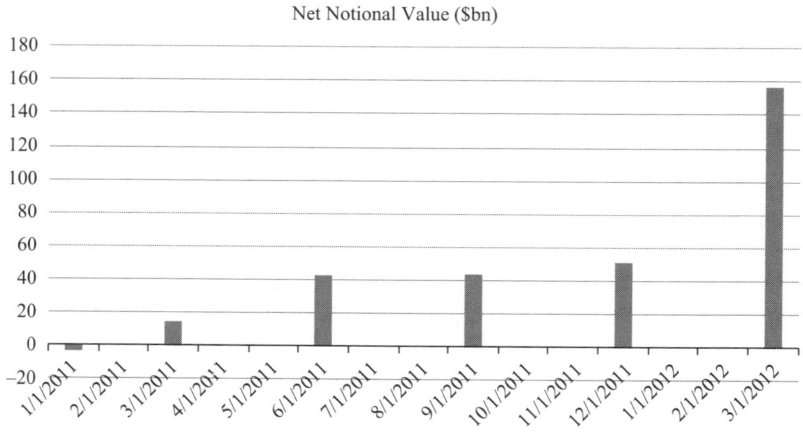

FIGURE 6.1. US Senate, Exhibit 15.

JPMorgan (though not for American Airlines), the CIO won this bet at the eleventh hour, in December 2011. The American Airlines trade was outright speculation, not a hedge. Nearly all of the SCP's $453 million of 2011 revenue came from that one risky, proprietary bet. Overall, the CIO contributed 8 percent of JPMorgan's net income for 2011, a substantial amount.

The complaint also described an early 2012 CIO bet in precisely the opposite direction, against the bankruptcy of Eastman Kodak. When Eastman Kodak filed for bankruptcy on January 19, 2012, the CIO suffered an estimated $50 million loss. As the complaint alleged: "The fact that the CIO placed two large and complex bets in opposite directions on whether a single company would go bankrupt, all within a matter of weeks, demonstrates that the CIO was not engaged in conservative trading or hedging in its synthetic credit derivatives positions. Instead, it was running a risky, proprietary trading operation, like a gambler who first bets that a roulette ball will land on a red number, and then quickly switches to a bet on black."[31]

The facts about these particular trades in the *JPMorgan* complaint are should-have-known allegations. How should they be assessed? On one hand, plaintiffs are required to plead facts with particularity, and there were no facts directly showing the board was aware of these trades. On the other hand, inferences can be drawn from circumstantial facts. In essence, the *JPMorgan* complaint included two alternative sets of allegations:

(1) to the extent JPMorgan had "a reasonable information and reporting system," the board must have known the alleged facts, or (2) JPMorgan did not have a "reasonable information and reporting system."

The complaint included some facts supporting alternative 2. Most strikingly, although JPMorgan's risk management framework provided for a CIO chief risk officer, from the time the CIO first began trading complex synthetic credit derivatives in 2006 until January 2012, the position was vacant. According to the complaint, "[t]he Board ultimately was responsible for risk management, but it delegated that responsibility to an empty seat."[32]

In addition, the complaint alleged that the board encouraged the CIO's proprietary trades by rewarding the CIO's traders for taking on increasing risks: The CIO's traders were among the highest-paid employees at JPMorgan (the top CIO managers made more than $10 million in 2011). Although the court in *Goldman Sachs* rejected such a compensation-focused claim, the *JPMorgan* complaint included greater specificity and was focused not on compensation incentives generally throughout the firm but on the board's knowledge of very high payments to a handful of employees in a supposedly low-risk part of the firm.

The complaint also alleged that the CIO breached its risk limits more than 330 times during the first four months of 2012, beginning on January 16, 2012, when the CIO's position caused the entire firm to breach its risk limits. The board ultimately became aware of these breaches, although the timing was not clear. The complaint alleged that senior managers encouraged risk taking by allowing the CIO to start using new mathematical models to calculate risk in a way that made it appear the CIO's risks had declined when in fact they were increasing. Again, it was unclear when the board learned of this approach. The complaint allegations were that the board "should have known."

Finally, the complaint included several allegations about lack of independence, including allegations that a majority of directors had extensive personal loans, extensions of credit, interlocking directorates, or other conflicted relationships. In addition, instead of appointing an independent investigator to report on the facts and recommend action, the board appointed Michael J. Cavanaugh, a longtime friend and colleague of Jamie Dimon, the JPMorgan chief executive officer. Cavanaugh was employed by JPMorgan as co-CEO of its investment bank and was the firm's former chief financial officer. (In addition, a board review committee prepared a separate, shorter report.)

As noted above, Judge Daniels dismissed the *JPMorgan* complaint. He addressed several of the complaint's allegations directly. He dismissed the audit report warning to the board about "proprietary position strategies" and the 2010 OCC warning letter to the board because they "did not put the Board on notice of facially improper business risks or illegal activity pertaining to JPMorgan's CIO."[33] He distinguished the *JPMorgan* complaint from complaints in cases such as *Abbott Labs*,[34] in which there were allegations of repeated violations of law and an extensive paper trail documenting the violations.[35]

Judge Daniels further found that "the Complaint lacks particularized allegations that a majority of the Director Defendants knew of (much less approved) the trades by the CIO personnel in London that ultimately resulted in the large losses in 2012."[36] That standard—knowledge and approval of trades by the board—is a high standard that likely would preclude the possibility of any case alleging board oversight failures regarding financial risk. Judge Daniels did not draw any inferences of knowledge based on circumstantial facts, as I suggested above might be done. He was not persuaded by the various should-have-known allegations. Judge Daniels also dismissed the notion that the directors faced a substantial likelihood of liability for securities fraud. (JPMorgan and its board ultimately settled the related securities fraud class action allegations for $150 million.)

On September 19, 2013, JPMorgan entered into settlement agreements and paid more than $1 billion in fines to resolve investigations by the Securities Exchange Commission, the OCC, the Board of Governors of the Federal Reserve System, and the UK Financial Conduct Authority. In many such settlements, institutions neither admit nor deny the regulators' factual findings. But JPMorgan admitted to certain facts and acknowledged that its conduct violated the securities laws. Plaintiffs moved for reconsideration of Judge Daniels's dismissal in light of these new facts, or alternatively for leave to amend.

Several individual members of the JPMorgan board signed the consent order with the OCC on behalf of the board, admitting that JPMorgan's oversight and governance of the CIO's credit derivatives trading were inadequate to protect it from material risks. These directors admitted specifically that:

> The credit derivatives trading activity constituted recklessly unsafe and unsound practices. (OCC at 4)

> The Bank's oversight and governance of the credit derivatives trading conducted by the CIO were inadequate to protect the Bank from material risks in those trading strategies, activities and positions. (OCC at 3)
>
> The Bank's risk management processes and procedures for the credit derivatives trading conducted by the CIO did not provide an adequate foundation to identify, understand, measure, monitor and control risk. (OCC at 3)
>
> The Bank's valuation control processes and procedures for the credit derivatives trading conducted by the CIO were insufficient to provide a rigorous and effective assessment of valuation. (OCC at 3)
>
> The Bank's internal audit processes and procedures related to the credit derivatives trading conducted by the CIO were not effective. (OCC at 3–4)
>
> The Bank's model risk management practices and procedures were inadequate to provide adequate controls over certain of the Bank's market risk and price risk models. (OCC at 4)
>
> The credit derivatives trading activity constituted recklessly unsafe and unsound practices, was part of a pattern of misconduct and resulted in more than minimal loss.[37] (OCC at 4)

In response to the plaintiffs' motion to reconsider based on this additional evidence, Judge Daniels issued a four-page order. Concerning the details about risk limit violations, Judge Daniels cited *Citigroup* in holding that "[p]laintiffs' allegations do not show that a majority of the Directors were aware of any particular limit excession, or that knowledge of these few risk limit excessions would have alerted the Directors to facially improper risk-taking or illegal activity in CIO."[38] He noted plaintiffs' reliance on the above settlements and then, citing nothing, held: "However, these settlements did not contain any admissions with respect to the Board's awareness of improper risk or illegal activity in CIO."[39]

My argument here is straightforward: *JPMorgan* was wrongly decided. Neither *Caremark* nor *Citigroup* requires that a majority of directors be aware of "particular" risk limit violations or be alerted to "facially improper risk-taking or illegal activity." The *JPMorgan* complaint included numerous particularized allegations that the board failed in its oversight duties, including an "utter failure to attempt to assure a reasonable information and reporting system exists"—the *Caremark* standard. That should have been enough to survive a motion to dismiss under *Caremark*.

If *JPMorgan* is an accurate statement of the law in Delaware, then there is no room in *Caremark* for board oversight claims related to financial risk. Given the importance of board oversight failures during the financial crisis, the lack of judicial response to the financial crisis in other cases (Zaring 2014), and the ongoing importance of financial risk generally, that should not be the law. The typical policy reasons for deference to board oversight are not present in cases such as *JPMorgan*. Denying a motion to dismiss in such a case would not deter people from serving on boards. Moreover, even if Delaware judges lack expertise about business risk generally, they are experienced and astute about assessing financial risk. And that distinction is crucial: Financial risk cases are different from generalized business risk cases, because financial risk is different.

In a case like *JPMorgan*, where the board had knowledge of massive and increasing risks associated with complex financial instruments and became aware of extensive risk limit and risk management violations (including failures documented by its primary regulator) and yet not only did nothing to address those failures but paid the leaders of the group eight-figure compensation—and then admitted to oversight failures after the fact in regulatory settlements—a complaint should at least survive a motion to dismiss.

Conclusion

Someday, perhaps soon, another plaintiff will bring a new board oversight case related to financial risk under Delaware law. The defendant firm in that case undoubtedly will have a financial risk management system; every firm with significant exposure to financial risk does. But my argument here is that the mere existence of a risk management system should not be dispositive, as it was in *JPMorgan*. Instead, both *Caremark* and *Citigroup* wisely left room for judges to hold directors accountable for sustained and systematic conscious financial risk oversight failures when they have not implemented "a reasonable information and reporting system."

Courts deciding future board oversight cases might look to banking law for analogous guidance about treating financial risk differently. In the past, banks were regularly subject to judicial second-guessing. In *Bailey v. O'Neil*, a 1909 Arkansas state case, the court found a bank's directors liable for lending nearly half of the bank's assets to one local businessman.[40] In *FDIC v. Robertson*, a 1989 Kansas federal case, the court found a bank director liable for lending money to a new business that had "no proven track record of profitability."[41] While these are not *Caremark* cases, they are illustrative examples of how some courts have shown less deference to directors when financial risk is central.

Some scholars have taken the position, consistent with these past cases, that bank directors and officers should be subject to heightened duties. McCoy (1996) argues that such heightened duties were warranted because of the incentives for bank managers to put deposits at risk by purchasing risky assets. Indeed, McCoy found that courts had second-guessed the decisions of bank directors in negligence cases for a century (McCoy 1996 at 1032). Likewise, Macey and O'Hara (2003, 92) describe the rationale for applying a duty of care to bank directors. They argue that "the scope of the duties and obligations of corporate officers and directors should be expanded in the case of banks." The key to these scholars' arguments is that the reason for holding bank directors and officers to heightened duties centers on the differences between banks and nonbank firms, particularly with respect to concerns about safety and soundness and protecting depositors (concerns that revolve around financial risk).

These scholarly views and these cases were not based on *Caremark*, and they were limited to banks. But it is worth recalling that *Litwin v. Allen*,[42] the classic New York derivative case on the duty of care not only involved bank directors, but J.P. Morgan & Co. itself. There is wisdom in noticing that the historic differences between banks and nonbanks resemble today's differences between financial risk and generalized business risk. The court in *JPMorgan* did not heed this wisdom, but perhaps a future court will.

In any event, financial risk is categorically different from business risk. That observation is not a snap reaction to the visceral impact of the financial crisis, which is almost a decade past at the time of this writing; the difference between financial risk and business risk has persisted through time. My central point in this chapter is that judges applying Delaware law should recognize this categorical difference.

Notes

Conflict disclosure: I was a consulting expert for plaintiffs' counsel in the *JPMorgan* derivative litigation, but I was not compensated in any way related to the writing of this chapter. I am grateful for comments on a draft from William Chandler, Steven Davidoff Solomon, Jill Fisch, Sean Griffith, Hillary Sale, Randall Thomas, and Robert Thompson.

1. *In re* Caremark Int'l Derivative Litigation, 698 A.2d 959 (Del. Ch. 1996).

2. *In re* Citigroup Inc. Shareholder Derivative Litigation, 964 A.2d 106 (Del. Ch. 2009). In that case, Chancellor Chandler dismissed all claims for failure to plead demand futility pursuant to Delaware Court of Chancery Rule 23.1, except for one count related to waste arising from the board's approval of a November 4, 2007, letter agreement awarding $68 million to Charles Prince upon his departure as Citigroup chief executive officer.

3. *In re* JPMorgan Chase & Co. Derivative Litigation, 12 Civ. 03878 (S.D.N.Y. Mar. 14, 2014). In a later order, Judge Daniels denied a motion to reconsider. *See In re* JPMorgan Chase & Co. Derivative Litigation, 12 Civ. 03878 (S.D.N.Y. Jul. 30, 2014) (hereafter cited as *JPMorgan Reconsideration*).

4. *See In re* Appraisal of Dell, C.A. No. 9322-VCL (Del. Ch. May 31, 2016) (Vice Chancellor Laster independently deriving fair value of Dell using a discounted cash flow analysis); *In re* ISN Software Corp. Appraisal Litigation, C.A. No. 8388-VCG (Del. Ch. Aug. 11, 2016) (Vice Chancellor Glasscock reaching an independent discounted cash flow valuation).

5. For example, Vice Chancellor Glasscock's description of the "London Whale" episode was far more nuanced and sophisticated than the description of that episode in *JPMorgan*, even though Vice Chancellor Glasscock did not even reach the ultimate question about demand futility in that case. *See* Asbestos Workers Local 42 Pension Fund v. Bammann, C.A. No. 9772-VCG at 9–29 (Del. Ch. May 22, 2015).

6. *See* RBC Capital Markets, LLC v. Jervis, 129 A.3d 816 (Del. 2015) (affirming $76 million verdict against Rural/Metro Corporation adviser, RBC).

7. Vice Chancellor Glasscock noted in Asbestos Workers Local 42 Pension Fund v. Bammann that "[b]usiness risk is the very stuff of which corporate decisions are constituted." *Asbestos Workers Local 42 v. Bammann* at 35. My argument is that financial risk can be of very different stuff than generalized business risk and, accordingly, should be assessed differently under *Caremark*. Because of the differences related to financial risk, the policy justification for deference to the business judgment of the board is less compelling.

8. *Citigroup* at 126.

9. *See* Office of the Comptroller of the Currency, The Director's Book: Role

of Directors for National Banks and Federal Savings Associations, July 2016, at 19, 49–58.

10. Federal Reserve Commercial Bank Examination Manual, "Duties and Responsibilities of Directors," Apr. 2013, at 1.

11. Caremark Def14A, Apr. 11, 1995, 13.

12. *See* Caremark, Form 10-K, Mar. 29, 1995, 30–33.

13. *Caremark.*

14. Thompson and Sale (2003) made this point more generally with respect to the idea of federal law as corporate governance.

15. *In re* Caremark Int'l Derivative Litigation, 698 A.2d 959, 971 (Del. Ch. 1996).

16. *Citigroup* at 128.

17. *Stone v. Ritter*, 911 A.2d 362, 370 (Del. 2006).

18. *Citigroup.*

19. The Financial Crisis Inquiry Report: Final Report of the National Commission on the Causes of the Financial and Economic Crisis in the United States (2010):1–633.

20. *Citigroup* at 126.

21. *Caremark.*

22. Nate Raymond & Bernard Vaughan, Judge Approves Citigroup $590 Million Settlement, Reuters, Aug. 1, 2013, at https://www.reuters.com/article/us-citigroup-settlement/judge-approves-citigroup-590-million-settlement-idUSBRE9700T420130801.

23. Just two weeks before *Citigroup*, then Vice Chancellor Strine had refused to dismiss the claims in *AIG v. Greenberg*, finding that two individual defendants who were "top dogs" in a "criminal organization" knowingly tolerated inadequate internal controls and knowingly failed to monitor their subordinates' compliance with legal duties. American International Group v. Greenberg, 965 A.2d 763, 796–99 (Del. Ch. 2009). The allegations in *AIG* were obviously much stronger, but the claims were markedly different.

24. *In re* Goldman Sachs Group Inc. Shareholder Litigation, No. 5215-VCG, 2011 WL 4826104 at *1, 23 (Del. Ch. Oct. 12, 2011).

25. US Senate Permanent Subcommittee on Investigations, "JPMorgan Chase Whale Trades: A Case History of Derivatives Risks and Abuses," Mar. 26, 2013.

26. *Asbestos Workers Local 42 v. Bammann.*

27. Second Amended Verified Shareholder Derivative Complaint for Breach of Fiduciary Duty, Unjust Enrichment, and Corporate Waste, In re JPMorgan Chase & Co. Derivative Litigation, No. 1:12-cv-03878-GBD, Apr. 25, 2013 (hereafter cited as *JPMorgan Complaint*).

28. *JPMorgan Complaint* at 45–46.

29. *Id.* at 29–32.

30. *JPMorgan*.
31. *Id.* at 48.
32. *Id.* at 37.
33. *JPMorgan* at 9.
34. In re: Abbott Lab. Derivative Shareholders Litigation, 325 F.3d 795 (7th Cir. 2003).
35. *JPMorgan* at 9 n.6.
36. *JPMorgan* at 10.
37. *See* Consent Order for a Civil Money Penalty, In the Matter of: JPMorgan Chase Bank, N.A., AA-EC-2013-75, Sep. 18, 2013, at 3–4.
38. *JPMorgan Reconsideration* at 3.
39. *JPMorgan Reconsideration* at 4.
40. Bailey v. O'Neil, 122 S.W. 503, 505–6 (Ark. 1909).
41. FDIC v. Robertson, No. 87-2623-S, 1989 U.S. Dist. LEXIS 9292 at *17 (D. Kan. July 24, 1989).
42. Litwin v. Allen, N.Y. Sup. Ct., 25 N.Y. S.2d 667 (1940).

References

Armour, John, and Jeffrey N. Gordon, 2014, "Systemic Harms and Shareholder Value," *Journal of Legal Analysis* 6:35–85.

Bainbridge, Stephen M., 2009, "*Caremark* and Enterprise Risk Management," *Journal of Corporation Law* 34:967–90.

Cox, James D., and Randall S. Thomas, 2016, "Corporate Darwinism: Disciplining Managers in a World with Weak Shareholder Litigation," *North Carolina Law Review* 95:19–65.

Davidoff Solomon, Steven M., and David Zaring, 2008, "Regulation by Deal: The Government's Response to the Financial Crisis," *Administrative Law Review* 61:463–541.

Egan, Mark, Gregor Matvos, and Amit Seru, 2016, "The Market for Financial Advisor Misconduct," working paper.

Fisch, Jill E., 2015, "The Mess at Morgan: Risk, Incentives and Shareholder Empowerment," *University of Cincinnati Law Review* 83:651–84.

Federal Reserve, 2013, Commercial Bank Examination Manual, "Duties and Responsibilities of Directors," 1–8.

Gabriel Stephen C., and C. B. Baker, 1980, "Concepts of Business and Financial Risk," *American Journal of Agricultural Economics* 62:560–64.

Gevurtz, Franklin A., 2010, "The Role of Corporate Law in Preventing a Financial Crisis: Reflections on In re Citigroup Inc. Shareholder Derivative Litigation," *Pacific McGeorge Global Business and Development Law Journal* 23:113–56.

Hill, Claire, and Brett McDonnell, 2013, "Reconsidering Board Oversight Duties after the Financial Crisis," *University of Illinois Law Review* 2013:859–79.

Jones, Renee M., and Michelle Welsh, 2012, "Toward a Public Enforcement Model for a Directors' Duty of Oversight," *Vanderbilt Journal of Transnational Law* 45:343–403.

Macey, Jonathan A., and Maureen O'Hara, 2003, "The Corporate Governance of Banks," *Economic Policy Review* 9:91–107.

McCoy, Patricia A., 1996, "A Political Economy of the Business Judgment Rule in Banking: Implications for Corporate Law," *Case Western Law Review* 47:1–80.

Miller, Robert T., 2010, "Oversight Liability for Risk-Management Failures at Financial Firms," *Southern California Law Review* 84:47–123.

Orenstein, Alec. 2011, "A Modified *Caremark* Standard to Protect Shareholders of Financial Firms from Poor Risk Management," *New York University Law Review* 86:766–803.

Pan, Eric J., 2009/2010, "A Board's Duty to Monitor," *New York Law School Law Review* 54:717–40.

Partnoy, Frank, 2009, *Infectious Greed: How Deceit and Risk Corrupted the Financial Markets* (PublicAffairs).

Partnoy, Frank. 2015, "Financial Systems, Crises, and Regulation," in *Oxford Handbook of Financial Regulation*, edited by Niamh Moloney, Eilis Ferran, and Jennifer Payne (Oxford University Press), 69–91.

Partnoy, Frank, and Jesse Eisinger, 2013, "What's Inside America's Banks," *The Atlantic*, January/February, 1–18.

Ricks, Morgan, 2016, *The Money Problem: Rethinking Financial Regulation* (University of Chicago Press).

Sale, Hillary A., 2014, "J.P. Morgan: An Anatomy of Corporate Publicness," *Brooklyn Law Review* 79:1629–55.

Thompson, Robert B., and Hillary A. Sale, 2003, "Securities Fraud as Corporate Governance: Reflections upon Federalism," *Vanderbilt Law Review* 56:859–910.

Tsuk Mitchell, Dalia, 2015, "The Import of History to Corporate Law," *Saint Louis University Law Journal* 59:683–700.

Zaring, David, 2014, "Litigating the Financial Crisis," *Virginia Law Review* 100:1405–81.

Zeissler, Arwin G., Daisuke Ikeda, and Andrew Metrick, 2015, "JPMorgan Chase London Whale," Yale Program on Financial Stability Case Study 2014-2A-V1:1–19.

CHAPTER SEVEN

Hedge Fund Activism, Poison Pills, and the Jurisprudence of Threat

William W. Bratton

Introduction

Hedge fund activism is to corporate law's early twenty-first century what the hostile takeover was to its late twentieth century. Like the hostile takeover, activism threatens incumbent managers and disrupts their business plans by successfully appealing to the shareholders' interest in immediate returns. Like the hostile takeover, activism occupies center stage in corporate law policy discussions, posing a choice between short-term gain and long-term investment. But there is a glaring point of distinction. Unlike the hostile takeover, activism has precipitated no significant changes in corporate law. Where the hostile takeover triggered structural changes in state corporate codes and the federal securities laws along with a root-and-branch reconfiguration of fiduciary duty, hedge fund activism largely leaves corporate law where it found it. The activists manage to play hostilely without bumping up against the defensive barriers erected in the late twentieth-century transformation of corporate law because they avoid attempting to take control. At the same time, law reform initiatives designed to constrain the new mode of hostile intervention have failed to gain traction.

There is but a single high-profile case in which twentieth-century antitakeover law has come to bear on a management defense against a twenty-first-century activist challenge: the Delaware Court of Chancery's decision in *Third Point LLC v. Ruprecht*,[1] better known as the

Sotheby's case. The board of directors of a target corporation, Sotheby's, lobbed a poison pill in the path of one of the more aggressive hedge funds, Third Point LLC, and its sharp-elbowed chief, Daniel Loeb. The pill had a low-threshold feature, capping a hostile challenger's block at 10 percent of outstanding shares rather than at the traditional 20 percent. It thereby disabled Third Point from enhancing its vote total in a short-slate proxy contest through additional purchases of target shares. The Chancery Court nonetheless sustained the pill under *Unocal v. Mesa Petroleum Co.*[2] The decision implicated an important policy question: whether a twentieth-century doctrine keyed to hostile takeovers and control transfers appropriately can be brought to bear in a twenty-first-century governance context in which the challenger eschews control transfer and instead makes aggressive use of the shareholder franchise.

Resolution of the issue entails evaluation of the gravity of two sets of threats, one at the doctrinal level and the other at the policy level. The doctrinal threats are exterior threats to corporate policy and effectiveness on which managers justify defensive tactics under *Unocal*. Because some threats have greater justificatory salience under *Unocal* than do others, a question arises as to the nature and characterization of the threats allegedly held out by activist intervention. The policy threats implicate the new balance of power between managers and shareholders. Hedge fund activism has operated as a catalyst that enables dispersed shareholders to surmount collective action problems so as to register preferences regarding corporate business plans in connection with voting on competing candidates for board seats. To the extent that managers wielding low-threshold poison pills disable activist challenges, the power balance could shift back in their favor, with potentially negative agency cost consequences.

This chapter appraises the threats. In regard to *Unocal*, it demonstrates a serious problem of fit. The most potent *Unocal* threats are those involving coercion of dispersed shareholders in connection with hostile tender offers or expropriation from dispersed shareholders by controlling blockholders. The threats, originally identified on 1980s control transfer fact patterns, show up only tangentially on the new fact patterns. To the extent that *Unocal* doctrine relies on the old threats in sustaining poison pills deployed against today's activists, it ends up as more of a formal rubber stamp than a substantive fiduciary inquiry.

The *Sotheby's* opinion, although for the most part staying inside the inherited framework of *Unocal* doctrine, does take a tentative step into the twenty-first century, suggesting that activists hold out a threat of "disproportionate influence," but without filling in any particulars about the influence's nature and negative effect. This chapter posits the missing details, conducting a thought experiment that reshapes and extends *Unocal* so that it provides a robust basis for sustaining management defense against activist hedge funds, even shielding poison pills with 5 percent triggers. The extension is radical. Up to now, *Unocal* has facilitated management actions that protect dispersed shareholders from being railroaded into selling the company for too little. Under the extension, *Unocal* would justify management actions that protect shareholders from the consequences of their own collective actions in casting uncoerced ballots at director elections. Many, perhaps most, observers would view the extension as a perversion of the governance system's heretofore jealous protection of the shareholder franchise to elect directors.

The chapter's refitted version of *Unocal* sharply poses the policy threat. Most observers would find the prospect of an easily justified 5 percent poison pill threatening. Indeed, they project that such a defense would inhibit activist intervention and thereby damage the corporate governance system. But the projection of harm rings hollow in the present posture of shareholder-manager politics. Even if structural changes inhibiting activism would in fact result in economic injury, no significant inhibition is likely to follow from judicial sanction of a 5 percent pill. A low-threshold pill deters activist block formation only to the extent that it is put in place in advance of the activist's appearance, so as to limit the activist block to 5 percent. A pill put in place after the activist passes the 5 percent level and makes its presence public comes too late, for so slow is the disclosure clock and so quick is the block accumulation process that the activist easily can hold 10 percent by the time the job gets done. These days few managers dare to promulgate such a "standing" pill in advance. So powerful have shareholders become in today's managerial cost-benefit calculus that the detriments of incurring the shareholders' wrath by traversing their governance preferences regarding charters and bylaws now outweigh a poison pill's insulating benefits.

Given that, it is worth asking whether 5 percent poison pills could provide policy benefits. The policy stakes are traversed in a debate in which activism is associated with value-destructive short-termism. The debate's participants argue back and forth based on assumed across-the-board tendencies. But questions about short-term value sacrifices cannot be resolved on an aggregate basis. It depends on the company. Some are appropriate targets for activist intervention, while others are not. This chapter suggests that company-by-company dialogue on the point would be good thing, exploring the possibility that a 5 percent standing pill could trigger useful information back to and between managers and institutional investors without simultaneously overdeterring activist intervention.

The next section assays the *Sotheby's* case. Then I situate *Unocal* threat doctrine in the context of hedge fund activism, showing a need for reformulation. This discussion is followed by a reformulation of *Unocal*, positing a theory supporting a poison pill with a 5 percent trigger. Finally, I consider the low-threshold pill's policy implications in the new world of empowered shareholders.

The Sotheby's Case

Third Point LLC v. Ruprecht denied a motion to enjoin deployment of a poison pill carefully tailored to target an activist hedge fund. The pill featured a two-tier trigger that sorted between passive and active blockholders.[3] Blockholders whose passive intentions were verified by a disclosure statement filed under a form 13G were capped at 20 percent of the stock, while an activist with aspirations to make changes at the company and so filing a form 13D under Rule 13d-1 faced a lower 10 percent cap on its block.[4] The drafting otherwise was scrupulous. The pill's duration was limited to a year. All cash, all shares tender offers were accepted,[5] showing that the board addressed only challenges in the activist hedge fund mode and did not seek to block a hostile control transfer on procedurally fair terms. Nor, as tends to be the case these days, was it a "standing" pill, put in place well in advance of a hedge fund challenge on a one-size-fits-all basis. It was instead promulgated by the target board after Third Point's campaign had been proceeding for months,[6] facilitating a situation-specific justification keyed to threats particular to Third Point.

The activist campaign was high-powered. At its commencement, a three-fund "wolf pack" demanded changes in Sotheby's business plan and governance arrangements, a demand backed up by a credible threat to launch a proxy fight for board seats. Third Point, which eventually accumulated 9.6 percent of the company's outstanding shares, took the lead, with Mercato (6.6 percent) and Trian (less than 5 percent) in tow.

Thus did the Sotheby's board already face a combined hostile block holding 20 percent before it promulgated its poison pill. The pill's bite lay in its containment of further stock acquisitions by Third Point, a bar that limited the fund's freedom either to add to its vote total by purchasing more shares in the heat of a close proxy contest or to campaign in concert with other hedge funds.

The litigation laid two new situations at the door of Delaware's poison pill jurisprudence. First, the 10 percent trigger amounted to a step-up in defensive intensity and, although not unprecedented in practice, had not been considered by a court. Poison pill drafters historically[7] had set the trigger applied to block accumulations at 20 percent, the rule-of-thumb magnitude thought to import sufficient influence to justify the attribution of "control block."[8] Second, never before had a hedge fund activist come to the Delaware Chancery Court attacking a pill deployed to inhibit a proxy contest.[9]

Even so, law sufficient to sustain the pill already was largely in place. Delaware parses review of defensive tactics into two categories. *Unocal* holds out the general rule, invalidating "preclusive" and "coercive" defenses on a per se basis, while subjecting all other management defenses to proportionality review, under which the measure must be reasonable in view of the threat posed.[10] A separate line of cases, grounded in *Blasius Industries, Inc. v. Atlas Corp.*,[11] applies to management actions primarily intended to interfere with or impede exercise of the shareholder franchise. These require a "compelling" justification, a standard unlikely to be met. Unsurprisingly, Third Point argued that a poison pill drafted with a discriminatory 10 percent trigger with a view to inhibit activist vote accumulation interfered with the franchise within *Blasius*.[12] But the cases already had restricted *Blasius* scrutiny to a small set of situations in which the defensive move has the effect of altogether precluding exercise of the franchise.[13] So long as the defense left the contestant free to put its candidates or proposition to the shareholders for an "effective" vote, the defense's effect of raising the bar to victory did not amount to "interference" within *Blasius*.[14] And nothing was preventing Third Point from conducting its proxy contest.

Meanwhile, the *Unocal* cases etched a profile of a threatening blockholder, the "creeping control" acquirer.[15] The "creeping" lies in the acquirer's gradual accumulation of a control block through open market stock purchases. By the time such a holder gets to 51 percent, the premium realizable in respect of a future control transfer appends to its block of stock rather than to the corporate entity and the shareholders as a group. The blockholder, who has not paid the selling shareholders a pro rata portion of control value in the course of its open market purchase program, effectively converts the premium potentially realized for the benefit of the shareholders as a group upon a sale of the whole. Such a block need not even amount to a majority stake, for the value of control begins to attach once the stake passes the 20 percent threshold. Thus do both the European Union and the United Kingdom require an accumulating blockholder to make an offer to buy 100 percent of the company's stock upon passing a 30 percent threshold.[16] Under the *Unocal* cases, a proxy challenger seeking less than a majority of board seats (a "short slate") and disavowing interest in control acquisition is nevertheless susceptible to a creeping control characterization to the extent the challenger can be shown to have either (1) made control acquisitions in the past implicating unequal outcomes or (2) made statements projecting a possible control transfer at the target, including a third-party merger.[17] Creeping control is thus a capacious category of threat.

Third Point and its principal, Daniel Loeb, perfectly fit the profile. In past activity, they had made acquisition bids for targets and negotiated defensive block repurchases by targets.[18] In present statements, Loeb had both discussed the possibility of pushing Sotheby's into a private equity buyout and projected that he would take operational control of the company and reorient its operations.[19] Potential damage to the business also was shown: Loeb's aggressive public statements were disturbing customer relationships in a heavily relational line of business.[20] It is hard to imagine an actor more ill suited to the role of plaintiff in a test case.

The Chancery Court, per Vice Chancellor Parsons, nonetheless characterized the case as close. The court inspected the pill as of two different dates, first upon promulgation prior to the commencement of the proxy contest and, second, at a later date in the midst of the solicitation process. The second look had been triggered by Third Point, which made a formal request to the Sotheby's board to waive the 10 percent threshold so as to permit it to buy up to 20 percent.[21] The court sustained creeping control as a validating threat only as of the earlier date. In the court's characterization, the promulgating board had faced a 20 percent wolf pack, the intentions of which could have included either control acquisition or a third-party control transfer.[22] As of the later date, however, the court held that a creeping control threat no longer was plausible. By then it was clear that the hostile attack devolved on a proxy contest for a few board seats with no control transfer in the offing.[23] Moreover, one of the Sotheby's directors, when asked on deposition what had motivated the board to refuse to waive the pill, said that minimizing the challenger's vote total was the prevailing concern.[24] Under *Unocal*, a primary motivation to retain one's position leads to prompt invalidation,[25] and it is one of the defending counsel's primary jobs to make sure that the board justifies its actions exclusively in terms of shareholder injury prevention. Such slips can be fatal.

But the Sotheby's board squeaked through, and Third Point's motion to enjoin the pill was denied for failure to make the requisite showing of a likelihood of success on the merits.[26] The Chancery Court devised two additional, albeit weaker, threat characterizations applicable on the later date. The first, "negative control," was relied upon as a basis for refusing the injunction: Even though Third Point could not be said to aspire to hold a control block, further acquisitions could import negative voting salience—a number of shares sufficient to veto a proposition subject to a supermajority vote.[27] The court added that, even if Third Point did not have enough shares to wield a unilateral negative block, moving up toward 20 percent could give it "disproportionate control and influence over major corporate decisions."[28] There was no further explication of what that meant.

Third Point lost the battle but not the war. Soon after the court refused the injunction, preliminary vote counts showed that Third Point was poised to win the proxy contest. The Sotheby's board cut its losses and settled, admitting Loeb and two of his nominees into the boardroom.[29]

Third Point also might have won the battle against the poison pill had the court analyzed the situation slightly differently. Previous cases had focused on creeping control. Once creeping control was off the table, alternative decisional possibilities opened up—most importantly, the option of giving decisive weight to the evidence concerning the motivation of the defending board. To the extent the Sotheby's directors were focused on the impending vote count, they arguably no longer lay in the zone of *Unocal* threat protection at all. It would have been a suitably narrow ground of decision. Alternatively, the court might have traveled the harder road and dismissed the secondary threats, negative control and disproportionate influence, as lacking in gravity.

But the court did not take that road, leaving us with two questions. The first involves the accuracy of the creeping control characterization in the activist context. The second question, which follows in the wake of a negative answer to the first, is whether activism otherwise holds out threats, however characterized, cognizable in *Unocal* contexts.

Hedge Fund Activism and Corporate Control

This section reconsiders *Unocal* and the creeping control threat in activist contexts. Stewart Gillan and Laura Starks have accurately defined shareholder activists as "investors, who dissatisfied with some aspect of the company's management or operations, try to bring about change within the company without a change in control."[30] Accordingly, one must massage the facts a little to support a creeping control characterization. Two factors have come to the fore: the wolf pack engagement pattern and the activists' interest in pushing their targets into third-party mergers. But the creeping control characterization remains problematic even given selective underscoring. There are three reasons for this: (1) Individual hedge funds almost never accumulate 20 percent; (2) wolf packs are not ubiquitous and tend to accumulate less than 20 percent, and (3) wolf packs that do accumulate a greater percentage result in a minority of cases and hold out no cognizable harm to shareholders. Control transfer by merger is a salient, but ancillary, possibility in the wake of activist intervention. When intervention does prompt a control transfer, the hedge fund is highly unlikely to be the acquiring party, and the proceeds of sale are shared pro rata with the shareholders as a group. It follows that the articulated basis for applying *Unocal* in activist contexts lacks substantial support in practice.

Share Accumulation

STAND-ALONE FUNDS. Hedge funds, even lead hedge funds, do not build control blocks. Only a handful of activist positions ever approach 20 percent. Boyson and Mooradian found a mean activist blockholding of 8.8 percent upon initial 13d-1 filing and a maximum accumulation mean holding of 12.4 percent.[31] Other studies offer a more granular picture. Brav, Jiang, Partnoy, and Thomas show, at the 75th percentile, an initial holding of 8.8 percent and a maximum holding of 13 percent. At the 95th percentile, they report an initial holding of 19.8 percent and a maximum holding of 25 percent.[32] More recently, Gantchev reports an initial filing maximum of 16 percent at the 95th percentile and a maximum holding of 18 percent[33]—that is, even the biggest accumulations by stand-alone funds fall short of 20 percent.

WOLF PACKS. Of course, even if stand-alone hedge funds almost never approach 20 percent, any threat still is magnified due to their tendency to attack in groups of two and three. Hedge fund wolf packs operate in the absence of formal agreements among their members, because formal agreement means a securities law "group" and enhances filing requirements.[34] Informal group activity nonetheless suffices for *Unocal* purposes—appropriately so, for consciously parallel courses of action are there for all to see.

There remains a question regarding the size and prevalence of group activity. The first sustained study, from Becht, Franks, Grant, and Wagner, appeared only recently.[35] Looking at 1,362 engagements, they find that 78.3 percent involve a stand-alone fund and 21.7 percent involve a wolf pack. Considering each target separately, they find that 88.2 percent faced a stand-alone fund while 11.8 percent faced a wolf pack.[36] The mean wolf pack stockholding is 13.4 percent compared with 8.3 percent for a stand-alone fund.[37] Group action does enhance influence. Given a wolf pack, the target's stock price rises 14 percent during the window period surrounding the activist's disclosure of its position compared with 6 percent for a stand-alone fund.[38] The probability of success is 78 percent with a wolf pack and 46 percent for an activist alone.[39]

The foregoing figures presuppose disclosure by each wolf pack member. But there are also silent fellow travelers who pile in when the lead fund discloses its holding but stay below the 5 percent reporting threshold. A recent study looks at share turnover at the time of lead fund disclosure and finds that trading volume is 325 percent above normal levels and then infers that 250 percent of the activity can be attributed to buyers other than the lead fund.[40] The study characterizes engagements in the top turnover quartile as wolf pack engagements and finds a 6 percent higher rate of success and a 9 percent higher rate of board seat acquisition for the subset.[41]

Wolf pack presence has been taken as the fact that validates a creeping control characterization of activism.[42] But what we see, in fact, is enhanced influence without control. Wolf packs matter because votes matter, and the objective continues to be minority board representation. While wolf pack formation makes victory more likely, it does not on average virtually assure activist success by trivializing the number of additional supporting shares needing to be solicited.[43] Given a mean holding of 13.4 percent, success still requires the support of a substantial number of passive shareholders, even assuming the presence of undisclosed fellow travelers.

MERGERS. Technically, a creeping control acquisition entails the accumulation and use of a control block with little or no sharing of the benefits of control with the noncontrolling shareholders.[44] There are a number of scenarios. A creeping controller can use its accumulated votes to take control of the board and then run the company, taking for itself the offices, compensation, and other spoils. To complete the game of exclusion, it can use its control power to cash out the minority in a later merger.[45] Alternatively, once in power, it can sell its control block to a third party, pocketing a premium price.[46]

None of these scenarios figures into the working picture of activism. The closest one gets is a case where an activist (or wolf pack) with a relatively large block successfully pushes a sale of the target to a third party. Any abuse lies in the activist's acquisition of shares prior to disclosing its own presence in a public filing. It thereby accumulates the block at a market price unreflective of the coming control transfer, in effect converting the later premium from the market sellers. Two questions follow. First, whether the scenario occurs frequently and, second, whether it is accurate to characterize it as wrongful conversion.

There is no question that activism prompts mergers. But different studies yield different figures. At the low end, Brav, Jiang, and Kim report a merger occurring in 12.2 percent of the cases in their database.[47] At the high end, Greenwood and Schor come in at 23 percent.[48] Becht, Franks, Grant, and Wagner fall between at 18.76 percent.[49] The largest and most recent study, from Boyson, Gantchev, and Shivdasani,[50] tends toward the high end. It shows a takeover bid occurring in 24 percent of the engagements—from third parties in 19.9 percent and from the activist itself in 3.4 percent.[51] A third-party bid is five times more likely to occur at an activist target than at a nontarget firm.[52] If the particular activist is categorized as aggressive, the probability of a bid is 29.0 percent; if the activist is categorized as experienced in causing mergers, the probability rises to 36.4 percent.[53] A bid also means significantly higher stock price returns from the engagement, with third-party bids offering larger premiums than those from activists.[54] Significantly, the stock price gain is shared pro rata.

The "victims" are those who sell to activist and wolf pack followers before and at the time the lead activist crosses the 5 percent reporting threshold. It appears that these sellers are noise-trading institutions making liquidity trades.[55] The sales are uncoerced and result from independent business decisions, often portfolio related. There is no loss, only an opportunity cost. Given widespread shareholder diversification, this opportunity cost is in the long run matched by a gain on a held investment in a different hedge fund target. There is no cognizable injury.

SUMMARY. There is a serious problem of fit between the classic creeping control picture of shareholder victimization and the ordinary incidents of activist intervention. Hedge funds almost never take control. Although intervention frequently results in a sale of control, the sale holds out a considerable upside for the target's other shareholders. The gains from sale are shared with the group as whole. And, of course, there is no sale in 76 percent (or more) of the cases. Any concerns about the premium paid when the activist itself bids can be dealt with under the separate line of fiduciary cases that begins with *Revlon, Inc. v. MacAndrews & Forbes Holdings, Inc.*[56] *Unocal*, in short, is being applied to sustain management defense against activist campaigns on a questionable basis that awkwardly cabins twenty-first-century hostile intervention in a twentieth-century mold.

Unocal and Activism Reconsidered

This section conducts a ground-up reconsideration of *Unocal* threats in the context of activist intervention. It suggests that the *Sotheby's* court's "disproportionate influence" notion can be amplified to fit the circumstances. The analysis takes corporate law into new territory. As restated, *Unocal* protects shareholder minorities from the business judgments of apparently unconflicted shareholder majorities, a reversal of the inherited conceptual framework.

The State of Play

The *Sotheby's* case stretches existing *Unocal* case law close to the breaking point. The court, once creeping control was off the table, was forced to improvise, formulating two new threats—negative control and disproportionate influence—in order to sustain the board's refusal to waive the pill.[57] The new threats hold out considerably less in the way of shareholder injury than would a genuine creeping control acquisition. The court made no attempt to warrant them otherwise, implying that low-threshold pills could be vulnerable under *Unocal* depending on a future case's particular facts. Meanwhile, there are companies implementing 10 percent and 15 percent standing pills that tend to include language calculated to pick up wolf pack formation—the pills apply to persons "acting in concert" or in "conscious parallelism" with a lead hedge fund.[58] Absent a lead activist with a clear creeping control profile like that of Third Point, these pills easily could fail inspection under a narrow reading of the *Sotheby's* opinion.

The poison pill drafter's holy grail, a 5 percent standing pill drafted for general application, thus seems unreachable. Coffee and Palia sensibly opine such a pill carries a cognizable risk of peremptory invalidation as "preclusive" within *Unocal*.[59] They nonetheless experiment with a justificatory strategy, positing a jump shift to a justification grounded in a public reporting benefit rather than in a threat to the target's business. They offer a 5.1 percent standing pill that would be triggered only if the purchaser failed to file a form 13D before purchasing stock in excess of the threshold.[60] That is, the activist could exceed a 5 percent holding only by making an immediate SEC filing upon reaching 5 percent and surrendering the option to continue to take advantage of Rule 13d-1's ten-day filing window to make further unreported stock purchases.[61] As a further modification designed to diminish the chance of invalidation, they suggest that this "window-closing pill" allow further acquisitions up to a 15 percent or 20 percent threshold in the event of timely filing.[62] The redirection of the justificatory theory away from traditional threats toward the supplementation of the Securities and Exchange Commission's block reporting regime and its ten-day filing window address a perceived policy need. Many think the SEC itself should shorten the filing period to a day or two, even as the SEC has remained unresponsive to such suggestions.[63] Coffee and Palia's window-closing pill would effect this change by private ordering. Significantly, it appears that Coffee and Palia do not think that hedge fund activism otherwise holds out a threat adequate to the task of justifying a 5 percent pill, presumably because the holding level is too low to implicate control transfer, creeping or otherwise.

Disproportionate Influence as a Unocal *Threat*

Suppose we extended the law of *Unocal* threats to acknowledge a cognizable activist threat without regard to prospects for control transfer. What would such a regime look like? We here project its possible parameters. So doing facilitates consideration of the policy question attending management actions that impede activist campaigns. If the projected justificatory threat rings hollow, management defensive responses should be deemed to be presumptively unreasonable under *Unocal*.

We begin with the two backstop threats invoked in the *Sotheby's* case—negative control and disproportionate influence. In the litigated case, the former did the work of justifying the board's refusal to waive the 10 percent cap, while the latter was mentioned only in passing. Now the roles are reversed. Negative control, while working better than creeping control in justifying defensive moves against activists, still holds out a problem of fit. Disproportionate influence, in contrast, provides a robust basis for reconfiguring *Unocal*, at least at a descriptive level.

Negative control amounts to a lightweight version of creeping control. It similarly looks to control acquisition, positing that hedge fund blocks potentially injure the general shareholder population by acquiring holdup power in respect of supermajority votes. But the theory also moves closer to the activist fact pattern, dropping the concern with the value consequences of a full control transfer and looking only toward distortionary effects on exercises of the shareholder franchise. Certainly, holdups by blockholders with selective incentives and private agendas conceivably could be a problem at some companies some of the time.[64] But, ultimately, there is little resonance with activist practice. Activist impact is not solely a function of the number of shares held. It follows from the support from similarly minded shareholders, whether or not they are activist hedge funds. Unilateral power to effect voting results, whether positively or negatively, does not figure into the model. Furthermore, the model looks to affirmative results. Holdups and side payments respecting matters submitted by management for shareholder approval (other than low-price mergers on the sell side and high-price mergers on the buy side) simply do not figure into the program.

The second threat, disproportionate influence, poses a more open-ended characterization of activism. Here there is no problem of fit. Disproportionate influence is what hedge fund activism is all about. Activists travel light, avoiding the large investments required for outright control purchase, instead buying smaller, more easily disposable blocks. They then leverage their small stakes into revisions of target business plans by soliciting the voting support of other shareholders. If activism poses a threat, this is where it lies—in change effected at the level of business policy, whether focused on an asset sale, additional borrowing, a stepped-up dividend, share repurchase activity, operating cost reductions, or a sell-side merger—change effected with the consent of a majority of the shares outstanding.

Of course, there is no threat if these activist-induced changes unequivocally add value. Empirical studies weigh in favor of the activists at this point, showing on an aggregate basis that their appearance causes enduring stock price increases[65] without simultaneously negatively impacting operating metrics in the long run.[66] But a threat characterization still can lie if we disaggregate target shareholders into two interest groups. Following the financial economics,[67] we distinguish those with short-term time horizons who take the full benefit of the stock price bump from those with long-term time horizons. The long-termers' interests are impaired to the extent that activist-induced change chokes off investment activity that would eventually enhance returns on the target's stock. Such value impairment is a distinct possibility at some companies some of the time, being more likely at twenty-first-century businesses that invest heavily in ideas and relationships and less likely at twentieth-century brick-and-mortar producers.[68] But long-term value sacrifice will not invariably result from activist victory, and, as noted, the present body of empirical studies shows no harm on an aggregate basis.

The company-specific threat amounts to a twenty-first-century recreation of the substantive coercion line of the *Unocal* doctrine. Substantive coercion is the threat held out by a procedurally uncoercive tender offer that holds out a substantial premium over the market price but nevertheless arguably sacrifices greater long-term value held out by the incumbents' business plan.[69] From the point of view of shareholder advocates, it is the weakest, least defensible of *Unocal* threats because it leaves the value choice with management rather than with the shareholders. And, like the threat being posed here, it divides the shareholders into short- and long-term constituencies and allows management to intervene defensively in the name of the latter group.

There is a significant point of distinction, despite the parallel. Although *Unocal* allows management to deploy a poison pill to block a premium tender offer, it ultimately only delays a persistent challenger.

The challenger can leave the offer on the table while conducting a proxy contest to gain control of the board with a view to withdrawing the pill and completing the acquisition. *Unocal* evolved on the theory that the shareholders still got a choice on control transfer through the exercise of their franchise. The implicit shareholder-protective justification was that the shift from the market for shares to the franchise and the resulting delay gave the competing parties time to lay out their cases and the shareholders a low-coercion context in which to evaluate the merits of the transaction. Any chilling effect on hostile takeover activity was disregarded, and, arguably, the shareholder interest has not been injured in the long run.

The new application of substantive coercion doctrine suggested here shifts the venue to that self-same shareholders' meeting. It thereby steps outside the received justificatory framework, which assumes that exercises of the shareholder franchise respecting board composition absolutely determine matters of business policy, even at the sacrifice of long-term value. The step is radical, for it disavows systemic reliance on indirect expression of shareholder business preferences in connection with director elections.

Here is a possible justification for the move. The situation can be described as a majority-minority shareholder conflict of interest: a long-term-oriented shareholder minority is being disadvantaged at the hands of a short-termist shareholder majority, which, due the parochial, skewed interests of agents of shareholder intermediaries, prefers a low-value short-term revision of the business plan to an arguably superior long-term value strategy. The majority-minority phrasing is conceptually comforting. But it still camouflages an implicit judgment that shareholder majorities cannot be trusted to determine business planning, even indirectly through the exercise of the board franchise. So let us color the picture of abuse a bit more intensely, recharacterizing the situation as one in which a short-termist minority exploits a long-termist majority. We get from here to there by disregarding the activists' shareholdings on the ground of interest in the outcome of the vote, analogizing to the majority-of-the-minority shareholder votes used to ratify self-dealing transactions between companies and large shareholders.

The new characterization imports more comfort, but still breaks with the inherited conceptual framework, for we are not, strictly speaking, discussing shareholder ratification of a self-dealing transaction. Indeed, there is no self-dealing in the fact pattern, even as there is pervasive self-interest. Concerning the duty of loyalty, the activist is no more interested in the outcome of the vote than are the defending board members, and the short-termist shareholders voting in favor of the activist are no more self-interested than are the long-termist shareholders supporting the board. The difference between the two shareholder groups is a mere incident of their holding periods. Furthermore, corporate law has always been comfortable with the notion that self-interest motivates shareholder voting—there is no shareholder-level duty to vote with a view to the corporation's best interests.[70]

The theory described is hypothetical. Even so, markers pointed in its direction are being put down in Delaware cases. Consider the following excerpt from Vice Chancellor Travis Laster's opinion in a case about a trade sale of a venture capital startup, *In re Trados Inc. Shareholder Litigation*:[71]

> A Delaware corporation, by default, has a perpetual existence. Equity capital, by default, is permanent capital. In terms of the standard of conduct, the duty of loyalty therefore mandates that directors maximize the value of the corporation over the long-term for the benefit of the providers of equity capital, as warranted for an entity with perpetual life in which the residual claimants have locked in their investment. When deciding whether to pursue a strategic alternative that would end or fundamentally alter the stockholders' ongoing investment in the corporation, the loyalty-based standard of conduct requires that the alternative yield value exceeding what the corporation otherwise would generate for stockholders over the long-term. Value, of course, does not just mean cash. It could mean an ownership interest in an entity, a package of other securities, or some combination, with or without cash, that will deliver greater value over the anticipated investment horizon. The duty to act for the ultimate benefit of stockholders does not require that directors fulfill the wishes of a particular subset of the stockholder base. . . . Stockholders may have idiosyncratic reasons for preferring decisions that misallocate capital. Directors must exercise their independent fiduciary judgment; they need not cater to stockholder whim.[72]

Vice Chancellor Laster makes an important move with this purposive alignment of corporate law's basic framework with the long-term side of the conflict between short- and long-term time horizons. Historically, such basic conceptual statements have elided the short-term/long-term distinction, treating the shareholder interest in unitary terms.[73] Vice

Chancellor Laster's formulation, which was quite unnecessary to the decision of the case, normatively situates corporate law firmly on the long-term side. As such, it builds a normative justification for management actions against disproportionately influential activists into corporate law's conceptual framework. Indeed, if the formulation was deployed foursquare in a litigated case, it would obviate any need to invoke the foregoing majority-minority characterization. The case becomes easy: To the extent that the core legal concept of the corporation includes a bias toward a long-term time horizon, there is no need to make reference to incentive impairments on the shareholders' part. Long-termism standing alone would suffice as a justification.

There remains a substantial question of whether we can ever expect to see Vice Chancellor Laster's statement deployed on the facts of a case so as to trump the conceptual framework's protection of shareholder voting discretion in board elections. But, for what is it worth, the statement is now embedded in the case law in neutral form, ready to be invoked to justify a 5 percent poison pill.

Practical Consequences

This chapter has posited a justification for a 5 percent general purpose poison pill, remodeling corporate law's conceptual framework to characterize activist employment of the shareholder franchise as a threat. It now must be noted that even if the law were to follow the course charted, it probably would not make much practical difference. Therein lies a hidden justification for the change suggested.

Standing Pills and Grandfathered Shares

Standing poison pills are disappearing, even as the level of activism continues to increase slightly, year by year. The reason is that managers now cater to the concerns of institutional investors and their informational intermediaries, all of whom dislike poison pills. In 2005, 35 percent of public companies had a poison pill in place. As of 2012, only 805 companies had standing pills, amounting to 22.6 percent of publicly traded companies. Ten percent of those pills were triggered at less than 15 percent, 61 percent were triggered at 15 percent, and 15 percent were triggered at more than 15 percent.[74] By 2015, there were only 471 companies with a standing pill—12.7 percent of public companies—of which only 25 were two-tier, low-threshold pills of the type seen in *Sotheby's*.[75]

It follows that, like the board in *Sotheby's*, defending managers adopt pills only once activists materialize with Rule 13d-1 filings or prefiling complaints and demands. These delayed pills have no effect on purchases in advance of promulgation (at least so long as selective ex post dilution of shareholder interests is impossible under corporate—and maybe property—law).

The delay substantially diminishes the pill's potency, for grandfathered activist purchases tend to be sufficient to support a serious challenge. Given the ten-day filing window under Rule 13d-1, the vast majority of purchases by the lead activist and any wolf pack members already have been made in advance of the filing of a form 13D and pill deployment. In fact, challengers do not even need the ten days of breathing space held out by the rule. In practice, market purchases above the 5 percent threshold are disproportionately concentrated on the day the threshold is crossed and the day after.[76] It seems that even undisclosed wolf pack members have their blocks in place by the second day.[77] Given this purchase pattern, a reduction of the 13d-1 filing window to even one day might have little practical deterrent effect.

A standing 5 percent pill has more bite, for it is triggered by purchases above 5 percent irrespective of the timing of a 13d-1 filing. Indeed, at present this is the only defense providing ex ante protection against activist intervention. But the deterrent effect is only marginal. A 5 percent per fund cap contains the intervention's impact by limiting the number of safe votes and giving a defensive proxy solicitation a higher probability of success. Perhaps more importantly, it also limits the arbitrage profit yielded on preannouncement share purchases by the postannouncement price bump. But it does not necessarily tip the cost-benefit scale against intervention.

A pill with something approaching preclusive effect would take a bit more. The drafter would have to sweep all wolf pack members into a defined group and then cap the group at 5 percent.[78] Problems of verification probably would limit such a provision's effectiveness, for the cap changes the activists' cost-benefit calculations concerning public disclosure. If every wolf in the pack held less than 5 percent, federal filing would no longer be required (at least so long as the federal group definition rules were not traversed).[79] The lead hedge fund presumably would disclose itself anyway, as an inevitable incident of the campaign. Any others could remain undisclosed, disabling the target from proving their participation and hence from enforcing its 5 percent group pill. A benefit still follows for the target, for, given undisclosed fellow travelers, the lead fund's clout would be more a matter of speculation than it is with a large disclosed wolf pack. But there would be no guarantee that any hedge funds working in parallel were in fact limited to an aggregate 5 percent.

Policy Considerations

Let us now step back and ask whether a *Unocal* regime that accepted a 5 percent standing pill (with or without a provision extending to groups) would be a bad thing.

THE CASE AGAINST. The potential downsides of the regime posited are clear to all—advocates of shareholder empowerment have set them out at length. For them, hedge fund activism is an unadulterated good and any increase in management insulation adds to agency costs.[80] And even if the shareholder advocates' absolute claims are unsustainable—there are costs and benefits on both sides, after all—the policy bottom line still resonates strongly. In the aggregate, hedge fund activism may very well do some good and has not been shown to do affirmative harm. Corporate law has accommodated it more or less without change. No change has been required, for activists work within the law's inherited framework, operating within the confines of board-centric governance. They effect changes in business plans by joining boards in a minority posture, not by displacing incumbents wholesale. Their opponents so far have not managed to prompt any disabling reform. Given all this, a root-and-branch revision of corporate law that makes it much more difficult for activists to join boards of directors needs to be justified by a showing of systemic damage to business plans and productivity. Arguably, no such showing can be made on the present record. It follows that we should adhere to the regulatory status quo.

From this point of view, most of the questions considered in *Sotheby's* in connection with a two-tier 10 percent standing pill never should have come up in the first place. Instead, the 10 percent trigger should been deemed invalid absent a compelling justification—*Blasius* rather than *Unocal* review. In this reframing of the law, the traditional 20 percent trigger becomes a line drawn in the sand, with the party seeking to step over it with a lower threshold bearing a heavy policy burden to discredit activism. The argument is powerful, for, as we have seen, creeping control and negative control—the theories thus far deployed to this end of sanctioning low-threshold pills—largely fail to grapple with the matters at hand and so import little policy traction against an argument favoring the 20 percent status quo.

A CASE IN FAVOR. Let us now attempt to justify a 5 percent poison pill in the teeth of the foregoing argument. The going is rough, for there is no aggregate evidence of injury from activism to support a policy case for across-the-board legal deterrence. Any case must be company-specific. To make such a case persuasively, one would have to avoid traditional *Unocal* factors, which tend to be beside the point. One instead would concentrate on the particular company's business plan, showing a capital-intensive investment program and a need to insulate long-term relationships with employees, customers, and suppliers from disruption. The case is more easily stated in theory than in practice, for its central empirical elements resist easy verification, even on a company-by-company basis. At the same time, the incentives of any managers making such a case are highly suspect.

Hypothesize a company whose managers can make an excellent case in all sincerity. Nothing would prevent them from submitting their pill to their shareholders for ratification, using the case to support the motion. Given shareholder approval and a pill of limited duration—say, no more than five years—fiduciary law arguably would hold out no basis for challenge. Shareholder approval simultaneously launders away any implication of management entrenchment and confirms the presence of a cognizable threat.

The scenario just posed holds out cold comfort to real-world managers operating under uncertainty. Shareholders dislike pills, and would be disinclined to take seriously even a valid case. Sincerity is unverifiable, and any management representations would be discounted for good reason. Even a case that remained persuasive net of a credibility discount still probably would fail. The institutional intermediaries who decide these questions are self-interested themselves and have a vested interest their own empowerment. Any discourse posing situational benefits from enhanced management insulation threatens their power structure by traversing the widely held assumption that insulation is never cost-beneficial due to stepped-up agency costs. Meanwhile, the very attempt to make the case in the context of a proxy solicitation to approve a poison pill holds out risks for management. A failed solicitation sends a signal of vulnerability even as the case itself reveals information of interest to a potential activist. It comes as no surprise that such solicitations are not seen in practice.

We could stop here, leaving management with the burden of persuading its shareholders as a condition to justifying an effective deterrent pill. But let's give it one more try, shifting the burden over to the shareholders on a penalty default theory. We leave the managers free to promulgate a 5 percent pill unilaterally in the absence of searching *Unocal* scrutiny, remitting the job of punishing the managers to their disgruntled institutional shareholders rather than to the courts.

This defensive shift in the structure that sets the balance of power between shareholders and managers could prove beneficial in the long run. The positive projection relies on the assumption that standing pills—even 5 percent pills without risk of *Unocal* invalidation—are very unlikely to be seen in practice because managers now cater to shareholder preferences. A management promulgating such a pill would have a lot of explaining to do, even absent the burden of conducting a successful proxy solicitation. Let us once again posit that the promulgating company is unsuitable for activist targeting and that management can make an excellent case by reference to the company's investment policy and relational commitments. Management promulgates the pill, simultaneously making the explanation. A set-to with Institutional Shareholder Services, Glass Lewis, and the large institutions no doubt would follow. The resulting dialogue could be beneficial—a learning experience for the institutional investor community.

Spinning the scenario out a bit, the poison pill emerges as a lever facilitating a productive sorting of companies among those well suited and ill suited to activist discipline, a sorting that will not occur under the present regime of *Unocal* scrutiny because managers have good reasons to avoid seeking shareholder ratification. It would achieve what anti-activist reformers tried and failed to get from the SEC—an activist baffler that deters purchases above 5 percent. It would be a superior means to the end because it would be a product of private ordering and would operate company by company.

The positive projection follows from the assumption that shareholder empowerment has waxed to the point at which most managers, even managers who believe in their own case, will refrain from taking advantage of available defenses to avoid retaliation from the intermediary community. If the assumption is unsound and a green light prompted a massive turn to standing pills without a beneficial informational back-and-forth, then the projection is unsound.

The projection's plausibility is remitted to the reader's judgment.

Conclusion

This chapter poses the question of whether *Unocal*, a twentieth-century doctrine keyed to hostile takeovers and control transfers, appropriately can be applied in a twenty-first-century governance context in which the challenger limits itself to the shareholder franchise and does not seek control. The answer clearly is no. The doctrine fixes on the wrong threat. It likely will retain this refractory framing even so. There is no emergency—the *Sotheby's* ruling does next to nothing to curb the strategies that determine most activist campaigns even as it strikes a blow for the defensive side. *Unocal* would have to be revamped conceptually to align itself with the right threat and so sustain a poison pill with enough bite even to begin to deter activism. A reformulation would have such radical implications for corporate law's conceptual framework as to open it to widespread and severe questioning. But the context is changing. Shareholder power has waxed sufficiently to make it plausible to contemplate the renovation. Management agency costs just aren't as big a deal as they used to be.

Notes

1. 2014 WL 1922029 (Del. Ch.).

2. 493 A.2d 946 (Del. 1985).

3. The poison in a poison pill is two-for-one dilution of the challenger's stock block. It follows that challengers avoid traversing the triggers, instead turning to the courts to ask for invalidation.

4. Third Point LLC v. Ruprecht, 2014 WL 1922029 (Del. Ch.), 9.

5. *Id.*

6. *Id.*

7. The pill in the original case, Moran v. Household International, Inc., 500 A.2d 1346 (Del. 1985), included a 20 percent block acquisition trigger. Lower thresholds did not come into use until recent years.

8. A 5 percent trigger was sustained in Versata Enterprises, Inc. v. Selectica, Inc., 5 A.3d 586 (Del. 2010), but the case was easily distinguished. The trigger

in question addressed a tax rule that removed loss carryforwards in the event of the appearance of a 5 percent blockholder. Given the tax angle, the court had no trouble sustaining the low-threshold pill by reference to the welfare of the shareholders as a group.

9. The closest case, Yucaipa American Alliance Fund II, L.P. v. Riggio, 1 A.3d 310 (Del. Ch. 2010), *aff'd* 5 A.3d 2318 (Del. 2011), concerned a fund and a defending board but did not implicate the standard fact pattern of dispersed target shares, a less than 20 percent activist hedge fund block, and a short slate proxy contest. The target in the case had a 30 percent blockholder, and the challenger was a private equity firm seeking to acquire a counterblock toward the end of redirecting the business plan.

It bears noting that several Delaware cases cast doubt on the operation of a similar defensive device in the context of hedge fund activism—the "poison puts" contained in bond and loan contracts. Poison puts are drafted in the same mold as poison pills, setting out triggers keyed to a list of control changes and control challenges. When the trigger goes off, holders of the securities covered by the debt contract receive a right to put the securities back to the issuer at face value. Depending on the drafting, activist challenges holding out acquisition of a majority of board seats can either trigger the pill or result in the defending board receiving discretion to trigger the pill. If the debt securities are trading at a discount to face value, exercise of the put injures the corporation by transferring value to the debtholders. A cash management disability can result even in the absence of a discount. The cases in turn disable the put's operation. *See* Kallick v. Sandridge Energy, Inc., 68 A.3d 242 (Del. Ch. 2013). The cases are easily distinguished. In a poison put case, the defensive device financially injures the company and thus its shareholders as a group for the benefit of the bondholders and the defending managers. In a poison pill case, the device injures the shareholders only by inference. It makes an activist challenge more expensive and difficult. But the deterrent effect injures the shareholders generally only to the extent that activism benefits them. Meanwhile, in a case like *Sotheby's*, the protected shareholders remain free to vote in favor of the activist slate at the annual meeting, arguably eliminating any direct threat of injury.

10. *See* Unitrin, Inc. v. American General Corp., 651 A.2d 1361 (Del.1995).

11. 564 A. 2d 651 (Del. Ch. 1988).

12. 2014 WL 1922029, 4–15.

13. *See* Stroud v. Grace, 606 A.2d 75, 91 (Del. 1992); Yucaipa American Alliance Fund II, L.P. v. Riggio, 1 A.3d 310 (Del. Ch. 2010), aff'd 5 A.3d 2318 (Del. 2011).

14. *See* MM Companies v. Liquid Audio, Inc., 813 A.2d 1118, 1130 (Del. 2003).

15. 2014 WL 1922029 at 16–18; Yucaipa American Alliance Fund II, L.P. v. Riggio, 1 A.3d 310, 350–51, 359–60(Del. Ch. 2010), *aff'd* 5 A.3d 2318 (Del. 2011).

16. Directive 2004/25/EC of the European Parliament and of the Council of 21 April 2004 on Takeover Bids, art 5 sec 1–4; UK Takeover Code Rules 9.1, 9.5.

17. Yucaipa American Alliance Fund II, L.P. v. Riggio, 1 A.3d 310, 348–350 (Del. Ch. 2010), *aff'd* 5 A.3d 2318 (Del. 2011).

18. 2014 WL 1922029, 5.

19. *Id.* at 4.

20. *Id.* at 7, 11.

21. *Id.* at 20.

22. *Id.* at 17–19.

23. It bears noting that one of the wolf pack members, Trian, had sold down its block a month after the board adopted the pill. *See* Carmen X. W. Lua, "Unpacking Wolf Packs," *Yale Law Journal* 125 (2016): 773, 780.

24. 2014 WL 1922029, 13.

25. 493 A.2d, 19 (plaintiffs must show a reasonable probability of demonstrating that the Board acted with "animus" or an "entrenchment motive").

26. 2014 WL 1922029, 21.

27. *Id.*

28. *Id.* at 22.

29. S. Michael J. de la Merced and Alexandra Stevenson, "Sotheby's Yields to Hedge Fund Mogul and Allies," *New York Times*, May 5, 2014, http://dealbook.nytimes.com/2014/05/05/sothebys-and-loeb-end-fight-over-board/?_r=0.

30. Stewart L. Gillan and Laura T. Starks, "The Evolution of Shareholder Activism in the United States," *Journal of Applied Corporate Finance* 19 (2007): 55.

31. Nicole M. Boyson and Robert M. Mooradian, "Experienced Hedge Fund Activists," working paper, April 3, 2012, http://ssrn.com/abstract=1787649.

32. Alon Brav, Wei Jiang, Frank Partnoy, and Randall Thomas.," Hedge Fund Activism, Corporate Governance, and Firm Performance," *Journal of Finance* 63 (2008): 1729, 1747.

33. Nikolay Gantchev, "The Costs of Shareholder Activism: Evidence from a Sequential Decision Model," working paper, August 2012, 47, www.ssrn.comabs=16464712012.

34. Section 13(d)(3) of the Securities Exchange Act of 1934 provides that "[w]hen two or more persons act as a . . . group for the purpose of acquiring, holding, or disposing of securities of an issuer, such syndicate or group shall be deemed a 'person' for the purposes of this subsection." 15 U.S.C. § 78m(d)(3) (2012). The leading case finding a group is CSX Corp. v. Children's Inv. Fund Mgmt. (UK), LLP, 562 F. Supp. 2d 511, 525 (S.D.N.Y. 2008).

35. Marco Becht, Julian Franks, Jeremey Grant, and Hannes Wagner, "The Returns to Hedge Fund Activism: An International Study," working paper, March 2015, www.ssrn.com/abs=2376271.

36. *Id.* at 51.

37. *Id.* at 32.

38. *Id.* at 5.

39. *Id.*

40. Yu Ting Forester Wong, "Wolves at the Door: A Closer Look at Hedge Fund Activism," working paper, January 2016, 3, http://ssrn.com/abstract=2721413.

41. *Id.* at 7.

42. John C. Coffee Jr. and Darius Palia, "The Wolf at the Door: The Impact of Hedge Fund Activism on Corporate Governance," *Journal of Corporation Law* 41 (2016): 545, 593.

43. *Id.* at 562–68.

44. *Id.* at 593.

45. Here fiduciary scrutiny minimizes the opportunity for unilaterally imposing a low price. *See* Weinberger v. UOP, Inc., 457 A.2d 701 (Del. 1983).

46. This was at one time the central problem of corporate fiduciary law. The leading case was Perlman v. Feldmann, 219 F.2d 173, *cert. denied* 349 U.S. 952 (1955). For the leading critique, *see* William D. Andrews, "The Stockholder's Right to Equal Opportunity in the Sale of Shares," *Harvard Law Review* (1965): 505, 515–22. The flow of case law has trailed off.

47. Alon Brav, Wei Jiang, and Hyunseob Kim, "Hedge Fund Activism: A Review," working paper, February 2010, 16, http://ssrn.com/abstract=1551953. Also at the low end are Bebchuk, Brav, and Jiang, who report that the rate of attrition due to merger for all public companies across a five-year period is 42 percent compared to 49 percent for their sample of activist targets. *See* Lucian A. Bebchuk, Alon Brav, and Wei Jiang, "The Long-Term Effects of Hedge Fund Activism," *Columbia Law Review* 115 (2015): 1085, 1104.

48. Robin Greenwood and Michael Schor, "Investor Activism and Takeovers," *Journal of Financial Economics* 92 (2009): 364, 368.

49. Becht et al., "Returns to Hedge Fund Activism," 54.

50. Nicole M. Boyson, Nickolay Gantchev, and Anil Shivdasani, "Activism Mergers," working paper, October 2015, http://dx.doi.org/10.2139/ssrn.2677416.

51. *Id.* at 34.

52. *Id.*

53. *Id.* at 16.

54. The twenty-four-month cumulative average returns work out as follows: targets in general, 9.8 percent; third-party bid, 38.9 percent; activist bid, 18.4 percent; failed bid, 17.7 percent. *Id.* at 19–24.

55. Nickolay Gantchev and Chotibhak Jotikasthira, "Institutional Trading and Hedge Fund Activism," working paper, November 2015, 3, http://ssrn.com/abstract=2139482.

56. 506 A.2d 173 (Del. 1986).

57. It is noted that influence can be found as a factor in Yucaipa American

Alliance Fund II, L.P. v. Riggio, 1 A.3d 310, 348 (Del. Ch. 2010), aff'd 5 A.3d 2318 (Del. 2011).

58. Coffee and Palia, "Wolf at the Door," 602.

59. *Id.*

60. *Id.*

61. The window is set under Rule 13d-1 under Section 13(d) of the Securities and Exchange Act of 1934. Sections 929R of the Dodd-Frank Wall Street Reform and Consumer Protection Act, Pub. L. No. 111–203, 124 Stat. 1376 (2010) explicitly authorize the Securities and Exchange Commission to shorten the filing window. *See* 15 U.S.C. § 78m(d)(1) (2012).

62. Coffee and Palia, "Wolf at the Door," 602.

63. *See* Letter from Wachtell Lipton Rosen & Katz to SEC Sec'y Elizabeth M. Murray (May 7, 2011), https://www.sec.gov/rules/petitions/2011/petn4-624.pdf (petitioning the SEC to shorten the ten-day window of the Williams Act); *see also* Adam O. Emmerich, Theodore N. Mirvis, Edward S. Robinson, and William Savitt, "Fair Markets and Fair Disclosure: Some Thoughts on the Law and Economics of Blockholder Disclosure and the Use and Abuse of Shareholder Power," *Harvard Business Law Review* 3 (2013): 135.

64. For discussion, *see* Zohar Goshen, "Controlling Strategic Voting: Property Rule or Liability Rule?" *Southern California Law Review* 70 (1997): 741, 769–71.

65. Activist intervention causes an immediate stock price increase that lasts for at least a year. The magnitude of the bump varies with the study. *See* Brav et al., "Hedge Fund Activism," 1729 (7 percent to 8 percent); April Klein and Emanuel Zur, "Entrepreneurial Shareholder Activism: Hedge Funds and Other Private Investors," *Journal of Finance* 64 (2009): 187, 188 (10.2 percent); Chris Clifford, "Value Creation or Destruction? Hedge Funds as Shareholder Activists," working paper, April 2008, 4–5, http://ssrn.com/abstract=971018 (3.39 percent), Robin Greenwood and Michael Schor, "Investor Activism and Takeovers," *Journal of Financial Economics* 92 (2009): 362, 366–68 (3.5 percent); Bebchuk, Brav, and Jiang, "Long Term Effects," 1122 (6 percent). Some studies show that positive cumulative abnormal returns continue to rise during the period following the activists' first appearance. *See* Greenwood and Schor, 366–68 (an additional 6.5% over 18 months); Klein and Zur, 188 (an additional 11.4 percent over one year).

66. The study of operations that takes the longest view comes from Bechuk, Brav, and Jiang, who purport to confirm that activist intervention adds long-term value. They run five-year postengagement return on assets and Tobin's Q figures for a set of engagements from 1994 to 2007. Bebchuk, Brav, and Jiang, "Long Term Effects," 1105.

67. *See, e.g.*, Francois Brochet, Maria Loumioti, and George Serafeim, "Speaking of the Short-Term: Disclosure Horizon and Managerial Myopia," working paper, May 2015, http://ssrn.com/abstract=1999484.

68. *See, e.g.*, Alex Edmans, "Does the Stock Market Fully Value Intangibles? Employee Satisfaction and Equity Prices," *Journal of Financial Economics* 101 (2011) 621, 622 (using appearance on the annual list of 100 Best Companies to Work for in America has a proxy for employee satisfaction); Brochet, Loumioti, and Serafeim, "Speaking of the Short-Term" (sorting companies between short- and long-term oriented by coding language used by senior managers and investors during quarterly conference calls); Jillian Popadak, "A Corporate Culture Channel: How Increased Shareholder Governance Reduces Firm Value," working paper, March 2014, http://ssrn.com/abstract=2345384 (quantifying corporate culture through textual analysis of a data set of over 1.8 million employee reviews).

69. *See* Unitrin, Inc. v. American General Corp., 651 A.2d 1361 (Del. 1995).

70. The only exception covers vote buying. *See* Goshen, "Controlling Strategic Voting," 789. For the suggestion that a fiduciary duty should apply, *see* Iman Anabtawi and Lynn Stout, "Fiduciary Duties for Activist Shareholders," *Stanford Law Review* 60 (2008): 1255.

71. 73 A.3d 17 (2013).

72. *Id.* at 37–38.

73. *See, e.g.*, *American Law Institute, Principles of Corporate Governance: Analysis and Recommendations* (St. Paul, MN: American Law Institute Publishers, 1994), § 2.01.

74. *See* Lucian A. Bebchuk, Alon Brav, Robert J. Jackson Jr., and Wei Jiang, "Pre-Disclosure Accumulations by Activist Investors: Evidence and Policy," *Journal of Corporation Law* 39 (2014): 1, 26–27.

75. Coffee and Palia, "Wolf at the Door," 30 n.67. The percentage figure assumes 3,700 publicly traded companies in 2015. *See* Barry Ritholtz, "Where Have All the Public Companies Gone?" *Bloomberg News*, June 24 2015, http://www.bloomberg.com/view/articles/2015-06-24/where-have-all-the-publicly-traded-companies-gone-.

76. Bebchuk et al., "Pre-Disclosure Accumulations," 23–25.

77. Wong, "Closer Look."

78. For drafting strategies, *see* Coffee and Palia, "Wolf at the Door," 601–2.

79. Rule 13d–5, promulgated under § 13 of the Exchange Act, provides: When two or more persons agree to act together for the purpose of acquiring, holding, voting or disposing of equity securities of an issuer, the group formed thereby shall be deemed to have acquired beneficial ownership, for purposes of Section 13(d) and (g) of the Act, as of the date of such agreement, of all equity securities of that issuer beneficially owned by any such persons.

80. *See* Lucian A. Bebchuk, "The Myth That Insulating Boards Serves Long-Term Value," *Columbia Law Review* 113 (2013): 163–67; Mark J. Roe, "Corporate Short-Termism—In the Boardroom and in the Courtroom," *The Business Lawyer* 68 (2013): 978–79.

CHAPTER EIGHT

Corporate Governance beyond Economics

Elizabeth Pollman

Introduction

US corporate law has an origin story. At the founding of the nation, and through the early nineteenth century, corporations served a quasi-public function. States granted charters to private property holders to fulfill a "public purpose," such as to provide infrastructure or local services such as transportation, banking, and insurance.[1] Profit and its distribution, while part of the expectations of early business corporation organizers, only became a meaningful part of categorizing corporate identity in the latter half of the nineteenth century.[2] Change occurred rapidly in both business and the law, and by the century's end, state corporate law as we know it today had started to take shape.

The quasi-public origin story of corporate law set the foundation for a debate about corporate purpose that has endured for decades, finding its way into legal opinions and serving as the subject for weighty academic discussions. Part of the classic canon of this debate is Adolf Berle and Gardiner Means' description of the twentieth-century public corporation involving a separation between ownership and control.[3] Their vision of a society dominated by management-controlled large corporations, with dispersed "owners of passive property,"[4] provided a paradigmatic view of the business corporation.[5] Their observations, moreover, raised the question of corporate accountability—both because of a potential conflict between those who own stock in the corporation and those who manage it and because of a concern about whether the public interest would be served by corporations dominating the US economy.

Throughout the twentieth century, corporate law developed with a focus on the allocation of power between shareholders and managers, and the model of the Berle and Means corporation largely persisted. The question of corporate purpose also remained a topic of perennial debate.[6] Case law reflects times in which the ultimate purpose of business corporations has been tested—ranging, for example, from when Delaware courts developed doctrine for dealing with defensive measures taken by target boards in the takeover context to the modern redux of the *Ford Motor Company* case involving directors pursuing goals other than shareholder value.[7] Courts navigated problems such as these with flexible and highly contextual judge-made standards. Notwithstanding significant ambiguity and meaningful dissent,[8] the dominant viewpoint that has emerged and remained relatively stable over decades is one of understanding corporate purpose and the corporate law framework in predominantly economic terms, and more specifically as focused on shareholder value.[9]

At the beginning of the twenty-first century, evidence of a changing corporate contract could move discourse beyond the classic corporate law canon. This change has come about with a demographic shift among shareholders in public corporations and the rise of institutional shareholders and shareholder activism—topics that have been extensively examined in recent literature.[10] This chapter explores the idea that we are also in an age of increased pressure on corporate law to serve as a mechanism for ordering or pursuing activity that has importance beyond its economic value.

Both state and federal law changes have added to this dynamic. On the federal front, recent US Supreme Court cases have put existing corporate law in a new quasi-constitutional light. In the landmark decisions of *Citizens United v. FEC* and *Burwell v. Hobby Lobby Stores, Inc.*, the Supreme Court has pointed to state corporate law as the means by which corporations determine their political and religious activity and resolve internal disputes.[11] These decisions rely on a view of business corporations that is, in many ways, at odds with long-standing notions from corporate law. In addition, Congress, the Securities and Exchange Commission, and federal courts have been embroiled in battles about the scope and appropriateness of regulating corporate speech and disclosures on topics such as conflict minerals and political expenditures that are driven principally by humanitarian and democratic goals rather than economic ones. On the state law front, a movement of social entrepreneurs has catalyzed a majority of states to adopt legislation for a new form of business entity—the benefit corporation. The public push for this form of corporate entity harkens back to early American law, permitting businesses to be chartered to pursue a "dual mission" of profits and a social, religious, or environmental goal.[12] The spread of benefit corporation legislation has occurred concurrently with but separately from the new federalizing force on corporate law—widening the potential impact of these developments.

We are in the early stages of understanding the significance of these developments, but they hold the potential to dramatically change the corporate landscape, just as the splintering of business corporations from nonprofits did in the nineteenth century. The chapter examines these developments and their implications and anticipates future challenges on the horizon.

Recent Federal and State Developments That Increase the Role of Corporate Law in Ordering Noneconomic Interests

Business corporations have always been embedded in society and have always involved natural persons who have a full range of interests and values—economic, social, political, religious—that may motivate their actions. Further, some significant corporate governance regulations, which have been in place for decades, implicate this range of motivations and concerns, such as proxy regulation and the shareholder proposal rule, SEC Rule 14a-8.[13]

Notwithstanding this general recognition that business corporations may have both economic and social aspects to their nature,[14] until recently federal regulation of corporate and securities law has focused predominantly on investor protection and the economic interests at stake.[15] And much of the corporate law literature and debate has continued to mine the classic questions of the nineteenth century regarding in whose interests the corporation should be run or has accepted an economic lens through which to theorize and analyze corporate law, treating corporations as economic entities designed to maximize value for their equity investors.[16]

Two significant developments have taken place in the past several years that have added complexity to this picture. First, a new federal influence on corporate governance has emerged that has increasingly placed into the spotlight the role of social, political, and religious values in business corporations. Second, the birth of benefit corporations has made visible the choice of some corporate organizers and investors to participate in a different type of corporate contract that expressly requires pursuing values beyond shareholder wealth. This section discusses each development in turn.

First Amendment Battles of Corporations and the Federalizing of Corporate Governance

Since the late 1970s, with little exception to the trend, courts have been expanding the First Amendment rights of corporations.[17] This trend has been in bold contrast to the pervasive regulation of corporate and commercial speech throughout US legal history and leading up to this point.[18] The recognition of corporate speech rights started with a focus on nonprofit and media corporations, but over time those decisions have been used as the foundation for recognizing the rights of business corporations more generally.[19] According to one study, "[n]early half of First Amendment legal challenges now benefit business corporations and trade groups, rather than other kinds of organizations or individuals."[20]

Two recent landmark decisions on the political spending rights and the statutory religious liberty rights of business corporations have significantly contributed to this trend: *Citizens United* and *Hobby Lobby*. These decisions—and other battles at the federal level about the political, religious, and social roles of corporations—have increased expectations that internal corporate governance will reconcile these changing rights and responsibilities. Business and constitutional law have thus intersected in ways that raise new issues for the future of corporate law.

In the 2010 case of *Citizens United*, the Supreme Court struck down as unconstitutional a significant campaign finance restriction and precedent that distinguished between the political speech of individuals and corporations.[21] The petitioner in the case, Citizens United, would have fit within an exception to the campaign finance prohibition at issue given its status as a nonprofit political advocacy corporation; however, it had funded the electioneering communication in question with a small portion of funds from for-profit business corporations.[22] Instead of ruling narrowly as to the corporation before the Court, it ruled broadly as to all corporations, freeing them to spend unlimited general treasury funds on independent political expenditures.

The Court based its ruling on the listeners' interest in hearing speech as well as on a characterization of corporations as "associations of citizens" and an implication that the First Amendment protection of corporations is equal to that of individuals.[23] The Court did not distinguish between various types of corporations in its reasoning and instead suggested an expressive or dignitary value in corporate speech.[24] Further, when rejecting an argument that the government had a compelling interest to regulate the political spending of business corporations to protect dissenting shareholders, the Court failed to look closely at the questions of whose voice is expressed through business corporations and what options exist for dissenting shareholders. The Court assumed that corporate law provided sufficient rules for ordering decisions about political spending and that expenditures would be transparent, as technology has enabled timely disclosure.[25] Thus, according to the Court, "[t]here is . . . little evidence of abuse that cannot be corrected by shareholders 'through the procedures of corporate democracy.'"[26]

To some, *Citizens United* represented an incremental loosening of restrictions on corporate political spending that had already begun in the 1970s;[27] others saw this as a dramatic move empowering business corporations to take on a new political role. Not all companies engaged in politics or cheered the *Citizens United* decision, but it provided many corporations and donors with what one campaign finance lawyer described as a "psychological green light," and "torrents of money, much of it anonymous" started flowing into electoral races.[28] The case became a cultural lightning rod as President Obama criticized it in his 2010 State of the Union address for having "reversed a century of law to open the floodgates for special interests . . . to spend without limit in our elections," to which Supreme Court Justice Samuel Alito mouthed in response, "It's not true."[29] Grassroots organizations sprung up to fight for a constitutional amendment overturning *Citizens United*.[30] Stories about the distorting impact of corporate political money, particularly in local elections, have continued to garner public attention.[31]

The additional latitude that *Citizens United* provided for business corporations to make political expenditures, and its reasoning based on the "procedures of corporate democracy," brought the fire and heat of the public controversy surrounding this decision into the realm of corporate governance. As Professor Larry Ribstein observed, "*Citizens*

United shifted the debate over corporate speech from corporations' power to distort political debate to the corporate governance processes that authorize this speech."[32]

The second recent blockbuster case adding to this federal overlay on corporate law is *Hobby Lobby*. The case arose out of challenges by three closely held corporations to a provision of the Patient Protection and Affordable Care Act of 2010 requiring employers to offer health insurance meeting certain minimum coverage standards, which the Department of Health and Human Services defined to include all FDA-approved contraceptive methods.[33] Families who were unanimous in their religious beliefs against certain contraception owned the stock of the three corporations in the case and argued that the Department of Health regulations violated the religious liberty rights of these corporations under the Religious Freedom Restoration Act (RFRA). The act prohibits the "Government [from] substantially burden[ing] a person's exercise of religion even if the burden results from a rule of general applicability" unless that action constitutes the least restrictive means of serving a compelling governmental interest.[34]

The Court held that business corporations are "persons" capable of the "exercise of religion" within the meaning of RFRA and that the Department of Health regulations violated RFRA as applied to these closely held corporations. The Court reasoned that extending RFRA protection to the corporations "protects the religious liberty of the humans who own and control these companies."[35]

In so reasoning, the Court alluded to corporate law as the mechanism for establishing the religious identity of a business corporation. The Court's language seemed to rely on a notion of shareholder agreement in a closely held corporation but left unspecified the precise qualifications for RFRA protection. Moreover, the Court acknowledged that "the owners of a company might well have a dispute relating to religion" but disposed of this concern by noting that "[s]tate corporate law provides a ready means for resolving any conflicts by, for example, dictating how a corporation can establish its governing structure."[36]

With *Citizens United*'s reference to the "procedures of corporate democracy" and *Hobby Lobby*'s reference to the "ready means" of state corporate law, the Court both expanded the political and religious rights of corporations and leaned on corporate law to provide the rules for corporations to determine whether and how to exercise such rights.[37]

Other battles at the federal level have added to the growing focus on corporations' political and social roles. For example, Congress included provisions in the Dodd-Frank Wall Street Reform and Consumer Protection Act of 2010 that used corporate disclosure as a tool for broader humanitarian or social goals. The conflict minerals provision, Section 1502 of Dodd-Frank, required public companies to investigate their supply chains, disclose the origins of certain minerals used in their products, and include a description of products not found to be "conflict-free." Congress explained the provision was aimed at helping to solve "an emergency and humanitarian situation" in the Democratic Republic of Congo, where "the exploitation and trade of conflict minerals . . . is helping to finance conflict characterized by extreme levels of violence . . . particularly sexual- and gender-based violence."[38] Shortly after the Securities and Exchange Commission implemented the law, three trade associations challenged it as unconstitutional compelled speech. The DC Circuit agreed with the trade associations, holding that whether the minerals were "conflicted" was a value judgment that the government could not force corporations to render under the First Amendment.[39]

Putting aside whether one views the conflict minerals rule as inappropriate overstepping by Congress or as an appropriate use of disclosure in the public interest, and whether rules such as these may have a short life expectancy in politically turbulent times, the point here is to observe that recent battles have added to the perception that there has been a "corporate takeover of the First Amendment."[40] As one observer explained: "Whether it is the corporate challenge to the Seattle minimum wage law where corporations were making a corporate equal protection argument or whether it is GMO labeling in Vermont . . . , corporate actors are using the First Amendment as a sword to fight democratic oversight of their conduct."[41] These battles increase the task of corporate law to order activity that is not only economic in nature and reduce the ability of government to regulate corporations as it has in the past.

The Birth of Benefit Corporations

In addition to—and arguably in tension with—these federal developments, a separate movement has arisen, reflecting the view that existing state corporate law is inadequate for businesses pursuing a social good besides shareholder wealth maximization. In 2010, the same year that the Supreme Court handed down its decision in *Citizens United*, Maryland became the first state in the United States to adopt a benefit corporation statute establishing a new form of business corporation in which the directors must consider the interests of all stakeholders and pursue a public benefit in addition to profits.[42] More than thirty states, including Delaware, currently have benefit corporation statutes.[43] Although the numbers are still modest, several thousand businesses have used these statutes, hundreds of millions of dollars of venture capital has been invested in benefit corporations, and several public corporations have subsidiaries that are benefit corporations.[44]

The catalyst for the benefit corporation movement is B Lab, a nonprofit started by social entrepreneurs with the belief that traditional corporate law does not provide a governance model that is fully consistent with operating business in a sustainable manner in the interests of all stakeholders. While some commentators have argued that a different form of corporation was unnecessary because traditional "C" corporations could be customized and corporate law gives directors discretion to consider stakeholder interests, particularly in states with constituency statutes,[45] the B Lab founders believed that it was necessary to create a new form of entity to lock into a company's DNA "mission-aligned governance" and to credibly prove to stakeholders that it was a firm commitment.[46]

The key concepts of benefit corporation legislation include requirements that the corporate charter must contain a clearly articulated public or social purpose, the directors must consider stakeholder interests beyond shareholder profit, and the company must report on its efforts to promote its purpose. Many states have adopted benefit corporation statutes based on the B Lab model legislation, but some variation exists—for example, with regard to the pursuit of a public or social benefit. Some states require the pursuit of a "general public benefit," which is defined as "a material positive impact on society and the environment, taken as a whole," whereas others leave it to the corporation to define its mission, and still others require or allow the corporation to identify a "specific social benefit."[47] Delaware, for example, defines public benefit to mean "a positive effect (or reduction of negative effects) on 1 or more categories . . . including, but not limited to, effects of an artistic, charitable, cultural, economic, educational, environmental, literary, medical, religious, scientific, or technological nature."[48]

Notwithstanding this variation, all benefit corporation statutes do not just allow the pursuit of social goals other than profit maximization, but in fact *require* them to do so, and this requirement is backed up by certain accountability and transparency mechanisms.[49] The ultimate goal of this movement appears to extend not only to spreading the benefit corporation form but to the ideals it embodies, of pursuing goals beyond economic value to shareholders, and the hope this will be embraced by business more broadly.[50]

Responses, Challenges, and Future Implications

The above discussion argues that the expanded federal rights of corporations and the birth of benefit corporations put new pressure on corporate law to serve as an ordering mechanism for interests and values beyond economics. Because the federal developments are not cabined within the benefit corporation movement, we have a broader push toward a reshaping of the rights and roles of corporations.

The next section examines some of the issues these developments have posed and identifies potential controversies that may still lie ahead. In particular, the discussion considers the possibility that reform that is responsive to the changing rights and roles of business corporations will be slow and difficult to achieve, and the history of corporate rights suggests that corporations will likely push for further expansions of rights.

Revising the Corporate Contract

Citizens United and *Hobby Lobby* raised a host of important questions in their wake. Should the same corporate law rules apply for issues concerning economic and noneconomic values? What must a corporation do to be recognized as having a social or religious identity? Are changes to voting rules in order, such as supermajority protections or other means of protecting dissenting shareholders in a new age of corporate activity? Should nonshareholder participants in the corporation have a greater voice in governance?

Despite this substantial list of questions and an abundance of attempts at reform, the years immediately following *Citizens United* and *Hobby Lobby* have produced relatively little change to corporate law or governance. The struggles to bring about real transformation in response to these landmark decisions have illuminated the political infeasibility and practical difficulty of broad-based corporate change and the fact that consensus is lacking about how to even understand existing corporate law.

One of the pressing issues post–*Citizens United* has been whether federal legislation, changes to state corporate law, or private ordering of corporations might bring governance in line with the "corporate democracy" and transparency to shareholders that the opinion had invoked in its reasoning. Although public disapproval of *Citizens United* was high,[51] reform efforts stalled in Congress. For example, a proposal by several US senators to amend the Constitution failed, as did multiple attempts at passing the Shareholder Protection Act, which would have required public companies to disclose and obtain shareholder approval of corporate political spending and to have board oversight of such spending.[52] A few states succeeded in adopting modest measures that require corporations to get board approval of corporate political expenditures,[53] but many more states considered bills requiring disclosure or shareholder approval of corporate political spending that have failed to become law.[54]

In addition, attempts to spur the Securities and Exchange Commission to mandate public companies to disclose political expenditures have so far failed. Record-breaking support for an SEC mandate has continued to grow, with a petition for public company political spending disclosure amassing more than a million public comments, including the support of many institutional investors and politicians.[55] However, under significant political pressure, then SEC chair, Mary Jo White, removed the request for rule making from the agency's agenda in 2013, and Congress buried a policy rider in the omnibus budget agreement that prevented the SEC from using fiscal year 2016 funds to finalize a rule on the topic.[56] Whether one agrees or disagrees on the merits of this result, it is notable that former Justice Anthony Kennedy, the author of the majority opinion in *Citizens United*, has expressed concern that corporate disclosure of political spending is "not working the way it should."[57]

Meanwhile, shareholders have endeavored to get political spending and disclosure rules through firm-by-firm private ordering and have had some limited and spotty success. Shareholder proposals on corporate political spending and disclosure increased significantly after *Citizens United*—hundreds of such proposals have been introduced in the past several years and a small handful have received majority shareholder support over board opposition.[58] Shareholder proposals are often negotiated behind the scenes, however, and thus much of what is known about public companies' political expenditures comes from voluntary disclosures or disclosures pursuant to privately negotiated agreements.[59] These private mechanisms have therefore brought about some increase in corporate political spending disclosure, but the broader picture remains that there have been no substantive changes to "the procedures of corporate democracy" that the Supreme Court blindly relied upon in *Citizens United*. Furthermore, shareholder proposals typically fail or proceed through opaque processes, and the information available to shareholders (and citizens) regarding corporate political spending remains incomplete.

Whereas the aftermath of *Citizens United* reflects the political infeasibility and practical difficulty of broad-based corporate change, the aftermath of *Hobby Lobby* reveals that consensus is lacking about how to even understand existing corporate law. After the Court handed down its decision in *Hobby Lobby*, the Department of the Treasury, the Department of Labor, and the Department of Health and Human Services published a proposed rule seeking comments on defining which for-profit corporations are eligible to claim religious exemptions under the decision. The Court itself had pointed to the term "closely held corporation" and state corporate law to provide guidance about how corporations may choose a religious identity. Comments flowed in, revealing that corporate law experts disagreed about how to best interpret the Court's language and reconcile it with state corporate law—belying the Court's claim that state corporate law provides a "ready means" for resolving disputes that may arise regarding which corporations have a religious identity.[60] For purposes of implementing the *Hobby Lobby* decision as to corporations claiming a religious accommodation, the three departments issued a final rule that defined eligible closely held corporations.[61] Subsequent courts have begun to grapple with whether and how to apply *Hobby Lobby*'s ruling and reasoning in different contexts beyond allowing business corporations to opt out of the contraception requirements under the Affordable Care Act.[62]

In sum, efforts to respond to *Citizens United* and *Hobby Lobby* have been limited in their effect. The Supreme Court can move relatively quickly in recasting corporate roles and rights, but responsive legislative change and private ordering are often difficult to achieve and narrower or piecemeal in scope. One of the boldest changes in corporate law in recent years has been the benefit corporation movement itself—yet it provides the choice of a separate corporate form rather than clarifying the purpose of traditional corporations or moving them toward greater transparency or improved governance.[63] Significant issues remain to be worked out to reconcile the increased social, political, and religious activity of business corporations.

Controversies on the Horizon

As state and federal law reshapes the rights and roles of business corporations, new controversies come into focus. The continued expansion of the constitutional and statutory rights of business corporations, as we saw in *Citizens United* and *Hobby Lobby*, portends potential future challenges concerning speech and association.

First, the expanded political speech rights of corporations call into question the boundaries with other areas, such as commercial speech, and the applicability of concerns about compelled speech with regard to business corporations. Although the Supreme Court has recognized a limited measure of protection for commercial speech since 1976 on the basis of the rights of listeners to be informed,[64] the Court and lower federal courts may have already lost sight of this limited basis for protection.

The recent DC Circuit conflict minerals disclosure case, discussed above, illustrates this point. There, the court found a First Amendment right against compelled speech by assuming that a value exists in protecting the autonomy of corporate speakers rather than recognizing that commercial speech is only constitutionally valuable to the extent that it provides factual information to an audience.[65] As Robert Post has explained, "Regulations that force a speaker to disgorge *more* information to an audience do not contradict the constitutional purpose of commercial speech doctrine. They may even enhance it."[66] Notably, the conflict minerals case is not an outlier; a growing number of circuit court decisions have used the doctrine of "compelled commercial speech" to strike down laws mandating commercial disclosures.[67] With changing views of corporations and the values they pursue, courts could increasingly see commercial speakers as having autonomy interests to protect.

Furthermore, in a 2011 case, *Sorrell v. IMS Health Inc.*, the Supreme Court applied "heightened" scrutiny to a commercial regulation, striking down a Vermont law that prohibited the sale, disclosure, and use of pharmacy records that reveal individual doctors' prescribing practices.[68] The majority opinion noted that "[c]ommercial speech is no exception" to the principle that "[t]he First Amendment requires heightened scrutiny whenever the government creates a regulation of speech because of disagreement with the message it conveys."[69] Justice Breyer understood the majority's ruling as a troubling turn and warned in his dissent: "At best the Court opens a Pandora's Box of First Amendment challenges to many ordinary regulatory practices that may only incidentally affect a commercial message. At worst, it reawakens *Lochner*'s pre–New Deal threat of substituting judicial for democratic decisionmaking where ordinary economic regulation is at issue."[70]

This line of cases may presage future First Amendment challenges to securities regulation and other long-standing pillars of corporate regulation. Scholars foretold this possibility decades ago,[71] and the law has moved closer in this direction. In a 2015 case, *Reed v. Town of Gilbert*, the Supreme Court cited *Sorrell* for the expansive proposition that "Government regulation of speech is content based if a law applies to particular speech because of the topic discussed or the idea or message expressed."[72] As Supreme Court commentator Adam Liptak wryly observed: "Securities regulation is a topic."[73] Indeed, taken literally or to its logical conclusion, the Supreme Court's language suggests a view of all mandatory commercial disclosures as content-based restrictions that would be subject to searching constitutional review.[74]

Another area that is ripe for new controversy in light of recent corporate developments is the Supreme Court's freedom of association doctrine, which has long recognized that expressive associations may claim institutional autonomy with respect to membership and internal governance.[75] Although an explicit dichotomy has not been drawn, commercial associations have been understood in the past as entitled only to minimal constitutional protection from regulation.[76] Justice Antonin Scalia, for example, once explained: "The robust First Amendment freedom to associate belongs only to groups 'engage[d] in 'expressive association . . .' The Campbell Soup Company does not exist to promote a message, and 'there is only minimal constitutional protection of the freedom of *commercial* association.'"[77]

Will this distinction hold in coming years? Justice Scalia referred to Campbell Soup Company simply as shorthand for what he seemed to take as a basic understanding that ordinary commercial associations are not formed to engage in First Amendment activities. But recent times have seen the developments discussed in this chapter, and we can observe that even Campbell Soup, for example, has acquired Plum Organics, a benefit corporation that "was founded by a group of parents on a mission to give the very best food to our little ones."[78]

Scholars have long criticized the distinction between expressive and commercial associations, arguing that it is unprincipled or that at least some commercial businesses deserve the same level of constitutional protection as expressive associations.[79] Their arguments are strengthened by the developments discussed in this chapter pushing corporate governance toward focusing on noneconomic values and the increasingly politicized consumer and investor markets. Benefit corporations have explicit social, religious, and environmental missions. Corporations are increasingly taking political and religious stances in the marketplace—from small businesses claiming religious liberty protections to discriminate in providing their services to major corporations pushing back against state religious liberty and anti-LGBTQ laws. Indeed, as of this writing, a case raising issues about state antidiscrimination law and the First Amendment is pending before the Supreme Court.[80]

As these trends continue, categorizing corporate activity may prove difficult. Professor Ronald Colombo posed the question: "Consider decisions to grant or deny employee benefits to unmarried domestic partners, or to purchase parts and supplies from foreign companies known to violate domestic standards regarding child labor. Could not these choices, however they are made, be deemed to some 'socially responsible,' to others 'political,' and to still others 'strictly business'"?[81]

Yet a great deal is at stake in these coming controversies. If courts "ignore[] the reality that nonhuman corporations are fundamentally distinct from their ultimate human investors,"[82] the rights of business corporations will expand and the sphere in which government can act will narrow. Indeed, "[i]f there were a First Amendment right to associate to form ordinary commercial corporations, . . . every aspect of state corporate law would be subject to strict First Amendment scrutiny."[83] Paradoxically, while some corporations echo earlier times in US history, when corporations were understood as pursuing private and public values, states and the federal government may have a smaller sphere than ever before in which they can regulate corporations.

Conclusion

Corporate governance, the "corporation's operating system," is complex and subject to continual change.[84] This chapter gathers some of the threads of recent legal change at the federal and state levels that challenge a view of corporate law as simply ordering the private economic interests and relations of shareholders and managers.

In the federal courts, First Amendment battles have increasingly placed into the spotlight the role of social, political, and religious values in business corporations. In particular, the Supreme Court's decisions in *Citizens United* and *Hobby Lobby* put weight on state corporate law to provide decision-making rules for corporate political spending and religious identity. Other federal court decisions suggest further controversy ahead with respect to corporate commercial speech and freedom of association. In a separate development, a social entrepreneurship movement has spread across the states, establishing the benefit corporation as a new form of business entity that expressly requires the pursuit of both profits and another purpose in the social, religious, or environmental realm.

A difficult question at the heart of these developments is whether there is, or could ever be, a clear and meaningful distinction between the economic and the noneconomic aspects of the business corporation or whether that distinction will always be hard to draw—or even illusory. But regardless of whether one sees these developments as increasing the role of business corporations and corporate law in ordering activity that is fundamentally noneconomic in nature or rather that simply has dimensions beyond the economic, these are important trends to pull together and examine.

As this chapter points out, understanding business corporations as institutions embedded in society, as sites of both public and private values, is not new but rather deeply rooted in history. What is new is a willingness to translate this understanding into expansions of rights for business corporations. Courts have allowed the logic of earlier decisions that set limits on the rights of corporations to fade and have embraced previously eschewed notions of autonomy and dignity interests in business corporations. There is a Pandora's box quality to this jurisprudence, as Justice Breyer observed, because it may open the door to future challenges and lines of reasoning that prove harmful. Together with the arrival of benefit corporations, these developments suggest that participants in business corporations face a changing corporate contract and will need to do more work to decide how they should operate, what activities they should engage in, and what differences in purposes and rights these varied business corporations will have.

Notes

Thanks to Sarah Haan, Benjamin Means, James Nelson, Jennifer Rothman, and Verity Winship for helpful conversations and comments, and to our excellent editors, Steven Davidoff Solomon and Randall Thomas.

1. J. W. Hurst, The Legitimacy of the Business Corporation in the Law of the United States 1780–1970 at 15–17 (1970); *see also* Alfred D. Chandler, *The Visible Hand: The Managerial Revolution in American Business* 28 (1977); Henry Hansmann and Mariana Pargendler, *The Evolution of Shareholder Voting Rights: Separation of Ownership and Consumption*, 123 Yale L. J. 948, 954–85 (2014). Notably, what constituted the public good was fiercely contested at the time. Eric Hilt, *Early American Corporations and the State*, in Corporations and American Democracy 37, 38 (Naomi R. Lamoreaux and William J. Novak eds., 2017) ("[E]arly American politics was riven by debates over business corporations, and what exactly constituted the 'common interest.'").

2. Jonathan Levy, *From Fiscal Triangle to Passing Through: Rise of the Nonprofit Corporation*, in Corporations and American Democracy 213, 217 (Naomi R. Lamoreaux and William J. Novak, eds., 2017); James J. Fishman, *The Development of Nonprofit Corporation Law and an Agenda for Reform*, 34 Emory L. J. 617, 635–36 (1985).

3. Adolf A. Berle Jr., and Gardiner C. Means, The Modern Corporation and Private Property (1932).

4. *Id.* at 356.

5. *See* Gerald F. Davis, *The Twilight of the Berle and Means Corporation*, 34 Seattle U. L. Rev. 1121 (2011).

6. Notable early works include the Berle-Dodd debate: Adolf A. Berle Jr., *Corporate Powers as Powers in Trust*, 44 Harv. L. Rev. 1049 (1931); E. Merrick Dodd Jr., *For Whom Are Corporate Managers Trustees?* 45 Harv. L. Rev. 1145 (1932); Adolf A. Berle Jr., *For Whom Corporate Managers Are Trustees: A Note*, 45 Harv. L. Rev. 1365 (1932). For a discussion of the Berle-Dodd debate, *see* William W. Bratton and Michael L. Wachter, *Shareholder Primacy's Corporatist Origins: Adolf Berle and the Modern Corporation*, 34 J. Corp. L. 99 (2008). More recent works in the corporate purpose literature include: Margaret M. Blair and Lynn A. Stout, *A Team Production Theory of Corporate Law*, 85 Va. L. Rev. 247 (1999); Stephen M. Bainbridge, *Director Primacy: The Means and Ends of Corporate Governance*, 97 Nw. U. L. Rev. 547 (2003); William W. Bratton, *Framing a Purpose for Corporate Law*, 39 J. Corp. L. 713 (2014).

7. *See, e.g.*, Revlon, Inc. v. MacAndrews & Forbes Holdings, Inc., 506 A.2d 173 (Del. 1986); Paramount Commc'ns Inc. v. QVC Network Inc., 637 A.2d 34 (Del. 1994); eBay Domestic Holdings, Inc. v. Newmark, 16 A.3d 1 (Del. Ch. 2010).

8. *See, e.g.*, William T. Allen, *Ambiguity in Corporation Law*, 22 DEL. J. CORP. L. 894 (1997); Christopher M. Bruner, *The Enduring Ambivalence of Corporate Law*, 59 ALA. L. REV. 1385 (2008); Kent Greenfield, THE FAILURE OF CORPORATE LAW 127 (2006); Lynn Stout, THE SHAREHOLDER VALUE MYTH: HOW PUTTING SHAREHOLDERS FIRST HARMS INVESTORS, CORPORATIONS, AND THE PUBLIC (2012).

9. *See* Henry Hansmann and Reinier Kraakman, *The End of History for Corporate Law*, 89 GEO. L. J. 439 (2001); Leo E. Strine Jr., *Our Continuing Struggle with the Idea That For-Profit Corporations Seek Profit*, 47 WAKE FOREST L. REV. 135 (2012); Steven M. Bainbridge, *Director Primacy: The Means and Ends of Corporate Governance*, 97 NW. U. L. REV. 547, 574 (2003).

10. *See, e.g.*, Usha Rodrigues, *Corporate Governance in an Age of Separation of Ownership from Ownership*, 95 MINN. L. REV. 1822, 1828 n.27 (2011); Myron T. Steele, *Lecture: Continuity and Change in Delaware Corporate Law Jurisprudence*, 20 FORDHAM J. CORP. & FIN. L. 352 (2015); Paul H. Edelman, Randall S. Thomas, and Robert B. Thompson, *Shareholder Voting in an Age of Intermediary Capitalism*, 87 S. CAL. L. REV. 1359, 1387–92 (2014); INSTITUTIONAL INVESTOR ACTIVISM: HEDGE FUNDS AND PRIVATE EQUITY, ECONOMICS AND REGULATION (William W. Bratton and Joseph A. McCahery eds., 2015); Ronald J. Gilson and Jeffrey N. Gordon, *The Agency Costs of Agency Capitalism: Activist Investors and the Revaluation of Governance Rights*, 113 COLUM. L. REV. 863 (2013); Randall S. Thomas, *The Evolving Role of Institutional Investors in Corporate Governance and Corporate Litigation*, 61 VAND. L. REV. 299 (2008); Marcel Kahan and Edward B. Rock, *Hedge Funds in Corporate Governance and Corporate Control*, 155 U. PA. L. REV. 1021 (2007).

11. Citizens United v. FEC, 558 U.S. 310 (2010); Burwell v. Hobby Lobby Stores, Inc., 573 U.S. _, 134 S. Ct. 2751 (2014).

12. *See, e.g.*, Lyman Johnson, *Pluralism in Corporate Form: Corporate Law and Benefit Corps.*, 25 REGENT U. L. REV. 269 (2013).

13. *See* Henry N. Butler and Larry E. Ribstein, THE CORPORATION AND THE CONSTITUTION, 93–95 (1995) (discussing the political nature of proxy speech and proxy regulation); Cynthia A. Williams, *The Securities and Exchange Commission and Corporate Social Transparency*, 112 HARV. L. REV. 1197 (1999) (arguing that the SEC can and should require social and financial disclosure by public companies to promote corporate social transparency).

14. William T. Allen, *Our Schizophrenic Conception of the Business Corporation*, 14 CARDOZO L. REV. 261 (1992).

15. For example, the substantive corporate governance mandates of Sarbanes-Oxley Act of 2002 included provisions that require independent audit committees, executive certifications of financial statements, and restrictions on purchasing nonauditing services from the corporation's auditors and a prohibition on corporate loans to officers. *See, e.g.*, Roberta Romano, *The Sarbanes-Oxley*

Act and the Making of Quack Corporate Governance, 114 YALE L. J. 1521 (2005).

16. *See, e.g.*, Colin Mayer, FIRM COMMITMENT: WHY THE CORPORATION IS FAILING US AND HOW TO RESTORE TRUST IN IT (2013); Lynn Stout, THE SHAREHOLDER VALUE MYTH: HOW PUTTING SHAREHOLDERS FIRST HARMS INVESTORS, CORPORATIONS, AND THE PUBLIC (2012); Kent Greenfield, THE FAILURE OF CORPORATE LAW (2006); Lucian Arye Bebchuk, *The Case for Increasing Shareholder Power*, 118 HARV. L. REV. 833 (2005).

17. Ciara Torres-Spelliscy, CORPORATE CITIZEN? AN ARGUMENT FOR THE SEPARATION OF CORPORATION AND STATE 6 (2016); John C. Coates IV, *Corporate Speech and the First Amendment: History, Data, and Implications*, 30 CONST. COMMENT. 223 (2015).

18. Coates, *Corporate Speech* at 223; Amanda Shanor, *The New* Lochner, 2016 WIS. L. REV. 133, 140.

19. Margaret M. Blair and Elizabeth Pollman, *The Derivative Nature of Corporate Constitutional Rights*, 56 WM. & MARY L. REV. 1673 (2015).

20. Coates, *Corporate Speech* at 224.

21. 558 U.S. 310, 319 (2010). Specifically, the Court struck down a provision of the Bipartisan Campaign Reform Act that prohibited corporations from using general treasury funds to make expenditures for electioneering communications within a certain period of a federal election, and it overruled Austin v. Michigan Chamber of Commerce, 494 U.S. 652 (1990).

22. *Citizens United*, 558 U.S. at 319, 327–29; *see also* FEC v. Mass. Citizens for Life, Inc., 479 U.S. 238 (1986).

23. *Citizens United*, 558 U.S. at 349, 354.

24. *See id.* at 340–41 ("By taking the right to speak from some and giving it to others, the Government deprives the disadvantaged person or class of the right to use speech to strive to establish worth, standing, and respect for the speaker's voice.").

25. *Citizens United*, 558 U.S. at 370 ("With the advent of the Internet, prompt disclosure of expenditures can provide shareholders and citizens with the information needed to hold corporations and elected officials accountable for their positions and supporters. Shareholders can determine whether their corporation's political speech advances the corporation's interest in making profits, and citizens can see whether elected officials are in the pocket of so-called moneyed interests.") (internal quotation marks omitted).

26. *Id.* at 361–62 (quoting First Nat'l Bank of Boston v. Bellotti, 435 U.S. 765, 794 (1978)).

27. *Bellotti*, 435 U.S. 765; Justin Levitt, *Confronting the Impact of Citizens United*, 29 YALE L. & POL'Y REV. 217, 217 (2010) (arguing "that although the decision was a bold stroke in many ways, its impact on the scope of permissible campaign finance regulation is far less substantial than commonly assumed").

28. Michael Luo, *Money Talks Louder Than Ever in Midterms*, N.Y. Times (Oct. 7, 2010), http://www.nytimes.com/2010/10/08/us/politics/08donate.html?pagewanted=all. Notably, a significant portion of post–*Citizens United* expenditures have come from wealthy individuals. *See* Matea Gold and Anu Narayanswamy, *The New Gilded Age: Close to Half of All Super-PAC Money Comes from 50 Donors*, Wash. Post (Apr. 15, 2016), https://www.washingtonpost.com/politics/the-new-gilded-age-close-to-half-of-all-super-pac-money-comes-from-50-donors/2016/04/15/63dc363c-01b4-11e6-9d36-33d198ea26c5_story.html?utm_term=.6c840f9bbfb7; Nicholas Confessore et al., *The Families Funding the 2016 Presidential Election*, N.Y. Times (Oct. 10, 2015), http://www.nytimes.com/interactive/2015/10/11/us/politics/2016-presidential-election-super-pac-donors.html.

29. Adam Winkler, *Alito Was Rude (But Right)*, Huffington Post (May 25, 2011), http://www.huffingtonpost.com/adam-winkler/alito-was-rude-but-right_b_440207.html.

30. *See* Susanna Kim Ripken, *Corporate First Amendment Rights after* Citizens United*: An Analysis of the Popular Movement to End the Constitutional Personhood of Corporations*, 14 U. Pa. J. Bus. L. 209 (2011).

31. *See, e.g.*, Ciara Torres-Spelliscy, *Why Is Chevron Spending Millions on a Municipal Election?* Brennan Center for Justice (Oct. 21, 2014), https://www.brennancenter.org/blog/why-chevron-spending-millions-municipal-election.

32. Larry E. Ribstein, *The First Amendment and Corporate Governance*, 27 Ga. St. U. L. Rev. 1019, 1021 (2011).

33. 134 S. Ct. 2751, 2762 (2014).

34. 42 U.S.C. § 2000bb-1(a), (b)(2012). In *Employment Division v. Smith*, the Supreme Court held that "the right of free exercise does not relieve an individual of the obligation to comply with a 'valid and neutral law of general applicability.'" 494 U.S. 872, 879 (1990). RFRA is a legislative response to *Smith*, with a stated purpose to "restore the compelling interest test" as set forth in pre-*Smith* case law. § 2000bb(a)(4), (b)(1).

35. 134 S. Ct. at 2768.

36. *Id.* at 2775.

37. Elizabeth Pollman, *Constitutionalizing Corporate Law*, 69 Vand. L. Rev. 639 (2016).

38. Dodd–Frank § 1502(a), 124 Stat. 2213.

39. Nat'l Ass'n of Mfrs. v. SEC, 748 F.3d 359, 371 (D.C. Cir. 2014); Nat'l Ass'n of Mfrs. v. SEC, 800 F.3d 518, 530 (D.C. Cir. 2015) ("[W]e continue to agree with NAM that [r]equiring a company to publicly condemn itself is undoubtedly a more effective way for the government to stigmatize and shape behavior than for the government to have to convey its views itself, but that makes the requirement more constitutionally offensive, not less so.") (internal quotation marks and footnote omitted).

40. Coates, *Corporate Speech*.

41. Torres-Spelliscy, CORPORATE CITIZEN at 76–77 (quoting interview with Elizabeth Kennedy, Counsel, Demos (Aug. 12, 2015)).

42. Frederick H. Alexander, *The Capital Markets and Benefit Corporations*, AMERICAN BAR ASS'N (July 5, 2016), http://www.americanbar.org/publications/blt/2016/07/05_alexander.html; Brett McDonnell, *Benefit Corporations and Strategic Action Fields (or the Existential Failing of Delaware)*, 39 SEATTLE U. L. REV. 263, 280 (2016) ("These statutes sit atop the basic business corporation statute. That is, benefit corporations *are* business corporations, subject to all of the rules of the business corporation statute, except insofar as the benefit corporation statute provides different or additional rules.").

43. Alexander, *Capital Markets*; *State by State Status of Legislation*, B LAB, http://benefitcorp.net/policymakers/state-by-state-status.

44. Alexander, *Capital Markets*; Leo E. Strine Jr., *Making It Easier for Directors to "Do the Right Thing"?* 4 HARV. BUS. L. REV. 235, 253 (2014); *see also* Jesse Finfrock and Eric Talley, *Social Entrepreneurship and Uncorporations*, 2014 U. ILL. L. REV. 1867, 1867 (arguing that using limited liability company uptake as a comparative historical benchmark suggests "that there is hope that these new social enterprise corporations will see an increasing rate of uptake in the future").

45. *See, e.g.*, Lyman Johnson, *Unsettledness in Delaware Corporate Law: Business Judgment Rule, Corporate Purpose*, 38 DEL. J. CORP. L. 405, 405–6 (2013) ("Delaware's new benefit corporation law laudably advances the goal of institutional pluralism, but does so at the ironic risk of reinforcing a belief that business corporations themselves are legally permitted only to maximize profits.").

46. Alexander, *Capital Markets*; Mark J. Loewenstein, *Benefit Corporations: A Challenge in Corporate Governance*, 68 BUS. LAW. 1007, 1036 (2013).

47. Michael Vargas, *The Next Stage of Social Entrepreneurship: Benefit Corporations and the Companies Using This Innovative Corporate Form*, AMERICAN BAR ASS'N (July 5, 2016), http://www.americanbar.org/publications/blt/2016/07/01_vargas.html.

48. Del. Code Ann. Tit. 8 § 362(b) (2013).

49. McDonnell, *Benefit Corporations* at 280.

50. Strine, *Making It Easier* at 253.

51. For example, in a *Washington Post–ABC News* poll, eight in ten respondents opposed the decision, with 65 percent "strongly" opposed. Dan Eggen, *Poll: Large Majority Opposes Supreme Court's Decision on Campaign Financing*, WASH. POST (Feb. 17, 2010), http://www.washingtonpost.com/wp-dyn/content/article/2010/02/17/AR2010021701151.html.

52. James R. Copland and Margaret M. O'Keefe, *Political Spending and Lobbying*, PROXY MONITOR (2016), http://www.proxymonitor.org/Forms/2016

Finding3.aspx#notes. For an argument that political speech decisions are different from ordinary business decisions and necessitate special corporate law rules, *see* Lucian A. Bebchuk and Robert J. Jackson Jr., *Corporate Political Speech: Who Decides?* 124 HARV. L. REV. 83 (2010).

53. La. Rev. Stat. Ann. 18:1505.2(F); Mo. Ann. Stat. 130.029; Ia. Stat. 68A.404(2); *see also* Iowa Right to Life Comm., Inc. v. Tooker, 717 F.3d 576 (8th Cir. 2013) (reviewing Iowa's campaign finance law).

54. Torres-Spelliscy, CORPORATE CITIZEN at 279–80.

55. Lucian A. Bebchuk and Robert J. Jackson Jr., *Hindering the S.E.C. from Shining a Light on Political Spending*, N.Y. TIMES (Dec. 21, 2015), http://www.nytimes.com/2015/12/22/business/dealbook/hindering-the-sec-from-shining-a-light-on-political-spending.html.

56. *Id.*

57. *Id.*

58. Sarah C. Haan, *Shareholder Proposal Settlements and the Private Ordering of Public Elections*, 126 YALE L. J. 262, 294 n.122 (2016).

59. *Id.* at 262, 264–66.

60. *See* Lyman Johnson et al., Comments on the HHS' Flawed Post-Hobby Lobby Rules (UCLA School of Law Research Paper No. 14-18, 2014), https://papers.ssrn.com/sol3/papers.cfm?abstract_id=2512860; Robert P. Bartlett III et al., Comment on the Definition of "Eligible Organization" (Oct. 8, 2014), http://ssrn.com/abstract=2507305 (authored by UC Berkeley corporate law professors); Katherine Franke et al., Comment on the Definition of "Eligible Organization" (Oct. 21, 2014), https://web.law.columbia.edu/sites/default/files/microsites/gender-sexuality/prpcp_comments_on_proposed_regs_corp_law_profs_for_submission.pdf (authored by the Columbia Conscience Project and corporate law professors).

61. *Administration Issues Final Rules on Coverage of Certain Recommended Preventive Services without Cost Sharing*, HHS.GOV (July 10, 2015), http://www.hhs.gov/about/news/2015/07/10/administration-issues-final-rules-on-coverage-of-certain-recommended-preventive-services-without-cost-sharing.html.

62. *See, e.g.*, EEOC v. R.G. & G.R. Harris Funeral Homes, Inc., 201 F. Supp. 3d 837, 863 (E.D. Mich. 2016) (citing *Hobby Lobby* in holding that a closely held corporation that terminated a transgender employee for sex-based considerations was eligible to claim RFRA protection from Title VII).

63. *See* Kevin V. Tu, *Socially Conscious Corporations and Shareholder Profit*, 84 GEO. WASH. L. REV. 121, 127 (2016) (arguing that "[i]n the absence of additional action, traditional for-profit corporations see little, if any, improvement from the addition of Benefit Corporations").

64. Va. State Bd. of Pharmacy v. Va. Citizens Consumer Council, Inc., 425 U.S. 748 (1976); Cent. Hudson Gas & Electric Corp. v. Pub. Serv. Comm'n, 447 U.S. 557 (1980); *see also* Robert C. Post, CITIZENS DIVIDED: CAMPAIGN

Finance Reform and the Constitution 74 (2014) ("[T]he speech is protected only because it promotes informed public decision making.").

65. Robert Post, *Compelled Commercial Speech*, 117 W. Va. L. Rev. 867, 874–79 (2015).

66. *Id.* at 877; *see also* Shanor, *The New* Lochner at 151–52.

67. *See, e.g.*, Nat'l Ass'n of Mfrs. v. NLRB, 717 F.3d 947 (D.C. Cir. 2013); R.J. Reynolds Tobacco Co. v. FDA, 696 F.3d 1205 (D.C. Cir. 2012); Authentic Beverages Co. v. Tex. Alcoholic Beverage Comm'n, 835 F. Supp. 2d 227 (W.D. Tex. 2011).

68. 564 U.S. 552 (2011).

69. *Id.* at 566 (internal quotation marks omitted).

70. *Id.* at 602–3 (Breyer, J., dissenting).

71. *See, e.g.*, Butler and Ribstein, The Corporation and the Constitution at 79–106.

72. 135 S. Ct. 2218, 2227 (2015).

73. Adam Liptak, *Court's Free-Speech Expansion Has Far-Reaching Consequences*, N.Y. Times (Aug. 17, 2015), http://www.nytimes.com/2015/08/18/us/politics/courts-free-speech-expansion-has-far-reaching-consequences.html; *see also* Torres-Spelliscy, Corporate Citizen at 97.

74. Other related issues include defining the boundaries of what constitutes commercial speech and the tests and levels of scrutiny applied to laws that restrict versus compel commercial speech. Compare Cent. Hudson Gas & Electric Corp. v. Pub. Serv. Comm'n, 447 U.S. 557 (1980) with Zauderer v. Office of Disciplinary Counsel, 471 U.S. 626 (1985).

75. Roberts v. U.S. Jaycees, 468 U.S. 609, 622 (1984) ("[W]e have long understood as implicit in the right to engage in activities protected by the First Amendment a corresponding right to associate with others in pursuit of a wide variety of political, social, economic, educational, religious, and cultural ends."); Boy Scouts of Am. v. Dale, 530 U.S. 640, 655 (2000) ("An association must merely engage in expressive activity that could be impaired in order to be entitled to protection.").

76. James D. Nelson, *The Freedom of Business Association*, 115 Colum. L. Rev. 461, 462 (2015).

77. Wash. St. Grange v. Wash. St. Repub. Party, 552 U.S. 442, 467 (2008) (Scalia, J., dissenting).

78. Press release, *Campbell to Acquire Plum Organics, A Leading Premium, Organic Kids Nutrition Company*, Campbell Soup Co. (May. 23, 2013), http://www.campbellsoupcompany.com/newsroom/press-releases/campbell-to-acquire-plum-organics-a-leading-premium-organic-kids-nutrition-company/.

79. *See, e.g.*, Ronald J. Colombo, The First Amendment and the Business Corporation (2014); Richard A. Epstein, *The Constitutional Perils of Moderation: The Case of the Boy Scouts*, 74 S. Cal. L. Rev. 119 (2000); John D.

Inazu, *Factions for the Rest of Us*, 89 WASH. U. L. REV. 1435 (2012); Jed Rubenfeld, *The First Amendment's Purpose*, 53 STAN. L. REV. 767 (2001); Robert K. Vischer, *How Necessary Is the Right of Assembly?* 89 WASH. U. L. REV. 1403 (2012).

80. Craig v. Masterpiece Cakeshop, Inc., 370 P.3d 272 (Colo. App. 2015), *cert. granted*, Masterpiece Cakeshop, Ltd. v. Colo. Civil Rights Comm'n, 2017 WL 2722428 (June 26, 2017), _ U.S. _ (2018); *see also* Petitioners' Petition for A Writ of Certiorari, http://www.scotusblog.com/wp-content/uploads/2016/08/16–111-cert-petition.pdf ("Petitioner Masterpiece Cakeshop, Ltd., is a small Colorado corporation owned by Petitioner Jack Phillips, an individual and citizen of Colorado, and his wife").

81. Colombo, THE FIRST AMENDMENT at 100–101. *See also, e.g.*, Virginia Harper Ho, *"Enlightened Shareholder Value": Corporate Governance Beyond the Shareholder-Stakeholder Divide*, 36 J. CORP. L. 59 (2010) (discussing the "enlightened shareholder value" approach which views the effect of corporate operations on the environment, employees, and other stakeholders as key to long-term financial performance and risk management). For example, in its 2015 Global Governance Principles, public pension fund CalPERS included "sustainability" as one of its "core principles" for long-term value creation and described it as including concern for governance, the environment, and social issues pertaining to human capital such as fair labor practices and workplace and board diversity. It further listed "corporate social responsibility—eliminating human rights violations" as another of its "core principles." *See* CalPERS Global Governance Principles, Mar. 16, 2016, https://www.calpers.ca.gov/docs/forms-publications/global-principles-corporate-governance.pdf.

82. Leo E. Strine Jr. and Nicholas Walter, *Conservative Collision Course? The Tension between Conservative Corporate Law Theory and* Citizens United, 100 CORNELL L. REV. 335, 386 (2015).

83. Post, CITIZENS DIVIDED at 70.

84. Ronald J. Gilson, *From Corporate Law to Corporate Governance*, in Jeffrey N. Gordon and Wolf-Georg Ringe, THE OXFORD HANDBOOK OF CORPORATE LAW AND GOVERNANCE(Oxford 2018), https://papers.ssrn.com/sol3/Papers.cfm?abstract_id=2819128.

CHAPTER NINE

The Many Modern Sources of Business Law

Colleen Honigsberg and Robert J. Jackson Jr.

Introduction

This book grapples with an important question that has largely eluded systematic study: whether American law is keeping up with the businesses it seeks to govern. The question is important, because the increasing pace of technological change[1] naturally gives rise to the concern that the law—created and enforced by actors who lack innovators' powerful incentives[2] to adapt to changed markets—will fall behind, imposing unproductive rules from another era on modern businesses.[3] From the common law of mergers and acquisitions to securities regulation, our colleagues' chapters help us better understand how the law might adapt to better serve corporate law's many constituents.[4]

In this chapter, we have a much less ambitious goal. We merely observe that, for many of today's most innovative corporations, there are so many sources of what can be called corporate law—each the subject of different political economy, policy objectives, and institutional sources—that there cannot be said to be a single, unified business law for these firms. Instead, "business law" at these companies consists of a complex ecosystem of federal, state, and local rules, all of which can be expected to change in response to emerging business models.[5] For that reason, we argue, understanding those interactions, and how the different sources of law can challenge companies by creating inconsistent pockets of law, is the true challenge for lawmakers who hope to ensure that law facilitates, rather than impedes, innovation.

We begin by illustrating this idea through a contemporary case study of an innovative industry that emerged against the backdrop of existing law arguably designed for another era: marketplace lending. These fast-growing finance firms seek to match prospective borrowers to willing lenders, enabling fast, cost-effective funding decisions, and are expected to issue over $150 billion in loans within the decade.[6] Yet marketplace lenders face extraordinary uncertainty about the law that will govern their operations at both the federal and state levels. Indeed, as we explain, marketplace lenders cannot meaningfully be said to face a single, unified corporate law.

We apply the insights from our case study of marketplace lending to the broader topic of this book: whether corporate law is keeping up with our economy's most innovative firms. We explain that the concept of corporate law encompasses not only federal securities law and the work of Delaware's famed judiciary but also a wide range of federal and state agencies tasked with protecting consumers, investors, and the broader public. For us, then, the question is not whether corporate law is keeping up with innovation; it is whether the interdependent evolution of the institutional sources of corporate law can be expected to produce an environment in which productive innovation will occur. Understanding the interplay between these different sources of regulation is critical, because confusion over the state of the law can, and often does, stifle socially valuable innovation.

This chapter proceeds as follows. The next section describes the emergence of marketplace lenders and the uniquely complex legal challenges that have arisen in response to their business model. A later section explains how the marketplace-lending experience can inform our thinking about the evolution of the institutional sources of corporate law in response to innovation. Finally, we offer a brief conclusion.

The Evolving Law of Marketplace Lending

The emergence of the marketplace-lending industry over the past decade offers a unique case study for this book's broader project. The business model draws heavily on technology to reduce the information and coordination costs of an ancient industry: lending. But that innovation also makes it difficult to know what institution—among the many that now regulate traditional lending—should have principal responsibility for the companies that use this increasingly popular business model.

Marketplace lending platforms use websites to match willing lenders with borrowers. The three largest platforms alone coordinated some $12 billion in loans in 2015.[7] And the industry is growing quickly: Observers expect that the industry will issue more than $150 billion in loans annually by 2025.[8] So the economic stakes over whether the law has kept up with this industry are significant.

Although there is some variance among platforms, marketplace lending generally works as follows.[9] A borrower submits an application with certain information, including her credit profile, employment history, and the intended use of the loan proceeds. Then, using a proprietary algorithm, the platform assigns a risk score to the application. Next, the application is posted to the platform's website, where investors can review the borrower's information and conduct their own risk assessment—investors are provided with significant detail, but any information that would allow the borrower to be personally identified is omitted. The investors then elect whether to fund all, or a portion, of the loan at the offered terms.

If enough investors are willing to fund the loan, the platform arranges for the loan to be approved. The loan itself will be issued by a federally insured national bank, typically pursuant to an agreement between the platform and that bank.[10] Pieces of this loan are then sold to the investors that have agreed to fund the commitment. The platform makes money by charging an origination fee along with a servicing fee throughout the loan's lifetime.[11]

By expanding the pool of potential lenders and providing exceptionally fast funding decisions, marketplace platforms hold some promise of expanded access to credit.[12] Further, platforms typically charge lower rates than those charged by traditional banks for credit cards—and, of course, the platforms' existence exerts competitive pressure that may lower rates more generally.[13] And, since most marketplace-lending consumers use the proceeds of their loans to repay higher-interest credit card debt,[14] the presence of marketplace lending can save some consumers the difference between credit card rates and marketplace rates. Especially for lower-quality borrowers, this difference may be substantial.

The nature of the marketplace-lending business, however, makes it difficult to situate in the existing, and extensive, legal regime governing lending. At the federal level alone, at least ten statutes governing banking, credit reporting, securities, and lending raise questions about marketplace-lender compliance.[15] For example, because marketplace platforms often facilitate the sale of pieces of loans, the Securities Act of 1933 is implicated.[16] And the Investment Company Act of 1940 is also relevant because the platforms assess the credit risk of particular loans.[17]

Emphasizing the federal statutes that raise risks for marketplace lenders, however, obscures the true source of legal constraints on their operations at the federal level: regulators. In late 2015, the Federal Deposit Insurance Corporation (FDIC) issued a prominent letter to financial institutions addressing "effective risk management" of purchased loans; as practitioners noted, "the timing of [the letter's] issuance suggested that one of the focal points was marketplace lending."[18] Under this guidance, financial institutions participating in marketplace lending are required to conduct extensive due diligence and monitoring of the lender's activities; according to our conversations with industry participants, this additional diligence has imposed significant costs for platforms and banks alike.[19] Nor is the FDIC alone: the Consumer Financial Protection Bureau recently announced that it is accepting consumer complaints about marketplace lending and issued guidance to consumers considering such loans.[20]

Recognizing that the phalanx of laws and regulatory agencies that apply to marketplace lending generate both regulatory gaps and market uncertainty, the US Treasury Department sought to coordinate the many potential legal responses to the industry's emergence.[21] In an unusual step, the department called for public comment in summer 2015, posing more than a dozen questions to industry, including those relating to "the risks arising from data-driven processes relative to those used in traditional lending, the provisions in place in the event of a downturn, and the potential harms to businesses and consumers."[22]

In a white paper released a year later, the Treasury Department noted that public comments "reflected a diverse set of viewpoints on the best role of the federal government" in marketplace lending: Some comments "called for a uniform regulatory regime for marketplace lenders," while others "argued that existing regulations are adequate to safeguard against the risks posed by the industry."[23] Nearly all seemed to agree, however, that "regulatory clarity could benefit the market."[24] It was ironic, then, that just weeks after the Treasury issued its white paper, the Office of the Comptroller of the Currency—an agency that is itself a bureau of the Treasury Department[25]—unveiled a new proposal requiring nationwide licensing of marketplace lenders[26] that had barely been mentioned by the Treasury.

Quite apart from the federal level, extensive state laws on both lending and securities raise concerns for marketplace lenders.[27] In particular, state usury laws, which cap the interest rate that a lender may charge on loans and are as low as 5 percent in some states,[28] have recently become a source of significant legal risk for these lenders.[29] The consequences for violating usury statutes are significant: In nearly all states with such a law, the lender is required to return to the borrower any interest paid above the usury cap.[30] And in some states, including New York and Connecticut, a loan above the usury cap is null and void; the borrower is entitled to keep the principal as a gift.[31]

Until recently, these state usury laws were not a significant concern for the industry because marketplace lenders relied on preemption of state usury statutes by the National Bank Act of 1864 (NBA), which permits national banks to charge interest up to the rate permitted in the state "where the bank is located."[32] NBA preemption is partly why many banks, and especially those that focus on consumer lending, are chartered in states such as South Dakota, which has no usury limit.

At the turn of the century, as securitization grew in popularity, a question arose when a loan was *issued* in compliance with the applicable usury cap of that state but was later sold to a lender in another state. Under traditional usury law, the rule is that loans are "valid when made": So long as the loan complies with the relevant usury statute at the time it is issued, a change in the loan's owner does not alter its compliance with usury law.[33] Federal courts facing usury law challenges to securitized loans consistently extended this rule to NBA preemption.[34] Thus, marketplace lenders—by arranging for loans to be issued by a national bank—assumed that their loans would not be subject to state usury caps by dint of such preemption.

In 2015, however, the Second Circuit shocked marketplace platforms and their investors by concluding in *Madden v. Midland Funding LLC* that National Bank Act preemption does *not* apply to loans initiated by a national bank but later sold to a nonbank third party.[35] As a result, the decision rendered marketplace loans above usury caps of questionable enforceability.[36] Upon reviewing the decision, one large New York law firm remarked: "Given that non-bank purchasers will be unable to enforce the terms of a loan according to the original agreement between bank and borrower, [*Madden*] will undoubtedly chill the market for . . . securitizations and bank loan programs with third parties," such as marketplace lending.[37]

Consistent with this prediction, our prior work evaluated the effect of the *Madden* decision on marketplace lending in the Second Circuit.[38] We found that the decision significantly reduced the volume of loans issued to riskier borrowers, who are more likely to borrow at rates above usury limits.[39] Such a result is not surprising when one considers the harsh repercussions for issuing usurious loans, particularly in states such as New York and Connecticut. Indeed, one leading marketplace lender now includes disclosures in registration statements for its sale of loans, describing the decision as a significant risk factor.[40] Another lender changed the financial structure of its transactions—requiring the originating bank to hold a small portion of the underlying loan—in an effort to accommodate the ruling.[41]

At present, the fate of the Madden decision remains uncertain. In a petition for certiorari, Midland previously argued that *Madden* "threaten[ed] to inflict catastrophic consequences on secondary markets that are essential to the operation of the national banking system."[42] Although the solicitor general agreed with the petitioners in later briefing that the *Madden* "decision is incorrect," it concluded that the Supreme Court's review was unwarranted.[43] The Court eventually agreed, denying review and leaving the *Madden* decision in place.[44] As a result, in New York, Vermont, and Connecticut, marketplace lenders currently cannot expect that the NBA will preempt state usury statutes.

We offer the narrative of the law of marketplace lending not merely to plead, as the Treasury Department has done, for legal clarity. We think that there is more to learn from the story. It shows how regulators, legislators, and judges will scramble—and struggle—to keep up as business innovation blurs long-standing lines dividing responsibility for legal decision making. That is why, just weeks after the Treasury Department produced a detailed study of a new industry, the Office of the Comptroller of the Currency proposed a nationwide licensing scheme in considerable tension with that study.[45] That is why federal judges find themselves in the awkward, and institutionally untenable, position of regulating interest rates for marketplace loans.[46] And that is why, as explained in the next section, it cannot be said that there is a single source of law governing the United States' most innovative companies.

Corporate Law and Innovation

The legal and institutional dynamics that have shaped the law of marketplace lending can help us better understand how corporate law has evolved in response to innovation. In short, because that evolution reflects interdependent decisions of regulators, lawmakers, judges, and private actors at both the state and federal levels, it cannot meaningfully be said today that there is a single corporate law governing America's most innovative companies.

We will begin with a discussion of the relationship between federal sources of corporate law—such as securities law—and the dominant source of US corporate law, Delaware's General Corporation Law, and the decisions of its courts. As Mark Roe famously observed, we can expect these institutions to develop law dynamically, each adjusting its position on a particular issue in light of its prediction about what the other will do.[47] Because "Washington can take away any, or all," of Delaware's authority to make law, "[w]hen Delaware fears a federal trump, Washington can affect what it does." As a result, Professor Roe explained, Delaware's resolution of disputes among its many interest groups depends in part on how Delaware imagines the federal government will respond to its decisions.[48]

Nor is this a one-way ratchet, with the federal government intervening only in areas where it is unsatisfied with Delaware's response. Delaware, too, has filled perceived gaps in corporate law when, in the views of its judges, federal agencies have failed to act. Take, for example, the law governing the disclosures shareholders receive in connection with mergers and acquisitions. For decades, that law was provided principally by the Securities and Exchange Commission through regulations interpreting the 1934 Securities Exchange Act. But when Delaware's jurists became convinced that SEC rules—and practitioners' interpretations of them—failed to provide investors with adequate information regarding advisor conflicts in the mergers and acquisition context, chancery judges stepped in with decisions requiring additional disclosure as a matter of directors' fiduciary duties.[49]

As that example shows, corporate law today is made in the shadow of a complex set of interactions between state and federal institutions. Consider, for example, the law governing activist shareholders. Delaware's cases have recently evinced some sympathy to the possibility that these investors might, especially when acting in concert, endanger the interests of shareholders more generally.[50] But those cases have developed against an ongoing debate at the Securities and Exchange Commission about whether the federal securities rules governing disclosure of significant activist stakes in public corporations should be tightened.[51] And, as one of us has pointed out, *that* debate itself has been profoundly influenced by the emergence, in the decades since the passage of the relevant securities statutes, of state corporate law authorizing takeover defenses that give managers significant latitude in blocking unfriendly acquisitions.[52] The law of shareholder activism, then, is best conceived not as a single area of corporate law but as an ongoing exchange among federal and state legislators, regulators, and judges.

But even that description fails to capture the many dynamics that define the development of modern corporate law. The reason, of course, is that the agenda for policy makers' exchanges in corporate law is typically set by private actors—corporate directors, investors, and their respective counsel. An instructive case study in this respect is the tale of so-called golden leashes—that is, compensation arrangements between activist investors and their director nominees designed to incentivize those directors to maximize the activist's return.

As Matthew Cain, Jill Fisch, Sean Griffith, and Steven Davidoff Solomon explained in recent work, the golden leash emerged as an innovation among high-profile activist investors.[53] Corporate counsel soon responded with an innovation of their own: a bylaw, adopted by some thirty large public companies, prohibiting the use of such arrangements.[54] *That* innovation, in turn, was then challenged, but not in any court of law: Institutional Shareholder Services concluded that it would recommend that shareholders withhold votes from directors at firms adopting such a bylaw, and soon the bylaw was repealed at twenty-eight of the thirty firms.[55] In sum, the authors concluded, "intermediaries," such as corporate counsel and institutional investors, "play an important role in channeling . . . innovation" in corporate law.[56]

Like the law of marketplace lending, corporate law today is the product of extensive exchanges among state and federal legislators, regulators, and judges, all of whom must scramble to respond to institutionally driven innovations. For that reason, we think, there is no single source of corporate law that can be said, to borrow the parlance of this volume's title, to be keeping up with America's most innovative corporations. Instead, the institutions responsible for the path of corporate law are merely participants in a complex interaction that produces the legal environment in which those corporations must operate. As the students of the golden leash put it, the development of corporate law today is a "complex story involving the actions and reactions not only of the firm and its shareholders"—legislators, regulators, and courts—"but of a variety of intermediaries and interest groups that have agendas of their own."[57]

Importantly, the interaction among these sources of law can have real effects on innovation throughout the US economy. As we have shown in our work on marketplace lending, legal uncertainty in this area has deprived American consumers of new sources of credit. But this is just one example of the effects of legal uncertainty on innovation. Consider, for example, the investment incentives now facing entrepreneurs interested in the sale and distribution of marijuana, who face a phalanx of state laws authorizing those businesses and the very real prospect that the federal government will seek to shut them down.[58] Even Tesla—the automobile manufacturer thought to be among the most innovative companies in the United States, worth more than $50 billion as of this writing—faces uncertainty as to whether its direct-to-consumer sales model violates state laws purporting to ban that approach.[59] In this way, uncertainty about the interactions among the many institutional sources of business law has had—and, we think, will continue to have—significant effects on innovation throughout the economy.

Conclusion

This book asks an important question: whether American business law is keeping up with the rapid technological change characterizing businesses throughout the US economy. Our colleagues' chapters help us better understand how the classic components of corporate law, from appraisal to securities law to the purpose of the corporate form itself, might grapple with that change. In this chapter, however, we offer a narrower claim: that the modern firm faces so many sources of business regulation that there cannot be said to be a single corporate law for those firms. Business law at today's most innovative companies, we have shown, consists of a complex web of federal, state, and local rules made and enforced by a wide range of institutions—all scrambling to keep up with the changing businesses they regulate.

Using the experience of marketplace lenders as a case study, we explain why emerging industries may face constantly changing, and frequently inconsistent, legal mandates from rule makers and judges alike at both the federal and state levels. Similarly, we argue that today's corporate law consists not only of Delaware judicial decisions and federal securities rules but of a complex interaction among a wide range of government agencies, intermediaries, and institutions—all with their own interests in the course of US business law.

In our view, the course that law will take—whether, and how, it keeps pace with the innovations driving the economy—is unlikely to depend on the decisions of any particular lawmaker. Instead, the path of US corporate law today depends fundamentally on how the wide range of institutions that produce business law interact with one another—and the firms they seek to govern.

Notes

This chapter benefited a great deal from conversations with Zohar Goshen, Joshua Mitts, Randall Thomas, and Steven Davidoff Solomon. We are grateful to the Columbia Law School and the Stanford Law School for financial support.

1. *See, e.g.*, Rita Gunther McGrath, THE END OF COMPETITIVE ADVANTAGE 44 (2013) (contending that increasingly rapid adoption of new technologies endangers traditional sources of competitive advantage); *see also* Michael DeGusta, *Are Smart Phones Spreading Faster Than Any Technology in Human History?* MIT TECH. REVIEW (May 9, 2012) (concluding that, while the telephone took some thirty-nine years to achieve 40 percent consumer penetration, the smart phone achieved this in fewer than five years).

2. *See, e.g.*, Jones v. Harris Associates, L.P., 527 F.3d 627, 633 (7th Cir. 2008) (Easterbrook, J.) ("Competitive processes are imperfect but remain superior to a 'just price' system administered by the judiciary. However weak competition may be at weeding out errors, the judicial process is worse—for judges can't be turned out of office or have their salaries cut if they display poor business judgment.").

3. For one helpful articulation of this concern, *see* The Brookings Institution, PHDs, POLICIES AND PATENTS: INNOVATION AND AMERICA'S FUTURE, PANEL DISCUSSION: OBSTACLES AND OPPORTUNITIES FOR AMERICAN SCIENCE AND INNOVATION 5 (Washington, DC, 2011) ("Work changes not at the pace of the new enabling technologies that enter . . . but at the pace that bureaucracies change to take them up. . . . And that's slower. It's slower to change bureaucracies around.") (statement of Professor Timothy Bresnahan, Landau Professor of Technology and the Economy, Stanford University).

4. *See* Steven Davidoff Solomon and Randall S. Thomas, "The Rise and Fall of Delaware's Takeover Standards," chap. 2 in this volume; Verity Winship, "Litigation Rights and the Corporate Contract," chap. 12 in this volume.

5. Because our chapter focuses on the narrow questions raised by the increasingly important interplay among various sources of corporate law, we put to one side broader issues related to the social purposes served by corporation law and the corporation itself. Instead, we refer the reader to the detailed treatment given to those questions by our colleagues in this volume. See Elizabeth Pollman, "Corporate Governance beyond Economics," chap. 8 in this volume.

6. PricewaterhouseCoopers, PEER PRESSURE: HOW PEER-TO-PEER LENDING PLATFORMS ARE TRANSFORMING THE CONSUMER LENDING INDUSTRY (2015).

7. Miriam Segal. Small Business Administration, PEER-TO-PEER LENDING: A FINANCING ALTERNATIVE FOR SMALL BUSINESSES 3–4 (2015), https://www.sba.gov/sites/default/files/advocacy/Issue-Brief-10-P2P-Lending_0.pdf.

8. PricewaterhouseCoopers, PEER PRESSURE at 4.

9. For a more detailed description of the institutional workings of a typical marketplace platform, *see generally* United States Department of the Treasury, OPPORTUNITIES AND CHALLENGES IN ONLINE MARKETPLACE LENDING (2016), https://www.treasury.gov/connect/blog/Documents/Opportunities_and_Challenges_in_Online_Marketplace_Lending_white_paper.pdf.

10. The bank used by many marketplace platforms, WebBank, is a federally chartered bank located in Utah. *See id.* at 4.

11. *Id.*

12. *Banking without Banks*, THE ECONOMIST (March 1, 2014), http://www.economist.com/news/finance-and-economics/21597932-offering-both-borrowers-and-lenders-better-dealwebsites-put-two; *see also* United States Department of the Treasury, OPPORTUNITIES AND CHALLENGES at 1 (summarizing public comments on the Treasury's request for information about marketplace lending as "suggest[ing] that online marketplace lending is expanding access to credit in some segments by providing loans to certain borrowers who might not otherwise have received capital").

13. *See, e.g.*, Vermont Department of Financial Regulation, PEER-TO-PEER LENDING 4–6 (2015) (describing this possibility), http://www.dfr.vermont.gov/sites/default/files/2015%20Peer%20To%20Peer%20Lending%20Study.pdf.

14. *See* PricewaterhouseCoopers, PEER PRESSURE at 4.

15. *See* National Bank Act, 12 U.S.C. § 85 (2016) (preempting state usury statutes for national banks); Truth in Lending Act, 15 U.S.C. § 1601 *et seq* (prescribing uniform methods for calculating the cost of credit and providing borrowers with disclosures on that subject); Equal Credit Opportunity Act, 15 U.S.C. § 1691 *et seq* (prohibiting lenders from discriminating against applicants); Fair Credit Reporting Act, 15 U.S.C. § 1681 *et seq* (establishing circumstances under which a lender can request a credit report); Gramm-Leach-Bliley Act, 15 U.S.C.

§ 6801 *et seq* (restricting disclosure of personal information about a credit applicant to third parties); Electronic Fund Transfer Act, 15 U.S.C. § 1693 *et seq* (establishing the rights and responsibilities of those overseeing or participating in electronic funds transfers); Bank Secrecy Act, 12 U.S.C. §§ 1951–1959 (requiring certain financial institutions to implement anti–money laundering procedures); Fair Debt Collection Practices Act, 15 U.S.C. §§ 1692 *et seq* (restricting what third parties may do in connection with collection of a debt).

16. For a detailed description of these issues from a practitioner perspective, *see generally* Peter Manbeck and Marc Franson, Chapman and Cutler LLP, The Regulation of Marketplace Lending: A Summary of the Principal Issues 13–31 (2016) (noting that, in the wake of a 2008 enforcement decision by the Securities and Exchange Commission, many marketplace lenders choose to register their loans under the Securities Act of 1933, 15 U.S.C. § 77b *et seq* or, because "registration of [marketplace loans] is an expensive and time-consuming process," offer their loans in private placements exempt from registration under Section 4(a)(2) of that act).

17. Under that act, an "investment company" must register with the SEC before selling any of its securities to the public, and the act defines an "investment company" as an entity holding securities having a value of more than 40 percent of the total value of its assets; *see* 15 U.S.C. § 3 *et seq.* As a result, marketplace lenders must either register or avail themselves of an exemption to the act. Although to date the SEC has not required registration of any marketplace lender, practitioners still view the act as a source of regulatory risk for these businesses. See Manbeck and Franson, Regulation of Marketplace Lending at 27.

18. *Id.* at 6; see also Federal Deposit Insurance Corporation, Financial Institutions Letter FIL-49-2015 (Nov. 6, 2015).

19. In one interview, a prominent industry participant told us that the costs associated with compliance with the FDIC guidance had been sufficient to drive several banks interested in marketplace underwriting out of the industry altogether.

20. *See* Consumer Financial Protection Bureau, CFPB Now Accepting Complaints on Consumer Loans from Online Marketplace Lender (March 2016) (announcing that the bureau "is also releasing a consumer bulletin that . . . outlines tips for consumers who are considering taking out loans from these types of lenders"), http://www.consumerfinance.gov/about-us/newsroom/cfpb-now-accepting-complaints-on-consumer-loans-from-online-marketplace-lender/.

21. A wide range of federal agencies attempted to play a similar role in convening industry and other commenters in an effort to address legal uncertainty in marketplace lending. For example, in 2016 alone, the Federal Reserve hosted a conference designed to "bring together academics, industry participants, and policymakers to discuss . . . innovations in online lending and its impli-

cations for borrowers, traditional lenders, . . . and regulatory policy." Board of Governors of the Federal Reserve, FINANCIAL INNOVATION: ONLINE LENDING TO HOUSEHOLDS AND SMALL BUSINESSES (Dec. 2, 2016), https://www.federalreserve.gov/newsevents/conferences/online-lending-to-households-and-small-businesses-about-201612.htm. The Federal Trade Commission hosted a similar forum designed to address "the range of marketplace lending models . . . and the applicability of consumer protection laws to market participants." Federal Trade Commission, FINTECH SERIES: MARKETPLACE LENDING (June 9, 2016), https://www.ftc.gov/news-events/events-calendar/2016/06/fintech-series-marketplace-lending?utm_source=govdelivery. And—not to be left out—the House Financial Services Committee hosted a hearing on the subject. United States House of Representatives Committee on Financial Services, HEARING ON THE DEVELOPMENT OF ONLINE MARKETPLACE LENDING (July 12, 2016), http://financialservices.house.gov/uploadedfiles/071216_fi_memo.pdf.

22. United States Department of the Treasury, OPPORTUNITIES AND CHALLENGES at 3.

23. *Id.* at 26 (citing, among other commentators favoring a uniform regulatory regime, letters from the American Bankers Association and Consumer Bankers Association and citing, among others urging that existing law is sufficient, a letter from WebBank).

24. United States Department of the Treasury, OPPORTUNITIES AND CHALLENGES at 26. Indeed, the Treasury Department took the opportunity in that document to clarify that certain risk retention requirements implemented pursuant to the Dodd-Frank Act; *see, e.g.*, Credit Risk Retention, 76 Fed. Reg. 24,090, 24,095–96 (April 29, 2011), which had limited application to securitizations in the marketplace-lending context; *see* United States Department of the Treasury, OPPORTUNITIES AND CHALLENGES at 27 ("The risk retention requirements apply only to the securitizer in the securitization of marketplace lending notes, not to the originator selling the notes.").

25. *See* Office of the Comptroller of the Currency, ABOUT THE OCC: MISSION, https://www.occ. treas.gov/about/what-we-do/mission/index-about.html.

26. *See* Office of the Comptroller of the Currency, EXPLORING SPECIAL PURPOSE NATIONAL BANK CHARTERS FOR FINTECH COMPANIES, https://www.occ.treas.gov/topics/bank-operations/innovation/comments/special-purpose-national-bank-charters-for-fintech.pdf.

27. *See, e.g.*, Manbeck and Franson, REGULATION OF MARKETPLACE LENDING at 20 ("[a]ny [platform] that intends to engage in a broad public offering [of its loans] must register its securities in multiple states and pay the associated filing fees").

28. *See* Ga. Code Ann. § 7-4-18 (West 2016). *See also, e.g.*, Ala. Code § 8–8-1, Minn. Stat. Ann. § 334.01 (West), 41 Pa. Stat. Ann. § 201 (West) (establishing a usury limit of 6 percent for loans below $50,000).

29. A majority of states have usury laws, which date back at least to the Old Testament. *See, e.g.*, Robert Shanks, *Practical Problems in the Application of Archaic Usury Statutes*, 53 VA. L. REV. 327 (1967).

30. *See, e.g.*, Victor G. Lopez, *When Lenders Can Legally Provide Loans with Effective Interest Rates above 1,000 Percent, Is It Time for Congress to Consider a Federal Interest Cap on Consumer Loans?* 42 J. LEGIS. 101, 103 table 1 (2016) (describing the consequences for making a usurious loan across the United States).

31. *See* N.Y. GEN. OBL. L. § 5-501(1); *see also* Seidel v. 18 East 17th Street Owners, 598 N.E. 2d 7, 9 (N.Y. 1992): "The consequences to the lender of a usurious loan [in New York] can be harsh: the borrower is relieved of all future payment—not only interest but also outstanding principal."

32. 12 U.S.C. § 85 (2016) (permitting national banks to "charge on any loan . . . interest at the rate allowed by the laws of the State, Territory, or District where the bank is located, or at a rate of 1 per centum in excess of the discount on ninety-day commercial paper in effect at the Federal reserve bank in the Federal reserve district where the bank is located, whichever may be the greater").

33. For an early acknowledgment of this principle in the Supreme Court (although outside the context of the National Bank Act), *see* Nichols v. Fearson, 32 U.S. (7 Pet.) 103, 109 (1833).

34. Before the rise of marketplace lending, Judge Richard Posner, among others, concluded for the Seventh Circuit that the valid-when-made rule should extend to NBA preemption. *See* Olvera v. Blitt & Gaines, PC, 431 F.3d 285 (7th Cir. 2005): "once assignors were authorized to charge interest, the common law kicked in and gave the assignees the same right, because the common law puts the assignee in the assignor's shoes, whatever the shoe size"; *see also* Krispin v. May Department Stores Co., 218 F.3d 939 (2000) (applying the same principle to credit receivables sold to a department store).

35. 786 F.3d 246, 250.

36. As noted earlier, usurious loans are void in states such as New York and Connecticut. The question for the courts is therefore whether the loans are usurious. At present, the parties in *Madden* are trying to resolve two independent legal bases on which the loan in *Madden* itself, and cases like it, may be able to avoid being deemed usurious. First, the parties will address whether choice-of-law provisions should be given effect. Although these provisions are almost always enforced in commercial agreements between sophisticated parties, their enforcement is less consistent in the consumer context (Honigsberg et al., 2014). Second, the parties are debating whether the common law of New York might separately embrace the valid-when-made doctrine. If New York law itself incorporates the valid-when-made rule, Madden-like claims that loans can be rendered usurious by virtue of the identity of the lender will likely be dismissed.

37. Paul Hastings LLP, *MADDEN V. MIDLAND FUNDING, LLC*: POTENTIALLY

Far-Reaching Implications for Non-Bank Assignees of Bank Originated Loans (2015), http://www.paulhastings.com/publications-items/details/?id=e695e469-2334-6428-811c-ff00004cbded.

38. Colleen Honigsberg, Robert J. Jackson Jr., and Richard Squire, *How Does Legal Enforceability Affect Consumer Lending? Evidence from a Natural Experiment*, 60 J. Law and Econ. 473 (2017).

39. *See id.* at 29 (finding that, "after *Madden*, [marketplace] loans to borrowers with FICO scores below 644"—that is, borrowers with fair to poor credit—"virtually disappeared").

40. *See, e.g.*, Prosper Funding LLC, $1,500,000,000 Borrower Payment Dependent Note, Registration Statement at 43 (disclosing, as a risk factor, that "it is possible that state usury laws may impose liability that could affect an . . . investor who purchases . . . [l]oans" from being able "to continue to charge borrowers the interest rates they agreed to pay," and citing the *Madden* decision as one basis for this concern), https://www.prosper.com/Downloads/Legal/Prosper_Prospectus_2016-05-24.pdf.

41. Peter Rudegeair and Telis Demos, *LendingClub to Change Its Fee Model*, Wall St. J. (2016), http://www.wsj.com/articles/fast-growing-lending-club-to-change-its-fee-model-1456488393.

42. Pet. for Cert. in *Midland Funding LLC v. Saliha Madden*, No. 15-610 (Nov. 10, 2015).

43. Brief for the United States as amicus curiae in *Midland Funding LLC v. Saliha Madden*, No. 15-610 (2016), http://www.scotusblog.com/wp-content/uploads/2016/06/midland.invite.18.pdf.

44. Midland Funding LLC v. Madden, 136 S. Ct. 2505 (June 27, 2016).

45. *See* note 25 and the text accompanying it.

46. *Cf. Jones v. Harris Associates* at 633 (critiquing, for just this reason, a "'just price' system administered by the judiciary").

47. *See generally* Mark J. Roe, *Delaware's Politics*, 118 Harv. L. Rev. 2491, 2492 (2005).

48. *See id.*; *see also* Mark J. Roe, *Delaware's Competition*, 117 Harv. L. Rev. 588 (2003) (making a similar argument about the competition between Delaware and other states competing with Delaware in the market for incorporation). As Delaware's chief justice has observed, the federal government's growing role in matters of corporate governance poses a particularly significant channel through which federal lawmakers have exerted their influence over Delaware law. *See, e.g.*, Leo E. Strine Jr., *The Delaware Way: How We Do Corporate Law and Some of the New Challenges We (and Europe) Face*, 30 J. Corp. L. 673 (2005).

49. For a description of this example, and its implications for the Delaware judiciary as a rule-promulgating institution, *see* David Friedman, Note, *The Regulator in Robes: Examining the SEC and the Delaware Court of Chancery's Parallel Disclosure Regimes*, 113 Colum. L. Rev. 1543 (2013).

50. *See, e.g.*, Third Point LLC v. Sotheby's, C.A. No. 9469-VCP (May 2, 2014); see also John C. Coffee and Darius Palia, THE WOLF AT THE DOOR: THE IMPACT OF HEDGE FUND ACTIVISM ON CORPORATE GOVERNANCE (Annuals of Corporate Governance 2015).

51. *See generally* Lucian Bebchuk and Robert J. Jackson Jr., *The Law and Economics of Blockholder Disclosure*, 2 HARV. BUS. L. REV. 39, 40 (2012); *see also* Letter from Wachtell, Lipton, Rosen & Katz to Elizabeth M. Murphy, Sec'y, U.S. Sec. & Exch. Comm'n (May 7, 2011), http://www.sec.gov/rules/petitions/2011/ (making the case that SEC rules promulgated pursuant to the Williams Act should be "modernized" so that activist investors are required to disclose their stakes and intentions more quickly than under current law).

52. *See* Bebchuk and Jackson, *Law and Economics of Blockholder Disclosure* at 56–57 (noting that "state law now allows companies to use poison pills selectively to disfavor some outside blockholders" and arguing that, in light of the emergence of such state law rules, federal rule makers should not make further changes to securities laws that would tip the balance of corporate law further toward management).

53. Matthew D. Cain et al., *How Corporate Governance Is Made: The Case of the Golden Leash*, 164 U. PA. L. REV. 649, 650 (2015).

54. *See id.* at 653 (noting that, soon after the emergence of the golden leash, "Martin Lipton of Wachtell, Lipton, Rosen & Katz," "a prominent law firm known for defending firms against activist interventions and hostile takeovers, issued a public memorandum recommending that corporations adopt bylaws prohibiting golden leash compensation arrangements").

55. *See id.* (citing Jones Day, GOVERNANCE PERSPECTIVES: ISS QUESTIONS DIRECTOR COMPENSATION BYLAW (2013)).

56. *Id.* at 655.

57. *Id.* at 649.

58. *See, e.g.*, John Bessonette, *Expert Analysis: Key Considerations for Investment in Marijuana Companies*, LAW360 (May 12, 2015), https://www.law360.com/articles/655026 (noting that, although an "increasing number of sophisticated investors are taking a closer look at opportunities in the marijuana industry," "the continuously evolving legal landscape is complicated and contradictory, and investments require a heightened level of due diligence").

59. *See, e.g.*, Mike Ramsey, *Tesla Weighs New Challenge to State Direct-Sales Bans*, WALL ST. J. (March 28, 2016), https://www.wsj.com/articles/tesla-weighs-new-challenge-to-state-direct-sales-bans-1459189069 (noting that Tesla's direct-to-consumer sales model is currently "prohibited by law in six states that represent about 18% of the new-car market" and that the company's strategy to address these concerns varies by state and ranges from litigation to lobbying for legislation).

CHAPTER TEN

Appraisal after *Dell*

Guhan Subramanian

Introduction

It is well known in corporate law circles that a revolution is under way with respect to appraisal rights. What used to be a sleepy backwater has become one of the hottest areas of transactional practice and Delaware doctrine. Chancellor Bill Chandler's 2007 opinion in *In re Appraisal of Transkaryotic Therapies, Inc.* opened the way for appraisal arbitrage, but the tactic did not materialize in a meaningful way until more recently. Sixty-two appraisal actions were filed in 2016, representing $1.9 billion in face-value claims, compared to sixteen actions, representing $129 million in face value, in 2012 (Hoffman 2017). Until December 2017, there were strong signs that this trend would continue: Merion Capital, Verition, and Magnetar Financial, among others, have made massive appraisal arbitrage plays in recent years, taking very large stakes in Delaware companies after the deal is announced but before the record date, with the intention of seeking appraisal of their shares. Then came *Dell.*

The starting point in the modern history of appraisal is the Delaware Supreme Court's 2010 pronouncement in *Golden Telecom v. Global GT*: "Requiring the Court of Chancery to defer—conclusively or presumptively—to the merger price, even in the face of a pristine, unchallenged transactional process, would contravene the unambiguous language of the statute and the reasoned holding of our precedent." This statement would seem to invite a *de novo*, roll-up-the-sleeves discounted cash flow analysis in every appraisal proceeding. Subsequent case law clarified, however, that the Delaware courts were willing to rely on the deal price in an arm's-length deal as the best evidence of "fair value."[1] This approach minimized appraisal risk as long as the deal process was good.

This trajectory was arguably disrupted with the Chancery Court's decisions in *Dell* and *DFC Global*. In *In re Appraisal of Dell, Inc.* (Del. Ch. May 2016), Vice Chancellor Travis Laster awarded dissenting shareholders $17.62 per share, which amounted to a 28 percent premium over the $13.75 per share deal price. Despite an ostensibly robust go-shop process, the court concluded that "[t]he sale process functioned imperfectly as a price discovery tool" and therefore afforded no weight to the $13.75 deal price. And in *In re Appraisal of DFC Global Corp.* (Del. Ch. July 2016), just two months after *Dell*, Chancellor Andre Bouchard awarded dissenting shareholders $10.21 per share, which was 7 percent more than the $9.50 per share deal price. In contrast to Vice Chancellor Laster's assessment of the process in *Dell*, Chancellor Bouchard concluded that DFC Global was sold in an "arm's-length sale," in a "robust" process that "lasted approximately two years and involved . . . reaching out to dozens of [potential buyers]" and "did not involve . . . conflicts of interest." Nevertheless, the court only afforded the deal price one-third weight in its fair-value assessment.

Brouhaha ensued. Wachtell, Lipton, Rosen & Katz wrote to its clients that "[t]he result [in *Dell*] reflects the remarkable view that 'fair value' in Delaware represents a price far higher than any buyer would have been willing to pay and that the merger price derived from an admirable sales process should be accorded no weight" (Lipton, Mirvis, Savitt, and McLeod 2016). The *Wall Street Journal* reported that "[t]he [*Dell*] decision is sending shudders all over Wall Street and the boardrooms of corporate America, because the court, in effect, overruled 'the market'" (Hoffman 2016). And Matt Levine (2016) stated in *Bloomberg View* (mostly tongue-in-cheek) that "[t]he proof that $17.62 was the fair price is that *no one was willing to pay it*" (emphasis in original).

At the March 2017 Tulane conference, Fried Frank attorney Scott Luftglass reported that private equity calls about appraisal risk were "pretty unlikely" five years ago. Now, he reported, "you get that call pretty frequently" (Naso 2017). And at the same conference, John Finley, chief legal officer of Blackstone, stated: "You look at *Dell*, and you look at the discrepancy there—it's terrifying" (Naso 2017). Transactional attorneys wondered out loud how they could provide any assurance (or even guidance) for their clients regarding appraisal risk.

In August 2017, the Delaware Supreme Court unanimously reversed

DFC Global. This was generally unsurprising in corporate law circles. In December 2017, the Delaware Supreme Court unanimously reversed *Dell.* This surprised (and even shocked) some practitioners and commentators, at least relative to their opinions before the Delaware Supreme Court's oral argument in the case.[2] In both cases, the Delaware Supreme Court effectively held that fair value should be the deal price.

This essay examines *Dell* and the current state of appraisal doctrine. With the one-two punch of *DFC Global* and *Dell*, the pendulum has clearly swung toward deal price as presumptive evidence of fair value. The next section of this essay examines (what turned out to be) the warm-up act of *DFC Global.* An examination of *Dell* follows. Later sections provide an assessment of the existing state of play regarding appraisal doctrine and describe implications for practitioners and courts.

The Warm-Up Act: *DFC Global*

In *DFC Global*, the Delaware Chancery Court awarded only a one-third weight to the deal price despite a robust market canvass and the absence of conflicts of interest. The decision jolted practitioners, who understood the general Delaware approach to be deference to the deal price if the deal process achieved adequate price discovery. Compounding the confusion in *DFC Global*, the company pointed out a clerical error to the court after the opinion was issued. Correcting this error would have reduced the discounted cash flow valuation from $13.07 per share to $7.70 per share, or 19 percent *below* the $9.50 per share deal price. Instead, the court corrected the error but simultaneously increased the perpetuity growth rate from 3.1 percent to 4.0 percent—which was beyond what even the petitioners' valuation expert had proposed—in order to return to the court's original valuation of $10.21 (DFC Global Opening Brief at 2; Frankel 2016).

In the *DFC Global* appeal in the Delaware Supreme Court, twenty-nine law and finance professors lined up on both sides with amicus briefs. By staking out the opposing ends of the appraisal spectrum, the dueling briefs provide a helpful framework for assessing the current state of play.

On one end of the spectrum, nine law and corporate finance professors submitted an amicus brief that urged reversal.[3] These well-respected scholars proposed that appraised value should depart from the deal price only "where the transaction price bears indications of misinformation or bias" (Bainbridge et al. 2017 at 16). With regard to misinformation, the professors explained that, "where material information is withheld from the market, discounted cash flow or other valuation analyses are necessary because the deal price will not reflect that inside information" (Bainbridge et al. 2017 at 17). With regard to bias, the professors invoked fiduciary duty doctrine, requiring only that "directors must make an informed decision about value" and "their decision must be disinterested" (Bainbridge et al. 2017 at 16).

At the other end of the spectrum, twenty professors of law, economics, and finance submitted an amicus brief that urged affirmance of *DFC Global*.[4] These equally well-respected professors argued that "Chancellor Bouchard found that the tremendous regulatory uncertainty surrounding DFC Global reduced the reliability of the negotiated price" and that this finding "should be treated as any other finding of fact" (Arlen et al. 2017). Arlen et al. further argued that "exclusive reliance on the merger price is *functionally equivalent to eliminating the appraisal remedy altogether*" (at 11; emphasis in original). Under their proposed approach, the weight afforded to the deal price by the Chancery Court should be disturbed only for abuse of discretion (Arlen et al. 2017 at 20).

In an earlier version of this essay, published before the Delaware Supreme Court issued its opinions in *DFC Global* and *Dell*, I argued that the Bainbridge et al. approach represented an overly broad reliance on the deal price (Subramanian 2017). In particular, the Bainbridge et al. approach would break from well-established Delaware doctrine by requiring a fiduciary duty breach in order to depart from the deal price in appraisal. Delaware courts have repeatedly acknowledged that the inquiry in a fiduciary duty proceeding is not the same as the inquiry in an appraisal proceeding, yet the Bainbridge et al. approach would have tethered these two things together. Similarly, requiring "misinformation" in order to depart from the deal price would set an unduly high bar.

I also argued that the Arlen et al. approach did not adequately acknowledge the imprecision of discounted cash flow methodologies. As commentators have repeatedly noted over the years (see, e.g., Subramanian 1998), valuation methods are notoriously imprecise in estimating fair value. In my recent mergers and acquisitions (M&A) executive education course at Harvard Business School, for example, experienced valuation practitioners deviated from one another by as much as 30 percent to 40 percent in valuing the same M&A target, even though they had access to multiple valuation methods to triangulate on value.

In an appraisal proceeding, Delaware Chancery Court judges are asked to engage in the artificially precise task of providing a point estimate of value. Even investment bankers, who are finance professionals, only provide a valuation range in their fairness opinions. By relying heavily on discounted cash flow approaches, and allowing courts to ignore market-based evidence when strong evidence exists, the Arlen et al. approach injects too much uncertainty in appraisal proceedings and would potentially deter value-creating deals. Transactional planners trying to provide deal certainty to their clients need more of a safe harbor against appraisal arbitrage than what the Arlen et al. approach provides.

I therefore proposed a middle ground between the Bainbridge and Arlen approaches: If the deal process involves a meaningful market canvass and an arm's-length negotiation, there should be a strong presumption that the deal price represents fair value in an appraisal proceeding;[5] but if the deal process does not include these features, then deal price should receive no weight (Subramanian 2017). The test is a stringent one: For example, an exclusive pre-signing negotiation followed by a go-shop process in which the buyer gets an unlimited match right would probably not qualify for deference to the deal price. Practitioners would need to earn the right to call their deal process arm's length, which would require more than (as one prominent Delaware practitioner put it to me) just a "good enough for fiduciary duty" deal process. But if they earn the right, the deal price should get 100 percent weight in appraisal proceedings.

Applying the competing approaches to both *DFC Global* and *Dell* highlights their differences. The Bainbridge et al. approach would have required reversal of both *DFC Global* and *Dell*, because there was no misinformation or bias in either deal process. As such, the deal price would govern in both deals. The Arlen et al. approach would have required affirmance of both cases (unless there was abuse of discretion) through deference to the finder of fact on the appropriate weight for the deal price. In contrast, my proposed approach suggested reversal of *DFC Global* and affirmance of *Dell*. This middle-ground approach would defer entirely to the deal price when the deal process is good (thus reversing *DFC Global*) but cast a hard look on whether the deal process included a meaningful market canvass and an arm's-length negotiation (as in the *Dell* Chancery Court opinion).

In July 2017, the Delaware Supreme Court reversed the Chancery Court's decision in *DFC Global*. Although the court declined to adopt an explicit presumption that fair value should be the deal price when the deal process is good, it stated that "the sale value resulting from a robust market check will often be the most reliable evidence of fair value, and that second-guessing the value arrived upon by the collective views of many sophisticated parties with a real stake in the matter is hazardous." In doing so, the court implicitly rejected the Arlen et al. approach. Commentators called it a "presumption in everything but name," and I agree with that assessment.

The question remained: How good would the deal process have to be in order to obtain deference to the deal price? Would the *Dell* court follow the Bainbridge et al. proposed approach—that a good-enough-for-fiduciary-duty process would mean that fair value was the deal price? Or, as I advocated, would something more be required to get deference to the deal price?

The *Dell* Decision

In December 2017, the Delaware Supreme Court reversed the Chancery Court's determination in the Dell appraisal. Although the case is technically remanded to the Delaware Chancery Court for a determination on fair value, the Supreme Court made clear that the deal price should govern: "[O]n this particular record, the trial court erred in not assigning any mathematical weight to the deal price. In fact, the record as distilled by the trial court suggests that the deal price deserved heavy, if not dispositive, weight" (Dell Supreme Court Opinion at 37). And just to make its point crystal clear, the court took an unprecedented further step: "[W]e give the Vice Chancellor the discretion on remand to enter judgment at the deal price if he so chooses, with no further proceedings" (Dell Supreme Court Opinion at 77).

In endorsing the deal price, the Supreme Court did not adopt the Bainbridge et al. approach that a fiduciary duty breach is required in order to depart from the deal price. In doing so, the court implicitly acknowledged that something more is required. But the Supreme Court departed from the Chancery Court in finding that the something more had been achieved. In effect, the Supreme Court engaged in a *de novo* review of the critical process choices rather than applying the required "abuse of discretion" standard. I therefore turn now to a review of the key aspects of the Delaware Supreme Court's factual determinations.

The Pre-Signing Process

The Chancery Court emphasized the fact that the Special Committee engaged in very limited pre-signing competition—reaching out only to private equity firms Kohlberg Kravis Roberts and Texas Pacific Group (in addition to Silver Lake, which teamed with Michael Dell to make its offer). The Special Committee did not reach out to other private equity firms—notably, Blackstone, which had just hired Dell's former M&A head, Dave Johnson; or Southeastern, which had originally proposed the management buyout idea to Michael Dell. Nor did the Special Committee reach out to Hewlett-Packard (HP), even though Evercore (one of the Special Committee's bankers) estimated $3 billion to $4 billion of synergies between Dell and HP. During this pre-signing phase, Evercore assured the Special Committee that there was no need to reach out to Blackstone and HP pre-signing, because it (Evercore) would reach out during the go-shop period; but Evercore was conflicted in this advice because it received a large contingent payment for any overbid it found during the go-shop period, and no such payment for a pre-signing overbid.[6]

Vice Chancellor Laster chastised the Special Committee for not engaging in more pre-signing competition:

> The Committee did not engage with Blackstone before signing, even though Blackstone approached the Company in January about a possible transaction. . . . [In addition,] [d]uring the pre-signing phase, the Committee did not contact any strategic buyers. . . . HP was the obvious choice.
>
> Without a meaningful source of competition, the Committee lacked the most powerful tool that a seller can use to extract a portion of the bidder's anticipated surplus. The Committee had the ability to say no, and it could demand a higher price, but it could not invoke the threat of an alternative deal. (Chancery Court Opinion at *37)

In contrast, the Delaware Supreme Court found that there had been adequate pre-signing competition, noting that Blackstone was aware that the company was for sale and crediting Evercore's testimony that "if there were any people out there who were actively interested, there was a good chance they would have already come forward" (Supreme Court Opinion at 11–12). In a footnote, the Supreme Court noted Evercore's conflict of interest in rendering this advice, "but other evidence in the record suggests that Blackstone *proposed* waiting until the go-shop on its own" (Supreme Court Opinion at 12 n.37; emphasis added). This is a highly convenient and important fact: Who could fault the Special Committee for not engaging with Blackstone pre-signing, if Blackstone did not *want* to be contacted pre-signing? But it happens to be false.

To support its claim, the court pointed to testimony from the (conflicted) Evercore banker and the Dell Special Committee minutes (which simply document what the Evercore banker told them). But even taking these statements at face value, the two sources only say that Blackstone wanted assurances of a meaningful go-shop,[7] not that "Blackstone proposed waiting until the go-shop on its own."

The actual factual record is not surprising, because the idea that Blackstone preferred to participate in the go-shop rather than the pre-signing process defies common sense. Why would a rational bidder wish to impose on itself a ticking clock, a go-shop termination fee, and a matching right when it could avoid all those impediments by engaging in pre-signing due diligence? It is like Usain Bolt saying he wants to give everyone else a five-meter head start in the 100 meters. What *is* surprising, however, is that the Supreme Court would misrepresent the testimony on such a critical point.

The claim that Blackstone wanted to wait until the go-shop period is also in tension with contemporaneous evidence indicating that Blackstone needed more time once it finally got access to the data room. During the go-shop period, Evercore reminded certain Dell employees: "[W]e all have to be mindful that Blackstone is looking to accomplish in 4–6 weeks what [S]ilverlake had 6 months to do, with the full support and insight of the CEO behind them." (Recall this is the same Evercore that recommended against contacting Blackstone pre-signing.) On April 1, 2013, six days after the go-shop period had expired, Chinh Chu, a senior managing director at Blackstone, e-mailed Michael Dell to identify seven "nuances and details [that] need to be explored in greater detail," including: "strategy for the PC business in light of eroding industry fundamentals" and "downside case for the PC business in the event that tablets continue to gain significant share, pricing erosion accelerates, Chrome is successful, and the transition to virtual desktop accelerates, which may further reduce ASPs [average selling prices]."[8] A news report three days later—and nine days after the go-shop period had expired—cited sources saying that "[Blackstone's] due diligence process is still in the early stages, and that Blackstone is just starting to put together a business plan" (Damouni and Gupta 2013). None of this catch-up needed to happen if Blackstone had participated in the pre-signing process, which makes the court's claim that "Blackstone *proposed* waiting until the go-shop on its own" both inconsistent with the record and inconsistent with common sense.

On Hewlett-Packard, the Delaware Supreme Court stated: "The likeliest strategic bidder, HP, signed a confidentiality agreement during the go-shop, but it did not even log into the data room" (Supreme Court Opinion at 48). One interpretation of this inaction is that HP was not interested in buying Dell, or at least not at a price higher than $13.65 per share. Another interpretation, equally consistent with the record, is that HP did not perceive a pathway to success in a bidding contest against Michael Dell, in which it would have forty-five days and Michael Dell would have had decades. Without explanation, the court ignores the second possible interpretation in favor of the first.

The Winner's Curse

Information asymmetry and winner's curse concerns become more pronounced when go-shop bidders have to play catch-up. Consistent with well-established economic theory, the Chancery Court found that winner's curse concerns might have deterred potential third-party bidders (Chancery Court Opinion at *42–*43). The Supreme Court dismissed these concerns because "the Court of Chancery did not point to any bidder who actually shied away from exploring an acquisition out of fear of the winner's curse phenomenon" (Supreme Court Opinion at 55).

This is a remarkable test. Perhaps the court would have been satisfied that a winner's curse existed if discovery had produced an e-mail from a prospective bidder: "We are considering bidding for Dell, Inc. against Michael Dell. The guy literally has his name on the door. What do we learn if we bid for Dell, Inc. and he decides not to match our bid?" In ten years of studying go-shops and twenty years of studying deal-jumping situations, I have never seen this kind of evidence. But it defies common sense and well-accepted economic theory to claim that the absence of such evidence means that a winner's curse concern does not exist.

In the Dell oral argument, Chief Justice Leo Strine argued that, "if you think the next move in a deal dynamic is that the next person who makes the price move will hurt themselves, is what you're saying that means you're already at fair value?" (Supreme Court Oral Argument transcript at 15). To which appellants' counsel, Greg Williams, responded: "It certainly is." Even though Chief Justice Strine did not author the Supreme Court's decision, this catechism made it into the opinion virtually verbatim: "If a deal price is at a level where the next upward move by a topping bidder has a material risk of being a self-destructive curse, that suggests the price is already at a level that is fair" (Supreme Court Opinion at 56).

In fact, this characterization of the winner's curse is not correct. Mr. Dell's match right meant that a potential third-party bidder was at least two bids away from winning, and potentially further if Mr. Dell obtained additional match rights. This means that a third party might not bid *even if the immediate offer on the table was below fair value*. It is simply incorrect that the winner's curse deters bidders only when the deal price already represents fair value. Sophisticated bidders "look forward and reason back" to identify a pathway to success before bidding in the first place.

Michael Dell's Value

The Supreme Court even rejected the Chancery Court's finding that Michael Dell added value to Dell, Inc. (Supreme Court Opinion at 57). When management is valuable, price discovery becomes more difficult because prospective third-party bidders can no longer free-ride on the inside bids (Subramanian 2016).

The idea that Michael Dell is valuable to Dell, Inc. would seem to need no explanation. At trial I nevertheless presented evidence showing that the market capitalization of Dell went *down* by $1.2 billion when Mr. Dell unexpectedly left the company in 2004, and went *up* by $2.5 billion when he unexpectedly rejoined the company in 2007 (Chancery Court Opinion at *43). In response to this evidence, the Supreme Court stated: "[I]t does not follow that such evidence showed his value six years later, in 2013" (Supreme Court Opinion at 57).

One would think that the burden should be on those who take the counterintuitive position that Michael Dell is *not* valuable to Dell, Inc. At least within the company, employees have told me over the years that he is viewed as a visionary and inspirational founder-CEO, in the same category as Steve Jobs and Bill Gates. This must have some value even if external assessments were mixed.

There is also evidence that Mr. Dell has been an extraordinary leader of Dell in the aftermath of the buyout. Management reported cost savings of $1.6 billion in April 2014, just sixteen months after the deal closed

(Chancery Court Opinion at *51), while concurrently making "investments of several hundred million dollars in areas with significant time horizons, such as cloud and analytics" (Dell 2014). In December 2014, *Bloomberg* reported that Michael Dell and Silver Lake had made "a paper gain of at least 90 percent on their investment" (Carey and Clark 2014). It is not clear why Mr. Dell was a valuable CEO in 2004, 2007, and since 2013, but was unimportant at the precise moment of the buyout. The Supreme Court correctly noted that "Blackstone had investigated possible replacements as CEO" (Supreme Court Opinion at 58), but the court does not mention that Michael Dell was still Blackstone's "preferred choice" to run the company (Damouni and Gupta 2013).

Putting aside the question of whether Michael Dell added value to Dell, Inc., the Supreme Court continued its steamroll over the Chancery Court's findings of fact: "[E]ven if one could accept the trial court's view that Mr. Dell's services as CEO added per-share value to the Company's stock, the record does not suggest that he would have stopped serving the Company if Blackstone, TPG, or another reputable buyer had prevailed. . . . Thus it is difficult to discern how 'Mr. Dell's unique value and his affiliation with the Buyout Group were negative factors that inhibited the effectiveness of the go-shop process'" (Supreme Court Opinion at 58, quoting Chancery Court Opinion at *44).

This argument ignores the finding by the Chancery Court that any overbid from an alternative bidder would have personally cost Mr. Dell more money. The Dell/Silver Lake offer planned for Mr. Dell to roll over his entire 16 percent equity stake into the new company; in addition, he would contribute $750 million of new equity. This means that Mr. Dell was a "net buyer" of shares, which means he would have a financial incentive to push the deal price down rather than up.

According to my calculations, Michael Dell would have to contribute approximately $250 million for each dollar increase in the deal price (and $1 billion for each dollar increase if bid increases were funded with all-equity) if he wanted to maintain his 75 percent ownership interest in the post-transaction company. If, instead, Mr. Dell allowed Silver Lake to fund bid increases, he would lose control at a deal price above approximately $15.70 per share (Chancery Court Opinion at *43 and n.43). The Chancery Court correctly observed: "Because Mr. Dell was a net buyer, any party considering an overbid would understand that a higher price would not be well received by the most important person at the Company" (Chancery Court Opinion at *43).

In a now-familiar move, the Supreme Court responded by noting that "the [Chancery] court did not identify any possible bidders that were actually deterred because of Mr. Dell's status" (Supreme Court Opinion at 59). This reasoning, yet again, sets an evidentiary bar that would be virtually impossible to meet. Perhaps the Supreme Court was looking for an internal e-mail from Blackstone like this: "We would like to partner with Michael Dell, but we're not sure he would be pleased to partner with us if our overbid costs him $1 billion personally." Third parties do not have to say this for it to be true. Even though Mr. Dell was formally required to consider the possibility of working with other bidders, the fact that it would cost him personally to work with someone else would certainly influence bidders' perceptions of the viability of that route.

Overall Effectiveness of the Deal Process

In general, the Dell deal process checked certain boxes to satisfy the indicia of a market canvass, but Vice Chancellor Laster looked beneath the surface to investigate whether this market canvass was meaningful. The limited pre-signing competition, the one-time match right, Evercore's conflicted advice, Mr. Dell's financial incentives, and the relatively tight (forty-five-day) go-shop window for a deal of this size did not adequately mitigate the inherent advantage of Michael Dell/Silver Lake; as such, the Chancery Court found that the market canvass received no weight.

In overruling the Chancery Court's ultimate determination on deal process, the Supreme Court relied in part on my testimony: "[E]ven the petitioners' expert characterized the structure here as 'rais[ing] fewer structural barriers than the norm' and found no disqualifying fault with the design of Dell's go-shop" (Supreme Court Opinion at 52). The problem with this description of my testimony is that it is wrong. As a relatively minor issue, the quoted language that is attributed to me comes from the Chancery Court opinion, not from my testimony. More importantly, my ultimate conclusion was the opposite of what the Supreme Court claimed: "Because the playing field was not level in the Dell MBO [management buyout], the go-shop process was not an effective market check for ensuring that fair value was paid to the non-continuing shareholders" (Subramanian Trial Demonstratives at 13). It is a mischaracterization of my testimony to claim that I "found no disqualifying fault with the design of Dell's go-shop."

In a presentation of an earlier version of this essay at Gibson, Dunn &

Crutcher in New York City, just before the *Dell* Supreme Court decision came down, some practitioners pointed to the Chancery Court's finding that the "[t]he [Special] Committee and its advisors did many praiseworthy things" to argue that this finding should be sufficient to find that the deal price represented fair value. But "many praiseworthy things" can be good enough for fiduciary duty but not good enough to meet the standard that is required to get deference to the deal price. As I put it at Gibson Dunn, "many praiseworthy things" can get you a B+, but the requirement for appraisal purposes should be at least an A−. Among other things, the Special Committee's reliance on a conflicted advisor (Evercore) on the critical decision of whether to solicit HP and Blackstone pre-signing; the failure to put in more potent deal process protections to counteract Mr. Dell's financial incentive to keep the deal price down; and the failure to mitigate the winner's curse problem (through, for example, information rights rather than match rights) should only get the Special Committee a B+.

The Delaware Chancery Court implicitly awarded the Dell process a B+, which was good enough to "sail through" a fiduciary duty analysis (Chancery Court Opinion at *29), but not good enough to provide evidence on fair value. The Delaware Supreme Court could have ruled that a B+ was sufficient to warrant deference to the deal price, as a matter of law. Instead, the court second-guessed the Chancery Court's findings of fact to award the deal process an A, or maybe even an A+ since the court seemed to find no fault whatsoever with the Dell deal process. Reasonable minds can differ on which grade is correct. But standards of review should matter. And the idea that Vice Chancellor Laster's grade for the *Dell* deal process amounted to an "abuse of discretion" defies credulity. If the dean of Harvard Law School scrutinized the faculty's grades in such a manner, there would be no point for faculty to provide grades in the first place.

The Current State of Play

Notwithstanding the Delaware Supreme Court's mischaracterization of the record in its *de novo* review of the deal process, the court left intact a critical piece of appraisal doctrine: Reliance on the deal price for appraisal purposes requires more than just fulfillment of fiduciary duties. The court had the opportunity to endorse the Bainbridge et al. approach—in which fair value would be the deal price unless there was a fiduciary duty breach—but declined to do so. A process that is "good enough for fiduciary duty" does not necessarily warrant deference to the deal price; something more is required. For this reason, appraisal remains alive in Delaware.

An important open question is what—exactly—is the something more that is required. This will no doubt get clarified through future case law. But there should be some distance between the requirements imposed by fiduciary duty and the hurdle for deference to the deal price in appraisal proceedings. This is particularly true after the near death of post-closing fiduciary duty litigation announced in *Corwin v. KKR Financial Holdings LLC* (Del. 2015). Appraisal is the only remaining check against a deficient deal process.

Another important open question is what weight deal price should receive if the deal process meets the more exacting standard described here. My proposed answer to this question is simple: 100 percent. One might reasonably ask why the test needs to be binary. Where the deal process is good but not perfect, why not acknowledge the shades of gray by awarding the deal price (say) one-third weight? This weighting system is a vestige of the pre-*Weinberger* "Delaware Block Method," where courts were instructed to attach weights to each of stock market value, earnings value, and net asset value. Although *Weinberger* explicitly rejected the Delaware Block Method in favor of "any techniques or methods which are generally considered acceptable in the financial community," the idea of a weighting approach continues to have intuitive appeal as a way to triangulate on fair value.

However, deal process is better assessed as a binary question: Was there a meaningful market canvass and an arm's-length negotiation? In this inquiry there can be no crossing the river halfway. To see why, consider a not-so-hypothetical deal process in which three financial buyers have reservation prices of $70, $80, and $90, and one strategic buyer has a reservation price of $100. The seller conducts a pre-signing auction solely among the financial buyers and reaches a deal with the high bidder among them, at $81. The seller then runs a go-shop, and the strategic buyer declines to bid because the financial buyer has an informational advantage and a match right. The deal closes at $81, and certain shareholders seek appraisal.

In that proceeding, the court concludes that the Special Committee erred in not reaching out to the strategic buyer pre-signing, and further erred in providing the financial buyer a match right. Now what? The court could nevertheless award some weight to the $81 deal price, on the grounds that the deal process was good but not perfect. But this stylized example illustrates why such a weighting approach would be a mistake, because it would be impossible to know what would have happened in the event of a meaningful market canvass. Put differently, the very nature of deal process design makes it impossible to determine what impact (if any) a flaw has on the deal price. In some endeavors (say, counting marbles) an after-the-fact reviewer can bracket the error term. This is not possible with deal process errors. The implication is that the weighting for deal price in appraisal proceedings should necessarily be an all-or-nothing affair.

Students of corporate law may recognize a similarity to the Delaware Supreme Court's refinements to freeze-out doctrine in *Kahn v. M&F Worldwide Corp* (Del. 2014). In that case, the Delaware Supreme Court held that approval by a special committee of independent directors and approval from a majority of the minority shares adequately cleansed the taint of conflict such that the business judgment rule should apply. In doing so, the Delaware Supreme Court converted a substantive inquiry (Was the deal price entirely fair to the minority shareholders?) into a procedural inquiry (Did the minority shareholders have adequate procedural protections?). Similarly, the approach proposed in this essay converts a substantive question (What is the fair value of the dissenting shares?) into a procedural question (Was the deal process good?).[9]

Nothing in this inquiry should necessarily turn on whether the transaction is conflicted. There can be meaningful price discovery in a management buyout, for example. Conversely, an ostensibly arm's-length deal can have process deficiencies sufficient to throw out the deal price. In the recent Norcraft appraisal, for example, the go-shop process required a Superior Proposal (not just Excluded Party status) within thirty days; the buyer (Fortune Brands) had an unlimited match right; the Norcraft CEO had an undisclosed interest in buying back one of the company's subsidiaries post-closing; and Fortune Brands' bankers actually called prospective go-shop bidders to dissuade them from participating in the go-shop. This appraisal is currently pending in the Delaware Chancery Court.[10]

Implications

On policy, the Delaware Supreme Court stated in *Dell*: "If the reward for adopting many mechanisms designed to minimize conflict and ensure stockholders obtain the highest possible value is to risk the court adding a premium to the deal price based on a discounted cash flow analysis, then the incentives to adopt best practices will be greatly reduced" (Supreme Court Opinion at 64–65). The court is clearly right that providing a safe harbor from appraisal litigation if the deal process is good will encourage practitioners to button up their deal processes. And the court is further correct to (implicitly) require an A−, which is to say, not perfection, but more than what is required by fiduciary duty. In awarding its A (or A+) in *Dell*, the court touts the "many mechanisms" that allegedly "minimize[d] conflict and ensure[d] stockholders obtain the highest possible value." In my opinion, this grade is too generous. The Special Committee could and should have done more to mitigate the massive informational and structural advantages that Mr. Dell had.

Without requiring practitioners to really earn the right to call their deal process arm's length, the best practices that the court rightly wants to promote will disseminate slowly at best. The reason is that appraisal is a buy-side cost, but the sell-side controls the deal process that determines whether the deal price represents fair value. In contrast, fiduciary duty claims are a sell-side risk, so the sell-side board has incentives to at least satisfy its fiduciary duties (at least pre-*Corwin*). Without demanding more in (buy-side) appraisal litigation, all we will get is good-enough-for-fiduciary-duty deal processes.

So buy-side advisors and their clients have an interesting tactical choice: They could encourage the sell-side board to have a good deal process (pre-signing auction, no matching rights, etc.) to reduce their post-closing appraisal risk, but that very same deal process might push up the price that the buyer has to pay to all shareholders. Better, in most cases, to allow a deficient process that gets the seller a good-enough-for-fiduciary-duty price, and then bear the consequences of appraisal. And even losing the appraisal case has a silver lining, because it means that the buy side got the vast majority of shares below fair value. The result of these practical realities is that dissemination of deal process best practices will be slow at best, unless appraisal remains a truly meaningful buy-side risk.

But more important than my evaluation of the Dell deal process or the pace of dissemination of deal process best practices is the question of who decides. And here the Supreme Court should have deferred to the Chancery Court on its numerous findings of fact regarding the deal process. In *DFC Global*, the Supreme Court accepted Chancellor Bouchard's findings of fact regarding the deal process (e.g., that the company was sold in an "arm's-length sale," in a "robust" process, and "did not involve . . . conflicts of interest") and clarified the legal implications of those findings under the appraisal statute. In *Dell*, the Supreme Court could have said that a B+ was sufficient as a matter of law. Instead, the court engaged in a *de novo* review of the Chancery Court's key factual determinations to award an A grade. Readers who might take issue with my substantive assessment of the Dell deal process for whatever reason—including the possibility of bias due to my involvement as the petitioners' deal process expert—might nevertheless agree that the Chancery Court deserves deference on findings of fact.

Without such deference, Chancery Court judges will take care to make their future appraisal cases appeal-proof, due to the prospect of a *de novo* review of factual determinations by the Delaware Supreme Court. Even if the deal process has many "praiseworthy things," they will not acknowledge those things if they wish to depart from the deal price. Chancery judges will award a C when a B+ might be more appropriate, just to make sure that the Supreme Court does not grab onto those "praiseworthy" findings of fact to require deference to the deal price. And Chancery Court judges will award an A+ when an A− is warranted, in situations where they believe deference to the deal price is appropriate. Shades of gray will disappear from deal process assessments in appraisal proceedings. Rather than calling it like they see it, chancery judges will rationally attempt to insulate their future appraisal opinions from reversal.

I close with an observation on the politics of *Dell*. Clearly the big winners are private equity firms (which benefit from reduced appraisal risk) and investment banks (which benefit from more deals). These are important customers for Delaware, Inc. For these constituencies, the "terrifying" specter of *Dell* that Blackstone's John Finley described after the Chancery Court's decision (Naso 2017) has been expunged.

On the losing side of *Dell* are minority shareholders. I have no illusions that the shareholders who seek appraisal are Grandma and Grandpa. Shareholders who engage in appraisal arbitrage tend to be "highly sophisticated shareholders engaging in a multi-round, high-stakes game with M&A practitioners and the Delaware courts" (Subramanian 2017). But all shareholders benefit from the improved deal processes that a meaningful appraisal remedy provides.

The law and finance literature demonstrates that protecting minority shareholders improves capital formation. The intuition for this empirical finding is that prospective investors in the *next* dorm room start-up will be wary to commit capital if they do not have adequate protections at exit. With the near death of post-closing fiduciary duty litigation in the post-*Corwin* world, appraisal remains the last check against a deficient and/or conflicted deal process. For this reason, the Delaware Supreme Court's decision in *Dell* represents a step in the wrong direction.

The title of this volume is *The Corporate Contract in Changing Times: Is the Law Keeping Up?* The answer, at least in the appraisal arena, is no.

Notes

An earlier version of this essay was posted on SSRN as *Using the Deal Price as Evidence of "Fair Value" in Appraisal Proceedings.* I thank Dami Seung of the Harvard Law School for excellent research assistance. I served as an expert witness for petitioners in the Dell and Norcraft appraisals, which are discussed in this essay, and currently serve as an expert witness for petitioners in other appraisal proceedings that are pending in the Delaware Chancery Court. Comments are welcome at gsubramanian@hbs.edu.

1. *See, e.g.*, Merion Capital LP v. BMC Software, Inc., 2015 WL 6164771 at *18 (Del. Ch. 2015); LongPath Capital, LLC v. Ramtron Int'l Corp., 2015 WL 4540443 at *20 (Del. Ch. 2015); Merlin Partners LP v. AutoInfo, Inc., 2015 WL 2069417 at *17–*18 (Del. Ch. 2015); *In re* Appraisal of Ancestry.com, 2015 WL 399726 at *23 (Del. Ch. 2015); Huff Fund Investment Partnership v. CKx, Inc. 2013 WL 5878807 at *13 (Del. Ch. 2013), *aff'd*, 2015 WL 631586 (Del. 2015). *See also* M.P.M. Enterprises Inc. v. Gilbert, 731 A.2d 790, 796 (Del. 1999) ("A merger price resulting from arms-length negotiations where there are no claims of collusion is a very strong indication of fair value."); *In re* Rural Metro Corp. S'holders Litig., 88 A.3d 54, 102 (Del. Ch. 2014) ("Ordinarily this court places heavy reliance on the terms of a transaction that was negotiated at arm's length, particularly if the transaction resulted from an effective pre- or post-agreement market canvas[s]."); Merion Capital LP v. Lender Processing Services, Inc., C.A. No. 9320-VCL (Del. Ch. 2016) at *73 (deferring to deal price because "[t]he Company ran a sale process that generated reliable evidence of fair value.").

2. At a conference of practitioners and academics held at Kirkland & Ellis in May 2017, which was a primarily respondent-friendly crowd, 62 percent of participants in an anonymous poll nevertheless predicted that *Dell* would be affirmed (and a similar percentage voted that *Dell* should be affirmed). However, at oral argument four months later, Chief Justice Leo Strine made clear his view that *Dell* should be reversed. *See, e.g.*, Dell Oral Argument Transcript (Sept. 27, 2017) at 6 ("[D]idn't the Trial Court actually . . . pick a price that no possible buyer in the world would pay?"); *id.* at 25 ("If there is no evidence that he [Mr. Dell] was going to walk out the door, then the entire [Chancery] opinion's emphasis on the uncertainty is totally incoherent."); *id.* at 29 ("[Y]ou don't steal something when you invite HP, other companies, every large private equity firm in, and you've volunteered your votes to them."). Then Chancellor Strine also seems to have formed certain impressions about the case as the judge in the 2013 fiduciary duty litigation. *See, e.g.*, In re Dell Inc. Shareholder Litigation Scheduling Office Conference on Plaintiffs' Motion for Expedited Proceedings and Rulings of the Court (June 19, 2013), transcript at 13 ("There was not only presigning competition among private equity firms, there was an active post signing go-shop with insubstantial deal protections."); *id.* at 36 (describing "a vibrant post-signing market check"); *id.* at 44 (describing "a full and vigorous market contest here").

3. The nine were (affiliations as noted in the brief): Stephen M. Bainbridge, William D. Warren Distinguished Professor of Law at UCLA School of Law; William J. Carney, Charles Howard Chandler Professor of Law Emeritus at Emory University School of Law; Lawrence A. Cunningham, Henry St. George Tucker III Research Professor of Law at George Washington University Law School; Hideki Kanda, Emeritus Professor at the University of Tokyo and Professor at Gakushuin University Law School; Michael Knoll, Theodore K. Warner Professor of Law and Academic Director for Legal Education Programs, Law School, Professor of Real Estate, the Wharton School, and Co-Director, the Center for Tax Law and Policy, at University of Pennsylvania; Fred S. McChesney, de la Cruz-Metschikoff Endowed Chair in Law and Economics at University of Miami School of Law; Keith Sharfman, Professor of Law and Director of Bankruptcy Studies at St. John's University School of Law; George B. Shepherd, Professor of Law at Emory University School of Law; and Thomas Smith, Professor of Law at University of San Diego School of Law.

4. The twenty were (affiliations as noted in the brief): Jennifer Arlen, Norma Z. Paige Professor of Law at New York University Law School; Robert Bartlett, Professor of Law at UC Berkeley School of Law; Antonio Bernardo, Professor of Finance at the UCLA Anderson School of Management; Bernard S. Black, Nicholas D. Chabraja Professor at Northwestern University, Pritzker School of Law, Institute for Policy Research, and Kellogg School of Management (Finance Department); Patrick Bolton, Barbara and David Zalaznick

Professor of Business and member of the Committee on Global Thought at Columbia University; Brian Broughman, Associate Dean for Research and Professor of Law at Indiana University, Maurer School of Law; Albert H. Choi Albert C. BeVier Research Professor of Law, University of Virginia School of Law; John C. Coffee Jr., Adolf A. Berle Professor of Law, Columbia Law School; Peter Cramton, Professor of Economics at the University of Maryland and European University Institute, and on the International Faculty at the University of Cologne; Jesse M. Fried, Dane Professor of Law at Harvard Law School; Jeff Gordon, Richard Paul Richman Professor of Law at Columbia Law School; Eric Maskin, Nobel Laureate and Adams University Professor, Harvard University; W. Bentley MacLeod, Sami Mnaymneh Professor of Economics, Professor of International and Public Affairs, Columbia; Justin McCrary, Professor of Law at UC Berkeley Law; Alan Schwartz, Sterling Professor at Yale University; Kathryn E. Spier, Domenico De Sole Professor of Law at the Harvard Law School; Eric L. Talley, Isidor and Seville Sulzbacher Professor of Law at Columbia Law School; Robert Thompson, Peter P. Weidenbruch Professor of Business Law at Georgetown Law; Mark Weinstein, Associate Professor of Finance and Business Economics at the University of Southern California Marshall School of Business; and Ivo Welch, Distinguished Professor of Finance and holds the J. Fred Weston Chair in Finance at UCLA Anderson.

5. This strong presumption might be overcome, for example, by evidence that the fair value at closing (which is what the Delaware appraisal statute requires) was different from fair value at the time the deal was announced; or that the deal price included some measurable and significant share of the synergies from the deal (which should be excluded for purposes of appraisal). But either of these would just require adjustments from the deal price rather than giving the deal price less than 100 percent weight.

6. *See also* Chancery Court Opinion at *11: "The petitioners observe correctly that Evercore would earn a contingency fee only from offers produced during the go-shop period, so it had an incentive to prefer that any additional bidder emerge during that phase."

7. *See* TRANSCRIPT OF WILLIAM HILTZ TRIAL TESTIMONY (Oct. 6, 2015) at A517 ("[W]e had been contacted by Blackstone indicating that they had an interest in participating in the go-shop and encouraging us to structure the go-shop in a manner that would make it easy for them to get their work done."); MINUTES OF SPECIAL COMMITTEE MEETING (Jan. 24, 2013) at A1640 ("Evercore received a telephone call from The Blackstone Group stating that it would expect to explore making a proposal to acquire the Company during a go-shop period, and seeking assurances that any definitive agreement the Company may be considering entering into would provide for a meaningful go-shop process."). The Supreme Court opinion does not include these quotes from the record in its footnote. It is interesting that the court set a high evidentiary bar with respect to

a winner's curse (see the sections in this essay on "The Winner's Curse" and "Michael Dell's Value") but did not require the same evidentiary bar for its own alternative facts.

8. E-MAIL FROM CHINH CHU, SENIOR MANAGING DIRECTOR OF BLACKSTONE, TO MICHAEL DELL (April 1, 2013) (JX 444).

9. This analogy does not mean to suggest that Special Committee approval and a majority-of-the-minority condition should create a presumption that deal price represents fair value for appraisal purposes in a freeze-out. What is lacking in the controlled company context, even with these procedural protections, is a meaningful market canvass. Only in the rare instance where the controller agrees to sell into an overbid, and the Special Committee takes up the invitation by engaging in a market canvass, should the combination of Special Committee approval and majority-of-the-minority approval create a presumption that the deal price represents fair value for appraisal purposes in a freeze-out.

10. As mentioned in the biographical note and acknowledgments, I served as petitioner's deal process expert in this case. The facts described here come from my demonstratives at trial.

References

Arlen et al., 2017, Brief of Law and Corporate Finance Professors as Amici Curiae, DFC Global Corp. v. Muirfield Value Partners, L.P. (Feb. 3).

Bainbridge, Stephen, et al., 2017, *Brief of Law and Corporate Finance Professors as Amici Curiae in Support of Reversal*, DFC Global Corp. v. Muirfield Value Partners, L.P. (Jan. 6).

Carey, David, and Jack Clark, 2014, *Dell, Silver Lake Said to Reap 90% Gain a Year after LBO*, BLOOMBERG (Nov. 6).

Damouni, Nadia, and Poornima Gupta, 2013, *DealTalk—Blackstone Heading to Texas to Firm Up Dell Strategy*, REUTERS (April 4).

In re Dell Inc. Shareholder Litigation Scheduling Office Conference on Plaintiffs' Motion for Expedited Proceedings and Rulings of the Court, 2013 (June 19).

Dell, Michael, 2014, *Going Private Is Paying Off for Dell*, WALL STREET JOURNAL (Nov. 24).

Frankel, Alison, 2016, *Gibson Dunn to Delaware Supreme Court: Fix Arbitrary, Imprecise Appraisal Rulings*, REUTERS (Dec. 15).

Hoffman, Liz, 2016, *Judge Finds Michael Dell, Silver Lake Underpaid for Dell in 2013*, WALL STREET JOURNAL (June 1).

Hoffman, Liz, 2017, Database of Appraisal Claims (last revised Jan. 31).

Levine, Matt, 2016, *Michael Dell Bought His Company Too Cheaply*, BLOOMBERG VIEW (June 1).

Lipton, Martin, Theodore N. Mirvis, William Savitt, and Ryan A. McLeod, 2016, *Delaware Court of Chancery Appraises Fully-Shopped Company at Nearly 30% over Merger Price*, Wachtell, Lipton, Rosen & Katz Memorandum to Clients (June 2).

Naso, Chelsea, 2017, *Four Takeaways from the 2017 Tulane Corporate Law Institute*, Law360 (April 3).

Subramanian, Guhan, 1998, *Note, Using Capital Cash Flows to Value Dissenters' Shares in Appraisal Proceedings*, Harvard Law Review 111, no. 7.

Subramanian, Guhan, 2016, *Deal Process Design in Management Buyouts*, Harvard Law Review 130, no. 2.

Subramanian, Guhan, 2017, *Using the Deal Price for Determining "Fair Value" in Appraisal Proceedings* (working paper), https://papers.ssrn.com/sol3/papers.cfm?abstract_id=2911880.

CHAPTER ELEVEN

Boilermakers and the Contractual Approach to Litigation Bylaws

Jill E. Fisch

Introduction

The contractual approach to corporate law has its roots in the work of leading economists such as Ronald Coase (1991) and Oliver Hart (1995).[1] Although scholars widely accept the utility of contract metaphor, they debate its implications for regulatory policy. Some argue that contract principles support substantial deference to the structural arrangements chosen by corporate participants (Easterbrook and Fischel 1989); others question the appropriate scope of this deference (Bebchuk 1989). Hart (1988), for example, observed that, within public corporations, contracts are particularly likely to be incomplete. Similarly, William Klein (1982) warned that acceptance of the contract metaphor did not mean that corporate participants should be "free to arrive at any bargain they consider mutually advantageous."

The contractual approach has become particularly influential in supporting deference to the participants' agreed-upon governance terms on both autonomy and efficiency grounds (Easterbrook and Fischel 1989). Commentators have argued that corporate law should adopt an enabling approach in which default corporate law rules can be freely modified by firm participants rather than imposing one-size-fits-all mandatory regulations (Paredes 2010).[2] Corporate participants use private ordering to customize their corporate governance by adopting issuer-specific terms (Smith et al. 2011). I have described this trend as the "new governance"

(Fisch 2016b). Recent examples include forum selection bylaws, majority voting bylaws, and advance notice bylaws.

Then Chancellor (now Chief Justice) Strine builds upon this well-developed contractual model of the corporation in *Boilermakers Local 154 Retirement Fund v. Chevron Corp.* As Chief Justice Strine explained in *Boilermakers*, "the bylaws of a Delaware corporation constitute part of a binding broader contract among the directors, officers, and stockholders formed within the statutory framework of the DGCL [Delaware General Corporation Law]."[3]

Chief Justice Strine's contractual model of the corporation, as articulated in *Boilermakers*, relies on two components. The first is a theory of implied consent. Shareholders who buy stock in a corporation in which the charter confers the power to amend the bylaws on the board of directors implicitly consent to be bound by board-adopted bylaws. The second, according to Chief Justice Strine, is "the indefeasible right of the stockholders to adopt and amend bylaws themselves."[4] Chief Justice Strine describes the shareholders' ability to do so as "legally sacrosanct."[5]

This broad conception of the shareholders' bylaw power is in tension with an earlier decision by the Delaware Supreme Court, however. In *CA v. AFSCME*, the court held that a shareholder-adopted proxy expense reimbursement bylaw was inconsistent with Delaware law because the shareholders' authority to adopt this type of bylaw is limited in scope.[6] Specifically, the court concluded that the board's statutory authority to manage the corporation operated as a constraint on shareholder power. As the court explained, "the internal governance contract—which here takes the form of a bylaw—is one that would also prevent the directors from exercising their full managerial power in circumstances where their fiduciary duties would otherwise require them to deny reimbursement to a dissident slate."[7]

The tension between *Boilermakers* and *AFSCME* poses a challenge to the contemporary understanding that the contractual nature of the corporate form warrants the high level of judicial deference to private ordering reflected in *Boilermakers*. Within the context of the new governance, the board's power to adopt and amend bylaw provisions may, for a variety of reasons, be greater than the corresponding shareholder power to do so. In turn, the resulting limit on the scope of the contract metaphor offers a reason to question the current judicial approach to litigation bylaws.

This chapter proceeds as follows. The next section briefly sketches the foundation for the contractual model of the corporation and its application to issuer-specific bylaws. Later, I identify constraints on shareholder power to adopt and amend bylaws that create a disparity between the board's power and that of the shareholders. Finally, I consider the implications of this disparity for litigation bylaws—the subject of the *Boilermakers* decision.

The Contractual Nature of Corporate Bylaws

The contractual model of the corporation has its origins in a strand of law and economics scholarship from the 1980s (Ayres 1992). Scholars characterized the relationship between managers and shareholders as contractual in nature and further argued that market discipline, imposed through stock prices, would lead to the adoption of optimal contract terms (Clark 1989).

Although not all corporate law scholars supported the contractual approach (Cox 2015; Klausner 2006), many law and economics scholars, including most prominently Frank Easterbrook and Dan Fischel (1991), argued that the contractual theory had two important implications for corporate law. First, corporate law should facilitate the contracting process by accepting a wide range of firm-specific customized contract terms. Second, and relatedly, corporate law should not mandate a one-size-fits-all approach, both because policy makers are unlikely to identify successfully the optimal corporate law rules and because a single rule is unlikely to be optimal for all issuers.

The contractual model of the corporation is premised on the idea that the parties to the corporate contract—typically the shareholders and management (although the relationship between a corporation and its creditors is contractual as well)—should be free to set the terms of the corporate contract and that this freedom of contract is more desirable than mandatory rules (Butler and Ribstein 1990). Commentators have used the term *private ordering* to describe this freedom of contract and have argued generally for a private ordering approach to corporate law (Smith et al. 2011). The corporate bylaws offer a mechanism by which shareholders (and directors) can engage in this private ordering.

By virtue of its largely enabling structure, Delaware corporate law is consistent with the private ordering approach (Fisch 2013). The Delaware statute contains relatively few mandatory provisions. Instead, most of the statute provides default rules that can be modified through an appropriate charter or bylaw provision (Strine 2002). Thus, for example, the statute contains an antitakeover provision restricting business combinations with an interested shareholder for a period of five years but provides various mechanisms by which a corporation can elect to avoid the application of that provision.[8] Similarly, the statute provides that the board of directors will be elected annually but allows a corporation to opt instead for a classified board through a charter provision or shareholder-adopted bylaw.[9]

In addition to enabling individual corporations to modify the statutory default rules, the Delaware statute facilitates private ordering by allowing corporations to customize their charters and bylaws through the inclusion of a variety of optional contract-like terms. One of the better-known provisions, DGCL 102(b)(7), allows corporations to adopt a charter provision that limits or eliminates certain director liability for monetary damages based on a breach of the duty of care (Reed and Neiderman 2004). Another provision authorizes corporations to adopt a charter provision renouncing an interest in specified business opportunities, thereby limiting potential claims under the corporate opportunity doctrine.[10] The statute also authorizes corporations to adopt supermajority voting requirements through the inclusion of an optional charter provision.[11]

Delaware law also allows corporations to customize their corporate governance through the adoption of bylaws. Under the Delaware statute, shareholders have the power to adopt, amend, and repeal the bylaws. The corporation may also confer this power on the directors through a charter provision, but such a provision does not remove that power from the shareholders.[12] The vast majority of Delaware corporate charters vest the board of directors with this authority (Lipton 2016).

The scope of potential governance bylaws is very broad. The Delaware statute authorizes corporations to adopt "any provision, not inconsistent with law or with the certificate of incorporation, relating to the business of the corporation the conduct of its affairs, and its rights or powers or the rights or powers of its stockholders, directors, officers or employees."[13] Because of this broad scope and because shareholders and boards can each adopt governance bylaws unilaterally, a substantial amount of private ordering in Delaware corporations takes place through the adoption of issuer-specific bylaws (Veasey 2007).

The Delaware courts have largely accepted the contractual theory of corporate law. As the Delaware Supreme Court explained in *Airgas*, "Corporate charters and bylaws are contracts among a corporation's shareholders."[14] The contractual theory provides a methodology for interpreting the charter and bylaws—they are to be interpreted using contract principles. It also provides support for a basis for enforcing them. As then Chancellor Strine explained in the *Boilermakers* decision, "the bylaws constitute a binding part of the contract between a Delaware corporation and its stockholders."[15]

Boilermakers concerned the validity of a board-adopted forum selection bylaw. In upholding the bylaw, the court relied on two factors. The first was a theory of implied consent. Chancellor Strine reasoned that the Delaware statute contemplates that directors will, if the charter so provides, have the authority to adopt bylaws unilaterally. Given the framework established by the statute, shareholders of a corporation in which the charter authorizes the board to amend the bylaws implicitly agree that they "will be bound by bylaws adopted unilaterally by their boards."[16] Shareholders consent through their decision to invest in the corporation.

Chancellor Strine found further support for the contractual analysis in the rights conferred on shareholders by the statute if they disagree with a board-adopted bylaw. First, as Strine noted, the shareholders possess a right, comparable to that of the board, to adopt or amend bylaws.[17] Second, shareholders have the further power to discipline boards that refuse to accede to a shareholder vote concerning a bylaw by removing recalcitrant directors from their position. Strine therefore concluded: "Thus, a corporation's bylaws are part of an inherently flexible contract between the stockholders and the corporation under which the stockholders have powerful rights they can use to protect themselves if they do not want board-adopted forum selection bylaws to be part of the contract between themselves and the corporation."[18]

The *Boilermakers* decision reflects a powerful endorsement of contractual freedom in corporate law. As such, it encouraged corporations to engage in private ordering through the adoption and amendment of the corporate bylaws. Corporations responded to this invitation. With respect to forum selection bylaws, which had been used to a limited extent prior to the *Boilermakers* decision, issuer adoption of the bylaws "rapidly accelerated" after *Boilermakers* (Romano and Sanga 2016).

Issuers also began to experiment with other governance bylaws. In

ATP, the Delaware Supreme Court upheld a board-adopted fee-shifting bylaw, reasoning that the contractual analysis in *Boilermakers* was similarly applicable.[19] Several issuers adopted director qualification bylaws to prohibit certain types of compensation agreements for activist-nominated director candidates (Cain et al. 2016). Commentators argued that the reasoning in *ATP* and *Boilermakers* allowed issuers to adopt bylaws compelling arbitration instead of litigation (Allen 2014). Several courts upheld the decision to adopt an arbitration bylaw by one issuer, a Massachusetts real estate investment trust, although the analysis did not implicate Delaware corporate law.[20]

Shareholders also increased their efforts to engage in private ordering through the adoption of governance bylaws. In recent years, shareholders have proposed various governance reforms—including majority voting, proxy access, and the right of shareholders to call a special meeting—through bylaw amendments (Fisch 2016b). These proposals have enjoyed considerable voting support. As of January 2014, for example, "almost 90% of S&P 500 companies ha[d] adopted some form of majority voting" (Choi et al. 2016). The year 2015 was a "breakthrough year" for proxy access shareholder bylaws, due in part to a shareholder proposal campaign by the New York City Comptroller (Kess 2015). Most proxy access proposals received support by a majority of shareholders, and a growing number of issuers are adopting some form of proxy access (Weil, Gotshal & Manges 2015).

Limits of the Contract Analogy

As noted above, boards and shareholders use private ordering to adopt issuer-specific governance bylaws. If these bylaws are properly understood as negotiated terms of a contract, then courts should give them broad deference.[21] The *Boilermakers* and *ATP* decisions relied on this rationale to uphold forum selection and fee-shifting bylaws, respectively.

The problem with the contractual analysis, however, is that, for various reasons, shareholder power to amend the bylaws is more limited than the *Boilermakers* decision suggests.[22] Although the board has broad power to adopt governance bylaws, shareholders do not enjoy analogous power. Accordingly, shareholders are limited in their ability to constrain board actions with which they disagree. This section identifies several key limitations on shareholder power over the corporations' bylaws. The next part considers the implications of these limitations for litigation bylaws.

Substantive Limits on Shareholder Power under Section 109

Although the *Boilermakers* and *ATP* opinions contain broad language concerning the shareholder power to adopt and amend bylaws under Delaware law, an earlier Delaware Supreme Court decision in *CA v. AFSCME* suggests a more limited shareholder role.[23] AFSCME, a union pension fund, submitted a shareholder proposal for the CA annual meeting, pursuant to Rule 14a-8,[24] seeking to amend the bylaws to require the issuer, under certain circumstances, to reimburse reasonable proxy solicitation expenses incurred by a stockholder who nominates one or more candidates for election to the board of directors.[25] CA sought to exclude the shareholder proposal from its proxy statement on the basis that the proposed bylaw was not a proper subject for shareholder action and, if adopted, would be illegal under Delaware law, specifically § 141(a).

In support of its request for no-action relief, CA submitted to the SEC an opinion letter from Delaware counsel arguing that the proposed bylaw was invalid because it would interfere with the board's authority under the statute and the charter to manage the corporation (Richards, Layton & Finger 2008). According to the letter, the board, not the shareholders, had the discretion to determine how to expend corporate funds, and the shareholders lacked the authority "unilaterally [to impose] limits on the Board's discretion." The letter also argued that the bylaw would "impede the Board's exercise of its fiduciary duties to manage the business and affairs of the Company."

The SEC sought guidance from the Delaware Supreme Court as to whether CA's argument was correct as a matter of Delaware corporate law.[26] The court used the occasion to provide several guiding principles about the scope of shareholder authority under Section 109. First, and perhaps most important, the court explicitly rejected the idea that the shareholder's power to adopt bylaws is coextensive with that of the board of directors. Instead, the court explained that shareholder power is limited by Section 141(a), which provides the board, but not the shareholder, with broad management power over the affairs of the corporation. The court explained that a shareholder-adopted bylaw would be invalid if it limited "the board's management prerogatives under Section 141(a)."[27]

The court's analysis drew upon an argument that commentators had developed in response to pill redemption bylaws (Hamermesh 1998). In the late 1990s, institutional investors attempted to adopt bylaws to restrict a board's use of a poison pill to resist a hostile tender offer (Coffee 1997). These bylaws took various forms, including requiring boards to redeem poison pills that had been adopted without shareholder approval and requiring boards to submit poison pills to the shareholders for approval. These bylaws generated substantial controversy among corporate law experts, many of whom argued that they were invalid because they exceeded shareholder power or interfered with the board's authority to run the corporation (Hamermesh 1998).

In a case involving an Oklahoma corporation, *International Bhd. of Teamsters v. Fleming Cos.*,[28] the Oklahoma Supreme Court upheld a bylaw requiring that the board submit a pill to its shareholders for ratification against the claim that the bylaw exceeded the shareholders' authority. Reading the Oklahoma corporation statute, the court concluded that, absent specific statutory language granting the board autonomy to adopt a pill such as a rights plan endorsement statute (which Oklahoma did not have), the shareholders were free to adopt a bylaw that limited board authority to implement such a plan. The court reasoned, in particular, that a pill was similar to stock option plans and that there was "authority supporting shareholder ratification of stock option plans."[29]

The Delaware courts did not have occasion to rule on whether a pill redemption bylaw was permissible under Delaware law, and whether they would have followed the Fleming court's approach is unclear (Macey 1998). Several prominent commentators argued that they would not have (Coates and Faris 2001). These commentators reasoned that Delaware law espouses a board-central model of the corporation. As Stephen Bainbridge (2003) has argued, various legal doctrines limit the control of shareholders of Delaware corporations over management decisions. Bainbridge (2006) has identified a variety of normative arguments in support of these limits, reasoning both that the corporate form involves the shareholders' decision to delegate this control to the board and that this delegation is efficient.

In the *CA* case, the court offered guidance on the permissible scope of corporate bylaws to analyze the relationship between board authority under Section 141(a) and shareholder power under Section 109.

As a starting point, the court recognized that the statutory language was only "marginally helpful in determining what the Delaware legislature intended to be the lawful scope of the shareholders' power to adopt, amend and repeal bylaws."[30] The court went on to explain that the proper function of bylaws was to address procedural issues rather than to mandate substantive business decisions and that this substance/procedure distinction could be used to demarcate the scope of a permissible bylaw under Delaware law. Using this concept, it then framed the answer to the first certified question as requiring it to determine whether an expense reimbursement bylaw was "process-related."[31] The court concluded that it was. Although the bylaw concededly involved the expenditure of corporate funds, the court reasoned that the expenditure was related to maintaining the integrity of the electoral process. The court concluded that, as such, the bylaw was a proper subject for shareholder action.

The substance/procedure distinction can be understood as a way to determine when a bylaw impermissibly infringes upon board authority under DGCL § 141(a). Section 141(a) vests the board with authority over substantive business decisions such that a substantive bylaw could be understood to usurp that authority. A bylaw that addresses the procedure by which a decision is made but leaves the ultimate decision to the board would presumably be less problematic than a bylaw that purports to limit the board's discretion.[32] This reasoning would have the effect of creating a different standard for board-adopted bylaws than for bylaws adopted by shareholders, because it would be unnecessary to limit the board to adopting only process-related bylaws.

The *CA* court's determination that the proxy reimbursement bylaw was process-based, and therefore legally permissible, did not conclude its analysis, however. The court went on to consider the second certified question—whether the proposed bylaw would cause CA to violate Delaware law. The court concluded that it would. Reasoning that the bylaw could, hypothetically, require the board to reimburse a stockholders' proxy expenses in a situation in which that reimbursement would violate the board's fiduciary duties, the court concluded this deficiency rendered the bylaw facially invalid.[33]

The court reached this conclusion by analogizing to situations in which courts had invalidated contracts that imposed obligations on a board that arguably were inconsistent with the board's fiduciary duties (Ursaner 2010). Although those situations involved contractual obligations that the board had voluntarily assumed, as opposed to obligations imposed by a shareholder-adopted bylaw, the court concluded that "the distinction is one without a difference."[34] The court's rationale was that, in either case, the result would be to limit the board's ability to exercise the full scope of its managerial authority. Again, the touchstone of the analysis was the board's broad authority under § 141(a).

Although the *CA* decision has been criticized (McDonnell 2008), and the Delaware legislature subsequently amended the statute explicitly to authorize both proxy expense reimbursement bylaws and proxy access bylaws,[35] the principle that shareholder authority under Section 109 is more limited than director authority appears to have survived. In a 2015 decision, Vice Chancellor Noble invalidated a bylaw that authorized shareholders to remove and replace corporate officers without cause.[36] Notably, the plaintiff in that case relied on statutory language that seemed expressly to authorize bylaws that dealt with the appointment and removal of corporate officers (Tiger and Oh 2015).[37]

Significantly, Vice Chancellor Noble relied on the *CA* decision for the proposition that "Stockholders' ability to amend bylaws is 'not coextensive with the board's concurrent power and is limited by the board's management prerogatives under Section 141(a).'"[38] The court further held that the touchstone for determining whether the bylaw infringed on the board's management function was the substance/procedure distinction developed by the *CA* court. Applying this standard, the court concluded that the bylaw was invalid, reasoning that it "would allow them to make substantive business decisions for the Company."[39]

Additional Statutory Limits on Shareholder Power

Although *CA* distinguishes between shareholder and board power to adopt and amend the bylaws, it is only one case.[40] The structure and language of the Delaware corporation statute provide additional reasons to view the scope of shareholder power under Section 109 as limited. One notable feature of the statute is that it contains provisions expressly authorizing bylaws that address particular issues. For example, Section 112 authorizes proxy expense reimbursement bylaws. Section 113 authorizes proxy access bylaws. Section 141(d) allows shareholders to adopt a bylaw to classify the board of directors. Section 216 permits a bylaw to implement majority voting, and Section 203(b)(3) authorizes shareholders to adopt a bylaw opting out of the state antitakeover statute.

Although the statute does not contain language indicating that shareholder-adopted bylaws are limited to subjects expressly authorized by the statute, there are two possible reasons to read the list of explicit statutory authorizations as limiting the scope of shareholder power. First, if, as Section 109 implies, shareholders can adopt bylaws containing "any provision, not inconsistent with law or with the certificate of incorporation, relating to the business of the corporation,"[41] the list of subject-specific authorizations is unnecessary.[42] Consequently, under a formalistic approach to statutory construction, the fact that the statute sets out a litany of subjects upon which a shareholder-adopted bylaw is permitted implies that, in the absence of statutory authorization, at least some types of shareholder-adopted bylaws are not allowed (Hamermesh 1998).

Second, the enabling provisions reinforce the idea that shareholder authority over corporate affairs is limited and that the statute vests all residual authority in the board of directors. This perspective is consistent with the argument identified earlier that board power to manage the corporation is, pursuant to Section 141(a), unlimited, but shareholders possess only those powers expressly conferred by the statute. It is also consistent with a statutory structure that confers specific and limited powers upon shareholders apart from their power to adopt bylaws. Thus, the Delaware statute allows shareholders to vote on a limited set of issues: the election of the board of directors, amendments to the certificate of incorporation, and the approval of mergers and other structural changes (Bebchuk 2005).

An additional concern with shareholder authority under Section 109 is that, in virtually all corporations, it is nonexclusive. While shareholders have the power to adopt and amend the bylaws, so does the board of directors. As a result, even if the shareholders adopt a bylaw, their action may be overturned by the board (Hamermesh 1998).

Although the Delaware statute contains provisions that explicitly protect a shareholder-adopted bylaw from board repeal, those provisions are applicable to only a few substantive issues, such as DGCL Section 216, which provides that a shareholder-adopted bylaw specifying the votes required for the election of directors "shall not be further amended or repealed by the board of directors." Absent language such as that found in Section 216, it appears that the board of a Delaware corporation is free to amend or repeal a shareholder-adopted bylaw with which it disagrees.

Furthermore, it is unclear whether the shareholders' attempt to prevent such a repeal would be valid (Bird 2008). Notably, the Delaware Supreme Court stated in dictum that a shareholder-adopted bylaw that purported to be insulated from board override would be void, reasoning that the limitation was "in obvious conflict" with the directors' "general authority to adopt or amend corporate by-laws."[43]

Delaware law differs in this regard from the Model Business Corporation Act (Bird 2008), which explicitly authorizes shareholders to insulate any shareholder-adopted bylaw from board override, providing that "A corporation's board of directors may amend or repeal the corporation's bylaws, unless . . . the shareholders in amending, repealing or adopting a bylaw expressly provide that the board of directors may not amend, repeal, or reinstate that bylaw."[44] As one commentator notes, Delaware could amend its statute to take a similar approach (Bird 2008). Alternatively, Delaware could reinforce its director primary position by explicitly granting the board the power to amend any shareholder-adopted bylaw. Either approach would increase predictability over the current legal uncertainty.

On the other hand, a broadly construed board power to amend the bylaws might provide a solution to the question of shareholder authority raised in *CA*. To the extent that a board retains the authority to repeal a shareholder-adopted bylaw that would infringe on the board's managerial authority or cause it to violate its fiduciary duties, arguably that power alone should save the bylaw from the infirmity identified in *CA*. At least at issuers in which the board has concurrent authority with the shareholders to amend the bylaws, its power to do so would seem to imply that a shareholder-adopted bylaw could not infringe on board authority under Section 141(a).

Then Vice Chancellor Strine implicitly made this point in dictum in *General Datacomm Indus. v. Wisconsin Inv. Bd.*[45] In considering whether a shareholder-proposed bylaw that prevented the board from repricing options without shareholder approval was valid under Delaware law, Vice Chancellor Strine observed that the board could repeal the offending bylaw at any time if it determined that it was necessary to do so. Accordingly, Vice Chancellor Strine concluded that the bylaw did not constrain board discretion in a way that would be analogous to a poison pill that could not be redeemed by a new board majority.[46]

Boards can also block shareholders' efforts to insulate a bylaw from board repeal by proactively adopting their own bylaw that does not preclude subsequent board amendment. Currently a number of issuer boards have used this approach with majority voting bylaws (Siegel 2011). Under the statutes of many states, a shareholder-adopted majority voting bylaw is insulated from board repeal, but this restriction does not apply to a board-adopted majority voting bylaw. As a result, boards can avoid the restriction on their power by adopting majority voting bylaws themselves. As one commentator notes, "In so doing, directors doubly benefit: they not only gain approval from shareholders who support majority voting, but the directors have also assured themselves the opportunity to repeal, unilaterally, their own bylaw" (Siegel 2011).

A related issue is whether shareholders indeed have the power, as Chancellor Strine suggested in *Boilermakers*, to amend or repeal a board-adopted bylaw with which they disagree. The issue is potentially problematic to the extent that, as suggested by *CA*, the board's bylaw authority is broader than that of the shareholders'. If the board adopts a bylaw pursuant to its authority under Section 141(a) that the shareholders could not have adopted on their own, it is not clear whether the shareholders would have the power to amend or repeal that bylaw. In other words, it is plausible that *CA* sets analogous limits on both the shareholders' power to adopt the bylaws and their power to amend or repeal board-adopted bylaws.[47] Although the Delaware courts have not had occasion to address this question, as corporations increase their efforts at private ordering and as shareholders become more willing to challenge board-adopted governance measures with which they disagree, the issue becomes more likely to arise (Allen 2012).

Shareholders, of course, have other ways of responding to an issuer's problematic governance provisions. One of the most powerful is withholding voting support from director candidates who adopt or fail to repeal an objectionable governance provision (Choi, Fisch, and Kahan 2008–9) The effectiveness of this approach has been enhanced by the role of the major proxy advisory firms Institutional Shareholder Services [ISS] and Glass Lewis (Choi, Fisch, and Kahan 2010). The proxy advisory firms have identified unilateral board actions that reduce shareholder rights and board failures to respond to shareholder demands as important considerations in their proxy voting policies (Weil, Gotshal & Manges 2014). ISS has specifically included both such actions as critical factors influencing its recommendations for director elections (Sullivan and Cromwell 2015). Shareholders take these recommendations very seriously (Choi, Fisch, and Kahan 2013). For example, one commentator reports that, of the various reasons for ISS issuing a negative recommendation for a director candidate, a "lack of 'responsiveness'" is "clearly the most impactful" (Sullivan and Cromwell 2015).

An example demonstrates the potential effectiveness of this approach. In 2013, ISS announced that it would recommend that shareholders withhold their votes from directors who had adopted a director compensation bylaw that limited a board candidate's ability to receive compensation from a third party (Cain et al. 2016). So-called golden leash bylaws were developed by the Wachtell law firm as a response to compensation arrangements between activist hedge funds and their director nominees. Following ISS's announcement, directors at Provident Bank, the first issuer affected by the ISS position, received a withhold vote of 34 percent. This withhold level was extremely high (Choi, Fisch, and Kahan 2013). Within the next six months, twenty-eight of the thirty-two issuers that had adopted golden leash bylaws repealed them. Notably, the threat of shareholder voting pressure was sufficient to cause the issuers in question to repeal their bylaws without the need to challenge the bylaws' validity.

The effectiveness of the shareholder vote on director elections has increased with the advent of majority voting. Under traditional plurality voting, it was not possible for shareholders to fail to elect a director candidate in an uncontested election (Choi et al. 2016). Under a majority voting rule, a director candidate must receive a majority of votes cast, and a large against or withhold vote can require the director to tender his or her resignation. Thus, majority voting theoretically gives the shareholder vote on the election of directors real teeth. In reality, however, even though a substantial percentage of issuers have adopted majority voting policies, the number of directors who fail to receive a majority vote is very small, and, of those, even fewer lose their jobs.

More importantly, although shareholders can use their voting power in director elections to apply pressure to board-adopted governance provisions, the ability to apply pressure in response to unwanted board actions is not the equivalent of consenting to those actions. The possibility that shareholders, if sufficiently mobilized, can pressure a board to amend or repeal an objectionable bylaw does not mean that shareholders have otherwise consented to the bylaw's adoption.

Finally, *Boilermakers* is, concededly, a Delaware case and is premised on the fact that under Delaware law, shareholder authority to amend the bylaws cannot be eliminated. Not every state corporation statute takes this approach, however. In some states, it is possible to structure a corporation so that directors have exclusive authority to amend the bylaws. In Texas, for example, a corporation may, through an appropriate provision in its charter, eliminate shareholder authority to amend the bylaws.[48] In Maryland, a corporation can grant the power to the board, the shareholders, or both.[49] Indeed, following the *Fleming* decision, the Oklahoma legislature amended its corporation statute to provide that, as a default rule, only the board of directors has the power to amend or repeal the corporation's bylaws, although a corporation may voluntarily grant this power to the shareholders as well.[50] The Indiana statute is similar.[51]

Even in states where shareholders have the power to amend the bylaws, this power may be restricted by limitations on the types of governance provisions that can be adopted through a shareholder-adopted bylaw. For example, although Delaware allows shareholders to adopt a majority voting rule by amending the bylaws, as of 2011, only nineteen states allowed shareholder-adopted majority voting bylaws without prior charter authorization or board approval (Siegel 2011). In a corporation in which shareholders lack the authority to adopt, amend, and repeal the bylaws, an essential predicate of the *Boilermakers* contractual approach is missing.

Practical Limits to Shareholder Power

In addition to legal limits on shareholder power to act through the adoption and amendment of the bylaws, shareholders face practical limits on their power to implement changes to the bylaws. Indeed, as Chief Justice Strine has noted, the "practical realities of stock market ownership have changed in ways that deprive most stockholders of both their right to voice and their right of exit" (Strine and Walter 2015). Strine and Walther have termed this a "separation of ownership from ownership."

One such limit is the standard collective action problem (Alces 2010). An extensive literature observes that shareholders of US public companies are dispersed; they face costs when they seek to act collectively; and shareholders, unlike directors, must typically bear those costs personally (Bainbridge 2006). Concededly, the rise of shareholder activism and intermediaries such as ISS have dramatically reduced these costs (Cain et al. 2016). In addition, activist hedge funds have taken on a role as governance intermediaries and are able to identify governance failures and then mobilize traditionally passive institutional investors to respond to those failures (Gilson and Gordon 2013). It is unlikely that governance issues are of sufficiently high value to attract the interest of hedge fund activists. Recent work supports the conclusion that hedge fund activism is focused on other areas, such as sale, capital structure, and corporate strategy (Krishnan, Partnoy, and Thomas 2016).

Supermajority voting requirements at specific issuers may limit shareholders' ability to amend or repeal a board-adopted bylaw (Klausner 2006). Delaware law allows a corporation to require "a supermajority vote for adopting any subsequent bylaw amendment" (Gill et al. 2014).[52] It is common for corporations to adopt supermajority voting requirements for some or all shareholder actions (Hirst 2017). Supermajority provisions are increasingly common in initial public offering (IPO) charters; such provisions were present in 88 percent of IPO charters in 2015 (Wilmer-Hale 2016). Although the incidence of such requirements has declined in S&P 500 companies, approximately 30 percent retained a supermajority requirement in 2013 (Gill et al. 2014). Notably, if an issuer's charter contains a supermajority requirement, that requirement can only be repealed by that same supermajority.[53]

Although shareholders can, in theory, obtain the necessary votes to adopt or amend a bylaw, even in a corporation with a supermajority voting requirement, such a requirement heightens the collective action problems. As Scott Hirst (2017) has documented, voter turnout varies substantially among issuers, and a substantial number of issuers regularly experience turnout levels that are below the supermajority thresholds. The problem of insufficient voter turnout has been exacerbated by the virtual elimination of broker discretionary voting (Fisch 2016a).

The impact of supermajority requirements is exacerbated by the standard vote-counting methodology. According to one study, more than half of large public companies count abstentions on shareholder proposals as no votes (Investor Voice 2015). Because a shareholder-initiated bylaw amendment must necessarily take the form of a shareholder proposal, this voting methodology has the effect of allowing issuers to treat some shareholder proposals as failing even if they receive a majority of votes cast (Herbert 2015). The study found sixty-three shareholder-sponsored proposals between 2004 and 2014 that were identified by issuers as failing but that would have passed under a so-called simple majority formula.[54]

A final practical impediment to shareholder power is the Securities and Exchange Commission's gatekeeping role. Shareholder resolutions seeking to amend the bylaws are typically presented to the issuer in the form of Rule 14a-8 shareholder proposals (Nagy 1998).[55] It is commonplace for issuers to seek SEC approval to exclude from the proxy statement shareholder proposals that they do not support (Palmiter 1994). One basis for excluding a shareholder proposal is if that proposal, if implemented, would cause the issuer to violate state law.[56] This leaves the SEC staff in the awkward position of attempting to determine the scope of shareholder bylaw authority despite the fact that, as noted above, Delaware law is somewhat unclear on the issue (Coffee 1997).

Although Delaware amended its constitution in 2007 to permit the SEC to certify questions regarding Delaware corporate law to the state supreme court[57]—the procedure that was used by the SEC in *CA*[58]—the SEC is not required to make use of the certification procedure, and the Delaware Supreme Court is not required to accept a request for a ruling.[59] As a result, the SEC staff is repeatedly called upon to determine whether a shareholder-proposed bylaw is permissible with only the submissions of the proponent and the issuer to guide it in making that determination.[60] Although a full analysis of the SEC's approach to this question is beyond the scope of this chapter, it is clear that the procedure has the practical effect of preventing many proposed bylaws from being presented to the shareholders (Nagy 1998).

Consequences of the Disparity for Litigation Bylaws

The foregoing discussion suggests that the contract analogy in *Boilermakers* is flawed in that shareholder power to act through the adoption, amendment, and repeal of the bylaws is, for various reasons, more limited than board power. The implications of this conclusion are that, at a minimum, courts should be wary of relying on contract principles as a basis for subjecting issuer-adopted governance provisions to limited oversight.

Forum selection bylaws, such as the one challenged in *Boilermakers*, are one of several types of governance provisions that issuers developed to respond to perceived excessive merger litigation. Other provisions include fee-shifting bylaws and arbitration bylaws. Elsewhere I have collectively termed these provisions *litigation bylaws* (Fisch 2016b). Issuers adopted litigation bylaws in response to the growth of merger litigation and, in particular, multiforum litigation (Cain and Davidoff Solomon 2015). The vast majority of these adoptions took place through unilateral board action and were not submitted to a shareholder vote. This part considers the application of the principles in the preceding section to litigation bylaws and suggests that, contrary to the perspective articulated in *Boilermakers*, existing corporate law and practice present serious obstacles to a shareholder effort to adopt or repeal such a bylaw. As a result, the role of the contract analogy in supporting the adoption of litigation bylaws may be overstated.

The merits of litigation bylaws have generated extensive debate. With exclusive forum and fee-shifting bylaws, the Delaware legislature intervened in 2015 by enacting legislation that explicitly authorized the adoption of exclusive forum bylaws (so long as a Delaware court was among the forums chosen).[61] The same legislation affirmatively prohibited issuers from adopting fee-shifting bylaws. Thus, on these two specific subjects, the issue of their facial validity has been put to rest.

Additional variations of litigation bylaws are possible, however, that extend beyond the 2015 statute (Winship 2016; Griffith 2017).[62] For example, one article has suggested a no-fees bylaw, which does not impose a fee obligation on a losing plaintiff but instead prohibits awarding fees to a successful plaintiff (Bayliss and Mixon 2015). Another option is a bylaw that imposes a minimum ownership requirement for a plaintiff to file a shareholder derivative suit on behalf of the issuer (LaCroix 2015). These have been termed *minimum stake to sue bylaws*.[63] Verity Winship (2016) has identified a variety of litigation provisions that could be incorporated into a firm's bylaws to affect the cost and availability of shareholder litigation, including limitations on discovery and provisions that require contemporaneous ownership or the posting of a bond.

Litigation bylaws arguably straddle the distinction between procedure and substance suggested by the *CA* decision. On the one hand, they address procedural aspects of litigation, such as the payment of attorneys' fees or the choice of forum rather than the substantive scope of litigation rights.[64] On the other hand, those procedural issues dramatically impact substantive rights—so much so that the Delaware State Bar Council (2015) observed, in proposing the 2015 legislation that fee-shifting bylaws such as that in *ATP* would make shareholder litigation "untenable" and "eliminate the only extant regulation of substantive corporate law."

Moreover, at least with respect to derivative suits, managing litigation involving the issuer is, quintessentially, a business decision.[65] The Delaware courts have repeatedly observed this fact and, consequently, have been reluctant to interfere with board decisions as to whether a particular lawsuit should proceed. As Professor and Dean Robert Clark (1986) observed, "Whether to sue or not to sue is ordinarily a matter for the business judgment of directors, just as is a decision that the corporation will make bricks instead of bottles." Similarly, again with respect to derivative litigation, Dooley and Veasey (1989) have observed that "no principled distinction can be drawn between a board's decisions relating to corporate litigation generally and those relating to other business matters." To the extent that litigation bylaws purport to address shareholder litigation generally, it is unclear whether shareholders have the power to restrict the board's discretion about the appropriate scope of litigation, at least litigation involving the issuer's rights.

To date, virtually all litigation bylaws have been board-adopted. Consequently, the Delaware courts have not had the opportunity to evaluate the validity of a shareholder effort to amend or repeal a board-adopted litigation bylaw.[66] As the foregoing analysis suggests, however, existing law raises serious questions about the scope of shareholder power with respect to litigation bylaws. For the contract principles on which *Boilermakers* relies to support judicial deference to the parties' agreed-upon terms, however, shareholders must have the power to respond to board-adopted litigation bylaws with which they disagree.

Finally, the SEC's role as gatekeeper of shareholder proposals imposes an additional potential limit on shareholder power to respond to board-adopted litigation bylaws. For shareholders to vote on a proposal to adopt or amend a litigation bylaw, the proposal would likely have to survive the SEC no-action process. Whether the SEC would allow an issuer to exclude a shareholder proposal involving a litigation bylaw remains unclear.

To date, the SEC has expressed some skepticism about whether shareholder proposals dealing with litigation are an appropriate subject for shareholder action under Rule 14a-8. In particular, the SEC allowed some issuers to exclude shareholder proposals dealing with litigation from the proxy statement on the basis that they deal with ordinary business issues and are therefore excludable pursuant to Rule 14a-8(c)(7).[67] The SEC's rulings on these issues have not been directed at the specific legality of litigation bylaws, however.

The validity of shareholder proposals concerning litigation bylaws has been presented to the SEC staff on only a few occasions. In *Pfizer*, the SEC had the opportunity to consider the scope of shareholder authority to adopt litigation bylaws but did not reach the issue of shareholder power.[68] A Pfizer shareholder submitted a proposal to amend the company's bylaws to provide that certain claims should be resolved through arbitration rather than litigation. As noted above, a few issuers have experimented with arbitration bylaws. Although Pfizer argued, inter alia, that the bylaw was inconsistent with state law, the SEC staff relied on an alternative argument—that the bylaw was inconsistent with the federal securities laws—and allowed Pfizer to exclude the proposal on that basis.

Previously a shareholder used Rule 14a-8 to propose a fee-shifting bylaw at 3Com corporation.[69] 3Com sought to exclude the bylaw, arguing that, among other things, the bylaw was inconsistent with the federal securities laws, was contrary to public policy, and addressed a matter of ordinary business operations. Because the shareholder subsequently withdrew the proposal, the SEC dismissed 3Com's request for no-action relief as moot.

On the other hand, in *Roper Industries*,[70] a shareholder submitted a Rule 14a-8 proposal requesting that the board repeal the issuer's board-adopted exclusive forum bylaw. Roper Industries sought to exclude the bylaw on the ground that it concerned the ordinary business operations of the issuer and was therefore excludable under SEC Rule 14a-8(c)(7). Specifically, the issuer argued that the proposal sought to manage the company's "litigation strategy and expenses" and that these were matters of ordinary business for the company. The SEC disagreed and refused to permit the exclusion of the proposal.

The bottom line of this analysis is that current law presents several obstacles to shareholders that might seek to initiate, limit, or overturn litigation bylaws. Apart from the specific bylaws addressed by the 2015 Delaware legislation, litigation bylaws offer an important example in which the limitations on shareholder bylaw authority arguably limit the shareholders' ability to overturn board action in the manner contemplated by *Boilermakers*. Given these limitations, it is not clear that *Boilermakers*' deferential approach to board adoption of these bylaws is warranted. More generally, the example of litigation bylaws offers reasons to question the scope of Delaware's true commitment to a contractual approach to corporate law.

Conclusion

The contractual approach to corporate law—which has been widely defended in legal scholarship for more than twenty-five years, has received strong judicial support in two recent Delaware decisions. The courts' apparent endorsement of freedom of contract appears to open the door to broad-based experimentation and implementation of new governance provisions tailored to issuer-specific needs.

At the same time, various legal and practical aspects of existing corporate law are in tension with the contractual approach upon which the *Boilermakers* decision is based. In particular, several aspects of existing law appear to limit the free participation of shareholders in the private ordering process. In the absence of true shareholder power to limit the board's adoption of unwanted governance provisions, the contractual analogy appears misplaced, and the resulting implication that board-adopted governance bylaws should enjoy substantial judicial deference appears unwarranted.

These concerns apply in particular to the still-nascent subject of litigation bylaws, whose potential scope and application remain unclear. As such, innovation and experimentation are to be encouraged. At the same time, judicial oversight of the field must reflect the legal and practical limitations on shareholder power discussed in this chapter.

Notes

I am grateful for helpful comments from Sean Griffith, Steven Davidoff Solomon, and Frank Partnoy. This chapter was originally published in CALIFORNIA LAW REVIEW 106 (2018).

1. *E.g.,* Coase (1991 at 56): "the firm is essentially a choice of contractual arrangements."

2. Other forms of business entity law are more explicit in providing the maximum effect to the participants' agreed-upon terms (see Ribstein 1991).

3. Boilermakers Local 154 Retirement Fund v. Chevron Corp., 73 A.3d 934, 939 (Del. Ch. 2013).

4. *Id.* at 956.

5. *Id.*

6. CA, Inc. v. AFSCME Emples. Pension Plan, 953 A.2d 227 (Del. 2008).

7. *Id.* at 239.

8. DGCL § 203(a).

9. DGCL § 141(d).

10. DGCL § 122(17).

11. DGCL § 102(b)(4).

12. DGCL § 109(a).

13. DGCL § 109(b).

14. Airgas, Inc. v. Air Prods. & Chems., Inc., 8 A.3d 1182, 1188 (Del. 2010).

15. Boilermakers Local 154 Retirement Fund v. Chevron Corp., 73 A.3d 934, 955 (Del. Ch. 2013).

16. *Id.* at 956.

17. *Id.*, quoting CA, Inc., 953 A.2d at 232.

18. *Id.*

19. ATP Tour, Inc. v. Deutscher Tennis Bund, 91 A.3d 554, 556 (Del. 2014).

20. Del. Cnty. Emps. Ret. Fund v. Portnoy, No. 13-10405-DJC, 2014 U.S. Dist. LEXIS 40107 (D. Mass. Mar. 26, 2014); Katz v. CommonWealth REIT, No. 24-C-13-001299 (Cir. Ct. Balt. City Aug. 31, 2015); Corvex Mgmt. LP v. CommonWealth REIT, No. 24-C-13-001111, 2013 Md. Cir. Ct. LEXIS 3 (Cir. Ct. Balt. City May 8, 2013).

21. These need not undercut the contractual approach completely. Instead, it may suggest the higher level of judicial scrutiny applicable in some contractual contests.

22. Justice Strine's argument that shareholders consent to the terms of the charter and bylaws also warrants further scrutiny. This chapter does not consider the extent to which the argument is valid. For further discussion of this point, *see* Winship (2016).

23. CA, Inc. v. AFSCME Emps. Pension Plan, 953 A.2d 227, 229 (Del. 2008). Prior to *CA*, the position of the Delaware courts on this issue was less clear. *See* Frantz Mfg. Co. v. EAC Indus., 501 A.2d 401 (Del. 1985) (upholding shareholder-adopted bylaw amendments that "required attendance of all directors for a quorum and unanimous approval of the board of directors before board action can be taken, and they thereby limited the functioning of the Frantz board" even though the amendments were intended to limit the board's "anti-takeover maneuvering").

24. 17 C.F.R. § 240.14a-8 (1988).

25. CA, Inc. v. AFSCME Emples. Pension Plan, 953 A.2d 227, 229–30 (Del. 2008).

26. *CA* used Delaware's newly adopted certification procedure. *See* 272S.B. 62, 144th Gen. Assem., Reg. Sess. (Del. 2007), http://delcode.delaware.gov/sessionlaws/ga144/chp037.

27. CA, Inc., 953 A.2d at 232.

28. International Bhd. of Teamsters v. Fleming Cos., 975 P.2d 907, 908 (Okla. 1999).

29. *Id.* at 911.

30. CA, Inc. v. AFSCME Emples. Pension Plan, 953 A.2d 227, 234 (Del. 2008). It is worth noting that the Delaware corporate law statute does not contain any language explicitly endorsing a contractual approach, particularly in light of the presence of such language in the Delaware LLC and LLP statutes.

See, e.g., Del. Code tit. 6, § 18-1101(b) (2011) ("It is the policy of this chapter to give the maximum effect to the principle of freedom of contract").

31. CA, Inc. at 236.

32. *See also* Hollinger Int'l, Inc. v. Black, 844 A.2d 1022, 1978–79 (Del. Ch. 2004) (stating that there is a "general consensus that bylaws that regulate the process by which the board acts are statutorily authorized").

33. The court explained that it was required to view the bylaw as inconsistent with the law if there was "any possible circumstance under which a board of directors might be required to act [and under which] the board of directors would breach their fiduciary duties if they complied with the Bylaw." *Id.* at 238.

34. *Id.* at 239.

35. See DGCL§§ 112, 113.

36. Gorman v. Salamone, 2015 Del. Ch. LEXIS 202.

37. Section 142(b) provides, "Officers shall be chosen in such a manner and shall hold their offices for such term as are prescribed by *the bylaws* or determined by the board of directors or other governing body.") (emphasis added).

38. *Id.* at *14, quoting *CA*.

39. *Id.* at 18.

40. *See also* Walther (2015) (arguing that *CA*'s "influence may be dwindling").

41. DGCL 109(b).

42. Put differently, a bylaw could be understood as inconsistent with the statute unless it deals with a subject upon which a bylaw is expressly permitted.

43. Centaur Partners, IV v. National Intergroup, Inc., 582 A.2d 923, 929 (Del. 1990).

44. Model Bus. Corp. Act § 10.20(b) (Am. Bar Ass'n 2010).

45. General DataComm Indus. v. Wisconsin Inv. Bd., 731 A.2d 818 (Del. Ch. 1999).

46. *Id.* (distinguishing the bylaw from the situation presented in Quickturn Design Sys., Inc. v. Shapiro, 721 A.2d 1281 (Del. Sup. 1998)).

47. The situation might be viewed by a court as analogous to that presented in Invacare Corp. v. Healthdyne Techs, Inc., 968 F. Supp. 1578 (N.D. Ga. 1997), in which the court held that, under Georgia corporate law, shareholders could not adopt bylaw to overturn a "dead-hand" provision of a poison pill because the law vested sole authority over the terms of a poison pill in the board of directors.

48. 2 Texas Bus. Orgs. Code Sec. 21.057. Bylaws: "(c) A corporation's board of directors may amend or repeal bylaws or adopt new bylaws unless: (1) the corporation's certificate of formation or this code wholly or partly reserves the power exclusively to the corporation's shareholders."

49. § 2-109(b).

50. 18 Okla. Stat. tit. 18, § 1013 (2015).

51. Indiana, IC 23-1-39-1 ("Unless the articles of incorporation or section 4

of this chapter provide otherwise, only a corporation's board of directors may amend or repeal the corporation's bylaws.").

52. *See* DGCL 102(b)(4). Other states similarly permit a corporation to include a supermajority vote requirement in its charter (Hirst 2017).

53. *E.g.*, 8 Del. C. § 242(b)(4).

54. A shareholder initiative has been seeking to persuade issues to shift to a "simple majority" formula for counting votes (Millman 2015).

55. *Cf.* Airgas, Inc. v. Air Prods. & Chems., Inc., 8 A.3d 1182, 1187 (Del. 2010) (describing Air Products' proposal of three bylaw amendments in conjunction with proxy contest "[a]s part of its takeover strategy.").

56. Rule 14a-8(i)(2), 17 C.F.R.

57. *See* Article IV, Section 11(8) of the Delaware Constitution, 76 Del. Laws 2007, ch. 37 § 1, effective May 3, 2007.

58. *See* CA, 953 A.2d 229, n.1 (noting that the case was the first submitted by the SEC to the court). *See also* Legal Opinion Letter of Richards, Layton & Finger to CA, Inc. (April 17, 2008) at 3 (arguing that proxy reimbursement proposal should be excluded under Rule 14a-8(i)(2).

59. *See* Baldon (2009) (observing that "The opportunity still exists for the SEC to go astray and continue to issue pronouncement of state law with minimal state guidance").

60. An issuer seeking exclusion under this provision is required to submit a supporting opinion of counsel. Rule 14a-8(j)(2)(iii).

61. Del. Code Ann. tit. 8, §§ 102(f), 109(b) (West 2015).

62. *See also* Choi (2016) (arguing that a balanced fee-shifting bylaw would be more effective in encouraging an appropriate level of litigation).

63. A related approach, adopted by Hemispherx Biopharma required plaintiffs in shareholder litigation to post a bond if they collectively owned less than 5 percent of the issuer's stock (Winship 2016).

64. *See* Boilermakers Local 154 Retirement Fund v. Chevron Corp., 73 A.3d 934, 951 (Del. Ch. 2013) (describing forum selection bylaw as "process-oriented, because they regulate where stockholders may file suit, not whether the stockholder may file suit or the kind of remedy that the stockholder may obtain on behalf of herself or the corporation.").

65. *See* Zapata Corp. v. Maldonado, 430 A.2d 779 (Del. Sup. 1981). One might argue that, even with respect to direct claims, the board should have some role because of the collective action problems associated with individual shareholder action. Such an argument would analogize to the generally accepted role of the board in responding to a tender offer. *See, e.g.*, Unocal Corp. v. Mesa Petroleum Co., 493 A.2d 946, 955 (Del. 1985) (recognizing the board's duty to protect "the corporation and its owners from perceived harm").

66. The Delaware courts are typically reluctant to consider the potential

validity of bylaws that have not yet been adopted. *See, e.g.*, Quickturn Design Sys., Inc. v. Shapiro, 721 A.2d 1281 (Del. Sup. 1998).

67. *See, e.g.*, NetCurrents, Inc. (May 8, 2001) (allowing exclusion of a proposal that would require the company to file a derivative suit) against certain officers for fiduciary violations); *cf.* Point Blank Solutions, Inc. (March 10, 2008) (concurring in the exclusion of a proposal seeking to direct the company's ongoing litigation strategy but also asking the company to initiate litigation).

68. 2012 SEC No-Act. LEXIS 161.

69. 1999 SEC No-Act. LEXIS 595.

70. 2012 SEC No-Act. LEXIS 302.

References

Alces, Kelli A., 2010, The Equity Trustee, *Arizona State Law Journal* 42: 717–81.

Allen, Claudia H., 2012, Exclusive Forum Provisions: Putting on the Brakes, http://www.nge.com/files/Uploads/Images/exclusive-forum-provisions-putting-on-the-brakes.pdf.

Allen, Claudia H., 2014, Bylaws Mandating Arbitration of Stockholder Disputes? *Delaware Journal of Corporate Law* 39: 751–818.

Ayres, Ian, 1992, Making a Difference: The Contractual Contributions of Easterbrook and Fischel, *University of Chicago Law Review* 59: 1391–420.

Bainbridge, Stephen M., 2003, Director Primary, The Means and Ends of Corporate Governance, *Northwestern University Law Review* 97: 547–606

Bainbridge, Stephen M., 2006, The Case for Limited Shareholder Voting Rights, *UCLA Law Review* 53: 601–36

Baldon, Junis L., 2009, Taking a Backseat: How Delaware Can Alter the Role of the SEC in Evaluating Shareholder Proposals, *Entrepreneurial Business Law Journal* 4: 105–31.

Bayliss, A. Thompson, and Mark Mixon, 2015, "No Pay" Provisions: The Forgotten Middle Ground in the Fee-Shifting Battle, *Harvard Law School Forum on Corporate Governance and Financial Regulation*, https://corpgov.law.harvard.edu/?s=forgotten+middle+ground.

Bebchuk, Lucian Arye, 1989, Limiting Contractual Freedom in Corporate Law: The Desirable Constraints on Charter Amendments, *Harvard Law Review* 102: 1820–59.

Bebchuk, Lucian Arye, 2005, The Case for Increasing Shareholder Power, *Harvard Law Review* 118: 833–912.

Bird, L. John, 2008, Comment: Stockholder and Corporate Board Bylaw Battles: Delaware Law and the Ability of a Corporate Board to Change or Overrule Stockholder Bylaw Amendments, *University of Pennsylvania Journal of Business and Employment Law* 11: 217–36.

Butler, Henry N., and Larry E. Ribstein, 1990, Opting Out of Fiduciary Duties: A Response to the Anti-Contractarians, *Washington Law Review* 65: 1–72.

Cain, Matthew D., Jill E. Fisch, Sean J. Griffith, and Steven Davidoff Solomon, 2016, How Corporate Governance Is Made: The Case of the Golden Leash, *University of Pennsylvania Law Review* 164: 649–701.

Cain, Matthew D., and Steven Davidoff Solomon, 2015, A Great Game: The Dynamics of State Competition and Litigation, *Iowa Law Review* 100: 465–99.

Choi, Albert, 2016, Optimal Fee-Shifting Bylaws, working paper.

Choi, Stephen J., Jill E. Fisch, and Marcel Kahan, 2008–9, Director Elections and the Role of Proxy Advisors, *Southern California Law Review* 82: 649–701.

Choi, Stephen J., Jill E. Fisch, and Marcel Kahan, 2010, The Power of Proxy Advisors: Myth or Reality? *Emory Law Journal* 59: 868–918.

Choi, Stephen J., Jill E. Fisch, and Marcel Kahan, 2013, Who Calls the Shots? How Mutual Funds Vote on Director Elections, *Harvard Business Law Review* 3: 35–81.

Choi, Stephen J., Jill E. Fisch, Marcel Kahan, and Edward B. Rock, 2016, Does Majority Voting Improve Board Accountability? *University of Chicago Law Review* 83: 1119–76.

Clark, Robert C., 1986, *Corporate Law* (Boston).

Clark, Robert C., 1989, Contracts, Elites, and Traditions in the Making of Corporate Law, *Columbia Law Review* 89: 1703–48.

Coase, Ronald H., 1991, The Nature of the Firm: Meaning, in *The Nature of the Firm: Origins, Evolution, and Development.*

Coates, John C. IV, and Bradley Faris, 2001, Second Generation By-Laws: Post-Quickturn Alternatives, *Business Lawyer* 56: 1357–66.

Coffee, John C. Jr., 1997, The Bylaw Battlefield: Can Institutions Change the Outcome of Corporate Control Contests? *University of Miami Law Review* 51: 605–21.

Cox, James D., 2015, Corporate Law and the Limits of Private Ordering, *Washington University Law Review* 93: 257–92.

Delaware State Bar Council, 2015, Explanation of Council Legislative Proposal, http://www.corporatedefensedisputes.com/files/2015/03/COUNCIL-SECOND-PROPOSAL-EXPLANATORY-PAPER-3-6-15-U0124513.pdf.

Dooley, Michael P., and E. Norman Veasey, 1989, The Role of the Board in Derivative Litigation: Delaware Law and the Current ALI Proposals Compared, *Business Lawyer* 44: 503–42.

Easterbrook, Frank, and Daniel R. Fischel, 1989, The Corporate Contract, *Columbia Law Review* 89: 1416–48.

Easterbrook, Frank, and Daniel R. Fischel, 1991, *The Economic Structure of Corporate Law.*

Fisch, Jill E., 2013, Leave It to Delaware: Why Congress Should Stay Out of Corporate Governance, *Delaware Journal of Corporate Law* 37: 731–82.

Fisch, Jill E., 2016a, Informed or Excluded: Advance Voting Instructions and Retail Investor Voting, working paper.

Fisch, Jill E., 2016b, The New Governance and the Challenge of Litigation Bylaws, *Brooklyn Law Review* 81: 1637–81.

Gill, Stephen M., Kai Haakon, E. Liekefett, and Leonard Wood, 2014, Structural Defenses to Shareholder Activism, *Review of Securities and Commodities Regulation* 47: 151–70.

Gilson, Ronald J., and Jeffrey N. Gordon, 2013, The Agency Costs of Agency Capitalism: Activist Investors and the Revaluation of Governance Rights, *Columbia Law Review* 113: 863–927.

Griffith, Sean J., 2017, Private Ordering Post-Trulia: Why No Pay Provisions Can Fix the Deal Tax and Forum Selection Provisions Can't in Steven Davidoff Solomon and Randall Thomas, The Corporate Contract in Changing Times (Chicago).

Hamermesh, Lawrence, 1998, Corporate Democracy and Stockholder Adopted By-Laws: Taking Back the Street? *Tulane Law Review* 73: 409–95.

Hart, Oliver D., 1995, *Firms, Contracts and Financial Structure.*

Hart, Oliver D., 1988, Incomplete Contracts and the Theory of the Firm, *Journal of Law, Economics and Organization* 4: 119–39.

Herbert, Bruce, 2015, Why Simple Majority Vote Counting Matters, *Corporate Governance*, http://www.corpgov.net/2015/03/simple-majority-vote-counting-initiative-for-proxies/.

Hirst, Scott, 2017, Frozen Charters, *Yale Journal on Regulation* 34: 91–166.

Investor Voice, 2015, Simple-Majority Standard for Use in Corporate Proxies, http://www.investorvoice.net/wp-content/uploads/2015/03/Vote-Counting_Synopsis_Version-9e_2015.0315.pdf.

Kess, Avrohom J., 2015, Proxy Access Proposals, *Harvard Law School Forum on Corporate Governance and Financial Regulation*, https://corpgov.law.harvard.edu/2015/08/10/proxy-access-proposals/.

Klausner, Michael. 2006, The Contractarian Theory of Corporate Law: A Generation Later, *Journal of Corporation Law* 31: 779–97.

Klein, William A., 1982, The Modern Business Organization: Bargaining Under Constraints, *Yale Law Journal* 91: 1521–64.

Krishnan, C. N. V., Frank Partnoy, and Randall Thomas, 2016, The Second Wave of Hedge Fund Activism: The Importance of Reputation, Clout, and Expertise, *Journal of Corporate Finance* 40: 296–314.

LaCroix, Kevin, 2015, Lawsuit Challenging Minimum Stake to Sue Bylaw Dismissed, *D&O Diary*, http://www.dandodiary.com/2015/10/articles/corporate-governance/lawsuit-challenging-minimum-stake-to-sue-bylaw-dismissed/.

Lipton, Ann, 2016, Manufactured Consent: The Problem of Arbitration Clauses in Corporate Charters and Bylaws, *Georgetown Law Journal* 104: 583–641

Macey, Jonathan R., 1998, The Legality and Utility of the Shareholder Rights Bylaw, *Hofstra Law Review* 26: 866–72.

McDonnell, Brett H., 2008, Bylaw Reforms for Delaware's Corporation Law, *Delaware Journal of Corporation Law* 33: 651–72.

Millman, James, 2015, Why Shareholder Proposals Win More Votes, Lose Anyway, *WSJ Risk & Compliance J.*, Mar. 20, 2015, https://blogs.wsj.com/riskandcompliance/2015/03/20/why-shareholder-proposals-win-more-votes-lose-anyway/.

Nagy, Donna, 1998, Judicial Reliance on Regulatory Interpretations in SEC No-Action Letters: Current Problems and a Proposed Framework, *Cornell Law Review* 83: 921–1013.

Palmiter, Alan, 1994, The Shareholder Proposal Rule: A Failed Experiment in Merit Regulation, *Alabama Law Review* 45: 879–926.

Paredes, Troy, 2010, Statement at Open Meeting to Adopt the Final Rule Regarding Facilitating Shareholder Nominations ("Proxy Access"), https://www.sec.gov/news/speech/2010/spch082510tap.htm.

Reed, John L., and Matt Neiderman, 2004, "Good Faith" and the Ability of Directors to Assert § 102(b)(7) of the Delaware General Corporation Law as a Defense to Claims Alleging Abdication, Lack of Oversight, and Similar Breaches of Fiduciary Duty, *Delaware Journal of Corporate Law* 29: 111–42.

Ribstein, Larry E., 1991, Unlimited Contracting in the Delaware Limited Partnership and Its Implications for Corporate Law, *Journal of Corporation Law* 16: 299–314.

Richards, Layton & Finger, 2008, Legal Opinion Letter to SEC, https://www.sec.gov/divisions/corpfin/cf-noaction/2008/ca062708-14a8-incoming.pdf.

Romano, Roberta and Sarath Sanga, 2017, The Private Ordering Solution to Multiforum Shareholder Litigation, *Journal of Empirical Legal Studies*, 14: 31–78, http://ssrn.com/abstract=2624951.

Siegel, Mary, 2011, The Holes in Majority Voting, *Columbia Business Law Review* 2011: 364–425.

Smith, D. Gordon, Matthew Wright, and Marcus Kai Hintze, 2011, Private Ordering with Shareholder Bylaws, *Fordham Law Review* 80: 125–88.

Strine, Leo E. Jr., 2002, The Inescapably Empirical Foundation of the Common Law of Corporations, *Delaware Journal of Corporate Law* 27: 499–518.

Strine, Leo E. Jr., and Nicholas Walter, 2015, Conservative Collision Course? The Tension between Conservative Corporate Law Theory and Citizens United, *Cornell Law Review* 100: 335–90.

Sullivan & Cromwell, 2015, 2015 Proxy Season Review.

Tiger, Paul M., and Carolyn Oh, 2015, Gorman v. Salamone: Delaware Court of Chancery Strikes Down Bylaw Granting Stockholders the Right to Remove and Replace Officers, *Cleary M&A and Corporate Governance Watch*, http://www.clearymawatch.com/2015/08/gorman-v-salamone-delaware-court-of-chancery-strikes-down-bylaw-granting-stockholders-the-right-to-remove-and-replace-officers/.

Ursaner, Sabrina, 2011, Keeping "Fiduciary Outs" Out of Shareholder-Proposed Bylaws: An Analysis of CA, Inc. v. AFSCME, *The Business Lawyer* 66: 361–63.

Veasey, E. Norman, 2007, The Shareholder Franchise Is Not a Myth: A Response to Professor Bebchuk, *Virginia Law Review* 93: 811–25.

Walther, Ben, 2015, Bylaw Governance, *Fordham Journal of Corporate and Financial Law* 20: 399–458.

Weil, Gotshal & Manges LLP, 2014, Alert: SEC Disclosure and Corporate Governance, http://www.weil.com/~/media/files/pdfs/pcag_alert_nov2014.pdf.

Weil, Gotshal & Manges, LLP, 2015, Heads Up for the 2016 Proxy Season Navigating Proxy Access: A Roadmap for the Board of Directors, https://corpgov.law.harvard.edu/2016/02/04/2016-proxy-season-engagement-transparency-proxy-access/.

Wilmer Hale, LLP, 2016, M&A Report, https://www.wilmerhale.com/uploadedfiles/shared_content/editorial/publications/documents/2016-wilmerhale-ma-report.pdf.

Winship, Verity, 2016, Shareholder Litigation by Contract, *Boston University Law Review* 96: 485–542.

CHAPTER TWELVE

Litigation Rights and the Corporate Contract

Verity Winship

Sometimes the term *corporate contract* is a metaphor for the relationship among corporate stakeholders. But the corporate contract can also be something more concrete: the agreement or set of agreements that articulate the terms of the relationship among shareholders, directors, and the corporation itself. These corporate organizational documents consist of the charter and corporate bylaws. Courts have referred, for instance, to charters and bylaws of a corporation as "contracts among a corporation's shareholders"[1] or as "part of a binding broader contract among the directors, officers, and stockholders."[2]

This chapter identifies one innovation within these corporate organizational documents that helps shape the future of the corporate contract. That innovation is the use of terms within the organizational documents that set the rules for resolving internal disputes, especially—but not only—for shareholder litigation. Contested examples are exclusive forum and fee-shifting clauses. This chapter analyzes how the emergence of corporate charter and bylaw provisions governing dispute resolution puts pressure on courts to define the nature and scope of the corporate contract.

The chapter details the emergence of dispute resolution clauses in corporate charters and bylaws, with their origins in exclusive forum clauses and their expansion to fee shifting. It then turns to the pressures that these clauses put on courts to define the limits of the corporate contract. Their use—and the aftermath of their contestation in court—pushes courts to answer three questions. First, to what extent should charters and bylaws be treated literally as corporate *contracts*? Second, what is the scope or subject matter of the corporate contract? The internal affairs of the corporation and corporate governance structure are at the contract's heart, but can the charter or bylaws specify, for instance, shareholders' rights in securities litigation? Third, is access to litigation part of the bundle of rights that shareholders purchase when they buy shares in a corporation? Each section concludes by considering how Delaware and other states might alter their corporate law in response to these pressures.[3]

Private Ordering of Shareholder Litigation

Dispute resolution provisions in corporate organizational documents set the rules for resolving disputes among corporate actors.[4] Exclusive forum, mandatory arbitration, and fee-shifting clauses are examples of this category that have been adopted and contested, but the category may also include other dispute resolution terms, such as jury waiver or percentage ownership requirements.

One step in analyzing the pressures these clauses put on the corporate contract is to identify how these clauses are new and distinctive. Although the boundaries of the category could be disputed,[5] these provisions are distinctive in that they expand the traditional function of corporate organizational documents, particularly of bylaws. Courts describe bylaws as "procedural" and "process-oriented."[6] Typical examples of the procedural rules that bylaws can dictate are "the procedures through which board and committee action is taken,"[7] such as corporate voting, meetings, or other internal processes of the organization. In contrast, dispute resolution provisions address how shareholders and other internal actors can enforce any rights they have within the corporation, often through external litigation. They are thus procedural in a newly expansive way.

The scope is also broader than that of other types of bylaw and charter provisions. Provisions that allocate voting rights, dictate the characteristics of shares, or detail the day-to-day workings of the corporation are generally governed by state corporate law and fit within the judicial definition of the internal affairs of the corporation. Dispute resolution provisions, however, claim new territory, sometimes trying to reach all of shareholders' potential disputes with the company or directors.[8] As noted below, the attempt to reach federal securities law claims in particular is one of the sources of pressure on courts to define the contract's scope.

The use of charter provisions and bylaws to shape litigation within a firm has some precedents in noncorporate forms. Limited liability company operating agreements, for instance, have contained a range of dispute resolution provisions, including forum choice, arbitration clauses, jury waivers, and other clauses that borrow from commercial contracts.[9] Antecedents can also be found in director indemnification bylaws and charter provisions that specify dispute resolution proceedings, including mandatory arbitration. The use of these terms in corporate charters and bylaws to limit shareholder litigation, however, has emerged more recently and is the form that puts pressure on courts to answer some fundamental questions about the corporate contract. Dispute resolution provisions are newly salient with the emergence of exclusive forum bylaws, the debate over arbitration clauses, and the (partially abortive) history of fee-shifting bylaws.[10]

Exclusive forum selection provisions provided the first testing ground for private ordering of intracorporate disputes. Historically, exclusive forum clauses were unnecessary to channel disputes within a firm to a particular forum because the internal affairs doctrine at one time limited intracorporate suits to the state of incorporation.[11] The legal doctrine later shifted so that it dictated only the governing law and not the forum. Even then, however, suits about the internal affairs of a corporation were routinely filed in the incorporating state as a matter of practice.[12] A shift toward multiforum deal litigation changed these practices, with some attorneys filing parallel actions outside the incorporating state beginning around 2002.[13] Defendant corporations called for consolidation, and the dominant response ultimately was for corporations to adopt exclusive forum charter provisions or bylaws designating the state of incorporation—often Delaware—as the exclusive forum for intracorporate disputes. This type of clause has become more accepted and commonplace. A study identified 746 public companies that had adopted such clauses by August 2014, with a movement toward standard inclusion in the initial public offering charters of Delaware corporations.[14]

Most significantly for this discussion, exclusive forum selection provisions were tested in Delaware Chancery Court in one of the two court opinions that define the terrain for dispute resolution bylaws. The first is the Delaware Chancery Court's 2013 decision in *Boilermakers v. Chev-*

ron, in which the court approved the use of a forum selection bylaw.[15] The court reasoned that the clauses at issue regulated disputes over corporate governance, which were a proper subject for bylaws under the Delaware corporate code.[16] It also concluded that they were valid as a matter of contract law, despite having been adopted unilaterally by the corporate board.[17]

The second definitive court opinion is *ATP Tour, Inc. v. Deutscher Tennis Bund*, a 2014 opinion in which the Delaware Supreme Court found a fee-shifting bylaw to be facially valid.[18] The issue arose in a federal court proceeding bringing antitrust and state law claims against a nonstock corporation organized in Delaware. Defendants won on all claims and invoked a fee-shifting bylaw to recover their legal costs from plaintiffs.[19] The federal court expressed doubts that Delaware courts would enforce such a bylaw, particularly in the context of federal antitrust claims.[20] To avoid deciding about preemption, the federal court certified a legal question to the Delaware Supreme Court, asking whether such a fee-shifting bylaw would be valid under Delaware law.[21] The Delaware court's answer surprised many: The fee-shifting bylaw was facially valid.[22] It was not contrary to any Delaware law, was binding on members (who were in a position analogous to shareholders of a stock corporation), and was within the permissible scope of section 109(b), which governs the content of bylaws under Delaware law.[23] Although *ATP Tour* concerned a nonstock corporation, it was widely viewed as being equally applicable to Delaware stock corporations.

ATP Tour ultimately triggered legislation explicitly designed to block that expansion to stock corporations.[24] The Delaware legislation prevented stock companies organized in Delaware from adopting fee-shifting charter provisions or bylaw provisions.[25] It also explicitly permitted these companies to adopt exclusive forum provisions, but the provisions could not exclude Delaware courts in favor of other states' courts or an arbitral forum.[26] Though influential in other states, Delaware corporate law does not reach non-Delaware entities. Moreover, the legislation applied only to stock corporations and affected only certain categories of dispute resolution provision (forum selection, fee shifting, and arbitration). The rest of the broad universe of dispute resolution provisions was left unregulated and relatively unexplored.[27]

Although exclusive forum provisions seem well established, future corporate appetite for other forms of private ordering of dispute resolution is difficult to predict. The pressure that these provisions put on courts to define the corporate contract does not turn, however, on what precisely happens next. Continuing use and innovation of these dispute resolution provisions could push courts, but this pressure is also exerted as part of the aftermath of the decisions that dealt with this type of provision (so the aftermath of *Boilermakers* and *ATP Tour*), even if adoption is not ultimately widespread. These pressures are the subject of the next section.

Pressures on the Corporate Contract

The emergence of private ordering of shareholder litigation raises some basic questions about the nature and form of the corporate contract. Courts are prompted, in particular, to address the extent to which courts treat (or should treat) corporate charters and bylaws literally as contracts, the proper subject matter of the contract, and whether shareholders have litigation rights. Each of these questions is taken up below.

Are Corporate Charters and Bylaws Literally Corporate Contracts?

Broad language in some court decisions equates corporate charters and bylaws with contracts, drawing some of its force from a long-dominant view of the corporation as a nexus of contracts.[28] Court decisions have stated, for instance, that "[c]orporate charters and by-laws are contracts among the shareholders of a corporation."[29] But are bylaws and charters literally contracts in all respects? For what purposes should courts treat them as analogous to commercial contracts?[30]

This section points to language in judicial opinions that describes corporate organizational documents as contracts among corporate actors. It examines how the emergence of private ordering of shareholder litigation and the judicial response put pressure on the courts to articulate the nature of these documents. It then draws on details of the decisions and the legislative context to suggest that, despite the rhetoric, a spectrum of how literally these are treated as contracts is already embedded in court opinions and legislation, and can be used as a basis for a more nuanced, hybrid view going forward.

Even courts that treat bylaws and charters as contractual acknowledge their differences from commercial contracts, especially differences in the nature and form of consent. Shareholders are not signatories. Moreover, when a provision is subject to a shareholder vote, shareholders are bound by a majority vote, regardless of whether they themselves dissented.[31] The terms of the bylaws in particular often can be changed unilaterally by the board of directors, even after a shareholder has bought shares.[32]

Nonetheless, language about the contractual nature of charters and bylaws has long been built into corporate law, and especially Delaware corporate law. Early cases declare that shareholders' rights are contract rights.[33] Explicit language that treats charters and bylaws as contracts was also central to the decisions in *Boilermakers* and *ATP Tour*. *Boilermakers*, for instance, called bylaws of a Delaware corporation "part of a binding broader contract among the directors, officers, and stockholders formed within the statutory framework of the DGCL [Delaware General Corporation Law]."[34] The court pointed to "an unbroken line of [Delaware Supreme Court] decisions dating back several generations" that "made clear that the bylaws constitute a binding part of the contract between a Delaware corporation and its stockholders."[35] Similarly, the court in *ATP Tour* relied on the premise that "corporate bylaws are 'contracts among a corporation's shareholders'" to conclude that the fee-shifting provision at issue was facially valid.[36]

A closer look at the decisions on which these cases rely suggests several qualifications to the broad rhetoric about the corporate contract. One of them is to distinguish between charters and bylaws. In general, corporate charters define "the broad and general aspects of the corporate entity's existence and nature,"[37] while bylaws govern the day-to-day mechanics. Under Delaware law, for instance, bylaws "may contain any provision . . . relating to the business of the corporation, the conduct of its affairs, and its rights or powers or the rights or powers of its stockholders, directors, officers or employees."[38]

These organizational documents have different modes of adoption and approval, with implications for shareholder consent.[39] On the one hand, shareholders vote on charter amendments,[40] bringing them closer to traditional notions of contractual consent. On the other hand, the charter is more difficult to change, and charters may be adopted before shares are offered to the public, giving notice to purchasing shareholders but not requiring shareholder approval for the initial terms.[41] Shareholders have indefeasible power to adopt bylaws,[42] but directors generally have the power to adopt, amend, and repeal corporate bylaws unilaterally.[43] The distinction between charter and bylaws accordingly matters when evaluating consent and whether these documents can be taken as contractual for all purposes.

The cases assessing dispute resolution provisions—*Boilermakers* and *ATP Tour*—evaluate the contractual validity of *bylaws*. However, some of the early cases on which *Boilermakers* relies focus on the charter rather than the bylaws.[44] One of the early cited cases found that a restriction on stock transfer was valid in part because of "the contractual relation existing between the corporation and its stockholders."[45] In support, it pointed to general recognition that "the *charter* of a corporation is a contract both between the corporation and the state and the corporation and its stockholders."[46] Courts have sometimes lumped together the charter and bylaws despite their different structures of shareholder consent.[47]

A closer look at the cases also reveals that courts equate the charter and bylaws with the corporate contract for particular purposes. One of the recurring applications of contract principles is to interpret the language of corporate organizational documents. The opinion in *Airgas* is widely cited in support of the contractual nature of charters and bylaws. It is also a useful example of broad rhetoric used in support of a more specific application of contract principles. The court in *Airgas* described bylaws as "contracts among a corporation's shareholders," but it did so as a prelude to applying contract principles to interpret the corporate bylaws at issue.[48] In fact, many Delaware cases that refer to charters or bylaws as contractual do so to justify the use of methods of contractual interpretation to interpret the terms of corporate organizational bylaws or charter provisions.[49]

Similarly, the courts in *Boilermakers* and *ATP Tour* used broad language about the "contractual nature of the stockholders' relationship with the corporation."[50] But even there, they did so for a particular application. In *Boilermakers*, plaintiffs argued that "express consent in a contract is a prerequisite to a valid forum selection provision," making the unilaterally adopted bylaws contractually invalid.[51] The emergence of dispute resolution provisions forced courts to address these arguments and accordingly be explicit about the rationale for binding shareholders to bylaws unilaterally adopted by the board. The courts' reasoning was essentially that shareholders have agreed to a governance structure, and these provisions (including bylaws adopted unilaterally by the directors) result naturally from that structure.[52] Delaware courts have also held that past and future shareholders are considered to be on notice and bound by the contract.[53] So the bylaws are contractual in that shareholders are bound, but they are not precisely contractual in that the overarching contract is for a governance system that usually allows unilateral amendment. It is an "inherently flexible" contract.[54]

The fight over fee-shifting bylaws also triggered Delaware legislation that implicitly addresses this question of whether charters and bylaws are contracts for all purposes. Delaware legislation banned fee-shifting clauses in stock corporations. At the same time, it also prevented Delaware stock corporations from including a mandatory arbitration clause in bylaws or charters. The implication is that, for some purposes, these charters and bylaws must not count as contracts. If they did, Delaware legislation preventing the enforcement of arbitration clauses in charters and bylaws might run counter to the Federal Arbitration Act's admonition to states not to pass legislation singling out arbitration clauses for disfavor.[55]

These examples are not exclusive. For instance, shareholders cannot generally sue other shareholders for violation of the bylaws, a right they would likely have if these were contracts in every sense.[56] In other words, these organizational documents are treated as contracts for some purposes (for instance, interpretation) but not for all (for instance, not to trigger the Federal Arbitration Act).

Precedent exists for a nuanced analysis of the application of contract principles to corporate organizational documents. Courts cannot be as literal as some of their language suggests; rather, they must sort out when contract principles apply and when they do not, asking whether the principles of contract interpretation apply or whom the organizational document binds. Contract principles are relevant, but equating charters and bylaws with other types of contracts—as some of the rhetoric does—oversimplifies their nature. The conclusion for Delaware and other courts is both descriptive and normative: that the contract label does not provide an answer to some of the more difficult questions about what can be in these organizational documents and, in some cases, masks judicial and legislative decisions about the rights of shareholders in the corporate context.

What Is the Subject Matter of the Corporate Contract?

So far this chapter has identified dispute resolution provisions in corporate charters and bylaws by referring to the disputing parties. The provisions set the rules for disputes among internal corporate actors—shareholders, directors, the corporation. This section takes up another aspect of the reach of these provisions: To which disputes do they apply? If a corporate contract exists, what is its subject matter?

Assuming these organizational documents can regulate dispute resolution, intracorporate disputes governed by state corporate law seems like the category most clearly reached. Current law reflects this intuition. The court in *Boilermakers* pointed to "suits brought by stockholders *as stockholders* in cases governed by the internal affairs doctrine" as "the kind of claims most central to the relationship between those who manage the corporation and the corporation's stockholders."[57] Provisions that set the rules for resolving these claims were accordingly at the heart of what can be included in corporate bylaws, at least under Delaware law.

An easy case also exists for what is definitely outside the scope of these corporate organizational documents. Provisions that affect shareholders' tort claims against the corporation are not covered. Nor do the terms of the corporate organizational documents govern claims based on a shareholder's separate commercial contract with the corporation. This area is another in which the emergence of dispute resolution provisions forced courts to be explicit about the scope of the corporate contract. The *Boilermakers* court, for instance, identified such shareholder tort and contract claims as "external" and thus beyond the permissible subject matter for corporate bylaws under Delaware's corporate code.[58]

Easy cases accordingly define each end of the spectrum. There is, however, a gray area in between. And it is a gray area that matters to litigants. Can terms of the corporate charter and bylaws set the rules for securities litigation? This is where the emergence of dispute resolution provisions puts particular pressure on courts to define the contract's scope, in part because of the financial significance and ubiquity of this type of litigation as well as long-standing controversy over its effectiveness. Corporations are interested in limiting this type of shareholder litigation. Many of the fee-shifting provisions were very broadly drafted to include securities claims and sometimes all shareholder claims, regardless of their legal source.[59] Some lawyers even pointed to securities litigation as the driver for adoption and for fights over these provisions' enforceability.[60]

Shareholders' securities claims are not the only ones in this gray area where it is unclear how far the corporate organizational documents can permissibly reach. Antitrust claims by shareholders are an example that became salient in *ATP Tour*. The court there found a fee-shifting provision to be facially valid even though it applied to claims based on federal antitrust statutes as well as state corporate law.[61] The implication is that the bylaws could permissibly set the rules for shareholder antitrust disputes—a very broad view of the corporate contract's scope. However, the opinion leaves some space for even Delaware courts to adopt a more limited interpretation, in part because of its peculiar procedural posture.[62]

Attempts to use private ordering to limit shareholder securities litigation in particular pushed courts to begin defining the subject matter of the corporate contract. The *Boilermakers* court, for instance, approved exclusive forum clauses that reached state law corporate governance disputes but indicated that tort claims cannot be reached for the "obvious" reason that they "would not deal with the rights and powers of the plaintiff-stockholder *as a stockholder*."[63] In a related context, the Delaware Chancery Court suggested that "[a] Rule 10b-5 claim under the federal securities laws is a personal claim akin to a tort claim for fraud."[64] Because shareholders' tort claims are clearly outside the scope of corporate organizational documents, this analogy suggests that securities fraud claims should likewise be beyond their reach.[65]

Though courts have taken steps toward defining the subject matter of the corporate contract, the task is not a simple one. Questions about the scope of corporate organizational documents implicate the division between federal securities law and state corporate law, a distinction in the United States that is fundamental but whose boundaries sometimes blur.[66]

Looking to the future, a fruitful approach would be to move to an "internal affairs" limit.[67] The subject matter of corporate organizational documents would be limited to the rules governing relationships among shareholders, directors, and the corporation that are at the core of state law corporate governance. This limit would borrow from the internal affairs doctrine, which determines which issues are governed by the law of the incorporating state. This approach would take the reasoning in *Boilermakers*—that exclusive forum provisions about internal affairs disputes were at the heart of what bylaws can prescribe—and make it an outer limit.[68] Broad descriptions of the internal affairs doctrine do not help courts draw bright lines: To call something "internal corporate affairs"[69] does not provide a clear rule about what counts. However, defining the outer boundary in reference to the internal affairs doctrine would take advantage of developed case law in this area. The doctrine may be disputed on the margins, but it has the advantage of providing multiple court decisions about what is within and beyond its scope.

Do Shareholders Have Litigation Rights?

The last question has to do with the fact that these dispute resolution charter provisions and bylaws govern what shareholders can do in legal actions against the corporation or other corporate actors. They are about the ability of shareholders to enforce other rights they have within a corporation. If directors violate their fiduciary duties, for instance, shareholder litigation is one way, however imperfect, to punish past behavior, recover compensation for losses, and deter corporations and possibly managers from misbehavior.

To what extent should this ability to litigate be considered a right? A full definition of legal right is beyond the scope of this chapter, but in some ways the term *litigation rights* is used here as shorthand for asking two questions. First, is access to litigation part of the bundle that a shareholder gets when he or she purchases shares? Should it be treated like shareholder voting rights or rights to sell? And, second, to what extent is this access fundamental? Can it be waived?

In some general sense, shareholders' court access could be labeled litigation rights. The *Boilermakers* court, for instance, had to evaluate whether the exclusive forum clause was within the legal definition of what bylaws may contain. One of the categories of bylaws permitted under the Delaware corporate code is bylaws that address the "'rights' of the stockholders."[70] The court suggested that forum selection bylaws fell in this category because "they regulate where stockholders can exercise their *right* to bring certain internal affairs claims against the corporation and its directors and officers."[71] The court points to this as a "matter of easy linguistics,"[72] suggesting that not much turns on their characterization as rights.

In other contexts, calling these litigation rights may be part of advocacy. Proxy firms that cautioned shareholders about the adoption of dispute resolution bylaws described "shareholders' ability to bring suit against the company" as "litigation *rights*."[73]

The question of whether shareholders' court access is a right has more bite, however, when the right is mandatory. To what extent is shareholders' access to litigation waivable? And, in particular, can it be waived through provisions in corporate organizational documents? Dispute resolution provisions prompted courts and legislatures to consider these questions because the fee-shifting provisions considered in *ATP Tour* were of a form that effectively prevented shareholder suits.[74] Under the fee-shifting bylaws adopted, suing shareholders would have to pay litigation costs any time that their action did "not obtain a judgment on the merits that substantially achieves, in substance and amount, the full remedy sought."[75] If given effect, this provision would almost always be triggered because shareholder litigation is routinely resolved through settlement—so almost never "on the merits"—and the "full remedy sought" is rarely obtained.[76] The clauses thus eliminated shareholder suits and effectively waived shareholders' substantive rights by preventing any enforcement of them.

In other areas of the law, courts have moved away from considering court access as a right.[77] Despite the prevalence of arbitration and other court exit elsewhere, however, corporate law might be (for now) a place where court access persists. In the corporate context, support exists for treating shareholders as having some litigation rights. Delaware's legislative response to the fee-shifting provisions is particularly striking in this regard. The statute prevented Delaware stock corporations from adopting fee-shifting provisions in their charters or bylaws. The rationale put forward by the legislation's drafters was that some versions of these clauses would chill shareholder litigation altogether.[78] The legislation deliberately preserved court access for shareholders, reasoning that it was necessary for policing agency costs and for developing corporate law.

The main effect of the legislation is to preserve corporate litigation in Delaware courts. The legislation banned fee shifting and allowed exclusive forum clauses as long as they did not exclude the incorporating state (Delaware). Regardless of one's view of the motivation for this legislation, the resulting court access may have systemic value. For instance, the availability of precedent may be a public good, particularly in the context of fiduciary duties, which depend on courts for their development.[79]

The other lesson from the legislative response is the approach it takes to the corporate organizational documents. It effectively established a heightened consent requirement for fee shifting. Corporations could adopt these through a shareholder agreement or other agreement actually signed by the shareholder.[80] In other words, they could be adopted only if shareholders expressly consented—a heightened consent requirement when court access is waived. Going forward, this heightened consent model might apply more broadly to prevent waiver of rights (litigation or other) through the charter or bylaws while still allowing such waiver when the provision is subject to shareholder approval.[81] Litigation rights would then be treated analogously to other shareholder rights of vote and exit in the sense that they trigger additional protections because of their centrality to corporate governance.[82] The relationship between litigation and other rights may also run the other way: The mechanism of heightened consent could be used to protect nonlitigation shareholder rights as well.

Conclusion

In some sense, this chapter is about corporate charter and bylaw provisions that set the rules for resolving disputes among corporate actors. This innovation piqued corporate interest and provoked controversy, particularly when corporate directors unilaterally set the rules for shareholder litigation. Court challenges to these provisions pushed courts and legislatures, especially in Delaware, to be newly explicit about the role of corporate organizational documents. The courts articulated the rationale, for instance, for binding shareholders to these documents' terms.

The innovation raised questions that go beyond dispute resolution provisions to all the ways the corporate charter and bylaws define the relationships within the corporation. The questions and the initial responses that this chapter outlines address fundamental aspects of the nature and scope of the corporate contract. The role of the dispute resolution provisions was to make them express and potentially urgent.

Notes

1. Airgas, Inc. v. Air Prods. & Chems., Inc., 8 A.3d 1182, 1188 (Del. 2010).
2. Boilermakers Local 154 Ret. Fund v. Chevron Corp., 73 A.3d 934, 938–

39 (Del. Ch. 2013); *see also, e.g.*, Merriam v. Demoulas Super Markets, Inc., 464 Mass. 721, 727, 985 N.E.2d 388, 394 (2013) ("Agreements in a corporation's articles of organization or bylaws are treated as contracts between the shareholders and the corporation.").

3. Delaware is the focus here because of its dominant position in incorporating US public companies and its influence on other states' corporate law. Moreover, many of the innovations discussed here began and were tested in Delaware companies and Delaware courts.

4. The terminology for this category varies and includes labels such as *litigation-regulating* provisions. *See, e.g.*, Corp. Law Council, Delaware State Bar Ass'n, Fee-Shifting FAQs, http://www.delawarelitigation.com/files/2015/03/COUNCIL-SECOND-PROPOSAL-FAQS-3-6-15-U0124511.docx. This chapter uses the label *dispute resolution provisions* because it is broad enough to encompass arbitration and other nonlitigation mechanisms.

5. For instance, exculpation charter provisions also shape how internal disputes are resolved, as do indemnification bylaws. Both are arguably dispute resolution provisions in that they determine what can be tested in separate litigation and who pays for these disputes. Moreover, both predate the history detailed here. Uncontested novelty is unnecessary, however, to the basic point of this chapter: that the emergence of dispute resolution clauses and their testing in court put pressure on courts to define the corporate contract's contours.

6. CA, Inc. v. AFSCME Employees Pension Plan, 953 A.2d 227, 235 (Del. 2008).

7. Hollinger Intern., Inc. v. Black, 844 A.2d 1022, 1078–79 (Del. Ch. 2004), *aff'd*, 872 A.2d 559 (Del. 2005).

8. *See generally* Verity Winship, *Contracting around Securities Litigation: Some Thoughts on the Scope of Litigation Bylaws*, 68 SMU L. REV. 913 (2015) (tracing the expanding scope of dispute resolution bylaws).

9. *See* Peter Molk and Verity Winship, *LLCs and the Private Ordering of Dispute Resolution*, 41 J. OF CORPORATION L. 795 (2016) (providing an empirical study of dispute resolution provisions in LLC operating agreements); *Boilermakers*, 73 A.3d at 953 (noting that the exclusive forum bylaws at issue could not "fairly be argued to regulate a novel subject matter . . . [as] in the analogous contexts of LLC agreements and stockholder agreements, the [Delaware] Supreme Court and this court have held that forum selection clauses are valid").

10. A detailed history can be found in Verity Winship, *Shareholder Litigation by Contract*, 96 BOSTON U. L. R. 481 (2016).

11. *See, e.g.*, N. State Copper & Gold Mining Co. v. Field, 20 A. 1039, 1040 (Md. 1885) (declining jurisdiction because "[o]ur courts possess no visitorial power" over the internal affairs of a foreign corporation).

12. Matthew D. Cain and Steven Davidoff Solomon, *Takeover Litigation*

in 2011 at 2 (Feb. 2, 2012) (unpublished manuscript), http://ssrn.com/abstract=1998482.

13. *See* Robert M. Daines and Olga Koumrian, Cornerstone Research, Shareholder Litigation Involving Mergers and Acquisitions 2 (2013), www.cornerstone.com/Shareholder-Litigation-Involving-M-and-A-Feb-2013.

14. Roberta Romano and Sarath Sanga, *The Private Ordering Solution to Multiforum Shareholder Litigation*, J. Empirical Legal Studies (forthcoming).

15. 73 A.3d 934, 938–39 (Del. Ch. 2013).

16. *Id.* at 939.

17. *Id.* at 954–56.

18. 91 A.3d 554 (Del. 2014).

19. Deutscher Tennis Bund v. ATP Tour, Inc., Civ. Act. No. 07-178, 2009 WL 3367041 at *1 (D. Del. Oct. 19, 2009), *vacated*, 480 F. App'x 124 (3d Cir. 2012).

20. Deutscher Tennis Bund v. ATP Tour Inc., 480 F. App'x 124, 127–28 and n.4 (3d Cir. 2012).

21. *Id.* at 126–27.

22. *ATP Tour*, 91 A.3d at 558.

23. *Id.* at 559–60.

24. S.B. 75, 148th Gen. Assemb., 1st Reg. Sess. (Del. 2015), signed into law June 24, 2015, effective Aug. 1, 2015 (amending § 109(b) and adding §§ 102(f) and 115).

25. *See* Del. Code Ann. tit. 8, §§ 102(f), 109(b) (2015).

26. *See id.*, § 115.

27. *See, e.g.*, Sean J. Griffith, *Private Ordering Post-Trulia: Why No Pay Provisions Can Fix the Deal Tax and Forum Selection Provisions Can't*, in The Corporate Contract in Changing Times (advocating the adoption of a "no-pay" charter provision or bylaw that would prevent corporate reimbursement for shareholder litigation).

28. *See, e.g.*, Frank H. Easterbrook and Daniel R. Fischel, *The Corporate Contract*, 89 Colum. L. Rev. 1416, 1417 (1989).

29. Centaur Partners, IV v. Nat'l Intergroup, Inc., 582 A.2d 923, 928 (Del. 1990).

30. Despite broad rhetoric in judicial opinions, this question has only more recently begun to be addressed in a systematic way in the literature. *See, e.g.*, James D. Cox, *Corporate Law and the Limits of Private Ordering*, 93 Wash. U. L. Rev. 257, 279–82 (2015) (pointing out, among other things, that the existence of fiduciary obligations undermines the notion of corporate organizational documents as a contract between arm's-length contracting parties whose expectations are limited to the four corners of the agreement).

31. *Boilermakers*, 73 A.3d at n.99.

32. Del. Code Ann. tit. 8, § 109(a).

33. Ellingwood v. Wolf's Head Oil Ref. Co., 27 Del. Ch. 356, 362, 38 A.2d 743, 747 (1944) ("The Courts of this State have held that the rights of stockholders are contract rights and that it is necessary to look to the certificate of incorporation to ascertain what those rights are."); Gaskill v. Gladys Belle Oil Co., 146 A. 337, 339 (Del. Ch. 1929) ("It is elementary that the rights of stockholders are contract rights.").

34. *Boilermakers*, 73 A.3d at 939.

35. *Id.* at 955.

36. *ATP Tour*, 91 A.3d 554, n.19 (Del. 2014) (quoting *Airgas*, 8 A.3d at 1188).

37. Gow v. Consol. Coppermines Corp., 165 A.136, 140 (Del. Ch. 1933).

38. Del. Code Ann. tit. 8, § 109(b).

39. Lawrence A. Hamermesh, *Consent in Corporate Law*, 70 Bus. Law. 161, 166 (2014) (analyzing shareholder consent).

40. Del. Code Ann. tit. 8, § 242(b)(1).

41. *See* Del. Code Ann. tit. 8, § 102.

42. Del. Code Ann. tit. 8, § 109(a). Practical barriers exist, but under the Delaware corporate code, directors may not divest shareholders of this power over bylaws. *Id.*

43. Delaware permits corporations to include a charter provision giving directors this power. Del. Code Ann. tit. 8, § 109(a). The language is standard in many charters. *See, e.g.*, Certificate of Incorporation (Short-form DE), Practical Law Standard Document 4-381-6417 (providing a standard form charter that "expressly authoriz[es]" the board of directors "to adopt, amend or repeal the By-laws or adopt new By-laws without any action on the part of the stockholders"). Under the Model Business Corporation Act, directors have this bylaw power over bylaws by default. *See* Model Bus. Corp. Act § 10.20(b) (Am. Bar Ass'n 2010) (giving corporate directors the power to adopt, amend, or repeal bylaws automatically unless a corporation opts out in its charter).

44. *Boilermakers*, 73 A.3d at 939 and n.7 (pointing to *Lawson* and *Airgas* as two cases, "eighty years apart," that made it clear that bylaws are part of a "binding broader contract among the directors, officers and stockholders").

45. Lawson v. Household Finance Corp., 152 A. 723, 726 (Del. 1930).

46. *Id.* at 727 (emphasis added) (noting that this proposition was so obvious that "[i]t is not necessary to cite authorities to support this proposition"); see also Morris v. Am. Pub. Utils. Co., 122 A. 696, 700 (Del. Ch. 1923) ("That a corporate charter is a contract has been long settled."); Benihana of Tokyo, Inc. v. Benihana, Inc., 906 A.2d 114, 120 (Del. 2006) ("It is settled law that certificates of incorporation are contracts"); In re Bicoastal Corp., 600 A.2d 343, 350 (Del. 1991) ("A certificate of incorporation is viewed as a contract among shareholders"); W. Foundry Co. v. Wicker, 403 Ill. 260, 267, 85 N.E.2d 722, 726 (1949) ("That a corporate charter is a contract has long been settled.").

47. Hamermesh, *Consent in Corporate Law* at 166.

48. *Airgas*, 8 A.3d at 1188.

49. *See* Centaur Partners, IV v. Nat'l Intergroup, Inc., 582 A.2d 923, 928 (Del. 1990) (stating that the charter and bylaws were a contract among shareholders, with the consequence that the rules of contractual interpretation applied); Harrah's Entm't, Inc. v. JCC Holding Co., 802 A.2d 294, 309 (Del. Ch. 2002) ("In general terms, corporate instruments such as charters and bylaws are interpreted in the same manner as other contracts."); Hill Int'l, Inc. v. Opportunity Partners L.P., 119 A.3d 30, 38 (Del. 2015) (same).

50. *Boilermakers*, 73 A.3d at 954.

51. Plaintiffs' Answering Brief in Opposition to Defendants' Motion for Judgement on the Pleadings, Boilermakers Local 154 Ret. Fund v. Chevron Corp., 2013 WL 435482 (Del. Ch.).

52. *Boilermakers*, 73 A.3d at 956–58; see also Kidsco, Inc. v. Dinsmore, 674 A.2d 483, 492 (Del. Ch. 1995).

53. *ATP Tour*, 91 A.3d at 560 (holding that bylaws normally apply to all members of a nonstock corporation regardless of whether the bylaw was adopted before or after the member in question became a member).

54. *Boilermakers*, 73 A.3d at 957.

55. 9 U.S.C. § 2. *See generally* Ann M. Lipton, *Manufactured Consent: The Problem of Arbitration Clauses in Corporate Charters and Bylaws*, 104 Geo. L. J. 583 (2016).

56. *See, e.g.*, Quantum Tech. Partners II, L.P. v. Altman Browning & Co., No. 08-CV-376-BR, 2009 WL 4826474 at *5 (D. Or. Dec. 8, 2009), *aff'd,* 436 F. App'x 792 (9th Cir. 2011) ("[T]he Court concludes neither *Centaur* nor the cases on which that court relied establish a shareholder may bring a breach-of-contract action under Delaware law for damages against other shareholders for violations of corporate bylaws.").

57. *Boilermakers*, 73 A.3d at 952 (approving a bylaw governing a state law corporate governance claims and noting that this type of suit was at the core of § 109(b)) (emphasis in original).

58. *Id.* (noting that bylaws would impermissibly regulate "external" matters if they "purported to bind a plaintiff, even a stockholder plaintiff, who sought to bring a tort claim against the company based on a personal injury she suffered that occurred on the company's premises or a contract claim based on a commercial contract with the corporation").

59. *See, e.g.*, Hemispherx Biopharma, Current Report (Form 8-K) (July 10, 2014) (applying a fee-shifting clause to various state law actions as well as "any action asserting a claim arising pursuant to any provision of the federal securities laws, and any regulation promulgated pursuant thereto"). Many of these intergalactic fee-shifting clauses persist, unaffected by Delaware legislation curtailing fee shifting in Delaware stock corporations. *E.g.*, Amended and Restated

Memorandum and Articles of Association of Alibaba Group Holding Limited, § 173, http://www.sec.gov/Archives/edgar/data/1577552/000119312514333674/d709111dex32.htm (including a fee-shifting provision covering all shareholder claims against the company).

60. Transcript of Scheduling Conference and Discussion Concerning Amendment of Bylaw at 20, Kastis v. Carter, No. 8657-CB (Del. Ch. Aug. 15, 2014), 2014 WL 4425407 (noting that related securities litigation was "really the central reason for adoption of the [fee-shifting] bylaw").

61. Complaint at 2, Deutscher Tennis Bund v. ATP Tour, Inc., Civ. Act. No. 07-178 (D. Del. Mar. 28, 2007), 2007 WL 4425678 at 36–48.

62. The Delaware Supreme Court's opinion in *ATP Tour* answered certified questions from the federal court, so was limited to matters of law. *See ATP Tour*, 91 A.3d at 555, 560. A court that wanted to limit the subject matter of the corporate contract to state law corporate governance could accordingly argue that the court in *ATP Tour* was not permitted to perform a granular analysis of the fees in the case. It was thus unable to distinguish between fee shifting in relation to state-law claims (permissible) and those in relation to federal antitrust claims (potentially impermissible).

63. *Boilermakers*, 73 A.3d at 952.

64. *In re* Activision Blizzard Inc. Stockholder Litig., 124 A.3d 1025 (Del. Ch. 2015) (distinguishing between personal claims and those that accompany a share as it is sold and resold, and indicating that "the right to bring a Rule 10b-5 claim is not a property right associated with shares").

65. *See also id.* (noting that the categories of shareholders and securities fraud plaintiffs are not coextensive: "Shareholders who do not buy or sell shares cannot sue under 10b-5, whereas they still count as shareholders for corporate governance purposes").

66. Although often state law controls corporate governance in the US system, some federal regulation of public companies (membership on boards, proxy solicitation and voting, insider trading rules, etc.) muddies the distinction.

67. Winship, *Contracting around Securities Litigation* (beginning to develop this argument).

68. *Boilermakers*, 73 A.3d at 939.

69. McDermott Inc. v. Lewis, 531 A.2d 206, 215 (Del. 1987).

70. Del. Code Ann. tit. 8, § 109(b).

71. *Boilermakers*, 73 A.3d at 950–51 (emphasis added).

72. *Id.*

73. *See, e.g.*, ISS, U.S. Summary Proxy Voting Guidelines 23–24 (2014), https://www.issgovernance.com/file/policy/2015ussummaryvotingguidelines.pdf.

74. As noted above, these were later defanged legislatively for Delaware stock corporations. *See* Del. Code Ann. tit. 8, §§ 102(f), 109(b) (2015). These fee-shifting provisions persist, however, because the Delaware legislation obviously

does not reach beyond state boundaries. Nor does it reach noncorporate forms of business organization.

75. Deutscher Tennis Bund v. ATP Tour Inc., 480 F. App'x 124, 126 (3d Cir. 2012) (quoting Article 23 of the Amended and Restated Bylaws of ATP Tour, Inc.).

76. Winship, *Shareholder Litigation by Contract* at 527–28.

77. Compare, *e.g.*, early cases viewing court access as a fundamental right, with the Federal Arbitration Act and court decisions enforcing consumer arbitration. *See, e.g.*, Ins. Co. v. Morse, 87 U.S. (20 Wall.) 445, 451 (1874): "Every citizen is entitled to resort to all the courts of the country [and may not] "barter away . . . his substantial rights"); 9 U.S.C. § 2.

78. Corp. Law Section, Del. State Bar Ass'n, Explanation of Council Legislative Proposal at 3–4 (2015), http://www.law.du.edu/documents/corporate-governance/legislation/delaware-stat-revisions/Council-Second-Proposal-Explanatory-Paper-3-6-15.pdf ("We have steadfastly declined to permit the fiduciary duties of corporate directors to be limited or eliminated by charter or bylaw provision, and we believe that permitting fee-shifting provisions would give corporations the authority to achieve essentially the same result.").

79. *Cf.* Jeffrey N. Gordon, *The Mandatory Structure of Corporate Law*, 89 COLUM. L. REV. 1549, 1591 (1989) (making the point that "a stock of precedents that construe the same provision" provides a public good).

80. Del. S.B. 75, Synopsis §§ 2–5.

81. *See* Winship, *Shareholder Litigation by Contract* at 524–28 (linking concerns about waiver to the nature of consent and proposing the use of a heightened consent requirement).

82. *See, e.g.*, Blasius Indus. v. Atlas Corp., 564 A.2d 651, 659 (Del. Ch. 1988) (pointing to the "central importance of the franchise" and thus requiring a stronger justification for impeding shareholder voting than simply that the board acted in good faith to defend control), cited in Cox, *Corporate Law and the Limits of Private Ordering* at 283–84.

CHAPTER THIRTEEN

Private Ordering Post-*Trulia*

Why No-Pay Provisions Can Fix the Deal Tax and Forum Selection Provisions Can't

Sean J. Griffith

Introduction

Not long ago, it was common to hear two complaints about merger litigation under Delaware corporate law. First, there was too much of it. Virtually every transaction was assessed the "deal tax"—that is, at least one shareholder suit, which typically settled for supplemental disclosures and, of course, attorneys' fees (Cain and Solomon 2016). And, second, this litigation, involving Delaware companies and Delaware law, was very often brought in alternative jurisdictions (Armour, Black, and Cheffins 2012a, 2012b; Cain and Solomon 2015).

Action followed on two fronts. First, the forum selection bylaw was put forward to solve the out-of-Delaware problem. Academics heralded the bylaw as a private ordering solution (Grundfest 2012; Grundfest and Savelle 2013). And Delaware agreed, blessing what came to be known as the "exclusive forum provision," first in judicial rulings, then by statute.[1] More recently, Delaware responded to the proliferation of merger litigation by taking aim at deal tax settlements, holding in the January 2016 *Trulia* opinion that settlements would be rejected unless they provided a "plainly material" benefit to the plaintiff class.[2] In this way, Delaware committed to both deterring nuisance litigation and guaranteeing the applicability of this regime through the exclusive forum bylaw. At least to some, both problems appeared to be solved.

This now appears to have been wishful thinking. Merger litigation remains extremely common, and claims are frequently brought in an alternative jurisdiction. In the fourth quarter of 2015 and first half of 2016, the percentage of litigated deals with claims filed in Delaware fell to 26 percent from 61 percent (Cornerstone Research 2016b). Similarly, complaints involving Delaware-incorporated targets were filed in Delaware just 32 percent of the time, down from 61 percent of the time in 2015 (Cain et al. 2017). Meanwhile merger filings in federal courts have expanded substantially. Merger lawsuits filed in federal court began increasing in the second half of 2015 (Cornerstone Research 2016a), and by all accounts continued to grow robustly in 2016 (Boettrich and Starykh 2017; Cain et al. 2017; Cornerstone Research 2017). Furthermore, exclusive forum provisions are not bringing the cases back to Delaware. Rather, many are settling (for supplemental disclosures) in alternative jurisdictions (Griffith and Rickey 2018).

The stampede of filings to alternative jurisdictions can plausibly be explained by the plaintiffs' bar's reaction to *Trulia* and to the cases leading up to it. Once it became clear that Delaware would act to curtail merger-related nuisance claims, these lawyers began to take their claims elsewhere. But defense counsel must be seen as complicit in the out-of-Delaware dynamic, because they have failed to exercise exclusive forum bylaws to bring the litigation back to Delaware. The problem is not that too few companies have adopted the provision. Like the poison pill, the exclusive forum bylaw can be adopted by unilateral action of the board at any moment. All Delaware firms should thus be regarded as having at least a "shadow" exclusive forum provision. As a result, the failure to invoke the provision must be seen as a revealed preference. It demonstrates defendants' continued interest in retaining the option of a cheap settlement and a broad release in an alternative jurisdiction (Griffith and Lahav 2013). As a result of this confluence of incentives, both sides of the merger litigation problem—the "deal tax" and the incentive to file and settle claims "anywhere but Chancery"—remain.

This chapter examines merger litigation post-*Trulia*. After demonstrating how *Trulia* succeeds in Delaware but fails outside Delaware, the chapter turns to the possibility of a private ordering solution. Exclusive forum provisions have failed, I argue, because these provisions in fact function as exclusive forum *options*. The provision will thus fail to solve the out-of-Delaware problem as long as defendants remain interested in steering claims to the "disclosure settlement bar" (Friedlander 2016). But the failure of the exclusive forum provision teaches an important set of lessons for how private ordering could successfully solve the problem of the deal tax. That solution, I argue, is the "no-pay" provision, a term barring corporations from paying attorneys' fees for specified litigation outcomes. After demonstrating the failure of the exclusive forum provision to cope with the assessment of the deal tax in alternative forums, this chapter demonstrates how the no-pay provision promises a more effective cure for what ails merger litigation.

Merger Litigation and the *Trulia* Decision

Merger litigation was, until very recently, ubiquitous. In each year from 2009 through 2015, somewhere between 85 percent and 95 percent of all merger transactions over $100 million attracted litigation (Cain and Solomon 2016). It has not always been so. A decade ago, a mere 39 percent of such deals attracted litigation. Filings remain common even after *Trulia*: In 2016, 73 percent of completed deals valued over $100 million attracted claims (Cain et al. 2017). This is down slightly from the high but still almost double the historical average.

Merger claims are typically resolved for no monetary recovery to the plaintiff class. Instead, the vast majority of such claims result in nothing more than supplemental disclosures—so-called disclosure settlements.[3] Although settling claims for supplemental disclosures entitles plaintiffs' attorneys to a fee for the supposed "benefit" they have produced, there is no evidence that such disclosures change shareholder voting behavior or alter deal outcomes in any way (Fisch, Griffith, and Solomon 2015).

Recognizing that the proliferation of such claims has been fueled by the near-automatic award of fees to plaintiffs' counsel for obtaining relief of little or no real value to the shareholder class, courts have recently reaffirmed the long-standing but inconsistently applied principle of materiality. Supplemental disclosures offered in connection with settlement are compensable only if they provide a material benefit to the shareholder class.[4] Information is material only "if there is a substantial likelihood that a reasonable shareholder would consider it important in deciding how to vote."[5] Judicial scrutiny of the materiality of disclosure settlements has increased markedly in recent years, culminating in the summer of 2015, when the Delaware Court of Chancery began a concerted effort to address disclosure-fueled nuisance litigation.[6]

In July 2015, Vice Chancellor Laster refused to approve a disclosure-only settlement where plaintiffs settled for "precisely the type of non-substantive disclosures that routinely show up in these types of settlements."[7] A few months later, Vice Chancellor Laster denied approval to another settlement, noting that plaintiffs provided inadequate representation to the class by filing litigation when "there wasn't a basis to file in the first place" and then failing to aggressively litigate when discovery turned up potentially valuable information.[8] At the same time, another line of Delaware Court of Chancery cases pledged to subject future disclosure settlements to more exacting scrutiny.[9] Other rulings, meanwhile, slashed the fees requested by plaintiffs' counsel in disclosure cases.[10] All these efforts culminated in Chancellor Bouchard's decision in *Trulia*.

Like most disclosure settlements, the plaintiffs in *Trulia* started out by challenging the deal price and the negotiation process, then shifted to challenging the adequacy of disclosures once the preliminary proxy statement was released, ultimately resolving all claims for supplemental disclosures and no payment to the plaintiff class.[11] After critiquing the parties' incentives to file and settle such claims, Chancellor Bouchard announced that the Delaware Court of Chancery would no longer be in the business of rubber-stamping disclosure settlements. Instead, "[P]ractitioners should expect that disclosure settlements are likely to be met with continued disfavor in the future unless the supplemental disclosures address a *plainly material misrepresentation or omission*. . . . In using the term 'plainly material,' I mean that *it should not be a close call that the supplemental information is material* as that term is defined under Delaware law."[12]

In applying a high standard of materiality as a condition for the approval of disclosure settlements, *Trulia* announced that such settlements are no longer welcome in Delaware. A lingering question, however, was whether they would be welcome elsewhere.

Trulia Outside Delaware

Merger claims can be brought in three places: in the state of incorporation, in the headquarters state, or in federal court. The substantive law of the state of incorporation will govern where the dispute is litigated (except when federal securities claims are raised, to which substantive federal law applies).[13] But when a company's headquarters state is different from its state of incorporation, as is almost always the case for companies incorporated in Delaware, the complaint can be heard in up to three different jurisdictions. Of course, facing litigation in multiple jurisdictions means defendants have a choice of where to settle. Defense counsel may take advantage of this situation to run a reverse auction (Griffith and Lahav 2013) or to steer litigation to members of the disclosure settlement bar (Krishnan, Solomon, and Thomas 2016). Setting up disclosure settlements is easy to do—as described by a practitioner: "One way to tee up a disclosure settlement is to hold back from disclosing in the preliminary proxy statement facts about financial advisor compensation, the full extent of a financial advisor's ties to a private equity buyer, components of the financial advisor's DCF [discounted cash flow] analysis, or compensation-related discussions between management and the buyer. The plaintiff disclosure settlement bar can be expected to look for supplemental disclosures on these topics to resolve the litigation" (Friedlander 2016).

Wherever the claim goes for resolution, there will be a fairness hearing prior to settlement. At the hearing, a judge will be asked to certify the class (making the settlement binding on absent class members) and review the fairness and reasonableness of the settlement. In this process: "If class action attorneys sell out their clients, the judge should perceive that the settlement does not live up to the value of the claims and reject it accordingly. Conversely, if class action attorneys file a frivolous case, the judge should perceive that the settlement is merely a nuisance payment, reject it for that reason, and dismiss the case" (Rubenstein 2006). *Trulia* enters at this point in the process, supplying the Delaware standard for judging the materiality of supplemental disclosures. If the settlement consideration is immaterial, it cannot be approved as fair and reasonable.

Unfortunately, judges are left to their own devices in settlement hearings. There is rarely any adversary process. The hearings are, instead, "pep rallies jointly orchestrated by plaintiffs' counsel and defense counsel" (Macey and Miller 2009). Objections are rare (Eisenberg and Miller 2004), and judges are left to parse the disclosures on their own—an exercise many judges, considering their heavy dockets, would likely prefer to avoid (Sale 2011). The question thus becomes whether and how *Trulia* will be applied by judges in other jurisdictions. And, just as there are multiple alternative jurisdictions for merger litigation, the question must be asked in multiple ways. First, how will *Trulia* be applied outside Delaware when the underlying substantive law is Delaware corporate law? And, second, how will *Trulia* be applied outside Delaware when the underlying substantive law is *not* Delaware corporate law?

Delaware Law, Non-Delaware Forum

Delaware-incorporated companies face corporate law litigation outside Delaware when a claim is brought in the company's headquarters state or when the claim is brought in federal court, either under diversity jurisdiction or when the corporate law claim is appended to a separate federal question claim. In such cases, Delaware law applies to matters of substance, and the law of the forum applies to matters of procedure (Griffith and Lahav 2013). So an initial question in this context is whether *Trulia* is substantive or procedural.

The rules governing the approval of settlement are procedural and therefore subject to the law of the forum. But, in the class action context at least, these rules are the same across jurisdictions (Rubenstein 2006). The court acts as a fiduciary for the class and, in that capacity, asks whether the settlement is "fair, reasonable, and adequate."[14] Courts may consider an array of factors in this analysis, but a crucial factor in all such analyses is the value received by the plaintiff class in the settlement. In the context of a disclosure settlement, that means courts must weigh the value of the disclosures. That much is procedural.

But what standard applies in analyzing the value of the disclosures? Delaware provides a substantive answer to this question, and that answer under *Trulia* is "plainly material." The internal affairs doctrine should thus lead a court applying Delaware substantive law to hew to the same plainly material standard despite an alternative standard (such as "useful" or "helpful") under the law of the forum.[15] *Trulia* therefore constitutes controlling authority for settlements involving Delaware companies outside Delaware.

But even if *Trulia* controls, the question becomes whether the judge in the alternative forum has ever heard of it. Non-Delaware judges, after all, have little incentive to remain abreast of developments in the Court of Chancery and must, as is typical in the adversarial system, rely on briefing from the litigants for information concerning the relevant legal standards. At settlement, however, there is no adversarial process. The litigants, recall, are interested in orchestrating a joint pep rally, not in subjecting their mutually agreed settlement to serious judicial scrutiny. Neither side has any incentive to raise *Trulia* to the judge either in the briefing or in the settlement hearing itself.

Still, even if the settlement proponents have no interest in raising *Trulia*, perhaps they have some obligation to do so. The rules of professional conduct may obligate counsel under some circumstances to disclose authority contrary to their position even if that authority is not raised by opposing counsel. For example, ABA Model Rule 3.3(a)(2) states that "[a] lawyer shall not knowingly . . . fail to disclose to the tribunal legal authority in the controlling jurisdiction known to the lawyer to be directly adverse to the position of the client and not disclosed by opposing counsel." *Trulia*, in its open hostility to disclosure settlements and in its announcement of a "plainly material" standard for supplemental disclosures, would seem to be adverse to the position of both settlement proponents. And, following the logic above, because Delaware law controls with regard to the materiality determination, *Trulia* should count as "authority in the controlling jurisdiction." Attorneys practicing in jurisdictions adopting a version of Model Rule 3.3(a)(2) would therefore seem to be under an ethical obligation to disclose *Trulia* to the court.

This, of course, does not mean that they always do so. As of this writing, I am aware of eight disclosure settlements involving Delaware-incorporated companies that have been presented in non-Delaware courts for approval since *Trulia* was decided.[16] I objected or filed papers in four of these cases and raised *Trulia* every time, always as the first party to do so.[17] In none of the four remaining cases, to my knowledge, did the parties raise *Trulia* to the court. In one, however, the court was already aware of the decision and denied preliminary approval to the settlement due in part to the parties' failure to address it.[18] Although my experience as an objector suggests that well-represented objectors can make a difference, objectors are rare, especially in this context where shareholders have no financial interest, either in the settlement itself or in objecting to it. As a result, the adversary element never enters the equation, leaving the judge to follow the path of least resistance and, very likely, approve the settlement without ever having heard of *Trulia*.[19]

Non-Delaware Law, Non-Delaware Forum

There are two ways non-Delaware law can apply to a merger claim, both of which involve a non-Delaware forum. First, the corporation can be incorporated somewhere other than Delaware and thus face non-Delaware law wherever the settlement occurs. Second, federal securities law can apply to the merger claim.

Merger Litigation Not Involving Delaware Companies

Trulia is not controlling authority for companies incorporated outside Delaware. However, because few, if any, jurisdictions see as many merger cases as Delaware, *Trulia* constitutes important persuasive authority regardless of where the case is brought and settled. Again, however, neither settlement proponent has any interest in citing *Trulia* at settlement, even in settlement papers otherwise rife with references to Delaware law as persuasive authority. It is more difficult to read Model Rule 3.3(a)(2) to compel disclosure in this situation. However, where Delaware law is widely cited by the settlement proponents as persuasive authority, failing to cite recent adverse authority in that jurisdiction arguably amounts to making a false statement of law to the tribunal, triggering a duty to correct under Model Rule 3.3(a)(1). This interpretation of the ethics rules would prevent settlement proponents from cherry-picking older Delaware case law supporting broad releases and large fees without also informing the court of Delaware's more recent rulings, especially *Trulia*.

The collapse of the adversary system at settlement, however, means that there is generally no one around to make these arguments. Considering the incentives of the settlement proponents in their jointly orchestrated pep rally, it would therefore not be surprising to find that *Trulia* is typically not cited in the briefing of settlements involving non-Delaware companies, even when the settlement proponents heavily cite Delaware law in support of the settlement and on other issues. And this, indeed, is what the preliminary data suggest. As of this writing, I am aware of seven disclosure settlements involving non-Delaware companies that have been presented for approval since *Trulia* was decided.[20] Of these, to my knowledge, *Trulia* was raised in only one case, *Corwin*, in which there was an objector.[21]

Merger Litigation under the Federal Securities Laws

The other context in which companies can face merger litigation under non-Delaware substantive law is when claims are brought under the federal securities laws. Merger claims can be filed in federal court by alleging fraud in the proxy statement under SEC Rule 14a-9, promulgated under Section 14(a) of the Securities Exchange Act of 1934. The rule proscribes false or misleading statements in a company's proxy materials. In the merger context, Rule 14a-9 claims allege that the target company did not fully and fairly disclose all material information in the merger proxy—essentially the same allegations underlying state law fiduciary duty claims to disclose. Additional state law claims, such as *Revlon* claims alleging defects in the merger process or the price, can be appended to the 14a-9 claims and brought in federal court. Alternatively, plaintiffs may simply file the 14a-9 claim and seek a disclosure settlement in federal court. In either case, Section 27 of the Securities Exchange Act guarantees that the 14a-9 claim can only be brought in federal court.[22]

Merger claims are increasingly being brought in federal court (Cornerstone Research 2016a). There is good reason for this: Settlement patterns in federal court mirror pre-*Trulia* settlement patterns in Delaware—that is, broad releases and substantial fees supported only by supplemental disclosures.[23] The plaintiffs' lawyers' expectation seems to be that easy settlement approvals will continue in federal court, changed practices in Delaware notwithstanding.

Federal judges presiding over fairness hearings in these cases face the same informational disadvantages as state law judges outside Delaware. Although *Trulia* is highly relevant persuasive authority, neither settlement proponent has any interest in raising it at the hearing and, except under the strong reading of Rule 3.3(a)(2), noted above, has no obligation to do so. Furthermore, objectors are no more likely to appear in federal court than they are in any other forum. There is evidence, however, that objectors can be successful. For example, in *In Re: Walgreen Co. Stockholder Litigation*, Judge Posner reversed a district court decision approving a disclosure settlement of litigation in the Walgreen-Boots merger.[24] In holding that the settlement should have been rejected because the disclosures provided no benefit to the plaintiff class, Judge Posner expressly endorsed the *Trulia* opinion and the plainly material standard, concluding that the district court on remand should "give serious consideration to either appointing new class counsel, or dismissing the suit."[25] As a result, *Trulia* via *Walgreen* now applies in the 7th Circuit, and, going forward, settlement proponents in that circuit have an obligation under Rule 3.3(a)(2) to raise it at the settlement hearing.

An alternative to spreading *Trulia* or *Walgreen* across the federal judiciary would be to direct the attention of federal judges to the wording of the Private Securities Litigation Reform Act—in particular, to what is now 15 U.S.C.A. § 78u4, which provides: "Total attorney fees and expenses awarded by the court to counsel for the plaintiff class" in securities class actions may "not exceed a reasonable percentage of the amount of any damages and prejudgment interest actually paid to the class." The provision, on its face, prohibits the award of attorneys' fees for nonpecuniary relief in 14a-9 claims.[26] However, consistent with the federal judiciary's disregard of the Private Securities Litigation Reform Act in other contexts (Henderson and Hubbard 2015), a federal district court rejected this reading of the provision the one time it was squarely presented, holding that Congress would not so glibly have altered the common benefit doctrine with respect to securities litigation.[27] The common benefit doctrine, of course, is common law (Griffith 2015). And in so holding, the judge implicitly hewed to the ancient maxim that statutes in derogation of the common law should be interpreted narrowly. Putting aside the viability of that maxim in an age when "statutes are the rule and common law the exception" (Eskridge and Frickey 1988, at 921), it is beyond doubt that Congress *could have* drafted a statute to alter the common law on this point. Moreover, precisely this reading of a parallel Texas statute was recently upheld in Texas state court, thereby banning fee awards for disclosure settlements in the state of Texas.[28]

The Exclusive Forum Option

If, as demonstrated above, there are strong reasons to suspect that *Trulia* will not apply consistently or at all to merger claims settled outside Delaware, the question becomes whether the exclusive forum provision will work to bring the claims back to Delaware, as indeed the *Trulia* court suggested it would.[29] The answer, unfortunately, is no. Some claims—most notably federal securities law claims—*cannot* be litigated in Delaware state courts. Although it may be possible to persuade a federal court to decline jurisdiction over state law claims appended to federal claims, it will typically not be worth the candle because Section 27 of the Securities Exchange Act requires that the core Rule 14a-9 claim be brought in federal court.[30] Exclusive forum bylaws therefore make no attempt to include federal claims,[31] which are, in any event, beyond their reach.[32] The doorway to federal court is therefore always open to merger claims and, potentially, disclosure settlements.

The more unsettling question to ask about exclusive forum provisions is not whether they could bring all merger litigation back to Delaware but whether, if they could, corporate defendants would want them to.[33] And once again, judging from the actual conduct of litigants, the answer is no. In cases where defendants *could* invoke exclusive forum provisions to bring litigation back to Delaware, they do not do so, but choose instead to settle in alternative jurisdictions. This becomes clear once the exclusive forum provision is recognized as an option that, thanks to the mechanism of adoption, could be invoked by defendants at any time and in any case. That it is not always invoked must be understood as a revealed preference of corporate defendants.

The exclusive forum provision preserves the optionality of defendants in two ways. First, waiver is expressly contemplated under the terms of the provision, which becomes inapplicable if the corporation consents in writing to another forum. Second, and more fundamentally, the provision is not self-enforcing but applies only when asserted by a defendant, typically in the form of a motion to dismiss filed in the alternative forum. Courts will not automatically dismiss or transfer litigation based on the mere existence of the provision. If the defendant does not assert the provision, nothing happens. The waiver language is thus redundant. Defendants can effectively waive the provision simply by choosing not to assert it.

This optionality for defendants was likely built into the bylaw to protect it against being invalidated as a breach of fiduciary duty. If asserting exclusive forum rights would somehow breach the board's fiduciary duty, then a contractual provision that purported to require it might be deemed invalid (Ursaner 2010). Drafters therefore built waiver and discretion into the provision as a kind of "fiduciary out" to protect it against judicial invalidation (Grundfest and Savelle 2013).

But the optionality inherent in the provision allows defendants to continue to choose where to settle, thus preserving defendants' prerogative to conduct a reverse auction or direct cases to the disclosure settlement bar. And defense counsel have been remarkably forthright in counseling their clients on this advantage: "[A] company may wish to wait to adopt Delaware selection bylaws until it becomes clearer whether other jurisdictions will continue to approve disclosure-only settlements; or may wish to adopt the bylaws now and then eliminate them if it becomes clear that other jurisdictions will continue to approve disclosure-only settlements. Further, *a company may wish to adopt the bylaws and then waive them in the context of an approved transaction when the company would prefer the certainty of a quick resolution over the prospect of lengthier litigation for vindication on the merits*."[34] The clear message here is that the optionality embedded within forum selection bylaw keeps the door open to disclosure settlements, notwithstanding *Trulia*.

There are plain examples of the opportunistic use of forum selection provisions by defendants—situations, that is, in which companies with forum selection bylaws have chosen not to assert them but have instead settled (for nonmonetary relief) in an alternative jurisdiction. For example, in the *CytRx* derivative litigation filed in Delaware and in federal court in California, the defendant corporation adopted a Delaware forum selection bylaw, pursuant to which it obtained dismissal of the California action, only then to negotiate a settlement in California rather than Delaware.[35] But instead of setting aside its dismissal to allow the settlement to proceed, the California federal court refused, noting:

> [W]e are skeptical of the Parties' motivation for attempting to settle here. The Delaware Court of Chancery has gained a reputation for rejecting shareholder class action and derivative settlements that do not have a monetary component yet include a broad release of claims and an award of attorneys' fees, similar to the proposed settlement here.
>
> . . . It is reasonable to infer that a motivation for seeking vacatur may be to avoid a forum that reviews critically the general type of settlement proposed by the Parties here. This inference is made all the more reasonable by Plaintiffs' counsel's recent failure to receive approval of a non-monetary settlement in the Chancery Court. We cannot ignore the possibility that the current Motion may be an attempt to shop for a more hospitable forum in which to settle the dispute.[36]

More basically, looking for evidence of opportunism by looking only at cases where the provision was *adopted and not invoked* undercounts the effective use of the provision in the same way that measuring takeover defenses by looking at firms that have *adopted* poison pills undercounts the number of companies that are effectively protected by the pill (Coates 2000; Catan 2016). As with the poison pill, forum selection bylaws are adopted by unilateral board action. Thus, surveying the number of firms that have adopted the provision fails to count those firms that could have the provision at their disposal in a moment's notice—as soon as the company receives a hostile bid in the case of a poison pill, or as soon as the company signs a merger agreement or engages in other transactions likely to lead to shareholder suits in the case of a forum selection bylaw. Thus, just as every Delaware company has a "shadow" pill, every Delaware company should also be regarded as having a "shadow" exclusive forum provision.

The scale of defense-side opportunism looks dramatically different if every firm is regarded as having a shadow exclusive forum provision. From this perspective, every case involving a Delaware corporation that settles outside Delaware raises the specter of a reverse settlement auction, especially disclosure settlements in the wake of *Trulia*. As should be clear from the discussion above, there are already many such settlements. This fact, post-*Boilermakers* and post-*Trulia*, can only mean that such outcomes are a revealed preference of defendants. Defendants have the option. If they wanted to bring litigation back to the forum that no longer accepts such settlements, they could. But they do not.

Corporations decry the state of merger litigation and denigrate plaintiffs' lawyers as holdup artists. But when given the choice, more often than not, they do not fight. They join hands and settle.

Substituting No-Pay Provisions for Exclusive Forum Provisions to Fix Merger Litigation

The failure of exclusive forum provisions to cure what ails merger litigation can be attributed to a disconnect in defense-side incentives ex ante and ex post. Ex ante, before entering into a merger transaction and facing the inevitable lawsuit filings, it is in every corporation's interest not to pay to settle frivolous claims to deter such claims from being brought in the first place. But ex post, once the corporation has become a defendant in merger litigation, that corporation has a strong incentive to buy the broad, cheap releases that disclosure settlements provide. The result is a kind of collective action problem brought on by the firm's inconsistent preferences over time. The problem can be solved through a precommitment strategy that binds the board to the mast and prevents it from changing its mind (Elster 2000; Posner 1997; Schelling 1985). The optionality embedded in exclusive forum bylaws, however, makes it impossible for boards to make a credible commitment not to settle.

Precommitment generally is a vexed issue under Delaware law. Several decisions suggest that boards may not bind themselves by contract in ways that inhibit the subsequent exercise of fiduciary duty.[37] These cases all involved takeovers, a particularly charged environment in which fiduciary duty requires the board to extract maximum value for shareholders, and the cases have attracted significant criticism (e.g., Bainbridge 2003; Griffith 2013). It is therefore unclear how broadly the cases apply to more banal contexts, such as the choice of forum.

Assuming some form of precommitment strategy would be enforceable in this context, a simple solution to the problem might be to strip the optionality from exclusive forum provisions, making them exclusive forum *mandates*. Companies would precommit to asserting Delaware forum wherever appropriate. To make the commitment binding, waiver could be prohibited and a shareholder vote requirement could be added to discourage ex post repeal. A narrow fiduciary out, allowing for waiver if enforcement would amount to a breach of the target board's fiduciary duty, could also be crafted if necessary. But even if fiduciary duty concerns could be allayed, an exclusive forum mandate cannot force federal securities claims to be litigated in the Court of Chancery. Even if all state law claims were brought back to Delaware, federal courts would retain exclusive jurisdiction over securities law claims. And because 14a-9 claims are perfectly serviceable substitutes for disclosure claims under state corporate law, the mandatory exclusive forum provision could not prevent disclosure settlements from being reached in federal court.

A second private ordering strategy closely related to the dynamics of the exclusive forum provision would be to incorporate terms into the merger agreement forcing target firms to fight rather than settle merger claims. Merger agreements could include provisions requiring companies to adopt an exclusive forum bylaw (a "must adopt" provision) as well as commitments to enforce and not waive the bylaw in the face of merger litigation (a "must enforce"/"don't waive" provision). But who would want these terms? Most acquirers, with the possible exception of repeat play acquirers, are likely to share targets' ex post incentives in favor of settlement, deal certainty, and release. Perhaps directors and officers (D&O) liability insurers, who are typically the ultimate source of funding in shareholder litigation, could insist that their insureds incorporate such terms in their merger agreements as a condition to coverage. Rewriting D&O policies to give insurers this level of control over litigation, however, would represent a significant deviation from current policies, which allocate the right to control the conduct of litigation to the insured, not the insurer (Baker and Griffith 2010). Moreover, any insurer that sought to take this level of control would likely be punished in the marketplace by rivals willing to underwrite policies without such features (Baker and Griffith 2010). In other words, the problem with this solution is that D&O insurers, at least in "soft" insurance markets, lack the power to implement it.

For private ordering to address the deal tax, it must address its dual nature. The problem is not just that plaintiffs' lawyers bring merger claims outside Delaware. It is that defense lawyers advise their corporate clients to pay for nuisance settlements to mitigate the risk that they may have done something wrong in the sale process. Paying for nuisance settlements perpetuates the cycle of litigation. The best way to break the cycle is therefore not to force the litigation into a single jurisdiction, but rather to precommit not to pay.

A no-pay provision would preclude the corporation from paying attorneys' fees and costs for a specified form of representative litigation. Corporations now customarily pay such fees and costs on the basis of the "corporate benefit" doctrine, which grew up as a common law corollary to the "common fund" doctrine (Griffith 2015). The common fund doctrine entitles plaintiffs' counsel to be paid from funds recovered in representative litigation. The corporate benefit doctrine extended the logic of the common fund doctrine to the derivative suit context, a form of representative litigation in which plaintiffs' counsel technically sues on behalf of the corporation. When a derivative suit results in nonmonetary relief, the common benefit doctrine allows plaintiffs' counsel to be paid by the corporation, the recipient of the benefit, and the party on whose behalf the lawyer was technically working. A further expansion of the doctrine led courts to apply the corporate benefit rationale to nonpecuniary relief in class actions as well as derivative suits. I have argued elsewhere that the metastasis of this doctrine is unwarranted and in no small part to blame for the growth of nuisance litigation (Griffith 2015). My argument here is that the mistake can be cured by contract, through a no-pay provision.

No-pay provisions could be crafted to preclude fees for shareholder litigation generally (Bayliss and Mixon 2015). Alternatively, no-pay provisions could be narrowed to preclude fees only for class action shareholder litigation (Griffith 2015). Or, even more narrowly, no-pay provisions could be written to preclude fees only for disclosure settlements. The provision is likely enforceable however broadly or narrowly it is written. The corporate benefit doctrine is a common law doctrine aimed at incentivizing litigation that is beneficial to shareholders. A no-pay provision amounts to shareholders collectively agreeing that, because specified forms of litigation provide them with no meaningful benefit, they will no longer pay for such claims to be brought. It is unclear why a court would override what amounts to shareholders' ex ante waiver of the right to recover their attorneys' fees from the corporation. The corporate benefit doctrine, in other words, ought to be understood as a default term of corporate law, not a statutory mandate.

No-pay provisions are consistent with the Delaware General Corporation Law's prohibition of fee shifting in bylaw and charter provisions.[38] The statute bars efforts to "impose liability on a stockholder for the attorneys' fees or expenses *of the corporation*" (emphasis added). As noted above, in the context of class actions, the corporation pays the attorney's fees *of shareholder plaintiffs*, not the corporation. As a result, a no-pay provision does not impose liability on any stockholder for the fees and expenses of the corporation. It merely forces the stockholder to bear his or her own fees and costs. Moreover, because no-pay provisions are not punitive—they do not seek to punish plaintiffs by imposing defense-side costs upon them—they do not raise any of the unsettling policy issues associated with fee-shifting provisions (e.g., Choi 2016). The provision is broadly supported by *ATP Tour v. Deutscher Tennis Bund*, which suggests broad acceptance of private ordering with regard to attorneys' fee arrangements.[39]

Furthermore, a no-pay provision has been upheld against shareholder challenge. In *Katz v. Commonwealth REIT*, a Maryland state court upheld a no-pay provision embedded in an arbitration bylaw.[40] The term provided: "[E]ach party involved in a Dispute shall bear its own costs and expenses (including attorneys' fees), and the arbitrators shall not render an award that would include shifting of any costs or expenses (including attorneys' fees), or, in a derivative case or class action, award any portion of the Trust's award to the claimant or the claimant's attorneys."[41] In upholding the provision, the court rejected the argument that the provision effectively eliminated the ability of shareholders to seek redress for even grievous wrongs, holding that the fact that "the Plaintiffs find the expense involved in proving their remedy is not worth the associated costs does not constitute the elimination of the right to pursue that remedy so as to render the bylaw invalid."[42] In so holding, the Maryland court invoked US Supreme Court precedent that "the fact that it is not worth the expense involved in *proving* a statutory remedy does not constitute the elimination of the *right to pursue* that remedy."[43]

An additional advantage is that, unlike exclusive forum provisions, which are impotent against federal securities law claims, no-pay provisions should be enforceable to bar the payment of attorneys' fees for disclosure settlements regardless of whether the settlement is reached under state corporate law or SEC Rule 14a-9. Attorneys' fees in federal securities law class actions are paid under the same common law corporate benefit doctrine as settlements under state law. Therefore, provisions that validly waive the doctrine under state law should be equally enforceable in federal court. Indeed, there is an elegance to the enforcement of a no-pay provision in the context of a Rule 14a-9 disclosure settlement, because it amounts to opting in to a right that is arguably already provided by statute.[44] A no-fee provision essentially contracts for the reading of the Private Securities Litigation Reform Act advanced above.

Finally, no-pay provisions solve the collective action problem created by corporate defendants' inconsistent preferences over time. As long as corporations adopt no-pay provisions on a clear day, when they are not subject to deal litigation, they have no incentive to defect from the collective interest in fighting nuisance litigation. Moreover, as long as the commitment is made binding—for example, in the form of a charter provision or, alternatively, in the form of a bylaw term requiring shareholder approval for waiver or amendment—the mere existence of the provision will deter litigation. If plaintiffs' lawyers cannot be paid for nuisance settlements, they will either stop bringing nuisance claims or, alternatively, abandon them upon concluding that the claims can yield only settlements for which they cannot be paid.

The downside of no-fee provisions, of course, is that companies will draft the provision so broadly as to amount to a de facto waiver of fiduciary duty. A provision forcing shareholders to bear their own fees regardless of the strength of the claim may have the effect of depriving shareholders of their only realistic remedy for fiduciary duty violations, thus leaving board misconduct largely undeterred. Nevertheless, it is important to recall that in relatively efficient equities markets, investors will discount suboptimal governance terms (Easterbrook and Fischel 1996), thus deterring boards from drafting overly broad or otherwise harmful provisions. Moreover, overly broad provisions could be invalidated by the Court of Chancery as a breach of fiduciary duty. That said, if the provision is appropriately tailored to disclaim fees only for nuisance litigation—defined perhaps as representative actions resulting in nonpecuniary relief or a *de minimus* monetary recovery—the provision will likely be upheld, at least in Delaware, where the judiciary demonstrated a willingness to tolerate the more radical form of fee shifting in *ATP*. Furthermore, no-fee provisions end forum-selection gamesmanship. The enforceability of governance provisions is a substantive aspect of corporate law to which the law of the state of incorporation applies. Because courts in other states must therefore follow Delaware law in enforcing the no-fee provision, there will be no more incentive to take shareholder litigation to other forums.

In sum, the no-fee provision has the potential to succeed where the exclusive forum provision has failed. The provision promises to radically reduce or even eliminate the deal tax.

Notes

I appeared as a shareholder objector, expert, or amicus curiae in several of the cases cited here. I have received no monetary compensation in any of these roles. I am grateful to Tom Bayliss, Jill Fisch, Joe Grundfest, Travis Laster, Vera Korzun, Anthony Rickey, Steven Davidoff Solomon, Leo Strine, and the participants at the April 2016 Berkeley conference for their thoughtful comments on earlier drafts of this chapter. Thanks also to Miranda Lievsay (FLS 2017) and Caitlin Kelley (FLS 2016) for superlative research assistance. The viewpoints and any errors expressed herein are mine alone.

1. Boilermakers Local 154 Retirement Fund v. Chevron Corporation, 73 A.3d 934 (Del. Ch. 2013); City of Providence v. First Citizens Bancshares, 99 A.3d 229 (Del. Ch. 2014). The forum selection bylaw was subsequently blessed by an amendment to the Delaware General Corporation Law expressly authorizing the certificate of incorporation or bylaws of a Delaware corporation to include a forum selection clause requiring that lawsuits asserting "internal corporate claims," including derivative actions, be brought solely and exclusively in the Delaware courts. See DGCL § 115 (eff. Aug. 1, 2015).

2. *In re* Trulia, Inc. S'holder Litig., 129 A.3d 884 (Del. Ch. 2016). I filed an

amicus curiae brief in the *Trulia* case. *See In re* Trulia, Inc. S'holder Litig., Brief of Sean J. Griffith As Amicus Curiae, 2015 WL 6391945 (Del. Ch., Oct. 16, 2015).

3. Cases resolved for disclosures alone are sometimes referred to as "disclosure only" settlements, while cases resolved for disclosures and additional nonpecuniary relief, such as a reduction in the termination fee, are sometimes referred to as "disclosure plus" settlements (Fisch, Griffith, and Solomon 2015). In this chapter I follow Friedlander (2016) in referring to both forms simply as "disclosure" settlements.

4. Chrysler v. Dann, 223 A.2d 384 (Del. 1966); Hoffman v. Dann, 205 A.2d 343, 345 (Del. 1964), *cert. denied* 380 U.S. 973 (1965).

5. Rosenblatt v. Getty Oil Co., 493 A.2d 929, 944 (Del. 1985) (adopting standard of TSC Indus., Inc. v. Northway, Inc., 426 U.S. 438, 449 (1976)). Said differently, information is material if, from the perspective of a reasonable stockholder, there is a substantial likelihood that it "significantly alter[s] the 'total mix' of information made available." Arnold v. Soc'y for Sav. Bancorp., 650 A.2d 1270, 1277 (Del. 1994).

6. For earlier Delaware cases scrutinizing settlement practices, *see In re* Transatlantic Holdings S'holders Litig., No. 6574-CS (transcript) (Del. Ch. Mar. 8, 2013) (refusing to approve settlement for lack of "any real investigation," disclosure of additional background information, and overwhelming vote in favor of the transaction); *In re* Medicis Pharmaceutical Corp. Shareholder Litigation, C.A. No. 7857-CS, transcript at 24 (Del. Ch. Feb. 26, 2014) (refusing to approve settlement and noting that "giving out releases lightly is something we've got to be careful about"); Rubin v. Obagi Medical Products, Inc., C.A. No. 8433-VCL transcript at 8 (Del. Ch. Apr. 30, 2014) (refusing to approve settlement and noting that "there are unknown unknowns in the world, and the type of global release . . . in this case and [similar] disclosure settlements provides expansive protection for the defendants against a broad range of claims, virtually all of which have been completely unexplored by plaintiffs"); *In re* Theragenics Corp. Stockholders Litigation, C.A. No. 8790-VCL, transcript at 69 (Del. Ch. May 5, 2014) (refusing to approve settlement and noting that "when a fiduciary action settles, I have to have some confidence that the issues in the case were adequately explored, particularly when there is going to be a global, expansive, all-encompassing release given").

For pre-*Trulia* cases outside Delaware applying rigorous scrutiny of settlement practices, *see* Gordon v. Verizon Communications, 2014 WL 7250212 (N.Y. Sup. Ct. Dec. 19, 2014) (emphasizing that "[e]nhanced or corrected disclosure, in order to support a settlement, must be a material improvement over what had been previously disclosed" and declining to either approve settlement or award fees); City Trading Fund v. Nye, 2015 WL 93894 at *19 (N.Y. Sup. Ct. Jan. 7, 2015) (denying approval of a settlement class and finding the proposed settlement was not in the best interests of the class because plaintiffs had not "alleged *material* omissions or settled for *material* supplemental disclosures"); *In re* Allied Health Care, 2015 WL 6499467 at *3 (N.Y. Supr. Oct. 23, 2015) (rejecting disclosure settlement and emphasizing that "[t]he willingness to rubber stamp class action settlements reflects poorly on the profession and on those courts that, from time to time, have approved these settlements"). I filed an expert affidavit for the objector in *Gordon*.

7. Acevedo v. Aeroflex Hldg. Corp., C.A. No. 9730-VCL at 73 (Del. Ch. July 8, 2015) (transcript).

8. *In re* Aruba Networks, Inc. Stockholder Litigation, Consol. C.A. No. 10765-VCL at 73 (Del. Ch. Oct. 9, 2015) (transcript).

9. *See, e.g., In re* Riverbed Technology, Inc. Stockholders Litigation, 2015 Del. Ch. LEXIS 241 at **20 (Del. Ch. Sept. 17, 2015): "If it were not for the reasonable reliance of the parties on formerly settled practice in this Court, . . . the interests of the Class might merit rejection of a settlement encompassing a release that goes far beyond the claims asserted and the results achieved." I was a shareholder objector in *Riverbed*.

10. *See id.* at *28 (cutting plaintiffs' fee award from the requested $500,000 to $329,881.61); *see also In re* Silicon Image, Inc. S'holders Litig., C.A. No 10601-VCG, at 55, 58 (Del. Ch. Dec. 9, 2015) (transcript) (approving fee request of $425,000 but noting that "[i]f this were a post-July [2015] case, I suspect strongly my decision here would be different"); *In re* Intermune, Inc. S'holder Litig., C.A. No. 10086-VCN, at 10, 15 (Dec. 29, 2015) (transcript) (cutting fee award from $470,000 to $325,000).

11. *Trulia*, 129 A.3d at 887 (describing the case as one wherein "[t]he only money that would change hands is the payment of a fee to plaintiffs' counsel").

12. *Trulia*, 129 A.3d at 898–99 (emphasis added, citations omitted).

13. As explained by the US Supreme Court, the internal affairs of a corporation include fiduciary duties owed to a corporation by its officers and directors and "matters peculiar to the relationships among of between the corporation and its officers, directors and shareholders." Edgar v. MITE Corp., 457 U.S. 624, 645 (1982). *See generally* Frederick Tung, *Before Competition: Origins of the Internal Affairs Doctrine*, 32 J. Corp. L. 33, 35–36 (2006) (explaining the internal affairs doctrine).

14. 4 Newberg on Class Actions § 11.41 (4th ed. 2002). Most state rules in this context—like Delaware Court of Chancery Rule 23—mirror Federal Rule of Civil Procedure 23(e).

15. See Vergiev v. Aguero et al. (*In re* Metalico Stockholders' Litigation), UNN-L-2276-15, Superior Court of New Jersey, Union County, Order and Statement of Reasons, June 6, 2016 (rejecting settlement and adopting *Trulia* into New Jersey law). I was the shareholder objector in *Vergiev*.

16. Those cases are: Suprina v. Berkowtiz, No. 1-14-CV-272358 (Ca. Super. Ct. Feb. 29, 2016); Saggar v. Woodward, No. CIV-532534 (Ca. Super. Ct. Apr. 4,

2016); Allan v. Micrel, Inc., No. 1-15-CV-280762 (Ca. Super. Ct. May 20, 2016); *In re* Pharmacyclics. Inc. Shareholder Litigation, No. 2015-1-CV-278055 (Ca. Super. Ct. Jul. 20, 2016); Vergiev v. Aguero et al. (*In re* Metalico Stockholders' Litigation), UNN-L-2276-15, Superior Court of New Jersey, Union County (June 6, 2016); Garcia v. Remy International, Inc., Civ. No. 1:15-cv-01385-TWP-TAB (S.D. Indiana, hearing scheduled Nov. 2, 2016); Dean Drulias v. 1st Century Bancshares, Inc., et al., 16-CV-294673 (Ca. Super. Ct. Nov. 18, 2016).

17. I objected in *Pharmacyclics*, *Vergiev*, and *Remy* and sought to provide an amicus curiae brief in *Saggar.*

18. *See, e.g.*, Dean Drulias v. 1st Century Bancshares, Inc., et al., 16-CV-294673, Superior Court of California, Santa Clara County, Order Denying Preliminary Approval of Settlement, Nov. 18, 2016 (denying motion for preliminary approval of settlement). In rejecting preliminary approval, the California court emphasized that:

> The Court also finds it very troubling that—despite urging that Delaware law governs the materiality of the disclosures in this case . . .—plaintiff does not discuss or even acknowledge a crucial new published opinion by the Delaware Court of Chancery on this subject, *In re Trulia, Inc. Stockholder Litigation* (Del. Ch. 2016) 129 A.3d 884. *Trulia* was filed in January 2016 and has been the subject of much commentary ever since. The Court doubts that practitioners of deal litigation like plaintiff's counsel would be unaware of this opinion, and counsel should be prepared to discuss their failure to address *Trulia* at the hearing on this matter.

Id. I had previously appeared before the *Drulias* court as an objector in the *Pharmacyclics* case, in which I cited and discussed *Trulia*.

19. When I have objected—always with the help of my law students and practitioners willing to represent me on a contingency basis—I have managed to disrupt disclosure settlements in several jurisdictions, proving that objectors can protect the integrity of the process. I have done this for no fee, but most objectors need an incentive. Courts can encourage meaningful objections by awarding fees to objectors' counsel and by other methods, such as the appointment of an expert to evaluate the settlement or an independent counsel to oppose it, taxing fees in either case to the settlement proponents.

20. These are McGill v. Hake, No. 1:15-CV-00217 (S.D. Ind. Mar. 10, 2016); *In re* Pall Corp. Stockholder Litig., No. 603314/2015 (N.Y. Super. Ct. Aug. 29, 2016); *In re* Meadowbrook Insurance Group, Inc. S'holder Litig., Nos. 5:15-CV-10057; 5:15-CV-10497 (E.D. Mich. 2016); *In re* Associated Estates Realty Corp. S'holder Litig., Nos. 1:15-CV-00857-DCN (N.D. Oh. Jun. 8, 2016); Leitz v. Kraft Foods Group, Inc., No. 3:15-CV-262-HEH (E.D. Va. Mar. 10, 2016); Corwin v.

British Am. Tobacco, No. 14-CV-8130, 2016 WL 635191 (Super. Ct. N.C. Feb. 17, 2016).

21. I filed an expert affidavit in *Corwin* on behalf of the objector, for which I received no monetary compensation.

22. Section 27 of the Securities Exchange Act of 1934 provides that federal courts "shall have exclusive jurisdiction" over "violations of [the Act] or the rules and regulations thereunder, and of all suits in equity and actions at law brought to enforce any liability or duty created by [the Act] or the rules and regulations thereunder." 15 U.S.C. § 78aa(a).

23. Typical disclosure settlements recently approved by federal courts include Taxman v. Covidien plc, 1:14-cv-12949 (D. Mass., Sept. 21, 2015); Leitz v. Kraft Foods Group, Inc., 3-15-CV-262-HEH (E.D. Va., Mar. 10, 2016); McGill v. Hake, 1:15-cv-00217-TWP-DKL (S.D. Indiana, Mar. 10, 2016); Li v. Bowers, 1:15-cv-373 (M.D. N.C., Mar. 22, 2016); *In re* Meadowbrook Ins. Grp., Inc., 5:15-cv-10057-JCO-MJH (E.D. Mich., Apr. 7, 2016). I was involved in *Covidien* as an expert for the objector but had no role in the other cases.

24. *In re* Walgreen Co. Stockholder Litigation (Hays, et al. v. Walgreen Co., et al.), No. 15-3799, (7th Cir., June 2, 2016).

25. *Id.* at 12.

26. An alternative reading of the provision is that it was intended to cap attorneys' fees in cases where there is both injunctive relief and damages to a reasonable percentage of the damages, not to prohibit fee awards for nonpecuniary relief. The prohibition of fees is the simpler reading, however, and the question is not clarified by the legislative history.

27. Taxman v. Covidien plc, 1:14-cv-12949 (D. Mass., Sept. 21, 2015) transcript at 48 ("[I]t is an awful lot of weight to read on that one sentence, that Congress rewrote the common benefit rule with respect to federal securities litigation in that sort of backhanded way, rather than directly. . . . I don't read the language quite as powerfully as you do.").

28. Kazman v. Frontier Oil Corp., 398 S.W.3d 377 (Tex. App., Houston, 2013).

29. *Trulia*, 129 A.3d 884, 899 (Del. Ch. 2016) ("It is within the power of a Delaware corporation to enact a forum selection bylaw to address this concern.").

30. A defendant with a forum selection bylaw may be able to argue under 28 U.S.C. Section 1367(c)(2) that the federal court should decline supplemental jurisdiction over the fiduciary duty claims on the grounds that those claims "substantially predominate" the federal law claim and, further, under Section 1367(c)(4) that the federal court ought to decline supplemental jurisdiction due to "compelling reasons" relating to the efficient disposition of claims involving the same underlying facts. However, federal courts do not easily decline jurisdiction, and the core 14a-9 claim would, in any event, remain in federal court. *See* Colo. River Water Conservation Dist. v. United States, 424 U.S. 800, 820 (1976) ("[W]e do not overlook the heavy obligation to exercise jurisdiction."); 17A

Charles Alan Wright et al, FEDERAL PRACTICE AND PROCEDURE § 4247 (3d ed. 2012) ("[I]n most cases [of concurrent jurisdiction] neither stay nor dismissal will be proper and the federal court will be obliged to exercise its jurisdiction.").

31. Bylaws typically provide for exclusive forum in the Delaware Court of Chancery for fiduciary duty claims, claims under the DGCL and the company's organizational documents, and claims governed by the internal affairs doctrine. A recent version of the provision provides:

> Unless the Corporation consents in writing to the selection of an alternate forum, the state courts of the State of Delaware in and for New Castle County (or, if no state court located within the State of Delaware has jurisdiction, the federal district court for the District of Delaware) shall be the sole and Exclusive Forum, to the fullest extent permitted by law, for (a) any derivative action or proceeding brought on behalf of the Corporation; (b) any action asserting a claim of a breach of fiduciary duty owed by any Director, officer or other employee of the Corporation to the Corporation or the Corporation's stockholders; (c) any action asserting a claim against the Corporation arising pursuant to any provision of the Delaware General Corporation Law or the Certificate of Incorporation or these Bylaws (in each case, as they may be amended from time to time); (d) any action seeking to interpret, apply, enforce or determine the validity of the Certificate of Incorporation or the Bylaws of the Corporation (in each case, as they may be amended from time to time); or (e) any action asserting a claim against the Corporation or any Director or officer or other employee of the Corporation governed by the internal affairs doctrine.

Amended and Restated Bylaws of Monster Worldwide, Inc. (as amended effective August 7, 2016), Art. 8, § 7, filed as Exh. 3.2 to Periodic Report on Form 8-K filed Aug. 9, 2016.

32. Not surprisingly, therefore, there are examples of litigants amending complaints to include a 14a-9 claim expressly to avoid removal on the basis of a forum selection bylaw. For example, in the Safeway-Albertsons merger in 2014, plaintiffs had filed merger claims in Delaware Chancery Court, California state court, and in federal court in the Northern District of California. When the target invoked its forum selection bylaw, the California state court action was dismissed, but the plaintiffs in California federal court avoided dismissal by amending their complaint to include a 14a-9 claim. See Steamfitters Local 449 Pension Fund v. Safeway, No. 14-cv01670-JSW (filed April 10, 2014). The claim was ultimately settled.

33. Where the provisions do apply, most judges in foreign jurisdictions have

upheld them when asserted as a basis for the motion to dismiss. Since *Boilermakers*, courts in New York, Illinois, Missouri, Ohio, Texas, and California have enforced forum selection bylaws in favor of Delaware for corporate law litigation. Courts in Oregon and California have refused. *See, e.g.*, Roberts v. TriQuint Semiconductor, No. 1402-02441 (Or. Cir. Ct. Aug. 14, 2014); Galaviz v. Berg, 763 F. Supp. 2d 1170 (N.D. Cal. 2011). However, the Oregon refusal was subsequently overturned by a decision of the Oregon Supreme Court, which recognized the validity of the provision. Roberts v. TriQuint Semiconductor, 358 Or. 413 (2015).

34. Fried Frank M&A Briefing: Delaware's Effort to Reduce Wasteful M&A Litigation—Should Companies Adopt Delaware Forum Selection Bylaws after Trulia? (Feb. 9, 2016) (emphasis added).

35. See Gordon Neidermayer, et al. v. Steven A. Kriegsman, et al. and CytRx Corp., C.A. No. 11800-VCMR, tr. ruling (Del. Ch. May 2, 2016) (oral ruling acknowledging novel issues raised by selective enforcement and waiver of a forum selection bylaw, but finding no evidence of gamesmanship in case at bar). *CytRx* is not a merger case.

36. *In re* CytRx Corp. Stockholder Derivative Litigation, C.A. No. 14-6414-GHK-PJW, order (C.D. Cal. Aug. 17, 2016).

37. *See, e.g.*, Carmody v. Toll Bros., 723 A.2d 1180, 1191–92 (Del. Ch. 1998) (voiding "dead hand" poison pill on the basis that it potentially disabled the board from redeeming the poison pill and going through with a hostile acquisition); Quickturn Design Sys., Inc. v. Shapiro, 721 A.2d 1281, 1291–92 (Del. 1998) (invalidating "slow hand" poison pill on the basis of its infringement of power of newly elected board to manage the corporation); Omnicare, Inc. v. NCS Healthcare, Inc., 818 A.2d 914 (Del. 2003) (voiding a no-out merger agreement as a breach of fiduciary duty on the basis that it prevented the board from engaging with a subsequent bidder offering a higher price).

38. Delaware General Corporation Law §§ 102(f) ("The certificate of incorporation may not contain any provision that would impose liability on a stockholder for the attorneys' fees or expenses of the corporation or any other party in connection with an internal corporate claim"), 109(b) ("The bylaws may not contain any provision that would impose liability on a stockholder for the attorneys' fees or expenses of the corporation or any other party in connection with an internal corporate claim"). See also Solak v. Paylocity Holding Corporation, C.A. No. 12299-CB, Dec. 27, 2016 (holding that a fee-shifting bylaw adopted to apply only to extra-forum litigation filed and maintained in contravention to an exclusive forum provision nevertheless violated the ban on fee-shifting provisions in 109(b)).

39. 91 A.3d 554 (Del. 2014).

40. Katz v. Commonwealth REIT, No. 24-C-13-001299, slip op. (Md. Cir. Ct. Feb. 19, 2014).

41. Commonwealth REIT, Amended and Restated Bylaws art. 16, Current Report (Form 8-K), Exhibit 3.2 (April 12, 2013).

42. Katz v. Commonwealth REIT, No. 24-C-13-001299, slip op. at 41 (Md. Cir. Ct. Feb. 19, 2014) (citing Am. Exp. Co. v. Italian Colors. Rest., 133 S.Ct. 2304, 2310–11 (U.S. 2013)).

43. Am. Exp. Co. v. Italian Colors. Rest., 133 S.Ct. 2304, 2310–11 (U.S. 2013) (emphasis in original).

44. On this point, compare Pritchard (2008) at 248 (suggesting that shareholders opt out of the "fraud on the market" presumption by stipulating to a disgorgement measure of damages in the corporate charter). *See also* Gilles (2005) (discussing how shareholders might opt out of the class action through the corporate charter).

References

ABA Model Rule 3.3(a) (1) and (2).

Armour, John, Bernard Black, and Brian Cheffins. 2012a. Delaware's Balancing Act, *Indiana Law Journal* 87:1345.

Armour, John, Bernard Black, and Brian Cheffins. 2012b. Is Delaware Losing Its Cases? *Journal of Empirical Legal Studies* 9:605.

Bainbridge, Stephen M. 2003. Precommitment Strategies in Corporate Law: The Case of Dead Hand and No Hand Pills, *Journal of Corporation Law* 29:1.

Baker, Tom, and Sean J. Griffith. 2010. *Ensuring Corporate Misconduct: How Liability Insurance Undermines Shareholder Litigation*. Chicago: University of Chicago Press.

Bayliss, A. Thompson, and Mark Mixon. 2015. "No Pay" Provisions: The Forgotten Middle Ground in the Fee-Shifting Battle, Harvard Corporate Governance blog, https://corpgov.law.harvard.edu/2015/06/01/no-pay-provisions-the-forgotten-middle-ground-in-the-fee-shifting-battle/.

Boettrich, Stefan, and Svetlana Starykh. 2017. *Recent Trends in Securities Class Action Litigation: 2016 Full-Year Review*. National Economic Research Associates, http://www.nera.com/content/dam/nera/publications/2017/PUB_2016_Securities_Year-End_Trends_Report_0117.pdf.

Cain, Matthew D., and Steven Davidoff Solomon. 2015. A Great Game: The Dynamics of State Competition and Litigation, *Iowa Law Review* 100:465.

Cain, Matthew D., and Steven Davidoff Solomon. 2016. Takeover Litigation in 2015, working paper, http://ssrn.com/abstract=2715890.

Cain, Matthew D., Jill E. Fisch, Steven Davidoff Solomon, and Randall S. Thomas. 2017. The Shifting Tides of Merger Litigation, working paper.

Catan, Emiliano M. 2016. The Insignificance of Clear-Day Poison Pills, working paper.

Choi, Albert H. 2016. Optimal Fee Shifting Bylaws, working paper.

Coates, John C. IV. 2000. Takeover Defenses in the Shadow of the Pill: A Critique of the Scientific Evidence, *Texas Law Review* 79:271.

Cornerstone Research. 2016a. Securities Class Action Filings: 2016 Midyear Assessment.

Cornerstone Research. 2016b. Shareholder Litigation Involving Acquisitions of Public Companies: Review of 2015 and 1H 2016 M&A Litigation.

Cornerstone Research. 2017. Securities Class Action Filings: 2016 Year in Review.

Easterbrook, Frank, & Daniel R. Fischel. 1996. *The Economic Structure of Corporate Law*. Cambridge, MA: Harvard University Press.

Eisenberg, Theodore, and Geoffrey Miller. 2004. The Role of Opt-Outs and Objectors in Class Action Litigation: Theoretical and Empirical Issues, *Vanderbilt Law Review* 57:1529.

Elster, Jon. 2000. *Ulysses Unbound: Studies in Rationality, Precommitment, and Constraints*. Cambridge, UK: Cambridge University Press.

Eskridge, William N., and Philip P. Frickey. 1988. *Cases and Materials on Legislation: Statutes and the Creation of Public Policy*. St. Paul, MN: West Publishing.

Fisch, Jill E., Sean J. Griffith, and Steven M. Davidoff Solomon. 2015. Confronting the Peppercorn Settlement in Merger Litigation: An Empirical Analysis and a Proposal for Reform, *Texas Law Review* 93:957.

Friedlander, Joel Edan. 2016. How Rural/Metro Exposed the Systemic Problem of Disclosure Settlements, *Delaware Journal of Corporate Law* 40:877.

Gilles, Myriam, 2005. Opting Out of Liability: The Forthcoming, Near-Total Demise of the Modern Class Action, *Michigan Law Review* 104: 373.

Griffith, Sean J. 2013. The Omnipresent Specter of Omnicare, *Journal of Corporation Law* 38:753.

Griffith, Sean J. 2015. Correcting Corporate Benefit: How to Fix Shareholder Litigation by Shifting the Doctrine on Fees, *Boston College Law Review* 56:1.

Griffith, Sean J., and Alexandra D. Lahav. 2013. The Market for Preclusion in Merger Litigation, *Vanderbilt Law Review* 66:1053.

Griffith, Sean J., and Anthony A. Rickey. 2018. Who Collects the Deal Tax, Where, and What Delaware Can Do About It, in *Research Handbook on Shareholder Litigation*, edited by Jessica Erickson, Sean Griffith, David Webber, and Verity Winship. Edward Elgar.

Grundfest, Joseph A. 2012. The History and Evolution of Intra-Corporate Forum Selection Clauses: An Empirical Analysis, *Delaware Journal of Corporate Law* 37:333.

Grundfest, Joseph A., and Kristen Savelle. 2013. The Brouhaha over Intra-Corporate Forum Selection Provisions: A Legal, Economic, and Political Analysis, *Business Lawyer* 68:325.

Henderson, Todd, and William H. J. Hubbard. 2015. Judicial Noncompliance with Mandatory Procedural Rules under the PSLRA, *Journal of Legal Studies* 44:S87.

Krishnan, C. N. V., Steven Davidoff Solomon, and Randall S. Thomas. 2016. Divided Loyalties? The Role of Defense Litigation Counsel in Shareholder M&A Litigation, working paper.

Macey, Jonathan R., and Geoffrey P. Miller. 2009. Judicial Review of Class Action Settlements, *Journal of Legal Analysis* 1:167.

Posner, Richard A. 1997. Are We One Self or Multiple Selves? Implications for Law and Public Policy, *Legal Theory* 3:23.

Pritchard, A. C. 2008. Stoneridge Investment Partners v. Scientific-Atlanta: The Political Economy of Securities Class Action Reform, *Cato Supreme Court Review* 2007–2008: 217–55.

Private Securities Litigation Reform Act, 15 U.S.C.A. § 78u4 (2018).

Rubenstein, William B. 2006. The Fairness Hearing: Adversarial and Regulatory Approaches, *UCLA Law Review* 53:1435.

Sale, Hillary A. 2011. Judges Who Settle, *Washington University Law Review* 89:377.

Schelling, Thomas C. 1985. Enforcing Rules on Oneself, *Journal of Law, Economics, and Organization* 1:357.

Ursaner, Sabrina. 2010. Keeping "Fiduciary Outs" out of Shareholder-Proposed Bylaws: An Analysis of CA, Inc. v. AFSCME, *New York University Journal of Law and Business* 6:479.

CHAPTER FOURTEEN

International Compliance Regimes

Stavros Gadinis

Introduction

Climate change was one of the most prominent issues in the 2016 proxy season. Shareholders brought a record-breaking 172 climate-related resolutions, mostly urging boards to assess their operations in light of the Paris Climate Summit's goal to limit global warming to below two degrees Celsius. In the two biggest US energy companies, Exxon and Chevron, such proposals garnered 38.1 percent and 40.8 percent of the votes.[1] In addition to illustrating the dynamism of shareholder activism in a broad range of issues besides core business strategies, these proposals are notable because they refer to an international instrument: the 2015 Paris Agreement. Environmental impact is hardly the only substantive area in which corporate conduct is shaped by international prototypes. Data management and privacy, intellectual property, human rights and labor laws, financial stability, anti–money laundering, and terrorism are just a few of the substantive areas where corporations increasingly adhere to legal frameworks designed to apply across borders.

A common feature of these international regimes is their emphasis on internal corporate governance reforms. Rather than simply setting a policy goal that the corporation must achieve—such as reducing emissions to a prescribed level—these regimes also detail a set of organizational arrangements designed to obtain the desired outcome. That international regimes choose to prioritize compliance is no surprise. By establishing a compliance infrastructure well suited to the underlying policy, international regimes can better accomplish uniform implementation around the world. Moreover, by committing all corporations to common procedures, international regimes can better address concerns about competitiveness or protectionism, which would result from varied implementation across borders.

But from a corporate law standpoint, prioritizing compliance as a key component of international regimes has important consequences that have been largely overlooked. An effective compliance infrastructure seeks to limit corporations' incentives to defect by devoting resources to specific monitoring, training, and sanctioning mechanisms. Often, compliance processes seek to bolster the position of internal control personnel. Compliance officials have extensive capabilities, operate under conditions of independence, and must adhere to strict guidelines that are intentionally hard to sidestep. From a legal design perspective, international regimes are better off strengthening ad hoc compliance processes rather than empowering preexisting corporate organs, since this obviates the risk of mismatches among diverse corporate laws. But for Delaware's corporate law framework, which entrusts the board with far-reaching decision-making powers, an internationally designed compliance infrastructure represents an important dent in the board's discretion to structure internal controls as it sees fit. Internationally designed compliance regimes, this chapter argues, erode boards' authority and strengthen alternative decision makers within the corporation.

The chapter proceeds as follows. The next section presents the argument theoretically, outlining how internationally designed processes operate to empower compliance officials at the expense of corporate boards. Yet boards often opt in to these regimes to enhance their reputation, gain certain regulatory benefits, or, in some cases, simply because they are required to do so by law. Three case studies support this argument. I then turn to an analysis of anti–money laundering compliance, which mandates financial institutions to report suspicious transactions and thus allows compliance officials significant say over important business choices. Global anti–money laundering laws follow a template enshrined in a nonbinding international instrument, the Forty Recommendations issued by the Financial Action Task Force (FATF). A discussion follows on environmental management systems, a compliance structure prototype delineated in ISO 14001, a nonbinding international instrument produced by a mostly private, industry-based standardization body. A later section examines the compliance process for removing copyright-infringing materials from online platforms such as

YouTube. Implemented in the United States in the context of the Digital Millennium Copyright Act (DMCA), this process reflects commitments adopted in a 1996 World Intellectual Property Organization (WIPO) treaty. Finally, the conclusion explains how these regimes empower company officials outside the board while also constraining boards' choices.

International Regimes and Corporate Compliance

Business conduct, traditionally understood as a predominantly domestic domain of legal practice, is increasingly becoming a key area of interest for international rule-making efforts. Internationally harmonized regimes have arisen in diverse areas of business activity, ranging from financial regulation to mining and from pharmaceuticals to labor standards. Sometimes, governments take the initiative of establishing a new international regime, either by concluding a legally binding international treaty or by supporting a nonbinding standard-setting effort. Other times, private industry spearheads the effort, creating model laws that governments can choose to adopt at a national level or to which businesses can voluntarily adhere. The motivations behind international standard-setting efforts and the reasons for their successes and failures have been the subject of a vast literature in international law and international relations. But for most scholars in this tradition, the analysis ends when corporations, either by law or voluntarily, become bound to internationally originated standards. Yet the impact of global harmonization efforts for corporate governance—that is, for the continuing function of the corporation past the point of adoption—has not received much attention.

This chapter explores the corporate governance implications of the international diffusion of laws. International lawmakers, regardless of provenance and legal background, seek to produce as harmonized a legal regime as possible. Given the many challenges of uniform implementation on the ground, international lawmakers often try to cement their regimes through institutional and procedural requirements. A typical set of institutional requirements involves the adoption of compliance processes specifically tailored to achieve the international regime's goals. The discussion below explores how compliance processes can support more uniform implementation, why they constitute a preferred technique for international lawmakers, and how they interact with domestic corporate law institutions, such as the board of directors.

Compliance as a Tool for Uniform Implementation

Generally, a compliance infrastructure includes certain processes that are geared toward implementing a particular legal mandate. Typical compliance processes include monitoring requirements, such as daily checks of chemical pollution levels or weekly checks on brokers' use of client funds; record-keeping requirements designed to constrain employees' discretion that may lead to mismanagement; and enhanced decision-making procedures, requiring employees to seek consent by supervisors in potentially questionable cases. Many compliance functions are performed by the company personnel regularly responsible for daily business, who often receive specifically designed training. However, managing the compliance function is typically the task of specialized compliance officials. This double-pronged approach—of detailed procedures run by designated professionals—is the keystone of international compliance regimes.

By incorporating guidelines about how to structure the compliance function, an international regime makes specific choices about implementation. Because compliance requirements are procedural in nature, they are relatively strict, constraining the flexibility of national decision makers. For example, compliance procedures may mandate a specific sequence of actions, some of which might demand a yes or no answer from the corporation, asking, for example, whether a transaction exceeds a certain amount or whether an applicant owns copyright over materials. Even when these answers are not immediately available, compliance procedures often impose a due diligence requirement for the corporation, which makes it harder to turn a blind eye on red flags. Typically, these compliance procedures generate a written record, which could provide damning evidence in a lawsuit against the corporation or the board. Thus, international regimes can specify standards of conduct for the corporation, determining both objective actions and subjective state-of-mind criteria. Moreover, ascertaining implementation of such requirements is relatively straightforward and transparent, irrespective of particularities in national legal and adjudicative systems.

Besides requiring specific compliance procedures, international regimes often mandate, or envision, that these procedures will be handled by specifically designated officers of the corporation—that is, compliance professionals. Tasked exclusively with supervisory goals, compliance professionals can become the torchbearers for the international regime within the corporation. Moreover, international lawmakers can shape the duties, actions, and obligations of compliance officers to best fit the goals of the international regime. However, as company employees, compliance officers are still subject to management influence. Thus, many international regimes seek to empower compliance professionals. Some introduce external certification schemes, which help buttress the position of internal compliance officers against management choices. Others strengthen the link between compliance officers and regulators—for example, by requiring compliance personnel to report problems to regulators with minimal management involvement. Finally, the more rigorous the procedural standards an international regime imposes, the more it strengthens the position of compliance officers against management. If the discretion of compliance officers is limited, there is little management can ask from them.[2]

That is not to say that compliance procedures and officers are sufficient, on their own, to elicit implementation from corporations across borders. While international regimes require corporate personnel to undertake specific actions, the results of these actions are still subject to exogenous influence. Procedural steps can be manipulated, reports can be whitewashed, records can be buried, and due diligence can be superficial. However, these requirements can increase the costs of misconduct for company employees or management, because they can make deviations from regulatory goals harder to accomplish ex ante and easier to detect ex post.

Why Emphasis on Compliance Makes Sense for International Harmonization Efforts

Detailed compliance procedures, especially when managed by dedicated officers, can facilitate the uniform implementation of a regulatory regime by the corporations it targets. Achieving uniformity is both more difficult and more desirable for a regulatory regime designed to apply across borders. Thus, it is little surprise that many international regimes include provisions about compliance procedures.

Compliance procedures can reduce the risk of national deviation, which is a significant threat for international regimes. International regimes are typically the product of painful compromises reached through extensive negotiations. But once called upon to implement these compromises, governments or corporations may have strong incentives to disregard their side of the bargain. Fears of only superficial implementation of international commitments, with little or no follow-up from local authorities, have dogged the literature on law diffusion. Concerns about protectionism or regulatory races are particularly acute in international regimes. Compliance procedures offer one way of addressing these problems, at least in part by intervening at the crucial stage of implementing the commitments previously reached. Thus, they increase the appeal of the international regime, because participants are more likely to trust each other to carry out their mutually agreed obligations.

Uniformity in approaches also helps coordination among different national authorities. Regulators can more effectively share resources by working together to formulate implementing rules and guidance, organizing cross-border cooperation in specific cases, and set up training programs. Lessons learned in one country can more readily travel across borders. Thus, compliance programs help better coordinate national enforcement efforts, pooling resources toward common goals.

Utilizing compliance regimes as engines of increasing coordination is a mechanism that international policy makers often use. Indeed, guidelines about compliance have been a mainstay of key efforts to establish global "best practices" on corporate governance. The G20/OECD Principles of Corporate Governance mention compliance as one of the key functions a board should fulfill.[3] The UN Global Compact, which seeks to mobilize corporations to pursue sustainable development through adherence to ten key principles, repeatedly emphasizes compliance as a tool for intervention in corporate culture.[4] By design, these initiatives leave boards significant leeway in designing their compliance framework. In contrast, other global standardization efforts provide specific guidelines on how to structure a compliance process. For example, they might include a specific reporting requirement to regulators or provide for a notice-and-comment process. These compliance processes are the focus of this chapter.

Implications for Corporate Governance

When called to implement a compliance regime specified in an international instrument, boards have significantly less flexibility than under current Delaware law doctrine. In *Caremark*,[5] Chancellor Allen recognized that the board's duties include an obligation to monitor employees for violations of the law. However, he also stated that only "a sustained or systematic failure of the board to exercise oversight" would suggest the lack of good faith necessary to generate liability.[6] As long as the board has established a reasonable system of oversight—for example, by hiring compliance officers, organizing training, or introducing reporting procedures—it will fulfill its monitoring duties in good faith. If these monitoring procedures, even though considered reasonable at the time, prove faulty or inadequate in the long run, the board will still not be deemed liable. To assess reasonableness, Delaware courts will examine the board's decision-making process to ensure that it demonstrated the appropriate level of care—for example, by hiring experts or referring to what other companies have done in similar cases. Thus, as long as the board carefully considers its options, it has significant flexibility in shaping its compliance procedures and can pick and choose different mechanisms of oversight as long as they remain within established market practices. Moreover, a *Caremark* obligation to build a compliance system is strictly limited to monitoring violations of law and cannot impinge on the board's autonomy to monitor company performance or exposure to business risk, as Delaware courts clarified in *Citigroup*.[7]

The reasonableness consideration mandated by Delaware law takes particular shape when compliance procedures are modeled after an international instrument. As an international regime sets out the key elements of a compliance system, it also provides a criterion for assessing the reasonableness of the system essentially followed. If the board adopts a system significantly different from the proposed international one, it is taking the risk that it may fail the reasonableness test. This constitutes a well-defined yardstick for board liability, particularly in comparison with more malleable market practice considerations. On the other hand, if the board does follow the international standard, it becomes much harder for plaintiffs to show a breach of fiduciary duty. In this case, the board's choices are in line with the suggestions of an internationally recognized standardization body and thus are more likely to be deemed reasonable ex post. Overall, the board cedes significant flexibility in setting up its compliance system—which may be different than its preferred one—but gains greater certainty that it complies with its legal and fiduciary obligations. This trade-off can be a desirable outcome for many boards.

Yet the real impact of the international regime unfolds once the compliance apparatus enters full operation. Presumably, the compliance department will provide the board with reports about potential violations by company personnel. Once the board receives alerts from the compliance department, its duty of care obligations mandate some reaction, proportionate to the severity of the problem alleged. Granted, the business judgment rule provides the board with ample leeway to frame its response, even when not protected by the 102(b)(7) waiver of liability. But, importantly, the board would be hard-pressed to do nothing and let the problematic situation continue to unfold. At a minimum, the duty of care would compel the board to further investigate the reported problem so that it can acquire a clearer and more complete picture of the problem. Thus, when it receives a compliance report with red flags, directors ought to spring into action or else face the risk of personal liability in the future.

Given that a reported problem swiftly imposes on directors a duty to react, the power to provide these reports turns compliance officers into significant nodes in the corporate governance structure. The compliance officer can push the board into accepting and addressing a legal violation that the board may not want to admit or that may be profitable for the company, at least in the short run. Or the compliance officer may decide that a report to the board is not warranted, thus never triggering any board duties or risking any liability. In *Stone v. Ritter*,[8] which involved failures in a bank's anti–money laundering compliance system, the board's good faith remained untainted because no reports of problems or gaps had previously reached it. In contrast, the board in *Stone* was deemed to have fulfilled its duty-of-care obligations after commissioning an independent assessment of its anti–money laundering program by KPMG that did not point to any weaknesses.

Given the implications of compliance officers' views and actions, and in particular their power to alter the liability landscape for the board, they enjoy significant influence and responsibility regardless of whether they are formally members of the board. Clearly, compliance officers remain employed by the company, and thus dependent on management, at least as far as their employment is concerned. On the other hand, the strict procedural requirements of international regimes might provide them with fallback, because they may require compliance officers to note and report problems and weaknesses. The tension between compliance and management is an important one to explore more closely in further research.

The International Anti–Money Laundering Regime

Fighting organized criminals and terrorists by limiting their access to the global financial system is a wide-ranging goal that requires the cooperation of criminal authorities, banking regulators, and private parties. Anti–money laundering laws became a global priority in the late 1980s, as drug wars were escalating and emerging markets were being more actively incorporated in the global economy.[9] To foster the development of appropriate regulatory and statutory frameworks, the G7 (Group of Seven, or Canada, France, Germany, Italy, Japan, the United Kingdom, and the United States) authorized the creation of the Financial Action Task Force, a transnational network of officials at treasury departments and ministries of finance.[10] In 1990, FATF released its Forty Recommendations for combating money laundering, which propose specific legislative and regulatory reforms designed as readily adaptable legislation models appropriate for diverse legal systems. The Recommendations have been amended extensively over the years, most notably in 2001, when their scope was extended to cover terrorist financing. Despite heavy government involvement in their design, the Recommendations constitute "soft law," because they are not rooted in international treaties and do not produce legally binding obligations for governments. However, more than 150 countries around the world have adopted anti–money laundering reforms in line with the Recommendations and have agreed to implementation monitoring by regional bodies.

A key component of FATF's Recommendations concerns the role that financial institutions should play in detecting money laundering among prospective or existing clients. The Recommendations center on customer due diligence, which requires financial institutions to make inquiries about the provenance of funds in connection with the identity and background of their clients. More importantly, financial institutions are required to report to authorities[11] any transaction that gives rise to *suspicions* of money laundering.[12] Suspicions arise when clients provide information with significant gaps or when their actions do not fit well with their stated goals. Generally, the suspicions threshold seeks to incentivize financial institutions to come forward even when they do not have the full picture of the client's activities, prioritizing alertness over certainty. For example, suspicions will arise when a client's conduct resembles patterns that have been associated with money laundering in the past or when the client deviates abruptly from established patterns of behavior. Clearly, the suspicions threshold is less demanding than the knowledge threshold, a standard typically required for establishing civil liability in financial regulation.

As a comparatively low liability threshold, reportable suspicions have transformed the relationship between the board, firm employees, and compliance officers. Suspicions can readily arise in many transactions, and thus financial institutions cannot rely only on high-level executives; they have to enlist the support of front-line employees who deal with clients directly. Moreover, given the likely high amount of potentially reportable conduct, employees will need support and guidance by experienced compliance officers, who can determine which case to further investigate, monitor, or report. As a result, financial institutions seeking to fulfill their customer due diligence obligations must establish expansive anti–money laundering compliance operations.[13] Large multinational banks employ thousands of officials to ensure compliance with anti–money laundering laws, while even the smallest banks tend to devote ten officials, on average, to this task. Moreover, financial institutions have invested significantly in detection technology, creating proprietary software that helps them identify suspicious transactions automatically. Overall, the board is required to take the necessary actions to establish and staff its anti–money laundering program, but these actions are shaped by agency rules, regulatory guidance, industry practice, and, in some cases, explicit agreements with regulators and prosecutors. Thus, board choices must fit within a highly prescribed set of options.

Once the compliance apparatus is set in motion, board involvement in suspicious reporting is typically very low. In many cases, it will be a computer or a front-line employee that will flag a transaction for investigation. As the red flag enters the compliance apparatus, it merits consideration. Compliance officials spend a significant amount of time assessing each flagged transaction and must then devote additional resources if they wish to investigate it further. At that stage, the case is typically presented to an oversight committee, which is ultimately responsible for determining whether to file a report. Reports must be well reasoned and justified, and compliance departments often employ highly specialized personnel, such as former law enforcement officials or investigators. In preparing the report, compliance officials produce extensive documentation, such as internal memos, e-mails, and other communications with harmed parties and potential perpetrators. This internal record supports compliance officers' decision to file a report and could be used to put management in a difficult position if they sought to overrule the compliance department. Ultimately, top compliance officials liaise with a board committee, typically comprised of independent members, and may present overview reports to the board as a whole.

In addition to internal review, financial institutions' anti–money laundering compliance is subject to extensive government oversight, both by specialized financial regulators and general criminal law enforcement authorities. US financial institutions and other regulated entities file about 1.6 million suspicious activity reports annually.[14] Regulators have established an extensive rule-making and guidance program, which provides standardized submission forms and thus further limits corporations' discretion. In addition, regulators have issued a manual specifying criteria and procedures that examiners will follow when assessing the adequacy of internal compliance departments.[15] Thus, regulators have further curtailed the discretion that boards enjoy under Delaware jurisprudence in setting up their compliance operations. When a financial institution fails to submit a report when doing so is warranted, the institution is likely to face severe sanctions, which have become increasingly harsh in recent years.[16] Moreover, banks have generally been subject to billion-dollar fines for assisting clients in money laundering: for example, $8.9 billion against BNP Paribas for transactions with links to countries targeted by US sanctions; $2.6 billion against J. P. Morgan in connection with the Madoff fraud; and $2.6 billion against Credit Suisse for transactions related to US tax evasion.[17]

This comprehensive, specialized, and actively enforced compliance framework is densely set out in statutes, rules, and industry practices. The requirements of this framework go further than the broad parameters of Delaware jurisprudence regarding internal compliance. Instead of entrusting the board with choosing how to best apply the law, this framework has fostered specialized professionals whose work is designed to curtail board involvement. Rather than following board directives, these professionals adhere to regulatory guidelines, set at a national or even an international level. Of course, boards remain in charge of significant decisions, such as how to staff their compliance departments. However, their decisions focus on implementing regulatory requirements rather than designing their preferred arrangements.

The ISO Standards for Environmental Management Systems

In recent years, environmental regulation has increasingly enlisted the support of private companies to promote environment-friendly goals through voluntarily adopted standards.[18] The most popular standard[19] is the ISO 14001 on environmental management systems, produced by the International Organization for Standardization (ISO). The ISO is an umbrella organization with more than 150 member states[20] that lead a diverse array of standardization efforts, ranging from textiles and equipment to biometrics and information technology.[21] To produce a standard, the ISO forms a technical committee, composed of representatives from national standardization bodies from its members, typically private industry groups.[22] Thus, the committee members producing the standards are experts in environmental issues but not necessarily experts in corporate law.

The goal of ISO 14001 is to standardize private firms' environmental compliance infrastructure. The ISO 14001 defines the key features of a successful environmental management system by instituting a coordinated set of procedures, routines, authority structures, and resource allocations.[23] Thus, the ISO 14001 advocates for a process-oriented approach to the complexities of environmental compliance. Implementing the standard requires a substantial commitment of financial and human resources from the firm to design, plan, apply, and review the processes. As a result, the standard requires top management involvement to trigger the adoption and launch the planning phase and to conduct an ongoing review of its operation. But, clearly, the goal of the procedures enshrined in the standard is to direct management's actions and to build an institutional infrastructure that constrains management choices. Once implemented, the standard envisages a new set of compliance professionals whose goal would be to secure compliance on a range of issues. By adopting ISO 14001, the board voluntarily ties its hands and commits to correct any failures that its management system brings to surface.

The empowerment of compliance staff through ISO 14001 is even more apparent when one considers the availability of a third-party certification process, one of its most prominent features. Certifiers are independent companies typically registered with a national association. The certification process is generally regarded as thorough and often involves reorganizing the firm's internal governance structure and expanding the resources available for environmental compliance. The certification process focuses on the adequacy of compliance checks throughout the corporate hierarchy and seeks to ensure that management promptly reacts to staff recommendations for corrective action.

Many private companies in the United States and around the world are voluntarily adopting ISO 14001 to improve their environmentally friendly reputations and, in some cases, secure preferential treatment from regulators. More than 267,000 companies have adopted ISO 14001 worldwide.[24] Leading studies among US companies illustrate that management sees the adoption of ISO 14001 as a way to enhance their reputation as environmentally conscious and better respond to their customers' demands.[25] The availability of third-party certification further strengthens their perceived gains. In addition to a reputational boost, the adoption of an environmental management system such as ISO 14001 brings some tangential benefits under US law. On the regulatory side, the Environmental Protection Agency offers a reduced inspection load and lighter reporting and monitoring obligations to companies that satisfy the agency's environmental management system requirements, such as companies that comply with ISO 14001. Moreover, in case of an environmental disaster with significant ramifications, the federal sentencing guidelines for organizations provide for a reduction in penalties if the company possesses a satisfactory compliance infrastructure, a criterion easily fulfilled by an ISO 14001 system.

Since compliance infrastructures focus on companies' internal processes rather than their actual impact on the environment, many fear that companies adopt them simply to "greenwash" their activities without intending to make any actual changes. In this logic, even after companies commit the resources necessary to obtain ISO 14001 certification, they do not respond to the weaknesses compliance professionals unearth, nullifying any impact they may have in practice. However, studies show that companies that adopt environmental management systems actually seem to change their behavior on the ground.[26] In particular, a study on ISO 14001 finds that third-party certified firms are more likely to both change their behavior in response to their internal processes and to experience better outcomes in terms of use of natural resources, waste, and water and air pollution.[27] Although exploring the causal links between internal compliance changes and environmental impacts is fraught with challenges, at least these initial findings suggest that compliance infrastructures are operational.

The example of ISO 14001 encapsulates the role of international standards in altering the shape of corporate hierarchies. Although ISO 14001 requires significant commitments and participation from board and management, it is clear in providing the leading role to compliance professionals. The standard's goal is to establish a specialized, well-run compliance infrastructure that will pursue environmentally friendly policies more effectively. In that respect, ISO 14001 not only supplements but curbs management discretion. Third-party certification enhances the reputational gains from compliance, and regulatory relief may provide additional incentives to comply.

The 1996 WIPO Treaty and DMCA

Among the three examples presented here, the structure for avoiding copyright infringement is the least intrusive in the internal governance of a company seeking to comply. Rather than requiring companies to proactively monitor for copyright infringing materials, the Digital Millennium Copyright Act only demands them to take down these materials upon notice of the infringement. Thus, the commitment of resources, staffing, and supervision required from management is less considerable, particularly compared with mandates of a preventive character, such as those discussed above in anti–money laundering and environmental compliance. However, even to pursue a relatively narrower mandate, the law deems it necessary to specify a compliance structure with some detail. Eventually, the DMCA goes further than current Delaware corporate law cases such as *Caremark* and *Stone*.

Similar to the anti–money laundering laws and ISO 14001, the DMCA has international origins. The DMCA implements into US law the provisions of a World Intellectual Property Organization treaty concluded in 1996 to address copyright challenges in the then-nascent digital era. WIPO is a specialized agency of the United Nations, established in 1967, with 189 member-states. At the time of the 1996 WIPO treaty, of particular concern was the wide availability of potentially infringing material on service providers, and especially popular websites that rely on user uploads, such as YouTube. As the use of online services proliferated, services providers were concerned that potential liability for copyright infringement was significant, but closer policing of individual users would prove exceedingly difficult. In response, Article 12 of the WIPO treaty struck a compromise: Liability against service providers would arise only if they *knowingly* distribute infringing materials. While the WIPO treaty leaves to national legislatures the choice of means for ascertaining knowledge, it clearly envisages some process that would allow copyright owners to at least stop the ongoing violation of their rights.

In response to US obligations under the WIPO treaty, DMCA § 512 establishes a safe harbor for online service providers who offer to take down infringing materials expeditiously after they become aware or receive notice of the infringement.[28] Known as the "red flag" doctrine, this approach establishes a presumption of good faith in favor of the online service provider unless there are clear red flags—for example, the posting of a pirate version of a movie by an unauthorized user. The red flag doctrine mirrors similar requirements for board monitoring potentially illegal employee actions under Delaware law.[29] Yet, while Delaware case law leaves ample discretion to the board to formulate procedures for identifying red flags and establishing knowledge of illegality, the DMCA specifies a process that all online service providers must follow. Under the DMCA regime, an important precondition for the safe harbor is that the service provider designates an agent responsible for receiving and processing notices of infringement by copyright owners.[30] The agent does not necessarily have to be an employee of the company, and some service providers outsource this task to their attorneys. Once the agent receives a notice of infringement and a request to take down the related materials, she or he must notify the original uploader and offer an opportunity to respond. Today, these procedures have been to a large extent automated, as specialized software monitors uploads and initiates automatic takedown notices to providers.

For all these reasons, compliance with the DMCA § 512 safe harbor has tangible benefits for companies, who can significantly reduce the risk of liability for copyright infringement. To do so, companies need to set up a governance structure authorized by, but ultimately outside the control of, the company's board. This governance structure, although simpler than in previous examples, still calls for a commitment of resources and effort according to requirements specified in the law.

Conclusion

International compliance regimes prescribe detailed procedural requirements and allocate tasks to specialized compliance officers. These requirements are designed to ensure greater uniformity in implementation across borders. But from a corporate governance perspective, these regimes constrain the flexibility of the board to set up its own control systems under Delaware law. Granted, boards that comply with these requirements can more convincingly claim that they have satisfied their monitoring obligations, which emanate from their fiduciary duties to shareholders. Often, to abide by international compliance regimes, companies must invest significant resources in staffing and technology and intensify their enforcement efforts. Of course, this strategy has produced noticeable enforcement results, such as the increase in suspicious activity reports that alert regulators about potential money laundering or the constant removal of copyright-infringing material from online platforms. Less clear is whether boards would have chosen to expend the resources necessary to build these compliance regimes, absent legal pressure to do so. Moreover, these compliance obligations are likely to gain a greater share of the company's enforcement budget than other areas of the law.

Perhaps the most far-reaching consequence of these international regimes is the continuous empowerment of internal control personnel. Ultimately, compliance officers have the responsibility—and the power—to report to the board weaknesses or gaps in the compliance mechanism as well as violations by other employees if they have occurred. *Stone* makes clear that, had the plaintiff not conceded that the board did not know of any red flags, the court would have taken a different path. Yet whether fact patterns amount to a red flag is a decision that is typically at the hands of compliance officers. As heads of internal controls, compliance officers aggregate all monitoring information and choose what to report to the board, when to submit their report, and what information to include. In effect, compliance officers can alter the liability landscape for the board, which allows them to be particularly influential players in the corporate governance structure. Such reports would trigger the board's duty of care, demanding some reaction from the board. In some cases, the board may have to investigate further, having to face unpleasant realities. In other cases, the board may have to take even more drastic measures, such as firing employees or making public acknowledgments of problems. Thus, this power can bring compliance officers in tension with the board. As corporate scandals continue to generate headlines, these tensions are only going to grow stronger.

Notes

I am grateful to my colleagues Holly Doremus and Molly van Houweling, whose thoughtful questions in a faculty workshop at Berkeley urged me to uncover the international origins of compliance regimes in diverse areas of law.

1. Bradley Olson and Nicole Friedman, *Exxon, Chevron Shareholders Narrowly Reject Climate-Change Stress Tests*, WALL ST. J., May 25, 2016.

2. International legal instruments have often used the technique of prescribing precise procedures in order to achieve greater uniformity in implementation of treaty commitments and reduce the flexibility of local decision makers. For a discussion, see Kenneth W. Abbot, Robert O. Keohane, Andrew Moravcsik, Anne-Marie Slaughter, and Duncan Snidal, *The Concept of Legalization* 54 INT'L ORG. 401 (2000); Kal Raustiala, *Form and Substance in International Agreements* 99 AM. J. INT'L L. 581 (2005).

3. G20/OECD PRINCIPLES OF CORPORATE GOVERNANCE at 47, http://www.oecd-ilibrary.org/governance/g20-oecd-principles-of-corporate-governance-2015_9789264236882-en.

4. *See, e.g.,* Global Compact LEAD, A NEW AGENDA FOR THE BOARD OF DIRECTORS, https://www.unglobalcompact.org/docs/news_events/9.1_news_archives/2012_01_27/Lead-board-loresR.pdf.

5. *In re* Caremark Int'l Inc. Deriv. Litig., 698 A.2d 959 (Del. Ch. 1996).

6. *Id.* at 971.

7. *In re* Citigroup Inc., Shareholder Derivative Litigation, 964 A.2d 106 (2009).

8. 911 A.2d 362 (2006).

9. *See, e.g.*, Basel Committee on Banking Supervision, PREVENTION OF CRIMINAL USE OF THE BANKING SYSTEM FOR THE PURPOSE OF MONEY-LAUNDERING (1988), http://www.bis.org/publ/bcbsc137.pdf.

10. For more information on the creation of FATF and the spread of its Forty Recommendations around the world, see Stavros Gadinis, *Three Pathways to Global Standards: Private, Regulator, and Ministry Networks*, 109 AM. J. INT'L L. 1 (2015).

11. In the United States, the agency receiving these reports is the Department of Treasury, which runs a specialized division, the Financial Crimes Enforcement Network.

12. Annunzio-Wylie Anti-Money Laundering Act of 1992 §§ 1513, 1517(b), 31 U.S.C. § 5318(g) (2014).

13. For a discussion of the implementation of anti–money laundering laws in the United States, see generally Stavros Gadinis and Colby Mangels, *Collaborative Gatekeepers*, 73 WASH. & LEE L. REV. 797 (2016).

14. US Department of Treasury Financial Crimes Enforcement Network, SAR STATS TECHNICAL BULLETIN 1 (2014), http://www.fincen.gov/news_room/rp/files/SAR01/SAR_Stats_proof_2.pdf.

15. Federal Financial Institutions Examination Council, BANK SECRECY ACT ANTI-MONEY LAUNDERING EXAMINATION MANUAL, https://www.ffiec.gov/bsa_aml_infobase/pages_manual/OLM_002.htm.

16. David Zaring and Elena Baylis, *Sending the Bureaucracy to War*, 92 IOWA L. REV. 1359, 1414 (2007).

17. Stephen Grocer, *A List of the Biggest Bank Settlements*, WALL ST. J. MONEYBEAT, June 23, 2014, http://blogs.wsj.com/moneybeat/2014/06/23/a-list-of-the-biggestbank-settlements/.

18. Michael P. Vanderbergh, *Private Environmental Governance*, 99 CORNELL L. REV. 129 (2013).

19. Oren Perez et al., *The Dynamic of Corporate Self-Regulation: ISO 14001, Environmental Commitment, and Organizational Citizenship Behavior*, 43 LAW & SOC'Y REV. 593 (2009).

20. David A. Wirth, *The International Organization for Standardization: Private Voluntary Standards as Swords and Shields*, 36 BOSTON COLL. ENVIRONMENTAL AFFAIRS L. REV. 79, 80–81 (2009).

21. Tim Büthe and Walter Mattli, THE NEW GLOBAL RULERS: THE PRIVATIZATION OF REGULATION IN THE WORLD ECONOMY chap. 6. (Princeton 2011)

22. *Id.* chap. 7.

23. Timothy F. Malloy, *Regulation, Compliance, and the Firm*, 76 TEMP. L. REV. 451, 493 (2003).

24. International Standards Organization, THE ISO SURVEY OF MANAGEMENT SYSTEM STANDARD CERTIFICATIONS—2011 at 1 (2012), http:// www.iso.org/iso/iso_survey2011_executive-summary.pdf.

25. Matthew Potoski and Aseem Prakash, *Green Clubs and Voluntary Governance: ISO 14001 and Firms' Regulatory Compliance*, 49 AM. J. POL. SCI. 235 (2005).

26. For a discussion of the related literature, see Vanderbergh, *Private Environmental Governance* at 189–90.

27. Nicole Darnall and Younsung Kim, *Which Types of Environmental Management Systems Are Related to Greater Environmental Improvements?* 72 PUBLIC ADMIN. REV. 351 (2012).

28. 17 U.S.C.A. § 512(c)(1).

29. Graham v. Allis Chalmers.

30. 17 U.S.C.A. § 512(c)(2).

Contributors

David J. Berger is Partner, Wilson Sonsini Goodrich & Rosati.

William W. Bratton is Nicholas F. Gallicchio Professor of Law and Co-Director, Institute for Law and Economics, University of Pennsylvania Law School.

Michael B. Dorff is Downer Chair of Corporate Law and Professor of Law, Southwestern Law School.

Jill E. Fisch is Perry Golkin Professor of Law, University of Pennsylvania Law School.

Stavros Gadinis is Professor, University of California, Berkeley, School of Law.

Sean J. Griffith is T. J. Maloney Chair and Professor of Law, Fordham Law School.

Colleen Honigsberg is Assistant Professor of Law, Stanford Law School.

Robert J. Jackson Jr. is Professor of Law and Director, Program on Corporate Law and Policy, Columbia Law School.

Frank Partnoy is George E. Barrett Professor of Law and Finance, University of San Diego.

Elizabeth Pollman is Professor of Law, Loyola Law School, Los Angeles.

Hillary A. Sale is Walter D. Coles Professor of Law and Management, Washington University in St. Louis.

Steven Davidoff Solomon is Professor, University of California, Berkeley, School of Law.

Guhan Subramanian is Joseph H. Flom Professor of Law and Business, Harvard Law School, and H. Douglas Weaver Professor of Business Law, Harvard Business School.

Randall S. Thomas is Professor and John S. Beasley II Chair in Law and Business, Vanderbilt University School of Law.

Robert B. Thompson is Peter P. Weidenbruch Jr. Professor of Business Law, Georgetown University Law Center.

Verity Winship is Professor of Law, University of Illinois, Urbana-Champaign.

Index

Page numbers in italics refer to figures and tables